EXCEL
HACKS™

Other resources from O'Reilly

SECOND EDITION

EXCEL HACKS™

David and Raina Hawley

O'REILLY®

Beijing · Cambridge · Farnham · Köln · Paris · Sebastopol · Taipei · Tokyo

Excel Hacks™

by David and Raina Hawley

Copyright © 2007 O'Reilly Media, Inc. All rights reserved.
Printed in the United States of America.

Published by O'Reilly Media, Inc., 1005 Gravenstein Highway North,
Sebastopol, CA 95472.

O'Reilly books may be purchased for educational, business, or sales promotional use. Online editions are also available for most titles (*safari.oreilly.com*). For more information, contact our corporate/institutional sales department: (800) 998-9938 or *corporate@oreilly.com*.

Editors: Brian Sawyer and Brian Jepson
Technical Editor Tom Sgouros
Production Editor: Adam Witwer
Copyeditor: Derek Di Matteo
Proofreader: Tolman Creek Design

Indexer: Tolman Creek Design
Cover Designer: Hanna Dyer
Interior Designer: David Futato
Illustrators: Robert Romano
and Jessamyn Read

Printing History:

March 2004:	First Edition.
June 2007:	Second Edition.

RepKover. This book uses RepKover™, a durable and flexible lay-flat binding.
ISBN-10: 0-596-52834-5
ISBN-13: 978-0-596-52834-8
[M]

For our girls, Aleisha and Kate

Contents

Credits xiii

Preface xv

Chapter 1. Reducing Workbook and Worksheet Frustration 1

  1. Create a Personal View of Your Workbooks   5

  2. Enter Data into Multiple Worksheets Simultaneously   8

  3. Prevent Users from Performing Certain Actions   11

  4. Prevent Seemingly Unnecessary Prompts   15

  5. Hide Worksheets So That They Cannot Be Unhidden   19

  6. Customize the Templates Dialog and Default Workbook   21

  7. Create an Index of Sheets in Your Workbook   23

  8. Limit the Scrolling Range of Your Worksheet   26

  9. Lock and Protect Cells Containing Formulas   30

  10. Find Duplicate Data Using Conditional Formatting   34

  11. Find Data That Appears Two or More Times Using Conditional
       Formatting   35

  12. Tie Custom Toolbars to a Particular Workbook   36

  13. Outsmart Excel's Relative Reference Handler   38

  14. Remove Phantom Workbook Links   39

  15. Reduce Workbook Bloat   42

  16. Extract Data from a Corrupt Workbook   45

Chapter 2. Hacking Excel's Built-in Features 48

  17. Validate Data Based on a List on Another Worksheet   48

  18. Control Conditional Formatting with Checkboxes   50

19. Identify Formulas with Conditional Formatting 54

20. Count or Sum Cells That Meet Conditional Formatting Criteria 56

21. Highlight Every Other Row or Column 58

22. Create 3-D Effects in Tables or Cells 60

23. Turn Conditional Formatting and Data Validation On and Off with a Checkbox 62

24. Support Multiple Lists in a ComboBox 64

25. Create Validation Lists That Change Based on a Selection from Another List 66

26. Use Replace... to Remove Unwanted Characters 68

27. Convert Text Numbers to Real Numbers 68

28. Extract the Numeric Portion of a Cell Entry 70

29. Customize Cell Comments 71

30. Sort by More Than Three Columns 73

31. Random Sorting 74

32. Manipulate Data with the Advanced Filter 75

33. Create Custom Number Formats 79

34. Add More Levels of Undo to Excel for Windows 84

35. Create Custom Lists 84

36. Boldface Excel Subtotals 85

37. Convert Excel Formulas and Functions to Values 89

38. Automatically Add Data to a Validation List 91

39. Hack Excel's Date and Time Features 94

40. Enable Grouping and Outlining on a Protected Worksheet 98

41. Prevent Blanks/Missing Fields in a Table 100

42. Provide Decreasing Data Validation Lists 101

43. Add a Custom List to the Fill Handle 102

Chapter 3. Naming Hacks **105**

44. Address Data by Name 105

45. Use the Same Name for Ranges on Different Worksheets 106

46. Create Custom Functions Using Names 108

47. Create Ranges That Expand and Contract 112

48. Nest Dynamic Ranges for Maximum Flexibility 118

49. Identify Named Ranges on a Worksheet 121

Chapter 4. Hacking PivotTables 124

    50. PivotTables: A Hack in Themselves   124

    51. Share PivotTables but Not Their Data   129

    52. Automate PivotTable Creation   131

    53. Move PivotTable Grand Totals   135

    54. Efficiently Pivot Another Workbook's Data   137

Chapter 5. Charting Hacks 140

    55. Explode a Single Slice from a Pie Chart   140

    56. Create Two Sets of Slices in One Pie Chart   142

    57. Create Charts That Adjust to Data   144

    58. Interact with Your Charts Using Custom Controls   148

    59. Four Quick Ways to Update Your Charts   152

    60. Hack Together a Simple Thermometer Chart   157

    61. Create a Column Chart with Variable Widths and Heights   160

    62. Create a Speedometer Chart   164

    63. Link Chart Text Elements to a Cell   171

    64. Hack Chart Data So That Empty or FALSE Formula Cells Are Not Plotted   173

    65. Add a Directional Arrow to the End of a Line Series   175

    66. Place an Arrow on the End of a Horizontal (X) Axis   177

    67. Correct Narrow Columns When Using Dates   180

    68. Position Axis Labels   181

    69. Tornado Chart   184

    70. Gauge Chart   186

    71. Conditional Highlighting Axis Labels   188

    72. Create Totals on a Stacked Column Chart   190

Chapter 6. Hacking Formulas and Functions 193

    73. Add Descriptive Text to Your Formulas   193

    74. Move Relative Formulas Without Changing References   194

    75. Compare Two Excel Ranges   195

    76. Fill All Blank Cells in a List   197

    77. Make Your Formulas Increment by Rows When You Copy Across Columns   199

    78. Convert Dates to Excel Formatted Dates   202

79. Sum or Count Cells While Avoiding Error Values — 203

80. Reduce the Impact of Volatile Functions on Recalculation — 205

81. Count Only One Instance of Each Entry in a List — 206

82. Sum Every Second, Third, or Nth Row or Cell — 208

83. Find the Nth Occurrence of a Value — 210

84. Make the Excel Subtotal Function Dynamic — 212

85. Add Date Extensions — 214

86. Convert Numbers with the Negative Sign on the Right to Excel Numbers — 215

87. Display Negative Time Values — 217

88. Use the VLOOKUP Function Across Multiple Tables — 219

89. Show Total Time As Days, Hours, and Minutes — 221

90. Determine the Number of Specified Days in Any Month — 222

91. Construct Mega-Formulas — 224

92. Hack Mega-Formulas that Reference Other Workbooks — 226

93. Hack One of Excel's Database Functions to Take the Place of Many Functions — 227

94. Extract Specified Words from a Text String — 233

95. Count Words in a Cell or Range of Cells — 234

96. Return a Worksheet Name to a Cell — 236

97. Sum Cells with Multiple Criteria — 239

98. Count Cells with Multiple Criteria — 243

99. Calculate a Sliding Tax Scale — 246

100. Add/Subtract Months from a Date — 251

101. Find the Last Day of Any Given Month — 253

102. Calculate a Person's Age — 255

103. Return the Weekday of a Date — 256

104. Evaluate a Text Equation — 258

105. Lookup from Within a Cell — 259

Chapter 7. Macro Hacks **263**

106. Speed Up Code While Halting Screen Flicker — 263

107. Run a Macro at a Set Time — 264

108. Use CodeNames to Reference Sheets in Excel Workbooks — 266

109. Connect Buttons to Macros Easily — 267

110. Create a Workbook Splash Screen — 268

111. Display a "Please Wait" Message 270

112. Have a Cell Ticked or Unticked upon Selection 271

113. Count or Sum Cells That Have a Specified Fill Color 273

114. Add the Microsoft Excel Calendar Control to Any Excel Workbook 274

115. Password-Protect and Unprotect All Excel Worksheets in One Fell Swoop 276

116. Retrieve a Workbook's Name and Path 279

117. Get Around Excel's Three-Criteria Limit for Conditional Formatting 280

118. Run Procedures on Protected Worksheets 282

119. Distribute Macros 283

120. Delete Rows Based on a Condition 289

121. Track and Report Changes in Excel 293

122. Automatically Add Date/Time to a Cell upon Entry 297

123. Create a List of Workbook Hyperlinks 298

124. Advanced Find 300

125. Find a Number Between Two Numbers 306

126. Convert Formula References from Relative to Absolute 310

127. Name a Workbook with the Text in a Cell 315

128. Hide and Restore Toolbars in Excel 316

129. Sort Worksheets 319

130. Password-Protect a Worksheet from Viewing 320

131. Change Text to Upper- or Proper Case 322

132. Force Text to Upper- or Proper Case 324

133. Prevent Case Sensitivity in VBA Code 328

134. Display AutoFilter Criteria 329

Chapter 8. Cross-Application Hacks **331**

135. Import Data from Access 2007 into Excel 2007 331

136. Retrieve Data from Closed Workbooks 336

137. Automate Word from Excel 344

138. Automate Outlook from Excel 349

Index **355**

Credits

About the Authors

David and Raina Hawley provide business applications, software, development, consultancy, training, and tutoring in all aspects of Excel and VBA for Excel through OzGrid Business Applications in Western Australia.

David Hawley has spent the last 15 years creating business applications using Excel and VBA for Excel on a day-to-day basis. He produces a monthly newsletter containing information on the use of Excel and VBA for Excel. He runs and maintains one of the largest Excel forums in the world on the OzGrid web site.

Raina Hawley lectures in industry and in the college education system, and is a registered workplace assessor. Raina runs the OzGrid office, administration, consultancy, development, and training side of the business, and works in Excel solutions alongside her husband.

David and Raina offer hundreds of Excel Add-Ins and business software designed for data analysis in all industry areas through their web site at *http://www.ozgrid.com*. The web site contains over 50,000 pages of free Excel information. They live in Bunbury, Western Australia, with their two children.

Contributors

The following people contributed their hacks, writing, and inspiration to this book:

- Andy Pope is a programmer working in London. He has been using computers since the mid '80s. His current role involves writing customized solutions for reporting projects utilizing the MS Office products via VBA. Andy also runs his own web site (*http://www.andypope.info*). His contributions to the Excel community have been recognized by Microsoft, which has awarded Andy with MVP status for the past four years.

- Dennis Wallentin has been working as an independent Excel consultant since the late '80s. He utilizes MS Excel and other tools to develop professional solutions for all sizes of companies, including the public sector both in Sweden and internationally. He is currently focused on Visual Studio Tools for Office System (VSTO). Dennis has a Masters in Business and Management Accounting. He runs an English web site (*http://www.excelkb.com*) and a blog (*http://xldennis.wordpress.com*).

Acknowledgments

First and foremost, we would like to thank our parents, Walter and Beryl Fenlon and Mike and Marlene Hawley, for without their love and support, we never would have made it through.

Thanks must also go to the team at O'Reilly, first and foremost Brian Sawyer, for all the hard work that he has put into this book. Andy Pope and Dennis Wallentin must be thanked also for the hacks they contributed, and we have to mention all the visitors to our web site and forum, who helped us to identify some of the most common issues that people face.

We would also like to say a special thanks to all moderators and Oz MVPs on our free Q/A forum who share their time and knowledge in such an unselfish way. Finally, we must thank Aleisha and Kate, as always, our inspiration. Their understanding and extra efforts to be good while the book was in progress will be remembered!!

Preface

Millions of Microsoft Excel users are busy creating and sharing spreadsheets every day. Indeed, the spreadsheet has grown from a powerful convenience to a transformative foundation for many businesses, driving decision-making around the planet.

Although Excel is a critical tool, many Excel users know only about a subset of its functionality. They utilize the pieces they need, often reusing more complex pieces from existing templates, and don't dive too deeply into everything Excel has to offer. Odds are good that no single user actually needs every feature in Excel, so this approach is pretty reasonable. At the same time, though, it means a lot of people never get far enough along the learning curve to see the techniques they can use to make their work much easier.

With the release of MS Office 2007 comes a new version of Excel. There are many changes with Excel 2007, the most obvious being the new user interface. The introduction of the *ribbon* provides a results-oriented interface that presents tools when you need them, in a clear and organized fashion. The size of a spreadsheet has also been greatly increased, with the number of columns now well over 16,000 and the number of rows over 1,000,000. The total amount of memory that Excel can use has also been increased and is limited only by the maximum available memory Windows will allow on your PC.

Other improvements include easier use of PivotTables, conditional formatting and named ranges, live visual previews, predefined style galleries, table formats, and SmartArt graphics allowing you to use more complicated graphics in your spreadsheets. As most of us are usually required to work across a range of applications, share workbooks, and connect with the Web, Excel 2007 makes this much more user-friendly and easy to manage.

we have again used real-life situations for the content. Excel
.een used as a base for almost all of the hacks, although most of
.s can be used in previous versions as well and a few are specific to
.r versions. Differences are highlighted in the text and most of the old
.enu items can still be found, just in a different place and possibly named
slightly differently.

Why Excel Hacks?

Although it's possible to accomplish an enormous amount of work using a
relatively simple subset of Excel's capabilities, the software offers a lot of
powerful techniques that can leapfrog your work beyond the ordinary without requiring that you spend years using and studying Excel. However, most
people focus on the content they create—data and formulas, with the occasional chart—so moving to more advanced levels of Excel usage seems
difficult.

There are lots of ways to take advantage of Excel's capabilities to greatly
extend your ability to create great spreadsheets, but that don't require years
of study. These tools, or *hacks*—quick and dirty solutions to problems, or
clever ways of doing things—were created by Excel users looking for simple
solutions to complex issues. The hacks in this book are designed to show
you what's possible and how to make them work immediately.

You can benefit from these hacks in two important ways. First, you can use
the hacks directly as you build and improve your spreadsheets. Second, by
studying the hacks and possibly learning a little Visual Basic for Applications (VBA) code, you can customize the hacks to meet your needs precisely.

Getting and Using the Hacks

To save you the time and effort of typing scripts and spreadsheets by hand, all
the hacks (except those that are only a few lines long or use only the GUI) are
available for download from the authors' web site at *http://www.ozgrid.com/
BookExamples/excel-hack2-examples.htm.*

You'll undoubtedly want to cut and paste from the examples and modify
their contents to make them fit your spreadsheets more precisely. Excel
spreadsheets are tremendously diverse, and you'll want to change things to
make them fit your work.

How to Use This Book

Although this book is divided into chapters, as described in the following
section, you can use it in a variety of different ways. One approach is to

think of the book as a toolbox and start by becoming familiar with the tools in each chapter. Then, when a need arises or a problem occurs, you can simply use the right tool for the job. Or, you might decide to browse through the book or read it from cover to cover, studying the procedures and scripts to learn more about Excel. Some of the hacks are helpful in this area because they contain tutorials about complex subjects or well-documented scripts. You also might pick one chapter and see what you find useful to your current situation or what you might find helpful in the future.

How This Book Is Organized

Whichever way you choose to use this book, you will probably want to familiarize yourself with the contents first, so here's a brief synopsis of each chapter and what you'll find:

Chapter 1, *Reducing Workbook and Worksheet Frustration*
Workbooks and worksheets are the primary interface to data in Excel, but sometimes this set of giant open grids doesn't do precisely what you want. These hacks enable you to manage how users interact with worksheets, help you find and highlight information, and teach you how to deal with debris and corruption.

Chapter 2, *Hacking Excel's Built-in Features*
Excel includes many built-in features for analyzing and managing data. However, these features often have limitations. The hacks in this chapter enable you to extend and automate these features, moving beyond the limited tasks they were designed to perform originally.

Chapter 3, *Naming Hacks*
Although cell references such as A2 and IV284:IN1237 are certainly useful, as spreadsheets become larger, it's often easier to reference information by name. These hacks show you not only how to name cells and ranges, but also how to create names that adapt to the data in your spreadsheet.

Chapter 4, *Hacking PivotTables*
For many Excel users, PivotTables already seem like a complicated but magical hack. The hacks in this chapter teach you how to get the most out of PivotTables by showing you how to extend them and avoid the problems that make them frustrating.

Chapter 5, *Charting Hacks*
Excel's built-in charting capabilities are very useful, but they don't always provide the best method for viewing spreadsheet data. These hacks teach you how to tweak and combine Excel's built-in charting capabilities so that you can create customized charts.

Chapter 6, *Hacking Formulas and Functions*

> Formulas and functions are at the heart of most spreadsheets, but sometimes the way Excel handles them just isn't quite what you want. These hacks cover subjects ranging from moving formulas around to dealing with datatype issues to improving recalculation time.

Chapter 7, *Macro Hacks*

> Macros (and VBA) are Excel's escape hatch, enabling you to build spreadsheets that go well beyond Excel's own capabilities or develop spreadsheets that look more like programs. These hacks help you make the most of macros, from managing them to using them to extend other features.

Chapter 8, *Cross-Application Hacks*

> Although most spreadsheets are self-contained, this chapter shows you how you can work with other Microsoft Office applications to get information into and out of your spreadsheets and into and out of other programs.

Windows, Macintosh, and Earlier Excel Versions

The hacks in this book were written for Excel 2007 and were tested on previous versions of Excel for Windows and on a Macintosh using Excel 2004. Where steps or menu options differ, the main text shows how to accomplish the task in Excel 2007, with instructions for "pre-2007" called out in notes or parentheses.

Most of the differences between the Windows and Mac platform versions are cosmetic, and most involve changes to key combinations and the occasional menu. Where the key combinations differ, they are written with the Windows modifier first, as in Alt/Command(⌘)-Q, which means Alt-Q for Windows and ⌘-Q on the Macintosh. There are a few cases, especially in the Visual Basic Editor (VBE), where the interfaces look different and have different menu choices, and these are explained on first encounter. There are also a few Windows-only hacks, using the Windows registry and other features that are supported only on Windows versions of Excel. These are noted in the text.

Macintosh users with one-button mice should also note that holding down the Control key while clicking is the equivalent of right-clicking. (Macintosh users with two or more buttons can just right-click.) Recent models of Apple MacBook and MacBook Pros allow you to specify a right-click by holding two fingers on the trackpad and clicking. You must enable this in System Preferences.

Most of the hacks should work with any version of Excel from Excel 97 onward; the text will indicate when this isn't the case. Whenever possible, screenshots were taken using Excel 2007, but the figures are not an indicator of which hacks work with which versions.

Conventions Used in This Book

The following typographical conventions are used in this book:

Plain text

> Indicates cell identifiers, named ranges, menu titles, menu options, menu buttons, and keyboard accelerators (such as Alt and Ctrl).

Italic

> Indicates new terms, URLs, email addresses, filenames, file extensions, pathnames, directories, and variables in text.

`Constant width`

> Used for commands, options, switches, variables, attributes, keys, functions, types, classes, namespaces, methods, modules, properties, parameters, values, objects, events, event handlers, XML tags, HTML tags, macros, the contents of files, and the output from commands.

`Constant width bold`

> Used to show commands or other text that should be typed literally by the user, as well as to emphasize important lines of code.

`Constant width italic`

> Used in examples, tables, and commands to show text that should be replaced with user-supplied values.

↵

> A carriage return (↵) at the end of a line of code is used to denote an unnatural line break—that is, you should not enter these as two lines of code, but as one continuous line. Multiple lines are used in these cases due to page width constraints.

You should pay special attention to notes set apart from the text with the following icons:

> This icon signifies a tip, suggestion, or general note.

> This icon indicates a warning or caution.

The thermometer icons, found next to each hack, indicate the relative complexity of the hack:

beginner   moderate   expert

The following icons, found below each hack, indicate which versions of Excel are compatible with the hack:

ALL

Works with all versions of Excel

2007

Works with Excel 2007

<2007

Works with versions of Excel prior to 2007

2003

Works with Excel 2003

2000

Works with Excel 2000

Using Code Examples

This book is here to help you get your job done. In general, you may use the code in this book in your programs and documentation. You do not need to contact us for permission unless you're reproducing a significant portion of the code. For example, writing a program that uses several chunks of code from this book does not require permission. Selling or distributing a CD-ROM of examples from O'Reilly books *does* require permission. Answering a question by citing this book and quoting example code does not require permission. Incorporating a significant amount of example code from this book into your product's documentation *does* require permission.

We appreciate, but do not require, attribution. An attribution usually includes the title, author, publisher, and ISBN. For example: "*Excel Hacks, Second Edition*, by David and Raina Hawley. Copyright 2007 O'Reilly Media, Inc., 978-0-596-52834-8."

If you feel your use of code examples falls outside fair use or the permission given above, feel free to contact us at *permissions@oreilly.com*.

Safari® Enabled

 When you see a Safari® Enabled icon on the cover of your favorite technology book, that means the book is available online through the O'Reilly Network Safari Bookshelf.

Safari offers a solution that's better than e-books. It's a virtual library that lets you easily search thousands of top tech books, cut and paste code samples, download chapters, and find quick answers when you need the most accurate, current information. Try it for free at *http://safari.oreilly.com*.

How to Contact Us

Please address comments and questions concerning this book to the publisher:

> O'Reilly Media, Inc.
> 1005 Gravenstein Highway North
> Sebastopol, CA 95472
> 800-998-9938 (in the United States or Canada)
> 707-829-0515 (international or local)
> 707-829-0104 (fax)

We have a web page for this book, where we list errata, examples, and any additional information. You can access this page at:

> *http://www.oreilly.com/catalog/9780596528348/*

A collection of spreadsheet files for each individual hack is available at:

> *http://www.ozgrid.com/BookExamples/excel-hack2-examples.htm*

Visit the official web site of the Hacks series of books:

> *http://www.hackszine.com*

To comment or ask technical questions about this book, send email to:

> *bookquestions@oreilly.com*

For more information about our books, conferences, Resource Centers, and the O'Reilly Network, see our web site at:

> *http://www.oreilly.com*

Reducing Workbook and Worksheet Frustration

Hacks 1–16

Excel users know that workbooks are a powerful metaphor. But many users are equally aware that dealing with workbooks can cause a huge number of snags. The hacks in this chapter will help you avoid some of these snags while taking advantage of some of the more effective but often overlooked ways in which you can control your workbooks.

Before we leap into the hacks, though, it's worth taking a quick look at some basics that will make it much easier to create effective hacks. Excel is a very powerful spreadsheet application, and you can do incredible things with it. Unfortunately, many people design their Excel spreadsheets with little foresight, making it difficult for them to reuse or update the spreadsheets they've so carefully built. In this section, we provide several tips you can follow to ensure that you're creating spreadsheets that are as efficient as possible.

The 80/20 Rule   *80% planning   20% implement*

Perhaps the most important rule to follow when designing a spreadsheet is to take a long-term view and never assume you will *not* need to add more data or formulas to your spreadsheet because chances are good that you will. With that in mind, you should spend about 80 percent of your time planning your spreadsheet and about 20 percent implementing it. Although this can seem extremely inefficient in the short run, we can assure you that the long-term gain will far outweigh the short-term pain and that the planning gets easier after you've done it for a while. Remember that spreadsheets are about making it easy for users to get correct information, not just about presenting information that looks good only once.

Structural Tips *Layout*

Without a doubt, the number one mistake most Excel users make when creating their spreadsheets is that they do not set up and lay out the data in the manner in which Excel and its features expect. Here are, in no particular order, some of the most common mistakes users make when setting up a spreadsheet:

- Unnecessarily spreading data over many different workbooks
- Unnecessarily spreading data over numerous worksheets
- Unnecessarily spreading data over different tables
- Having blank columns and rows in tables of data
- Leaving blank cells for repeated data

RULE The first three items on the preceding list add up to one thing: you should always try to keep related data in one continuous table. Time and time again we see spreadsheets that do not follow this simple rule and thus are limited in their ability to take full advantage of some of Excel's most powerful features, including PivotTables, subtotals, and worksheet formulas. In such scenarios, you can use these features to their full potential only when you've laid out your data in a very basic table.

RULE It is no coincidence that Excel spreadsheets can comprise 1,048,576 rows (65,536 pre-2007) but only 16,384 columns (256 pre-2007). With this in mind, you should set up tables with column headings going across the first row of your table and related data laid out in a continuous manner directly underneath their appropriate headings. If you find you are repeating the same data over and over for two or more rows in one of these columns, resist the temptation to use blank cells to indicate repetition.

Rule Make sure your data is sorted whenever possible. Excel has a rich set of lookup and reference formulas, some of which require that your data be sorted in a logical order. Sorting also will speed the calculation process of many functions significantly.

Formatting Tips *Cells*

Moving beyond structure, formatting also can cause problems. Although a spreadsheet should be easy to read and follow, this should rarely be at the expense of efficiency. We are big believers in "keeping it simple." Far too many people spend tremendous amounts of time formatting their spreadsheets. Although they don't necessarily realize it, this time frequently comes at the expense of efficiency. Often the overuse of formatting adds size to your workbook, and although your workbook might look like a work of art to you, it might look terrible to someone else. Some very good universal colors to consider using in your spreadsheets are black, white, and gray.

It is always a good idea to leave at least three blank rows above your table (*at least* three, preferably more). These can then be used for criteria for features such as Advanced Filter and Database functions.

People also tinker with the alignment of cell data. By default, numbers in Excel are right-aligned and text is left-aligned, and there are good reasons to leave it this way. If you start changing this formatting, you will not be able to tell at a glance if the contents of a cell are text or numeric. It is very common for people to reference cells, which look like numbers but in reality are text. If you have altered the default alignment, you will be left scratching your head. Perhaps headings are an exception to this rule.

Format cells as text only when completely necessary. All data entered into cells formatted as text become text, even if you meant for them to be numbers or dates. Worse still, any cell housing a formula that references a text-formatted cell also will be formatted as text. Generally, you do not want formula cells to be formatted as text!

Merged cells can also cause problems. The Microsoft knowledge base is full of frequently encountered problems with merged cells. As a good alternative, use "Center across selection," found under Home → Alignment Group. The arrow in the bottom right will display the Format dialog with the Alignment tab active. Use the Horizontal drop-down to select Center Across Selection or right-click and choose Format Cells from the shortcut menu (pre-2007, Format → Cells).

Formula Tips

Another enormous mistake users often make in Excel formulas is referencing entire columns. This forces Excel to examine potentially thousands, if not millions, of cells it otherwise could have ignored.

Assume, for example, that you have a table of data ranging from cell A1 to cell H1000. You might decide you want to use one or more of Excel's lookup formulas to extract the required information. Because your table might continue to grow (as you add new data), it is common to reference the entire table, incorporating all rows. In other words, your reference might look something like A:H, or possibly A1:H65536. You would use this reference so that when new data is added to the table, it will be referenced in the formulas automatically.

This is a very bad habit to form and you should almost always avoid it. You still can eliminate the need to constantly update your formula references to incorporate new data as it is added to a table by using dynamic named ranges.

Another common problem with poorly designed spreadsheets is painfully slow recalculation. Many people suggest that shifting calculation mode into Manual via the Office button → Excel → Formulas (pre-2007, Tools → Options → Calculations; Mac OS X, Excel → Preferences → Calculation) will solve this problem.

However, this is generally very poor advice, fraught with potential disasters. A spreadsheet is all about formulas and calculations and the results they produce. If you are running a spreadsheet in manual calculation mode, sooner or later you will read some information from your spreadsheet that will not have been updated. Your formulas might be reflecting old values and not the updated values because when you go into manual calculation mode, you must force Excel to recalculate by pressing the F9 key (⌘-= on Mac OS X). However, it is very easy to forget to do this! Think of it this way. If your car brakes were rubbing and slowing down your car, would you disconnect the brake pedal and rely on the hand brake instead of fixing the problem? Most of us wouldn't dream of doing this, but many people don't hesitate to put their spreadsheets into manual calculation mode. If you need to run your spreadsheet in manual calculation mode, you have a design problem. Address it properly and do not use a "Band-Aid" approach.

Array formulas are another common cause of trouble. They are best suited to referencing single cells. If you use them to reference large ranges, do so as infrequently as possible. When large numbers of arrays reference large ranges, your workbook's performance will suffer, sometimes to the point where it becomes unusable and you are forced to run your spreadsheet in manual calculation mode.

Excel's database functions provide many alternatives to array formulas, as discussed in "Sum or Count Cells While Avoiding Error Values" [Hack #79]. Also, the Excel Help offers some good examples on how you can use these formulas on large tables of data to return results based on multiple criteria. Another alternative that is often overlooked is the use of Excel's PivotTable feature, discussed in Chapter 4. Although PivotTables might seem very daunting when first encountered, we highly recommend that you familiarize yourself with this powerful Excel feature because once you master PivotTables, you will wonder how you survived without them!

At the end of the day, if you remember nothing else about spreadsheet design, remember that Excel works best when all related data is laid out in one continuous table. That should make the rest of your hacking much easier.

Create a Personal View of Your Workbooks

ALL

Excel enables you to have multiple workbooks showing simultaneously, and to have a customized view of your workbooks arranged in different windows. Then you can save your view workspaces as *.xlw* files and use them when it suits you.

Sometimes when working in Excel, you might need to have more than one workbook open on your screen to make it easier to use or view data from multiple workbooks. The next few paragraphs describe how to do this in a neat and organized way.

First, open all the workbooks you will need.

> To open more than one workbook at a time, select the Office button → Open..., press the Ctrl key (⌘ key on the Mac) while selecting the workbooks you want to open, and then click Open (pre-2007, select File → Open).

From any of the workbooks (it doesn't matter which one), select Windows → View → Arrange All (pre-2007, select Window → Arrange). If "Windows of active workbook" is checked, uncheck it, and then select the window arrangement you prefer and click OK.

If you select Tiled, you will be presented with your workbooks in a tiled fashion, as shown with blank workbooks in Figure 1-1.

Selecting Horizontal gives you a view of your workbooks in a single stack, one on top of the other, as in Figure 1-2.

Checking the Vertical option will place all your open workbooks side by side, as shown in Figure 1-3.

Finally, as shown in Figure 1-4, selecting the Cascade option will layer all open workbooks one on top of the other.

Once your workbooks are displayed in your preferred view, you can easily move data between them (e.g., copy, paste, drag and drop).

If you think you might want to return to a view you created, you can save this preferred view as a *workspace*. To save a workspace, simply select Windows → Save Workspace (pre-2007, File → Save Workspace), enter the workspace's filename in the File Name box, and click OK. When saving your workspace, the file extension will be *.xlw* rather than the standard *.xlsx* of Excel 2007. To restore your Excel workspace to one full window of a particular workbook, just double-click the title bar (on the Mac, click the green

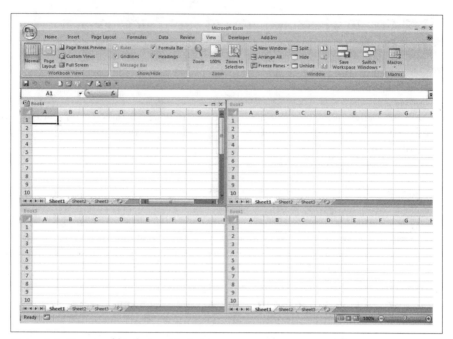

Figure 1-1. Four workbooks in a tiled view

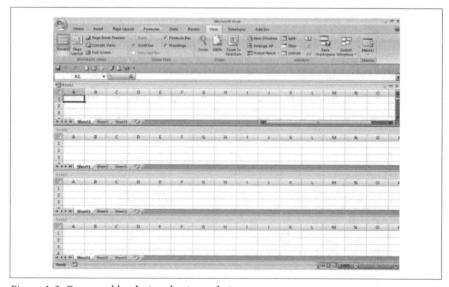

Figure 1-2. Four workbooks in a horizontal view

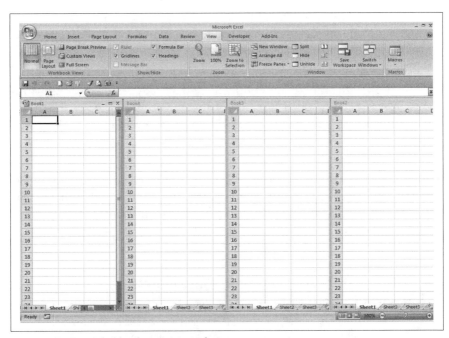

Figure 1-3. Four workbooks in a vertical view

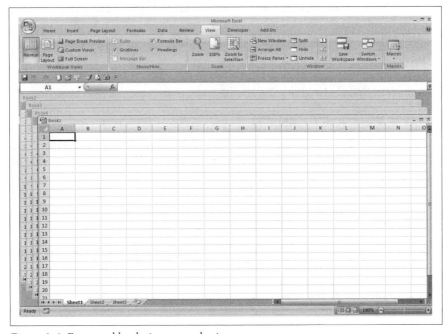

Figure 1-4. Four workbooks in a cascade view

Zoom button in the upper left of the window) appearing on any one of your workbooks. You can also click the Maximize button on any of the windows in your workspace. Close your workbooks as usual when you're finished.

Whenever you need to open those same workbooks, simply open the *.xlw* file, and the view you initially set up will be magically restored for all workbooks. If you need to open just one of those workbooks, open the file as usual. Any changes you make to the workbooks in the *.xlw* file will be saved automatically as you close the workspace as a whole, or you can save workbooks individually.

If you spend a small amount of time setting up some custom views for repetitive tasks that require multiple open workbooks, you'll find that these tasks become easier to manage. You might decide to use different views for different repetitive tasks, depending on what the task is or how you're feeling that day.

HACK #2 Enter Data into Multiple Worksheets Simultaneously

ALL It's fairly ordinary to need some data to be duplicated in multiple worksheets. You can use Excel's tool for grouping so that data entered in one workbook can be entered into multiple worksheets simultaneously. But therer is also a quicker and more flexible approach that uses a couple of lines of Visual Basic for Applications (VBA) code.

Excel's built-in mechanism for making data go to multiple places at once is a feature called *Group*. It works by grouping the worksheets together so that they're all linked within the workbook.

Grouping Worksheets Manually

To use the Group feature manually, simply click the sheet into which you will be entering the data, and press the Ctrl key (the ⌘ key on the Macintosh) while clicking the Name tabs of the worksheets where you want the data to go. When you enter data into any cells on your worksheet, they will be entered automatically in the other grouped worksheets. Mission accomplished.

To ungroup your worksheets, either select one worksheet that is not part of the group, right-click any Name tab and select Ungroup Sheets, or Ctrl/⌘-click the sheets you added to the group.

When your worksheets are grouped together, you can look up to the title bar and see the word *Group* in square brackets. This lets you know your worksheets are still grouped. Unless you have eagle eyes and a mind like a steel trap, however, it is highly likely that you won't notice this or that you'll forget you have your worksheets grouped. For this reason, we gently suggest you ungroup your sheets as soon as you finish doing what you need to do.

Although this method is easy, it means you need to remember to group and ungroup your sheets as needed or else you will inadvertently overtype data from another worksheet. For example, you might want the simultaneous entries to occur only when you are in a particular range of cells. However, simultaneous data entries will occur regardless of the cell you are in at the time.

 Grouping Worksheets Automatically

You can overcome these shortcomings by using some very simple VBA code. For this code to work, it must reside within the private module for the Sheet object. To quickly go to the private module, right-click the Sheet Name tab and select View Code. You can then use one of Excel's sheet events—which are events that take place within your worksheet, such as changing a cell, selecting a range, activating, deactivating, and so on—to move the code into the private module for the Sheet object.

In most cases, you will be taken directly to the private module when you right-click on a workbook or worksheet and select View Code. You can confirm that you're in the private module by looking at the state of the drop-down menu in the upper left of the code window—this window is usually labeled something like "Workbook - *sheetname* (Code)". If the drop-down menu says "Workbook" or "Worksheet," then you in the private module. If it says "(General)," change it before typing in the code.

To enable grouping, first name the range of cells you want to have grouped so that the data shows automatically on other worksheets.

Enter this code into the private module:

```
Private Sub Worksheet_SelectionChange(ByVal Target As Range)
  If Not Intersect(Range("MyRange"), Target) Is Nothing Then
```

```
'Sheet5 has purposely been placed first as this will
'be the active sheet we will work from
Sheets(Array("Sheet5", "Sheet3", "Sheet1")).Select
Else
Me.Select
End If
End Sub
```

In this code, we used the named range MyRange. (If you aren't familiar with named ranges, see "Address Data by Name" [Hack #44].) Change MyRange to the range name you are using on your worksheet. Also change the three sheet names in the code, as shown in Figure 1-5, to the sheet names you want to be grouped. When you're done, either click the View Microsoft Excel tool, close the module window, or press Alt/⌘-Q to get back to Excel, then save your workbook.

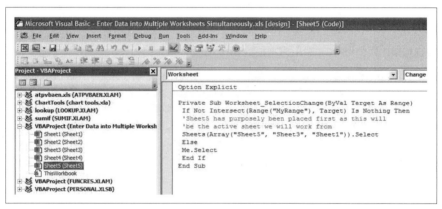

Figure 1-5. Code for automatically grouping worksheets

It is important to note that the first sheet name used in the array must be the sheet housing the code, and thus the worksheet on which you will enter the data.

Once the code is in place, each time you select any cell on the worksheet, the code checks to see whether the cell you selected (the target) is within the range named MyRange. If it is, the code will automatically group the worksheets you want grouped. If it isn't, it will ungroup the sheets simply by activating the sheet you are already on. The beauty of this hack is that there is no need to manually group the sheets and therefore run the risk of forgetting to ungroup them. This approach can save lots of time and frustration.

If you want the same data to appear on other sheets but *not* in the same cell addresses, use code like this:

```
Private Sub worksheet_Change(ByVal Target As Range)
If Not Intersect(Range("MyRange"), Target) Is Nothing Then
With Range("MyRange")
```

```
.Copy Destination:=Sheets("Sheet3").Range("A1")
.Copy Destination:=Sheets("Sheet1").Range("D10")
End With
End If
End Sub
```

This code also needs to live within the private module of the Sheet object. Follow the steps described earlier in this hack to get it there.

Prevent Users from Performing Certain Actions

Although Excel provides overall protection for workbooks and worksheets, this blunt instrument doesn't provide limited privileges to users—unless you do some hacking.

You can manage user interactions with your spreadsheets by monitoring and responding to events. *Events,* as the term suggests, are actions that occur as you work with your workbooks and worksheets. Some of the more common events include opening a workbook, saving it, and closing it. You can tell Excel to run some Visual Basic code automatically when any one of these events is triggered.

> Users can bypass all these protections by disabling macros entirely. Click the Office button and choose Excel Options → Trust Center → Trust Center Settings and press the Macro Settings Button (pre-2007, Tools → Macro → Security). If their security is set to "Disable all macros with notification" (Medium in pre-2007 versions), they'll be notified of macros in the workbook upon opening it and will be offered the opportunity to turn them off. A security setting of "Disable all macros without notification" (High in older versions) will simply turn them off automatically. On the other hand, if using the spreadsheet requires the use of macros, users might be more likely to have macros turned on. These hacks are a convenience and do not provide heavy-duty data security.
>
> On Mac OS X, you cannot control macro protection at this level of detail. Instead, you can select Excel → Preferences → Security and toggle the setting "Warn before opening a file that contains macros."

Preventing Save As... in a Workbook

You can specify that any workbook be saved as read-only by choosing Office button → Save → Tools Button → General Options and enabling the "Read-only recommended" checkbox (pre-2007, File → Save As → Tools [Options on the Mac] → General options in the Save options dialog). Doing so can prevent a user from saving any changes he might make to the file, unless he saves it with a different name and/or in a different location.

Sometimes, however, you might want to prevent users from being able to save a copy of your workbook to another directory or folder with or without a different name. In other words, you want users to be able to save on top of the existing file and not save another copy elsewhere. This is particularly handy when more than one person is saving changes to a workbook because you do not end up with a number of different copies of the same workbook, saved with the same name in different folders.

The *Before Save* event you'll be using has existed since Excel 97. As its name suggests, this event occurs just before a workbook is saved, enabling you to catch the user before the fact, issue a warning, and stop Excel from saving.

 Before trying this at home, be sure to save your workbook first. Putting this code into place without having saved will prevent your workbook from ever saving.

To insert the code, open your workbook and choose Developer → Visual Basic, then select View → Code, and double-click on ThisWorkbook in the Project Explorer (pre-2007, right-click the Excel icon immediately to the left of the File menu item on the worksheet menu bar, and select View Code, as shown in Figure 1-6).

 You might have to enable the Developer tab (not standard in Excel 2007) by selecting Office button → Excel Options → Popular, checking the option "Show Developer tab in the Ribbon" and clicking OK.

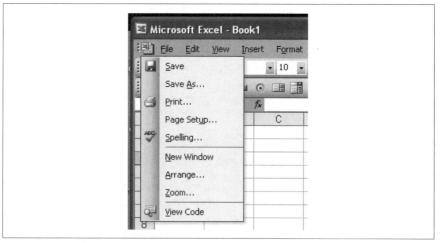

Figure 1-6. Quick access menu (in Excel 2003) to the private module for the workbook object

> This shortcut isn't available on the Mac. You'll have to open the Visual Basic Editor (VBE) by pressing Option-F11, or by selecting Tools → Macro → Visual Basic Editor. Once you're there, Ctrl-click or right-click This Workbook in the Projects window.

Type the following code into the VBE, as shown in Figure 1-7, and press Alt/⌘-Q to get back to Excel proper, then save your workbook:

```
Private Sub workbook_BeforeSave(ByVal SaveAsUI As Boolean, _
Cancel As Boolean)
Dim lReply As Long
  If SaveAsUI = True Then
lReply = MsgBox("Sorry, you are not allowed to save this " & _
"workbook as another name. Do you wish to save this " & _
"workbook?", vbQuestion + vbOKCancel)
Cancel = (lReply = vbCancel)
If Cancel = False Then Me.Save
Cancel = True
End If
End Sub
```

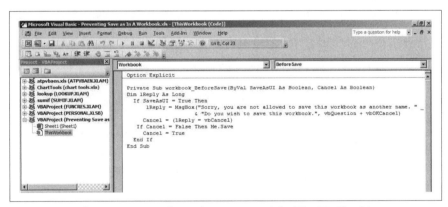

Figure 1-7. Code once it's entered into the private module (ThisWorkbook)

Give it a whirl. Select Office button → Save (pre-2007, File → Save) and your workbook will save as expected. However, select Office button → Save As (pre-2007, File → Save As...) and you'll be informed that you're not allowed to save this workbook under any other filename, unless you've disabled macros.

> Note that when you save a workbook in Excel 2007 and it contains either macros or code, you will be prompted to save your workbook as an Excel macro-enabled workbook (*.xlsm) and will be unable to save in the standard Excel file format (*.xlsx).

Preventing Users from Printing a Workbook

Perhaps you want to prevent users from printing your workbook—and probably having it end up in a recycling bin or left on a desk somewhere in plain sight. Using Excel's *Before Print* event, you can stop them in their tracks. Enter the following code, as before, into the VBE:

```
Private Sub workbook_BeforePrint(Cancel As Boolean)
  Cancel = True
  MsgBox "Sorry, you cannot Print from this workbook", vbInformation
End Sub
```

Press Alt/⌘-Q when you're done entering the code to get back to Excel, then save your workbook. Now each time users try to print from this workbook, nothing will happen. The MsgBox line of code is optional, but it's always a good idea to include it to at least inform users so that they do not hassle the IT department, saying there is a problem with their program!

If you want to prevent users from printing only particular sheets in your workbook, use this similar code instead:

```
Private Sub workbook_BeforePrint(Cancel As Boolean)
  Select Case ActiveSheet.Name
  Case "Sheet1", "Sheet2"
  Cancel = True
  MsgBox "Sorry, you cannot print this sheet from this workbook", _
vbInformation
  End Select
End Sub
```

Notice you've specified "Sheet1" and "Sheet2" as the only cases in which printing should be stopped. Of course, these can be the names of any sheets in your workbook; to add more sheets to the list, simply type a comma followed by the sheet name in quotation marks. If you need to prevent the printing of only one sheet, supply just that one name in quotes and drop the comma.

Preventing Users from Inserting More Worksheets

Excel lets you protect a workbook's structure so that users cannot delete worksheets, rearrange the order in which they appear, rename them, and so forth. Sometimes, though, you want to prevent just the addition of more worksheets, while still allowing other structural alterations.

The following code will get the job done:

```
Private Sub Workbook_NewSheet(ByVal Sh As Object)
  Application.DisplayAlerts = False
  MsgBox "Sorry, you cannot add any more sheets to this workbook", _
  vbInformation
```

```
    Sh.Delete
    Application.DisplayAlerts = True
End Sub
```

The code first displays the message box with the message and then immediately deletes the newly added sheet when the user clicks OK from the message box. The use of `Application.DisplayAlerts = False` stops the standard Excel warning that asks users if they really want to delete the sheet. With this in place, users will be unable to add more worksheets to the workbook.

Another way to prevent users from adding worksheets is to select Review → Changes → Protect Workbook, and then press the Protect Structure and Windows button (pre-2007, Tools → Protection → Protect Workbook..., ensure that the Structure checkbox is checked, and click OK). However, as mentioned at the beginning of this hack, Excel's worksheet protection is a rather blunt instrument and will also prevent many other Excel features from working.

Prevent Seemingly Unnecessary Prompts

HACK #4

ALL

Excel's chattiness can get a little old, always prompting you to confirm actions you just asked it to perform. Quit the conversation and let Excel get back to the action.

The types of prompts we are talking about are those that ask you whether you want to enable macros (when you do not have any), or whether you are sure you want to delete a worksheet. Here is how to get rid of the most common prompts once and for all.

Enabling Macros When You Don't Have Any

Excel's memory is like a steel trap when it comes to remembering that you recorded a macro in your workbook. Unfortunately, its memory of macros persists even though you might have since deleted one or more macros via Developer → Macros or Alt/Option-F8 (pre-2007, Tools → Macro → Macros). Reopen the workbook and you'll still be prompted to enable macros, even though there are none to enable.

You'll be prompted to enable macros only if your security level is set to "Disable all macros with notification" (Medium in pre-2007 versions). If it's set to "Enable all macros" (Low in pre-2007 versions), macros are enabled without a peep; if it's set to "Disable all macros without notification" (High in pre-2007 versions), macros are disabled automatically for your protection.

When you record a macro, Excel inserts a Visual Basic module to hold your commands and home-brewed functions. Upon opening a workbook, Excel checks for the presence of modules, whether empty or macro-filled. Deleting a workbook's macros deletes any code within the module, not the module itself—kind of like drinking the last of the milk, yet putting the empty carton back in the fridge. To avoid the unnecessary macro prompt, you need to remove the module. Here's how to do that.

Open the VBE by selecting Developer → Visual Basic under Code options or by pressing Alt/Option-F11 (pre-2007, Tools → Macro → Visual Basic Editor and select View → Project Explorer).

> On the Macintosh and in Excel 2007, the Projects window is always open, so you don't need to open the Project Explorer.

You'll see a window like the one shown in Figure 1-8.

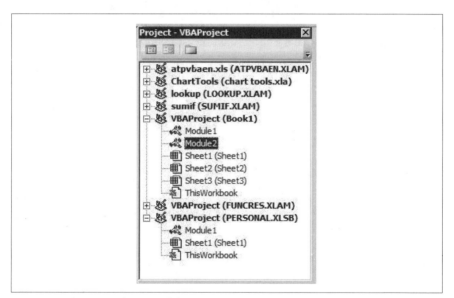

Figure 1-8. Project Explorer modules

Find your workbook in the Project Explorer and click the plus sign (+) to its left to expose the workbook's component parts, particularly the modules if they are not already showing. Right-click each module in turn and choose Remove Module from the context-sensitive menu. Decline the offer to export the modules. Before blithely removing modules that might contain useful code, double-click each module in turn to make certain you don't need them. Press Alt/⌘-Q as usual to get back to Excel's spreadsheet view.

Prompting to Save Nonexistent Changes

You might have noticed that sometimes simply opening a workbook and taking a look around is enough to trigger Excel to prompt you to save changes to your personal macro workbook—despite the fact that you've made no changes whatsoever. Whether you know it or not, you most likely have a volatile function within your personal macro workbook.

A *personal macro workbook* is a hidden workbook created the first time you record a macro (Tools → Macro → Record New Macro) and specify "Personal Macro Workbook" in the "Store Macro in" drop-down menu. It is opened each time you use Excel. A *volatile function* (or formula) is one that automatically recalculates each time you do almost anything in Excel, including opening and closing either the workbook or the entire application. Two of the most common volatile functions are the Today( ) and Now( ) functions.

So, although you might believe you've made no changes to the workbook at hand, those volatile functions running in the background might have. This counts as a change and triggers Excel's prompt to save said invisible changes.

If you want Excel to stop prompting you to save changes you didn't make, you have a couple of options open to you. The most obvious is not to store volatile functions within your personal macro workbook in the first place, and to delete any volatile functions that are already there. Or, if you need volatile functions, you can use this rather simple snippet of code to circumvent the check by tricking Excel into thinking your personal macro workbook has been saved the moment it opens:

```
Private Sub Workbook_BeforeClose(Cancel As Boolean)
    Me.Saved = True
End Sub
```

This code must live in the private workbook module of your personal macro workbook. To get there from any workbook, select View → Unhide under Window options (pre-2007, Window → Unhide), select *Personal.xls* from Unhide Workbook, and click OK. Visit the VBE and enter the aforementioned code. Press Alt/⌘-Q to get back to Excel when you're done.

Of course, if you have a volatile function that you want to recalculate and you want to save the changes, you need to explicitly tell Excel to do so:

```
Private Sub Workbook_BeforeClose(Cancel As Boolean)
    Me.Save
End Sub
```

This macro will save your personal macro workbook automatically each time it is opened.

Stopping Excel's Warning Prompts for Recorded Macros

One of the many drawbacks of recorded macros is that, although they're pretty good at mimicking just about any command, they tend to forget your responses to prompts. Delete a worksheet and you're prompted for confirmation; run a macro for the same and you'll still be prompted. Let's turn off those prompts.

Select Developer → Macros under Code options or Alt/Option-F8 (pre-2007, Tools → Macro → Macros) to bring up a list of your macros. Make sure "All Open Workbooks" is selected in the Macros In: box's pull-down menu. Select the macro you're interested in and click the Edit button. Put the cursor before the very first line of code—i.e., the first line without an apostrophe in front of it—and prepend the following:

```
Application.DisplayAlerts = False
```

At the very end of your code, append the following:

```
Application.DisplayAlerts = True
```

Your macro should look something like this:

```
Sub MyMacro( )
'
' MyMacro Macro
' Deletes the Active worksheet
'

    '
    Application.DisplayAlerts = False
    ActiveSheet.Delete
    Application.DisplayAlerts = True
End Sub
```

Note that you've turned alerts back on at the end of your macro to re-enable standard Excel prompts while working in Excel. Leave this out, and you'll see no alerts at all, not even those that might have been good to include.

 If your macro does not complete for any reason—a runtime error, for instance—Excel might never get to the line of code that turns alerts back on. If this happens, it's probably wise to quit and restart Excel to set things back to the way they were.

Now you know how to use Excel without prompts. Be aware, though, that these prompts are there for a reason. Make sure you fully understand the purpose of a prompt before summarily turning it off.

HACK #5

ALL

Hide Worksheets So That They Cannot Be Unhidden

Sometimes you want a place for information that users can't read or modify. Build a backstage into your workbook, a place to keep data, formulas, and other minutiae consumed by, but not seen in, your sheets.

A useful practice when setting up a new Excel workbook is to reserve one worksheet for storing information users do not need to see: formula calculations, data validation, lists, useful variables and special values, sensitive data, and so forth. Although you can hide the sheet by selecting View → Hide under Window options (pre-2007, Format → Sheet → Hide), it's a good idea to ensure that users can't unhide it by selecting View → Unhide under the Window options (pre-2007, Format → Sheet → Unhide...).

You can, of course, simply protect the worksheet. However, this still leaves it in full view—sensitive data, scary formulas, and all. Also, you can't protect a cell linked into any of the controls available to you from the Forms toolbar.

Instead, we'll fiddle with the worksheet's Visible property, making it xlVeryHidden. Go to Developer → Visual Basic or Alt/Option-F11 to get to the VBE (pre-2007, go to Tools → Macro → Visual Basic Editor and make sure the Project Explorer window is visible by selecting View → Project Explorer). Find the name of your workbook within the Project Explorer and expand its hierarchy by clicking the + to the left of the workbook's name. Expand the Microsoft Excel Objects folder within to reveal all your workbook's worksheets.

Select the sheet you want to hide from the Project Explorer and reveal its properties by selecting View → Properties Window (or by pressing F4). Make sure the Alphabetic tab is selected, and look for the Visible property at the very bottom. Click the value box on the right associated with the Visible property and select the last option, 2 - xlSheetVeryHidden, as shown in Figure 1-9. Press Alt/⌘-Q to return to Excel, then save your changes. The sheet will no longer be visible via the Excel interface and won't appear as a choice under View → Unhide under Window options (pre-2007, Format → Sheet → Unhide...).

Once you have selected 2 - xlSheetVeryHidden from the Properties window, it might appear as though your selection had no effect. This visual bug sometimes occurs and shouldn't concern you; if the sheet no longer appears when you select View → Unhide under Window options (pre-2007, Format → Sheet → Unhide...) you know it had the desired effect.

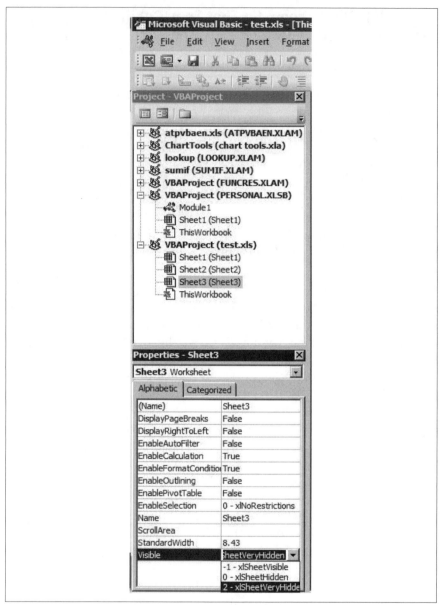

Figure 1-9. Properties window of a worksheet having its visible property set to 2 - xlSheetVeryHidden

To reverse the process, simply follow the preceding steps, this time selecting `-1 - xlSheetVisible`.

ALL

Customize the Templates Dialog and Default Workbook

If you tend to perform the same tasks or use the same spreadsheet layouts again and again, you can build your own Template tab into Excel's standard Insert Template dialog to provide a quick starting point.

Imagine you have a spreadsheet containing days of the year and formulas summarizing various data for the days. You have formatted this spreadsheet beautifully with your company colors, logo, and required formulas, and you need to use it on a daily basis. Instead of reinventing the wheel (or copying and deleting what you don't need) each day, you can save yourself a lot of time and trouble by creating a template.

Excel's worksheet and workbook templates provide you with a running start on your next project, enabling you to skip the initial setup, formatting, formula building, and so on. Saving a template worksheet simply means opening a new workbook, deleting all but one worksheet, and then creating the basic template you will be using. Once you're finished, select Office button → Save As... (pre-2007, File → Save As...) and choose Excel Template (Template on Mac OS X) from the dialog's Save As Type (Format on Mac OS X) drop-down list. If your template is to be a workbook template—i.e., it will contain more than one worksheet—again add a new workbook, make all the necessary changes, select Office button → Save As..., and save as an Excel template.

Template in hand, you can create a clone at any time by either selecting the Office button → New (pre-2007, File → New...; File → Project Gallery on the Mac) and selecting a workbook template, or by right-clicking the Worksheet tab and selecting Insert... from the context sensitive menu to insert a new worksheet from a template. Wouldn't it be nice, though, to have those templates available to you right from Excel's standard Insert Template dialog, or to set your preferred workbook as the default? You can, by creating your own Template tab.

This hack assumes you have a single installation of Excel running on your computer. If you have multiple copies or versions of Excel installed, this may not work.

Creating Your Own Template Tab

If you have a slew of templates—workbooks, worksheets, or both—that you use on a regular basis, you can group them together to make it easier for you to manage them.

From within any workbook, choose the Office button → Save As... (pre-2007, File → Save As...). Then, from the Files of Type pop-up menu, select Excel Template (*.xltx*); for older versions, select Template (*.xlt*). By default Excel will select the standard Templates folder in which all your home-grown templates are kept.

If you want to create tabs in which to store your templates, create a sub-folder by using the New Folder button.

 On Mac OS X, Excel 2004 defaults to your My Templates directory for saving new templates, so this step is not needed.

Now, go to the Office button, select New, and click the "My templates" option button (for Excel 2000 and above, choose General Templates from the New Workbook dialog that will appear; for older versions, select File → New... on the worksheet menu bar). You should now see the tab you created (named Ozgrid in the screen shot in Figure 1-10) on the dialog floating over your screen. You also should now see your Template workbooks and worksheets, as long as you saved them to this folder.

 In Excel 2007, as a default if you do not create any tabs, your templates are stored under "My templates" in the My Templates tab.

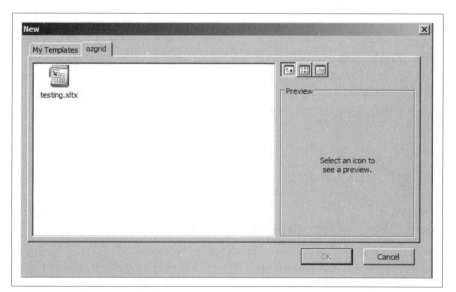

Figure 1-10. The Templates dialog

Using a Custom Default Workbook

Starting Excel opens a blank default workbook called *Book1* containing three blank worksheets. This is fine and dandy if you want a clean slate each time you start Excel. If you're like us, however, you tend to favor one workbook over the others. So, for us, opening Excel involves dismissing the default workbook and searching for our regular workbook. It sure would be handy to have that favored workbook open at the outset, ready for action.

To do so, save your default workbook (template) in the *XLSTART* folder (generally found in *C:\Documents and Settings\Owner\Application Data\ Microsoft\Excel\XLSTART* in Windows, and in *Applications/Microsoft Office 2004/Office/Startup/Excel* under Mac OS X). Once you have done this, Excel will automatically use whichever workbook(s) you have in there as the default.

> The *XLSTART* folder is where your personal macro workbook is created and saved automatically when you record a macro. The personal macro workbook is a hidden workbook. You also can have your own hidden workbooks open in the background if you want by opening the required workbook, selecting View → Hide under Window options (pre-2007, Window → Hide), closing Excel, and clicking Yes to save changes to the workbook you just hid. Now place this workbook in your *XLSTART* folder. All the workbooks you hide and place within the *XLSTART* folder will open as hidden workbooks each time you start Excel.
>
> Don't be tempted to place too many workbooks into this folder, especially large ones, as all of them will open when you start Excel. Too many open workbooks can greatly slow down Excel's performance.

Naturally, if you change your mind and decide to go back to a blank default workbook, simply remove the appropriate workbook or workbook template from the *XLSTART* folder.

HACK #7   Create an Index of Sheets in Your Workbook

ALL

If you've spent much time in a workbook with many worksheets, you know how painful it can be to find a particular worksheet. An index sheet available to every worksheet is a navigational must-have.

Using an index sheet will enable you to quickly and easily navigate throughout your workbook so that with one click of the mouse you will be taken exactly where you want to go, without fuss. You can create an index in a few ways: by hand, auto-generated by code, or as a context-sensitive menu option.

Creating an Index Sheet by Hand

You might be tempted to simply create the index by hand. Create a new worksheet, call it *Index* or the like, enter a list of all your worksheets' names, and hyperlink each to the appropriate sheet by selecting Insert → Hyperlink under Link options (pre-2007, Insert → Hyperlink...) or by pressing Ctrl/⌘-K. Although this method is probably sufficient for limited instances in which you don't have too many sheets and they won't change often, you'll be stuck maintaining your index by hand.

Auto-Generate an Index Using VBA

An alternative is to use VBA to auto-generate the index. The following code will automatically create a clickable, hyperlinked index of all the sheets you have in the workbook. The index is re-created each time the sheet that houses the code is activated.

This code should live in the private module for the Sheet object. Insert a new worksheet into your workbook and name it something appropriate—*Index*, for instance. Right-click the index sheet's tab and select View Code from the context menu or select Alt/Option-F11.

Enter the following Visual Basic code:

```
Private Sub Worksheet_Activate( )
Dim wSheet As Worksheet
Dim l As Long
l = 1
 With Me
 .Columns(1).ClearContents
 .Cells(1, 1) = "INDEX"
 .Cells(1, 1).Name = "Index"
 End With

 For Each wSheet In Worksheets
 If wSheet.Name <> Me.Name Then
 l = l + 1
 With wSheet
 .Range("A1").Name = "Start" & wSheet.Index
 .Hyperlinks.Add Anchor:=.Range("A1"), Address:="", SubAddress:= _
 "Index", TextToDisplay:="Back to Index"
 End With
 Me.Hyperlinks.Add Anchor:=Me.Cells(l, 1), Address:="", _
 SubAddress:="Start" & wSheet.Index, TextToDisplay:=wSheet.Name
 End If
 Next wSheet
End Sub
```

Press Alt/⌘-Q to get back to your workbook and then save your chan
To make the code run, you will first need to deactivate your worksho
(select another sheet) and select the index sheet.

Notice that in the same way you name a range of cells, the code names cell
A1 on each sheet Start, plus a unique whole number representing the index
number of the sheet. This ensures that A1 on each sheet has a different
name. If A1 on your worksheet already has a name, you should consider
changing any mention of A1 in the code to something more suitable—an
unused cell anywhere on the sheet, for instance.

> Be aware that if you select the Office button → Prepare →
> Properties → Document Properties → Advanced Properties
> ([pre-2007, File → Properties → Summary) and enter a URL
> as a hyperlink base, the index created from the preceding
> code might not work. A hyperlink base is a path or URL that
> you want to use for all hyperlinks with the same base address
> that are inserted in the current document.

Link to the Index from a Context Menu

The third way of constructing an index is to add a link to the list of sheets as
a context-menu item, keeping it just a right-click away. We'll have that link
open the standard workbook tabs command bar. You generally get to this
command bar by right-clicking any of the sheet tab scroll arrows on the bottom left of any worksheet, as shown in Figure 1-11.

16	
17	✓ Today's Stuff
18	This Weeks Figures
19	Sheet1
20	Sheet2
21	Sheet3
22	
23	Sheet4
24	Sheet5
25	Sheet6

Figure 1-11. Tabs command bar displayed by right-clicking the sheet scroll tabs

To link that tab's command bar to a right-click in any cell, enter the following code in the private module of ThisWorkbook:

```
Private Sub Workbook_SheetBeforeRightClick _
(ByVal Sh As Object, ByVal Target As Range, Cancel As Boolean)
```

```
Dim cCont As CommandBarButton
On Error Resume Next
Application.CommandBars("Cell").Controls("Sheet Index").Delete
On Error GoTo 0
Set cCont = Application.CommandBars("Cell").Controls.Add _
(Type:=msoControlButton, Temporary:=True)
With cCont
.Caption = "Sheet Index"
.OnAction = "IndexCode"
End With
End Sub
```

Next, you'll need to insert a standard module to house the IndexCode macro, called by the preceding code whenever the user right-clicks in a cell. It is vital that you use a standard module next, as placing the code in the same module as Workbook_SheetBeforeRightClick will mean Excel will not know where to find the macro called IndexCode.

Select Insert → Module and enter the following code:

```
Sub IndexCode( )
Application.CommandBars("workbook Tabs").ShowPopup
End Sub
```

Press Alt/⌘-Q to get back to the Excel interface, then save your workbook.

Now, right-click within any cell on any worksheet and you should see a new menu item called Sheet Index that will take you right to a list of sheets in the workbook.

HACK #8   Limit the Scrolling Range of Your Worksheet

If you move around your spreadsheet a lot, or if you have data you don't want readers to explore, you might find it convenient to limit the visible area of your spreadsheet to only that which has actual data.

All Excel worksheets created in Excel 2007 have a column limit of 16,384 (256, A to IV, in previous versions) and a row limit of 1,048,576 (65,536 pre-2007). More often than not, your worksheet uses only a small percentage of the cells available to you. A nice bit of spring cleaning limits the worksheet's scrollable area to just the part containing the data you want a user to see. You then can place data you do not want a user to see outside the scrollable area. Doing this also can make it less daunting to scroll around in a worksheet, as it is not uncommon for users to find themselves at row 50,000 and then start screaming that they are unable to find any data in a worksheet. You can do this by hiding rows and columns, by specifying a valid range, or by activating only the used range.

Hiding Rows and Columns

The easiest way to establish boundaries is simply to hide all the unused columns and rows. On your sheet, locate the last row containing data and select the entire row below it by clicking the row label. Press the Ctrl and Shift keys while pressing the down arrow to select all rows beneath. Select Home → Format → Hide & Unhide → Hide Rows or right click and select Hide (pre-2007, Format → Row → Hide) to hide them all. Do the same thing for unused columns; find the last-used column, select the entire column to the right of it, press the Ctrl and Shift keys while pressing the right arrow, and then again on the Home tab, select Format → Hide & Unhide → Hide Columns (pre-2007, Format → Column → Hide). If all went according to plan, your useful cells should be surrounded by a moat past which you cannot scroll.

Specifying a Valid Range

The second way to establish boundaries is to specify a valid range in the worksheet's Properties window. Right-click the sheet's tab at the bottom left of the window and select View Code from the context menu. If you are using a version of Excel before 2007, you may need to select View → Project Explorer (Ctrl-R) on Windows to visit the Project Explorer (it is always visible on the Mac). If the Properties window isn't visible, press F4 to make it appear. Select the appropriate worksheet and visit the ScrollArea property in the Properties window.

Now, from within the Project Explorer, select the worksheet you want the scroll area limited to, and then, from the Properties window (shown in Figure 1-12), go down to the ScrollArea property. In the associated value field to the right, enter the preferred boundaries of your worksheet— $A$1:$G$50, for instance.

You will be unable to scroll outside the area you have specified. Unfortunately, Excel will not save this setting after you close the window. This means you need a very simple macro to automatically set the scroll area to the desired range by placing some code in the worksheet_Activate event.

Right-click the Sheet Name tab on which the scroll area should be limited, select View Code, and then enter the following:

```
Private Sub Worksheet_Activate ()
Me.ScrollArea = "A1:G50"
End Sub
```

As usual, press Alt/⌘-Q to return to Excel proper and save your workbook.

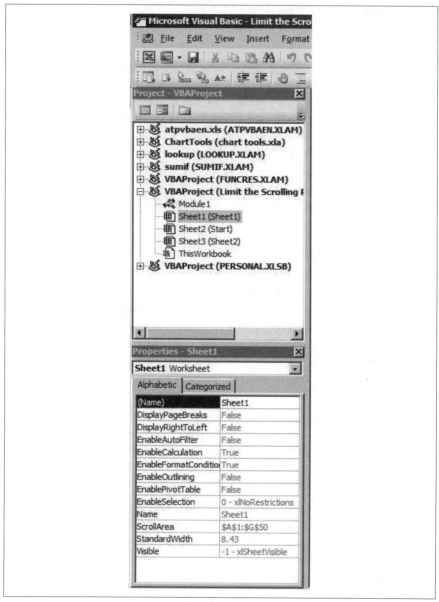

Figure 1-12. Project Explorer Properties window

Although you will not see a visible clue, such as the moat of the first method, you won't be able to scroll or select anything outside the specified area.

Any macro that tries to select a range outside this scroll area (including selections of entire rows and columns) will no longer be able to do so. This is true particularly for recorded macros, as they often use selections.

If your macros do select a range outside the scrollable area, you can easily modify any existing macros so that they are not limited to a specific scroll area while operating. Simply select View → Macros under Macro options, or Developer → Macros under Code options, or Alt/Option-F8 (pre-2007, Tools → Macro → Macros...), then locate your macro name, select it, and click Edit.

Place the following line of code as the very first line of code:

```
ActiveSheet.ScrollArea = ""
```

As the very last line of code in your macro, place the following:

```
ActiveSheet.ScrollArea = "$A$1:$G$50"
```

So, your code should look something like this:

```
Sub MyMacro( )
'
' MyMacro Macro
' Macro recorded 19/9/2007 by OzGrid.com
'

'
ActiveSheet.ScrollArea = ""
 Range("Z100").Select
 Selection.Font.Bold = True
ActiveSheet.ScrollArea = "$A$1:$G$50"
Sheets("Daily Budget").Select
ActiveSheet.ScrollArea = ""
 Range ("T500").Select
 Selection.Font.Bold = False
ActiveSheet.ScrollArea = "$A$1:$H$25"

    End Sub
```

Our recorded macro selects cell Z100 and formats it to boldface. It then selects the worksheet named Daily Budget, selects cell T500 on that sheet, and un-bolds it. We added ActiveSheet.ScrollArea = "" so that any cell on the worksheet can be selected and then the scroll area can be set back to our desired range. When we select another worksheet (Daily Budget), we again allow the code to select any cell on this worksheet and set the scroll area for this worksheet back to the desired range.

Activating Only the Used Range

A third method, the most flexible, automatically limits the scroll area to the used range on the worksheet within which you place the code. To use this method, right-click the Sheet Name tab on which you want the scroll area limited, select View Code, and enter the following code:

```
Private Sub Worksheet_Activate()
 Me.ScrollArea = Range(Me.UsedRange, Me.UsedRange(2,2)).Address
 End Sub
```

Now press Alt/⌘-Q or click the X in the top righthand corner to get back to Excel and save your workbook.

The preceding macro will run automatically each time you activate the worksheet in which you placed it. However, you might encounter a problem with this macro when you need to actually enter data outside the existing used range. To avoid this problem, simply use a standard macro that will reset your scroll area back to the full sheet. Select Developer → Visual Basic under Code options (pre-2007, Tools → Macro → Visual Basic Editor), then select Insert → Module, and enter the following code:

```
Sub ResetScrollArea()
 ActiveSheet.ScrollArea = ""
 End Sub
```

Now press Alt/⌘-Q or click the X in the top-righthand corner to get back to Excel and save your workbook.

If you want to, you can make your macro easier to run by assigning it to a shortcut key. Select the view tab, then Macros, or press Alt/Option-F8 (pre-2007, Tools → Macro → Macros...). Select ResetScrollArea (the name of your macro), click Options, and assign a shortcut key.

Each time you need to add data outside the established bounds of your worksheet, run the ResetScrollArea macro to readjust the borders. After you run the macro, make any changes you were unable to make while the scroll area was limited. When you're finished, activate any other worksheet and then activate the worksheet you just modified. Activation of the worksheet will cause the code to run and limit the scroll area to the desired range.

HACK #9   Lock and Protect Cells Containing Formulas

You may want to let users change cells that contain data without providing them access to change formulas. You can keep cells containing formulas under lock and key without having to protect your entire sheet or workbook.

ALL

When we create a spreadsheet, most of us need to use formulas of some sort. Sometimes, however, you might not want other users to tamper/delete/overtype any formulas you included on your spreadsheet. The easiest and most common way of barring people from playing with your formulas is to protect your worksheet. However, protecting your worksheet doesn't just prevent users from tampering with your formulas; it also stops users from entering anything at all. Sometimes you do not want to go this far. Three solutions are: locking the formula cells, using data-validation on the formula cells, and auto-toggling worksheet protection, although none of these solutions is bulletproof.

Locking Formula Cells

By default, all cells on a worksheet are locked; however, this has no effect unless worksheet protection has been applied. Here is a very easy way to apply worksheet protection so that only formula cells are locked and protected.

Select all cells on your worksheet, either by pressing Ctrl/⌘-A or by clicking the square at the intersecting point of column A and row 1. Then select Home → Format → Lock Cell (under Cells options, toggles to Lock/unlock cells), or if you prefer you can right-click and select Format Cells and on the Protection tab, uncheck the Locked checkbox to remove the tick (pre-2007, select Format → →Cells → Protection and uncheck the Locked checkbox to remove the tick). Click OK.

Now select any single cell, select Home → Find & Select → Go To Special or Ctrl-G, or F5 and click Special (pre-2007, Edit → Go To... → Special). You'll see a dialog box such as that in Figure 1-13.

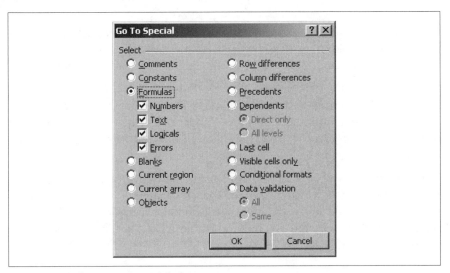

Figure 1-13. The Go To Special dialog

Select Formulas from the Go To Special dialog and, if needed, limit the formulas to the subtypes underneath. Click OK. With only the formula cells selected, under Cells options choose Format → Lock Cell (pre-2007, select Format → Cells → Protection, check the Locked checkbox to insert a tick), and click OK.

Now you need to protect your sheet. Select Format → Protect sheet under the Cells options (pre-2007, Tools → Protection → Protect Worksheet). Apply a password if required and click OK.

The preceding method certainly saves a lot of time and eliminates possible errors locating formulas so that you can protect them. Unfortunately, it can also prevent users from using certain features, such as sorting, formatting changes, aligning text, and many others you might not be concerned with, even when in an unlocked cell.

Data Validation

Using data validation doesn't rely on worksheet protection at all, and instead simply prevents accidental overtyping of formula cells.

> Data validation is far from bulletproof when it comes to preventing users from entering nonvalidated data into cells. Users can still paste into a validated cell any data they want and, in doing so, remove the validation from that cell unless the copied cell also contains data validation, in which case this validation would override the original validation.

To see what we mean, select any single cell, press Ctrl-G or select Home → Find & Select → Go to Special, or press F5 and click Special (pre-2007, Edit → Go To... → Special). Now select Formulas from the Go To Special dialog and, if needed, limit the formulas to the subtypes underneath. Click OK.

With only the Formula cells selected, select Data → Data Validation, under Data Tools options (pre-2007, Data → Validation). Then, select the Settings page tab, choose Custom from the Allow: box, and in the Formula box, enter ="", as shown in Figure 1-14. Click OK.

This method will prevent a user from accidentally overtyping into any formula cells, although, as stressed in the earlier warning, it is not a fully secure method and should be used only for accidental overtyping, etc. However, the big advantage to using this method is that all of Excel's features are still usable on the worksheet.

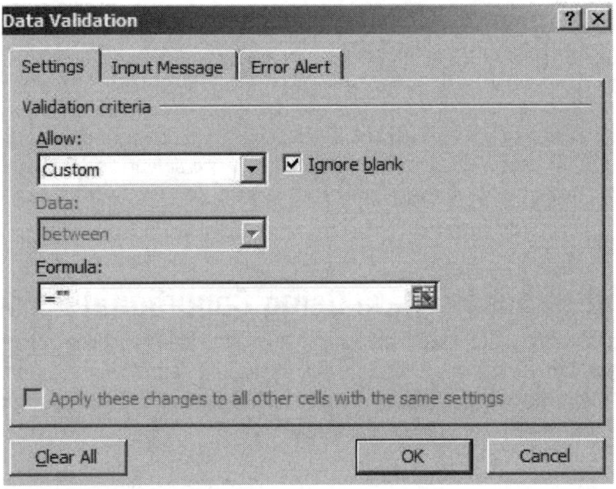

Figure 1-14. Validation formulas

Auto-Toggle Worksheet Protection

This method dynamically turns worksheet protection on and off, but will also enable you to use all of Excel's features when you are in a cell that is not locked. To start, ensure that only the cells you want protected are locked and that all other cells are unlocked. Right-click the Sheet Name tab, select View Code from the pop-up menu, and enter the following code:

```
Private Sub Worksheet_SelectionChange(ByVal Target As Range)
 If Target.Locked = True Then
 Me.Protect Password:="Secret"
 Else
 Me.Unprotect Password:="Secret"
 End If
End Sub
```

If no password is used, omit `Password:="Secret"`. If a password is used, change the word `Secret` to your password. Press Alt/⌘-Q or click the X in the top-righthand corner to get back to Excel and save your workbook.

> If you're worried about your users getting into the macro and disabling it, you can password-protect your macro by selecting Tools → VBAProject Properties, going to the Protection tab, selecting "Lock Project for Viewing", and entering a password.

Now, each time you select a cell that is locked, your worksheet will automatically protect itself. The moment you select any cell that is not locked, your worksheet will unprotect itself.

This hack doesn't work perfectly, though it usually works well enough. The keyword used in the code, Target, will refer only to the cell that is active at the time of selection. For this reason, it is important to note that if a user selects a range of cells (with the active cell being an unlocked cell), it is possible for him to delete the entire selection because the target cell is unlocked and, therefore, the worksheet will automatically unprotect itself.

HACK #10   Find Duplicate Data Using Conditional Formatting

<2007   Excel's conditional formatting is generally used to identify values in particular ranges, but we can hack it to identify duplicated data within a list or table. The improved functionality in Conditional Formatting in Excel 2007 makes this hack suitable for prior versions only.

People frequently have to identify duplicated data within a list or table, and doing this manually can be very time-consuming and error-prone. To make this job much easier, you can hack one of Excel's standard features, Conditional Formatting.

Take, for example, a table of data with a range of $A$1:$H$100. Select the top-left cell, A1, and drag it over and down to H100. It is important that A1 be the active cell in your selection, so don't drag from H100 to A1. Select Format → Conditional Formatting... and, in the Conditional Formatting dialog box, select Formula Is from the top-left pop-up menu. In the field to its right, enter the following code:

```
=COUNTIF($A$1:$H$100,A1)>1
```

Click the Format tab (that's the Format button under Mac OS X), followed by the Patterns tab, and select a color you want applied to visually identify duplicate data. Click OK to return to the Conditional Formatting dialog box and click OK again to apply the formatting.

All those cells containing duplicate data should be lit up like a Christmas tree in the color you chose, making it much easier to eyeball duplicate data and delete, move, or alter it as appropriate.

It is vital to note that as A1 was the active cell in your selection, the cell address is a relative reference and is not absolute (unlike your table of data, $A$1:$H$100). By using conditional formatting in this way, Excel automatically knows to use the correct cell as the COUNTIF criterion. By this we mean that the conditional formatting formula in cell A1 will read as follows:

```
=COUNTIF($A$1:$H$100,A1)>1
```

while in cell A2, it will read:

```
=COUNTIF($A$1:$H$100,A2)>1
```

in cell A3, it will read:

```
=COUNTIF($A$1:$H$100,A3)>1
```

and so forth.

HACK #11 Find Data That Appears Two or More Times Using Conditional Formatting

ALL

While Excel's Conditional Formatting is vastly improved in Excel 2007 and can easily take care of duplicated data, it still does not offer the facility to identify data that appears two or more times.

If you need to identify data that appears two or more times, you can use Conditional Formatting with as many conditions/rules as your system memory will allow (note that you can use up to three different conditions only in versions pre-2007) and color-code each condition for visual identification. To do this, select cell A1 (the cell in the top-left corner) and drag it down to H100. Again, it is important that A1 is the active cell in your selection.

Now, select Home → Conditional Formatting → New Rule under Styles options. For Select Rule Type, choose "Use a Formula to determine which cells to format" and then click in the white strip under "Format values where this formula is true."

> Pre-2007, select Format → Conditional Formatting... and, from the box containing the text Cell Value Is, select Formula Is. Click in the white box to the right of Formula Is.

Enter the following formula:

```
=COUNTIF($A$1:$H$100,A1)>3
```

Click the Format button, select a color you want to apply to identify data that appears more than three times, and click OK; or for pre-2007 versions, go to the Patterns page tab, select a color, and click OK.

Click New Rule (on the Mac, click Add>>) and repeat the previous steps, entering the following formula (pre-2007, use the Condition 2 box and select Formula Is) and selecting a different color this time:

```
=COUNTIF($A$1:$H$100,A1)=3
```

Instead of retyping the formula, highlight it after you have entered it, then press Ctrl/⌘-C to copy, then paste where necessary by pressing Ctrl/⌘-V to paste, and then change >3 to =3.

Click New Rule, repeat the steps a third time (pre-2007, from the Condition 3 box, select Formula Is), and add the following formula:

```
=COUNTIF($A$1:$H$100,A1)=2
```

Again, select a different color from those previously chosen. You will have different cell colors depending on the number of times your data appears within your table of data.

Again, it is vital to note that as A1 was the active cell in your selection, the cell address is a relative reference and is not absolute (unlike your table of data, $A$1:$H$100). By using conditional formatting in this way, Excel automatically knows to use the correct cell as the COUNTIF criterion.

In Excel 2007, your Conditions are limited only by your system memory, whereas in pre-Excel 2007 versions, the limit is 3 Conditions.

HACK #12 Tie Custom Toolbars to a Particular Workbook

<2007

Although most toolbars you build apply to just about any work you do, sometimes the functionality of a custom toolbar applies to only one workbook in particular. With this hack, you can tie custom toolbars to their respective workbooks. The Quick Access Toolbar options in Excel 2007 make this hack suitable for prior versions only.

If you've ever created a custom toolbar, you have no doubt noticed that the toolbar is loaded and visible regardless of which workbook you have open. What if your custom toolbar contains recorded macros meant only for a specific workbook? It's probably best to tie special-purpose custom toolbars to the appropriate workbooks to reduce both clutter and possible confusion. You can do this by inserting some very simple code into the private module of the workbook.

To get to this private module, right-click the Excel icon, which you'll find at the top left of your screen, next to File, and select View Code.

This shortcut isn't available on the Mac. You'll have to open the Visual Basic Editor (VBE) by pressing Option-F11 or by selecting Tools → Macro → Visual Basic Editor. Once you're there, Ctrl-click or right-click This Workbook in the Projects window.

Then, enter this code:

```
Private Sub Workbook_Activate()
 On Error Resume Next
 With Application.CommandBars("MyCustomToolbar")
 .Enabled = True
 .Visible = True
 End With
 On Error GoTo 0
End Sub

Private Sub Workbook_Deactivate()
 On Error Resume Next
 Application.CommandBars("MyCustomToolbar").Enabled = False
 On Error GoTo 0
End Sub
```

Change the text *MyCustomToolbar* to the name of your own custom toolbar. To get back to the Excel interface, close the module window or press Alt/⌘-Q, then save your workbook. Whenever you open or activate another workbook, your custom toolbar disappears and isn't accessible. Reactivate the appropriate workbook, and poof! The toolbar's back.

You even can take this down a level, making the custom toolbar available only to a specific worksheet within the workbook. Right-click the Sheet Name tab of the sheet on which you want the toolbar to be accessible and select View Code. Enter this code:

```
Private Sub Worksheet_Deactivate()
 On Error Resume Next
 Application.CommandBars("MyCustomToolbar").Enabled = False
 On Error GoTo 0
End Sub

Private Sub Worksheet_Activate()
 On Error Resume Next
 With Application.CommandBars("MyCustomToolbar")
 .Enabled = True
 .Visible = True
 End With
 On Error GoTo 0
End Sub
```

Now press Alt/⌘-Q or close the window to get back to Excel.

The first procedure, Worksheet_Deactivate( ), will fire automatically each time you leave that particular worksheet to activate another one. The firing of the code changes the Enable property of your custom toolbar to False so that it cannot be seen or displayed. The second procedure is fired each time you activate the worksheet and sets the Enable property of your custom toolbar to True so that it can be made visible. The line of code that reads Application.CommandBars("MyCustomToolbar").Visible = True simply displays your custom toolbar again, so the user can see it. Switch worksheets and the toolbar is gone; switch back and it reappears like magic.

HACK #13 Outsmart Excel's Relative Reference Handler

ALL

In Excel, a formula reference can be either relative or absolute, but sometimes you want to move cells that use relative references without making the references absolute. Here's how.

When a formula needs to be made absolute, you use the dollar sign ($) in front of the column letter and/or row number of the cell reference, as in $A$1. Once you do this, no matter where you copy your formula, the formula will reference the same cells. Sometimes, however, you may have already set up a lot of formulas that contain not absolute references, but relative references. You would usually do this so that when you copy the original cell formula down or across, the row and column references change accordingly.

If you already set up your formulas using only relative references, or perhaps a mix of relative and absolute references, you can reproduce the same formulas in another range on the same worksheet, another sheet in the same workbook, or perhaps even another sheet in a different workbook.

To do this without changing any range references inside the formulas, select the range of cells you want to copy and then select the Home tab → Find & Select → Replace (pre-2007, Edit → Replace...). In the Find What: box, type an equals sign (=) and in the Replace With: box, type an ampersand (&). (Of course, these could be any symbols you are sure are not being used in any of the formulas.) Click Replace All. The equals sign in all the formulas on your worksheet will be replaced with the ampersand sign.

You can now simply copy this range, paste it to its desired destination, select the range you just pasted, and select the Home tab → Find & Select → Replace (pre-2007, Edit → Replace...). This time replace the ampersand sign with an equals sign (don't forget to do this with the source range you just copied). Your formulas now should be referencing the same cell references as your originals.

Remove Phantom Workbook Links

#14   Ah, phantom links. You open your workbook and are prompted to "Update
Links," but there are no links! How can you update links when they don't
ALL   exist?

External links are links that reference another workbook. Unexpected external linking can occur for various reasons, many of them stemming from moving or copying charts, chart sheets, or worksheets into another workbook. Knowing why they're there doesn't always help you find them, though. Here are a few ways to deal with the spooky phantom link problem.

First, you need to see whether you have any real external links (nonphantom) that you forgot about. If you are not sure whether you have real external links, start looking in the most obvious place: your formulas. You can do this by ensuring no other workbooks are open and then searching for [*] within the formulas on each worksheet. Close all other workbooks to ensure that any formula links will include [*], where the asterisk represents a wildcard string.

 Excel 97 doesn't provide the option of searching the entire workbook, but you can search all worksheets in a workbook by grouping them. You do this by right-clicking any Sheet Name tab and choosing Select All Sheets. In later versions of Excel, Find... and Replace... provide the option of searching within the sheet or workbook.

Once you find the formula links, simply change the formula accordingly or delete it altogether. Whether you change the formula or delete it depends on the situation, and only you can decide which route to take.

You also might want to consider going to the Microsoft Office Download Center (located at *http://www.microsoft.com/downloads/Search.aspx?displaylang=en*) and downloading the Delete Links Wizard. The Delete Links Wizard is designed to find and delete links such as defined name links, hidden name links, chart links, Microsoft query links, and object links. However, in our experience, it does not find phantom links.

Once you're confident there are no formula links, you need to ensure that you don't have any nonphantom links lurking somewhere else. To do this, we like to start from within the Excel workbook containing the phantom links. Select Formulas → Name Manager under Defined Names options and check in the Refers To: column to make sure none of the names are referencing a different workbook (pre-2007, select Insert → Name → Define and scroll through the list of names, clicking to highlight each one and looking in the Refers To: box at the bottom).

Pre-2007 users, instead of clicking each name in the Define Name dialog, can insert a new worksheet and select Insert → Name → Paste. Then, from the Paste Name dialog, click Paste Link. This will create a list of all the names in your workbook, with their referenced ranges in the corresponding column.

Excel 2007 users can see all the names in the Define Name dialog easily, but if you wish to paste to a workbook, select Formulas → Use in Formula → Paste Names, then select the Paste List button from the Paste List dialog.

F3 will also bring up the Paste Name dialog and works in all versions.

If any of the names are pointing outside your workbook, you've found the source of at least one link that would prompt the updating question. Now it's up to you to decide whether you want to change this range name to refer only to the workbook itself or leave it as it is.

Another potential source of links is in your charts. It's possible that your charts have the same problem we just explained. You should check that the data ranges and the X-axis labels for the chart aren't referencing an external workbook. Once again, you get to decide whether the link you've found is correct.

Links also can lurk in objects, such as text boxes, autoshapes, etc. Objects can try to reference an external workbook. The easiest way to locate objects is to select any single cell on each worksheet and then select Home → Find & Select → Go to Special or click F5 and check the Objects option, then click OK (pre-2007, Edit → Go To... → Special, check the Objects option, and click OK). This will select all objects on the worksheet. You should do this on a copy of your workbook. Then, with all objects selected, you can delete, save, close, and reopen your copy to see whether this has eliminated the problem.

Finally, the last not-so-obvious place to check for real links is in the hidden sheets that you might have cleverly created and forgotten about. Unhide these sheets by selecting View → Unhide under Window options (pre-2007, Format → Sheet → Unhide). If the Unhide option on the right-click Sheet submenu is grayed out, that means you have no hidden sheets. (If you think there are sheets that don't turn up in the menu, see "Hide Worksheets So That They Cannot Be Unhidden" [Hack #5] for more information.)

Now that you have eliminated the possibility of real links, it's time to elimi-nate the phantom links. Go to the haunted workbook with the phantom links and select Data → Edit Links under Connection options (pre-2007, Edit → Links...). Sometimes you can simply select the unwanted link, click Change Source, and then refer the link back to itself. Often, though, you will be told that one of your formulas contains an error, and you will not be able to do this.

If you can't take the easy way out, note to which workbook Excel thinks it is linking (we'll call it the well-behaved workbook). Create a real link between the two by opening both workbooks. Go to the problem workbook and, in any cell on any worksheet, type =. Now click a cell in the well-behaved workbook and press Enter so that you have a true external link to the other workbook.

Save both workbooks, but don't close them yet. While in the problem work-book, select Data → Edit Links (pre-2007, Edit → Links...) and use the Change Source button to refer all links to the well-behaved workbook to which you just purposely created a link. Save your workbook again and delete the cell in which you created the true external link. Finally, save your file.

This often eliminates the offending phantom link, as Excel now realizes you have deleted the external link to the workbook. If this does not solve the problem, however, try these next steps, but make sure you *save a copy of your workbook first.*

The following process involves deleting data permanently. Therefore, before you begin, create a backup copy of your workbook. Neglecting to do so could create new problems for you.

With the problem workbook open, delete one sheet, save, and then close and re-open the workbook. If you are not prompted to update your missing links, the sheet you deleted contained the phantom link. This should solve the problem, but if it doesn't, repeat the first step for each sheet in the work-book. You will need to add a new sheet before you delete the last sheet, as any workbook must have at least one sheet.

If this technique worked, here's what you should do next. Open the copy of your workbook (the one that still has data in it) and make another copy. You've got to work with the problem worksheet (or worksheets) and use the process of elimination to discover where the problem is in the worksheet.

With the problem worksheet active, select a chunk of cells (about 10 x 10) and then select Home → Clear → Clear All under Editing options (pre-2007, Edit → Clear → All). Are you absolutely sure you saved a copy? Save, close, and reopen the problem worksheet. If you are not prompted to update those links, you found the problem and your reward is to redo that block of cells. If you are prompted to update the links, continue deleting cells until you are no longer prompted. Then redo the badly behaved cells.

We hope these techniques will save you some of the frustration that arises when those dreaded phantom links appear in your workbooks. They're not easy or fun to perform, but they can get you out of trouble.

HACK #15 Reduce Workbook Bloat

Ever notice that your workbook is increasing in size at an alarming rate for no apparent reason? There are several causes of workbook bloat, and some slimming solutions. The introduction of workbook size being limited only by the amount of memory your system in Excel 2007 will allow should eliminate workbook bloat; however, you may find some of the following tips handy if you have a particularly large workbook.

Have you ever eaten so much that you can't function properly? Workbook bloat in Excel is much the same thing. *Workbook bloat* is a term for a workbook that has had so much done to it that it has swollen to such a size that it no longer functions correctly.

We checked out the size of a typical workbook containing a fairly large amount of data. With data only, the workbook file size was 1.37 MB. Then we added a pivot table referencing four entire columns for its data source and noted that the file size increased dramatically to 2.4 MB. Add some formatting and your typical workbook size has blown out to almost double by performing a few actions.

One of the more common causes of file bloat, particularly in earlier versions of Excel, is the application of formats to entire columns or rows rather than to just the data range in use. Another mistake is referencing entire columns as the data source for charts and pivot tables rather than just the cells with actual data in them. To fix these problems, you will need to eliminate all the superfluous formatting and restrict your data source to only the useful range of cells.

> Before doing such refactoring, *always* make a copy of your workbook for safekeeping.

Eliminating Superfluous Formatting

The first step in eliminating superfluous formatting is to figure out where your worksheet's data ends—e.g., the bottom righthand corner of your data, if you will. Don't rely on Find & Select → Go To Special → Last cell, (pre-2007, Edit → Go To... → Special → Last Cell), as this might take you to the last cell containing formatting, not actual data. Having manually located the cell you know to be your last cell containing legitimate data, highlight the row immediately following it. While pressing the Ctrl and Shift keys, press the down arrow on your keyboard to highlight all rows beneath that row and select Home → Clear → Clear All to clear them (pre-2007, Edit → Clear → All).

Now apply the same logic to unwanted formatting lurking in your columns. Locate the cell in the last column containing data and click the column header of the column immediately to the right. Press Ctrl-Shift and the right arrow on your keyboard to highlight all other columns to the right and then select Home → Clear → Clear All under Edit options to clear them (pre-2007, Edit → Clear → All).

 Don't be tempted to actually delete these rows or columns rather than clearing them, as doing so often causes the dreaded #REF! error in any cells of any formulas that might reference them.

Save your workbook and take gleeful note of the change in its file size by selecting the Office button → Prepare → Properties → Document Properties → Advanced Properties (pre-2007, File → Properties... → General).

Clean Up Your Macros

If you have macros, now you need to address the modules that the macro code resides in. This is a fairly quick, painless, and straightforward process that entails exporting all modules (this functionality is not available on Mac OS X) and UserForms to your hard drive and then deleting the existing modules and UserForms, pressing Save, and importing the modules you exported.

To do this, go into the Visual Basic Editor and, from within the Project Explorer, right-click each module and select Remove Module1 (or whatever the name of the module happens to be). When you are asked whether you want to export your module before removing it, say Yes, taking note of the path.

Do this for each module in turn, as well as for any UserForms you might have. Don't forget the private modules of your workbook and worksheets if they house code as well. Once you have done all this, save the workbook. Then, select File → Import File and import each module and UserForm back into your workbook. Following this process will create a text file of each module and that, in turn, removes all extra baggage that the modules might be holding.

The Web contains some free utilities that will automate this task to some degree, but we have heard cases of these utilities making a mess of code or even increasing file sizes. If you do use one of them, always save a backup copy of your file first, as the developers will take no responsibility for any loss of data.

Honing Data Sources

If, after performing the previous steps, you still believe your file size is unrealistically large, another possible suspect is referencing unused cells in Pivot-Tables and PivotCharts. This is true particularly of PivotTables, as people frequently reference all rows in order to avoid manually updating ranges as new data is added. If this is your modus operandi, use dynamic named ranges [Hack #47] for your data sources instead.

Cleaning Corrupted Workbooks

If you still believe your workbook is too large, it is possible that your workbook or component sheets are corrupt. Unfortunately, determining a point of corruption requires a manual process of elimination.

> Again, we strongly advise you to save a copy of your workbook before proceeding.

To be sure you're not missing anything, unhide any hidden sheets by selecting View → Unhide under Window options or right click and select Unhide (pre-2007, Format → Sheet → Unhide). If this menu option is grayed out, you have no hidden worksheets to worry about. With all your sheets visible, start from the sheet on the far left and move one-by-one to the right. For each in turn, delete it, save your workbook, and note its file size by selecting the Office button → Prepare → Properties → Document Properties drop-down → Advanced Properties (or File → Properties → General in pre-2007 versions). If the file size drops dramatically considering the amount of data on that sheet, you've probably found your corruption.

To replace a corrupt sheet in your workbook, create a new worksheet, manually select the data in the corrupt sheet, and cut (do not copy) and paste it into the new sheet. Delete the corrupt sheet from your workbook, save, and repeat.

> By cutting rather than copying, Excel automatically will follow the data to the new sheet, keeping references intact.

Extract Data from a Corrupt Workbook

HACK
#16
ALL

Workbook corruption can mean the loss of vital data, costing you more than just money. This hack explores some methods that might recover your data.

Workbooks sometimes become corrupt for no apparent reason. This can cause all sorts of problems, especially if the workbook is vital and for whatever reason you have no backup. Lesson 1: Always back up your data somewhere. Realistically, though, this does not always happen, and corruption can, of course, occur right before your regularly scheduled backup.

To add to your frustration, even though you know your workbook is corrupt, you sometimes might still be able to open it and even perform certain actions in it.

If You Can Open Your Workbook

If you can open the offending workbook, before doing anything else, be sure to save a copy of it; otherwise, you might regret it. If you have a copy, you can always seek professional help!

Now, try opening the workbook in a later version of Excel and simply saving it again. Obviously this is not possible if you already are using the latest version of Excel.

If this doesn't work, try opening your workbook and saving the file in HTML or HTM format (see the "What You Lose in HTML or HTM" sidebar for a warning about these formats), then close the file and reopen it, this time saving again in the format you require—e.g., *.xlsx*.

Finally, try opening your file and saving it in SYLK (*.slk*, for symbolic link) format. Note that when you save a workbook in this format, only the active worksheet is saved. So, you will have to do the same for each worksheet. Reopen the file and save it in a desired format such as *.xlsx*.

What You Lose in HTML or HTM

When saving in HTML or HTM format, the following features will be lost in Excel 2007:

- New Excel 2007 features
- PivotTables and charts (they can be saved, but are lost when the file is opened in this format again in Excel)
- VBA Projects

If you are using a pre-2007 version, the following features will be lost:

- Unused number formats
- Unused styles
- Data consolidation settings
- Scenarios
- Natural language formulas (they are converted to standard range references)
- Custom function categories
- Strikethrough, subscript, and superscript elements
- Change History
- Customized page setup settings for charts that are embedded on a worksheet
- List settings for ListBoxes and ComboBoxes from the Forms toolbar
- Conditional formatting that is stored on an XLM macro sheet

Also, shared workbooks in versions of Excel before Excel 2007 will no longer be shared. The "Value (Y) axis crosses at category number" setting on the Scale tab of the Format Axis dialog box is not saved if the "Value (Y) axis crosses a maximum category" checkbox is checked. The "Vary colors by point" setting in the Format Data Series dialog box is not saved if the chart contains more than one data series.

If You Cannot Open Your File

If your workbook is corrupt to the point that you cannot even open it, open your spreadsheet in Microsoft Word or via the Spreadsheet viewer, which can be downloaded from the Microsoft web site, then copy your data from the open file (note that much of your formatting, formulas, etc, will be lost).

Next, open a new workbook and create an external link to the corrupt workbook—e.g., ='C:\Documents and Settings\Raina\My Documents\[ChookSheet.xls]Sheet1'!A1. Copy this link down as many rows and across as many columns as needed. Do the same for each worksheet in the workbook. If you cannot remember any of the names of the worksheets, create any old sheet name using the correct filename path, and Excel will display the sheet names for you when you press Enter.

One final thing you can do is visit the OpenOffice.org web site and download the free version of OpenOffice.org. Except for different names for different tools and commands, OpenOffice.org is very similar to Excel. OpenOffice.org is based on the same basic spreadsheet structure as Excel, making it simple for Excel users to use. In fact, about 96 percent of the formulas used in Excel can be created and applied by using the spreadsheet in OpenOffice.org.

To download the free version of OpenOffice.org, go to *http://download. openoffice.org/index.html* and download it from the FTP site of your choice. Then install the program. OpenOffice.org is also available for Macs.

In many cases, your Excel data can be recovered. However, no VBA code can be recovered due to incompatibility between OpenOffice.org and Excel.

Sadly, if none of these methods works, you probably will have to pay to try to have your workbook recovered with special software. One source where such reputable software (for Windows) can be purchased belongs to the authors of this book and is located at *http://www.ozgrid.com/Services/ corrupt-file-recovery-index.htm*.

After purchase and installation, run the ExcelFix program. Click Select File, select a corrupt file, and then click Diagnose to recover the file. You should now see the recovered file in the workbook viewer. Click Save Workbook to save the workbook into a new readable file that you can open from Excel.

Also available is a demo version that does not enable you to save the file, but all versions of the program enable you to start again and recover as many files as you want.

CHAPTER TWO

Hacking Excel's Built-in Features
Hacks 17–43

Although Excel comes with a wide variety of standard features for managing and analyzing data, the boundaries of these features are often frustrating. The hacks in this chapter provide numerous ways in which you can escape these boundaries and make Excel a much more powerful tool.

HACK #17 ALL — Validate Data Based on a List on Another Worksheet

Data validation makes it easy to specify rules your data must follow. Unfortunately, Excel insists that lists used in data validation must appear on the same worksheet as the data being validated. Fortunately, there are ways to evade this requirement.

This hack provides two methods you can use to validate data based on a list on another worksheet. The first method takes advantage of Excel's named ranges (which are covered in more detail in Chapter 3), and the second uses a function call.

Method 1: Named Ranges

Perhaps the easiest and quickest way to overcome Excel's data-validation barrier is by naming the range where the list resides. To create a named range, select the cells containing the list and enter a name in the Name box that appears at the left end of the Formula bar. For the purposes of this example, we will assume your range is called MyRange.

Select the cell in which you want the drop-down list to appear and then, under the Data tab select Data Tools → Data → Validation (pre-2007, Data → Validation). Select List from the Allow: field, and in the Source: box enter =MyRange. Click OK.

Because you used a named range, your list (even though it resides on another worksheet) can now be used for the validation list.

Method 2: the INDIRECT Function

The INDIRECT function enables you to reference a cell containing text that represents a cell address. You then can use that cell as a local cell reference, even though it gets its data from another worksheet. You can use this feature to reference the worksheet where your list resides.

Assume your list resides on Sheet1 in the range $A$1:$A$8. Click any cell on a different worksheet where you want to have this validation list (pick list) appear. Then, under the Data tab, select Data → Data Validation (pre-2007, Data → Validation). Choose List from the Allow: field. In the Source: box, enter the following code:

```
=INDIRECT("Sheet1!$A$1:$A$8")
```

Ensure that the In-Cell drop-down checkbox is selected and click OK. The list that resides on Sheet1 should appear in your drop-down validation list.

If the name of the worksheet on which your list resides contains spaces, you need to use the INDIRECT function in the following way:

```
=INDIRECT("'Sheet 1'!$A$1:$A$8")
```

The difference here is that you type a single apostrophe immediately after the first quotation mark and another single apostrophe immediately before the exclamation point.

It is a good idea to always use the single apostrophe, regardless of whether your sheet name contains spaces. You will still be able to reference a sheet with no spaces in its name, and it makes it easier to make changes later.

The Pros and Cons of Both Methods

Named ranges and the INDIRECT function each have an advantage and a disadvantage.

The advantage of using a named range is that changes you make to the sheet name will have no effect on the validation list. This highlights the INDIRECT function's disadvantage—namely, that any change you make to the sheet name will not be reflected automatically within the INDIRECT function, so you will have to manually change the function to correspond to the new sheet name.

The advantage of using the INDIRECT function is that the range you specify will always be the same, whereas if you use a named range and you delete cells/rows from your range, then the named range will adjust accordingly.

HACK #18   Control Conditional Formatting with Checkboxes

Although conditional formatting is one of Excel's most powerful features, it's a nuisance to turn it on and off through the ribbon. Adding checkboxes to your worksheet that turn formatting on and off makes it much easier to read data in any way you want, whenever you want.

ALL

Conditional formatting, a feature available since Excel 97, applies formats to selected cells that meet criteria based on values or formulas you specify. Although conditional formatting is usually applied based on cell values, applying it based on formulas provides the flexibility to extend the conditional formatting interface all the way to the spreadsheet grid.

Setting Up Checkboxes for Conditional Formatting

The checkboxes from the Form Controls—found under the Developer tab by selecting Controls → Insert (Forms toolbar for pre-2007 versions)—return either a TRUE or FALSE value (checked/not checked) to their linked cell. By combining a checkbox from the Form Controls with conditional formatting using the "Use a formula to determine which cells to format" option (Formula Is in pre-2007 versions), as shown in Figure 2-1, you can turn conditional formatting on and off via a checkbox.

> When used in conjunction with a formula (such as the "Use a formula to determine which cells to format" option), conditional formatting automatically formats a cell whenever the formula result returns TRUE. For this reason, any formula you use in this hack must return either TRUE or FALSE.

To see what we mean, try this simple example, which hides data via the use of conditional formatting and a checkbox. For this example, we will use the range $A$1:$A$10, filled consecutively with the numbers 1-10. To obtain a checkbox from the Form Controls, go to the Developer Tab Controls options and select Insert (pre-2007, go to the Forms toolbar by selecting View → Toolbars → Forms) and click the checkbox, then click near cell C1 on your sheet to position the check. Right-click the checkbox and select Format Control → Control. Type **C1** in the Cell Link box, as shown in Figure 2-2, and click OK.

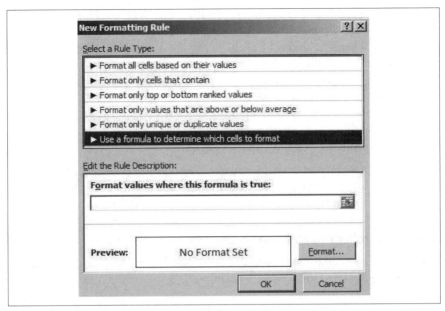

Figure 2-1. The Conditional Formatting dialog with the Formula option

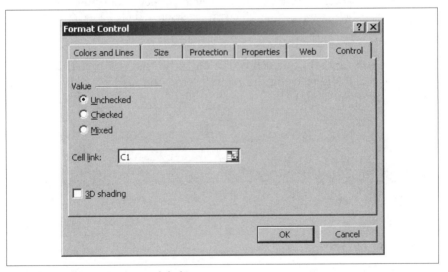

Figure 2-2. The Format Control dialog

When you select the checkbox floating over cell C1, it will return TRUE or FALSE to cell C1. As you do not need to see these values, select cell C1 and change the font color to white.

Now select cells $A$1:$A$10, starting with A1. Select the Home tab, then under the Styles options select Conditional Formatting → New Rule. Select the "use a formula to determine which cells to format" option—pre-2007, go to Format → Conditional Formatting..., and then select Formula Is (it will initially read Cell Value Is). Under "Format values where this formula is true" (in the Formula box to the right for pre-2007), type =$C$1. Next, click the Format button and select white under color (pre-2007, click the Format tab of the Conditional Formatting dialog, then the Font tab, and change the font color to white). Click OK, then OK again.

Select your checkbox so that it is checked, and the font color of the data in range $A$1:$A$10 will automatically change to white. Unchecking the checkbox will set it back to normal.

Toggling Number Highlighting On and Off

The ability to automatically highlight numbers that meet certain criteria can make it a lot easier to find the data you need in a spreadsheet.

> The ability to use conditional formatting to format numbers between certain ranges is available as a new feature in Excel 2007. However, the ability to toggle on and off via a checkbox as described in this hack is not.

To do this, start by selecting cell E1 (or any other cell you prefer) and name this cell *CheckBoxLink* using the name box at the far left of the Formula toolbar (see Figure 2-3).

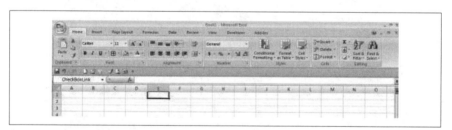

Figure 2-3. Cell E1 named CheckboxLink

Add a checkbox from the Form Controls (Forms toolbar for pre-2007) to cell F1. Set the cell link of this checkbox to the cell CheckBoxLink by right-clicking the checkbox and selecting Format Control... → Control. Then type **CheckBoxLink** in the Cell Link box and click OK.

Right-click the checkbox again, select Edit Text, and enter the words **Show Me**. In column A on another worksheet, enter the numbers 25 to 2500 in increments of 25. Name this range *Numbers* and hide this sheet by selecting View → Hide under the Windows options (pre-2007, Format → Sheet → Hide).

> To enter these numbers quickly, enter the number **25** in cell A1. Then, right-click (Control-click on the Mac) the fill handle (which appears as a small black square at the bottom right of the selection) and, while holding down the right mouse button, drag down to about row 100. Now release the left mouse button, select Series from the pop-up shortcut menu, enter **25** as the step value, and enter **2500** as the stop value. Then click OK.

Select cell B1 of the checkboxes worksheet and name this cell *FirstNum*. Select cell D1 and name this cell *SecondNum*. In cell C1, type the word **AND**. Now, select cell B1 (FirstNum), and press the Ctrl key while selecting cell D1 (SecondNum). Select the Data tab, go to Data Tools → Data Validation (pre-2007, Data → Validation → Settings), select List in the Allow: box, and type **=Numbers** in the Source: box. Ensure that the In-Cell drop-down item is checked and then click OK. This will give you a drop-down list of numbers 25 through 2500 in both cells.

In cell A1, type the heading **Amount**. Immediately below this, fill the range A2:A20 with any numbers that fall between the range 25 and 2500. Select cells A2:A20 (ensuring that you start from cell A2 and that it is your active cell in the selection), select Home → Styles → Conditional Formatting → New Rule (pre-2007, Format → Conditional Formatting...).

In the dialog box that appears, shown in Figure 2-4, select "Use a formula to determine which cells to format" (pre-2007, select Formula Is; it now should read Cell Value Is).

Then, in the "Format values when this formula is true" box (Formula box in pre-2007 versions), type the following formula:

```
=AND($A2>=FirstNum,$A2<=SecondNum,CheckboxLink)
```

Click Format and set any desired formatting or combination of formatting. Click OK, and then click OK again to dismiss the dialog boxes. Change the font color for cell E1 (CheckBoxLink) to white so that True or False will not show. From cell B1 (FirstNum), select any number and then select another number higher than the first from cell SecondNum (D1).

Check the checkbox, and the conditional formatting you just set will be applied automatically to the numbers that fall between the range you specified earlier. Deselect the checkbox and the formatting will revert to the default.

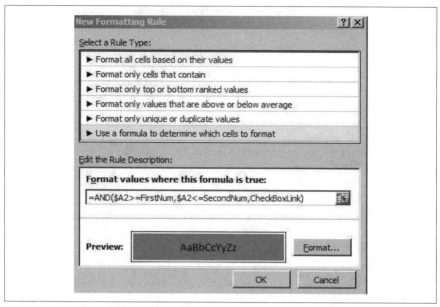

Figure 2-4. The New Formatting Rule dialog box

As you can see, by using a checkbox in combination with conditional formatting, you can do things most people would think is possible only through the use of VBA code.

HACK

#19

ALL

Identify Formulas with Conditional Formatting

Once a formula is entered into a cell, you can tell whether the cell is a static value or a value derived from a formula only by clicking in each cell and looking in the Formula bar, or by pressing Ctrl-~ (tilde). This hack fills that gap with a custom function.

The VBA code in this custom function (also called a *user-defined function*) enables you to identify cells that contain formulas without having to click through 10,000 cells and examine each one.

> You could select Conditional Formatting → New Rule (pre-2007, Format → Conditional Formatting → Formula Is) and use =CELL("Type",A1) in the "Use a formula to determine which cells to format" section, but you must be aware that this is a volatile function. This means that every time you make any changes at all in the workbook, or another workbook while the workbook containing the conditional formatting is still open, it will force all the cells using the CELL function to recalculate. These global recalculations can add considerably to your overhead in a large spreadsheet. This hack presents a better way.

To become a clever formula hunter, start by going to the Developer tab and selecting Code → Visual Basic (pre-2007, go to Tools → Macro → Visual Basic Editor) or Alt/Option-F11 and then select Insert → Module. Enter the following function into the window that appears:

```
Function IsFormula(Check_Cell As Range)
 IsFormula = Check_Cell.HasFormula
 End Function
```

Close the window (press Alt/⌘-Q, or use the Close button in the window's title bar). Now this function is available in any cell on any worksheet in this workbook when you enter the formula =IsFormula($A$1). You also can access the function by going to the Formulas tab, selecting Function Library → Insert Function (pre-2007, Insert → Function), selecting UserDefined from the Category option, and choosing IsFormula from the functions displayed.

The formula returns TRUE if the reference cell houses a formula and FALSE if it does not. You can use this Boolean result in conjunction with conditional formatting so that all formulas are highlighted automatically in a format of your choice.

One of the best things about using this method is that your spreadsheet's formula identification capabilities will be dynamic. This means that if you add or remove a formula, your formatting will change accordingly. Here we explain how to do this.

Select a range of cells on your spreadsheet—say, A1:J500—and incorporate some extra cells in case more formulas are added at a later stage.

 Avoid the temptation of selecting an entire worksheet, as this can add unnecessary overhead to your spreadsheet.

With these cells selected, and with A1 the active cell of the selection, select Home → Conditional Formatting → New Rule → "Use a formula to determine which cells to format," and enter the following in the "Format values where this formula is true" box (pre-2007, Format → Conditional Formatting... → change "Cell Value Is" to "Formula Is"):

```
=IsFormula(A1)
```

Click the Format option and choose any formatting you want to use to identify formula cells. Click OK, then OK again.

> Sometimes, when entering formulas into conditional format-
> ting, Excel will try to put quotation marks around the formu-
> las after you click OK. This means Excel has recognized
> what you entered as text, not as a formula. If this happens to
> you, go back into the Conditional Formatting dialog, remove
> the quotation marks, and click OK.

At this point, the specified formula should be applied to all cells on your
worksheet that contain formulas. If you delete or overtype a cell containing
a formula, the conditional formatting will disappear. Similarly, if you enter a
new formula into any cell within the range, it too will be highlighted.

This simple conditional formatting hack can make your spreadsheets a lot
easier to deal with when it comes time to maintain or modify them.

HACK #20 Count or Sum Cells That Meet Conditional Formatting Criteria

ALL

Once you can see the results of conditional formatting, you might want to
create formulas that reference only the data that was conditionally formatted.
Excel doesn't quite understand this in its calculations, but it can learn.

Excel users regularly ask, "How can I do calculations on only the cells that
have a specific background color?" This question arises so often because
Excel has no standard function for accomplishing this task; however, it can
be accomplished with a custom function [Hack #113].

The only trouble with using a custom function is that it does not pick up
any formatting that is applied using conditional formatting. With a bit of
lateral thinking, however, you can achieve the same result without bother-
ing with a custom function.

Say you have a long list of numbers in the range $A$2:$A$100. You applied
conditional formatting to these cells so that any numbers that fall between
the range 10 and 20 are flagged. Now you have to add the value of the cells
that meet the criterion you just set and then specify the sum of the values
using conditional formatting. You don't need to worry about what conditional formatting you applied to these cells, but you do need to know the
criteria that were used to flag the cells (in this case, cells with values between
10 and 20).

You can use the SUMIF function to add a range of cells that meet a certain criterion—but only one criterion. If you need to deal with more than one fac-
tor, you can use an array formula.

You use an array formula like this:

```
=SUM(IF($A$2:$A$100>10,IF($A$2:$A$100<20,$A$2:$A$100)))
```

When entering array formulas, *don't press Enter. Press Ctrl-Shift-Enter.* This way, Excel will place curly braces around the outside of the formula so that it looks like this:

```
{=SUM(IF($A$2:$A$100>10,IF($A$2:$A$100<20,$A$2:
$A$100)))}
```

If you enter these braces yourself, it won't work. You must allow Excel to do it for you.

Also, note that using an array formula can slow down Excel's recalculations if there are too many references to large ranges.

To read more about array formulas, visit *http://www.ozgrid.com/Excel/arrays.htm.*

An Alternate Path

Alternatively, you can use a spare column (for instance, column B) to reference the cells in column A. Your reference will return results into column B only if the value meets the conditions you set—e.g., >10, <20. To do this, follow these steps:

Select cell B1 and enter the following formula:

```
=IF(AND(A2>10,A2<20),A2,"")
```

Fill this formula into each cell, down to cell B100. Once the values are filled in, you should have values in column B that are between 10 and 20.

To quickly copy a formula down to the last used row in the column adjacent, enter the formula in the first cell (B2), reselect that cell, and double-click the fill handle. You also can do this by going to the Home tab and selecting Editing → Fill → Down (pre-2007, Edit → Fill → Down).

Now you can select any cell where you want your SUM result to appear and use a standard SUM function to add it up. (You can hide column B if you want so that you do not see an extra column full of the returned values of your formula.)

The preceding methods certainly get the job done, but Excel provides yet another function that enables you to specify two or more criteria. This function is part of Excel's database functions, and is called DSUM. To test it, use the same set of numbers in A2:A100. Select cells C1:D2 and name this range *SumCriteria* by selecting the cells and entering the name in the name box to the left of the Formula bar. Now select cell C1 and enter =$A$1, a reference to the first cell on the worksheet. Copy this across to cell D1, and you should have a double copy of your column A heading. These copies will be used as headings for your DSUM criteria (C1:D2), which you called SumCriteria.

In cell C2, enter **>10**. In cell D2, enter **<20**. In the cell where you want your result, enter the following formula:

```
=DSUM($A$1:$A$100,$A$1,SumCriteria)
```

DSUM is the preferred and most efficient method of working with cells that meet certain criteria. Unlike arrays, the built-in database functions are designed specifically for this purpose, and even when they reference a very large range and are used in large numbers, the negative effects they have on recalculation speed and efficiency are quite small compared to those of array formulas.

Highlight Every Other Row or Column

HACK #21

ALL

You've surely seen Excel spreadsheets that have alternating row colors. For instance, odd-numbered rows might be white, while even-numbered rows might be gray. Conditional formatting makes this easy.

Alternating colors or shading looks professional and can make data easier to read. You can apply this formatting manually, but as you can imagine, or might have experienced, it's a rather time-consuming task that requires constant updating as you add and remove data from the table. It also requires infinite patience. Fortunately, *conditional formatting* can reduce the amount of patience required and enhance your professional image.

We'll assume your data occupies the range A1:H100. Select this range of cells, starting with A1, thus ensuring that A1 is the active cell in the selection. Now select Home → Conditional Formatting → New Rule → "Use a formula to determine which cells to format," and type the following formula in the "Format values where this formula is true" box (pre-2007, go to Format → Conditional Formatting... → change "Cell Value Is" to "Formula Is"), as shown in Figure 2-5:

```
=MOD(ROW( ),2)
```

Click the Format button and choose the format you want to apply to every second row. Click OK, and then click OK again. The format you specified should be applied to every second row in the range A1:H100. You also should have some patience left for the rest of the day.

If you need to apply this to columns rather than rows, use this formula instead:

```
=MOD(COLUMN( ),2)
```

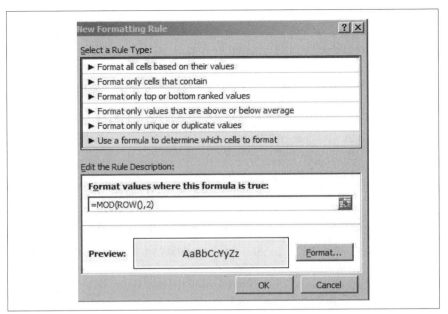

Figure 2-5. New Formatting Rule dialog containing the MOD formula to specify a format to every second row in a range

Although this method applies the formatting specified to every second row or column quickly and easily, it is not dynamic. Rows containing no data will still have the formatting applied. This looks slightly untidy and makes reading the spreadsheet a bit more difficult. Making the highlighting of every second row or column dynamic takes a little more formula tweaking.

Highlighting Dynamically *(INDIVIDUAL CELLS)*

Again, select the range A1:H100, ensuring that A1 is the active cell. Select Home → Conditional Formatting → New Rule → "Use a formula to determine which cells to format," and in the "Format values where this formula is true" box (pre-2007, go to Format → Conditional Formatting... → change "Cell Value Is" to "Formula Is"), type the following formula:

```
=AND(MOD(ROW( ),2),COUNTA($A1:$H1))
```

> Note that you do not reference rows absolutely (with dollar signs), but you do reference columns this way.

Click the dialog's Format option and select the desired formatting, then click OK, and OK again. Any row within the range A1:H100 that does not contain data will not have conditional formatting applied. If you remove data from a specific row in your table, it too will no longer have conditional formatting applied. If you add new data anywhere within the range A1: H100, the conditional formatting will kick in.

This works because when you supply a formula for conditional formatting, the formula itself must return an answer of either TRUE or FALSE. In the language of Excel formulas, 0 has a Boolean value of FALSE, while any nonzero value has a Boolean value of TRUE. When you use the formula =MOD(ROW( ),2), it will return either a value of 0 (FALSE) or a number greater than 0.

The ROW( ) function is a volatile function that always returns the row number of the cell it resides in. You use the MOD function to return the remainder after dividing one number by another. In the case of the formula you used, you are dividing the row number by 2, so all even row numbers will return 0, while all odd row numbers will always return a number greater than 0.

When you nest the ROW( ) function and the COUNTA function in the AND function, it means you must return TRUE (or any number greater than 0) to both the MOD function and the COUNTA function for the AND function to return TRUE. Note that COUNTA counts all nonblank cells.

HACK #22 Create 3-D Effects in Tables or Cells

ALL

Whenever you see a nifty 3-D effect in a program or application such as Excel, you are actually seeing an illusion created by specific formatting. It is easy to create this illusion yourself by applying formatting to a cell or range of cells. The release of Excel 2007 introduces cell styles, so you can create a 3-D effect and save it to use anytime you like.

To start off with a simple example, we'll give a cell a 3-D effect so that it appears raised, like a button. On a clean worksheet, select cell D5. (You're selecting D5 because it's not on an edge.) Under the Cells options on the Home tab, select Format → Format Cellst → Border (pre-2007, Format → Cells → Border). From the Line box, choose the second thickest line style. Ensure that the color selected is black (or Automatic, if you haven't changed the default for this option). Now click the right-hand border and then click the bottom border. Return to the color option and select white. The second thickest border still should be selected, so this time click the two remaining borders of the cell, the top border and the left border. Click the Fill tab (pre-2007, the Patterns tab) in the Format Cells dialog and make the cell shading gray. Click OK and deselect cell D5. Cell D5 will have a raised effect that gives the appearance of a button. You did it all with borders and shading.

If, for fun or diversity, you want to make a cell look indented or pushed in, select cell E5 (because it's next to D5 and it makes the next exercise work). Select Home → Cells → Format → Format Cells → Border (pre-2007, Format

→ Cells → Border) and choose the second thickest border from the line styles, and ensure that the color is black.

Apply the formatting to the top and left border of the cell. Select white for the color option and apply a white line to the right and bottom borders. Click the Patterns tab and change the cell's format to gray. Click OK. Cell E5 should appear indented. This works even better in contrast with cell D5, which has the raised effect.

> If you are happy with the cell style you have created, select Home → Styles → Cell Style → New Cell Style, give your Cell Style a name and click OK. Note that Cell Styles are saved to the current workbook, although you can merge Styles from other workbooks. This option is not available in versions before Excel 2007. If you want to save a cell style in prior versions, go to Format → Style.

Using a 3-D Effect on a Table of Data

Next, we'll experiment with this tool to see the sorts of effects you can apply to your tables or spreadsheets to give them some 3-D excitement.

Select cells D5 and E5, and click the Format Painter tool (the paintbrush icon) under Clipboard options on the Home tab (for pre-2007 users it's on the standard toolbar). While holding down the left mouse button, click in cell F5 and drag across to cell J5, then release.

Now select cells D5:J5 and again click the Format Painter tool. While holding down the left mouse button, select cell D6 and drag it across and down to cell J15, then release. This should produce the effect shown in Figure 2-6.

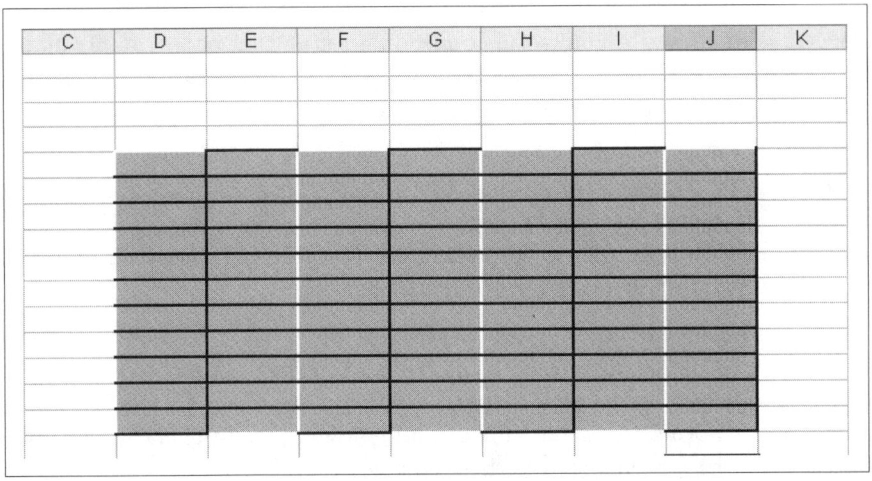

Figure 2-6. A 3-D effect applied to a range of cells

If you want to save your Table Style, select Home → Styles → Format as Table → New Table Style. You cannot save a Table Style in versions prior to Excel 2007.

We have used a fairly thick border to ensure that the effect is seen clearly; however, you might want to make this a little subtler by using a thinner line style. You also could use one of the other line styles to produce an even greater effect. The easiest way to find good combinations is to use trial and error on a blank worksheet to create the effect you want. You are limited only by your imagination and, perhaps, your taste.

Always keep in mind that 3-D effects can enhance readability and give spreadsheets a more professional look and feel, but when they're used in excess, they can have the opposite effect. Remember, use everything in moderation.

If you want to take this a step further and apply 3-D effects automatically and dynamically, you can combine the 3-D with conditional formatting, automating the application of the style choices you prefer.

HACK #23 Turn Conditional Formatting and Data Validation On and Off with a Checkbox

ALL   Data validation can make it far less likely that a user will accidentally enter incorrect data. Sometimes, however, you might need to make it easier to enter data that otherwise would be flagged as incorrect by conditional formatting or blocked completely by the validator.

Usually, you would enable users to enter data that otherwise would be flagged as incorrect by removing conditional formatting and/or data validation from the cells. There is an easier way, however: you can combine a simple checkbox from the Forms toolbar with data validation.

For this example, you'll apply conditional formatting to a range of cells so that any data appearing more than twice is highlighted for easy identification. We'll assume your table of data extends from cell $A$1:$H$100. To conditionally format this range of data so that you can identify cells with more than two duplicates requires a few steps.

Select cell K1 and name this cell CheckBoxLink by typing the name into the Name box to the left of the Formula bar and pressing Enter. Now click in cell I3 and select Developer → Insert → Form Controls → Check Box (pre-2007, if the Forms toolbar is not already showing, right-click any toolbar and select Forms, then click the checkbox icon).

Right-click the checkbox and select Format Control → Control. In the Cell Link box, type the name **CheckBoxLink** and click OK. Select cell A1, then drag and select a range down to cell H100. It is important that cell A1 is the active cell in your selection. Select Home → Conditional Formatting → New Rule → "Use a formula to determine which cells to format," and type the following in the "Format values where this formula is true" box, as shown in Figure 2-7 (pre-2007, Format → Conditional Formatting... → change "Cell Value Is" to "Formula Is"):

```
=AND(COUNTIF($A$1:$H$100,A1)>1,CheckboxLink)
```

Click the Format option and select the format you want to be applied to duplicated data. Click OK, then OK again.

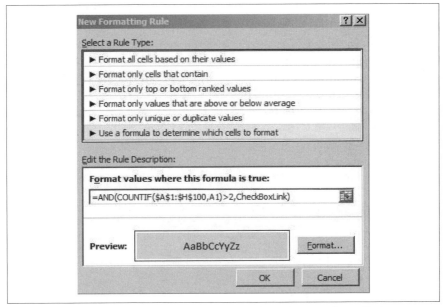

Figure 2-7. Conditional Formatting dialog showing formula to conditionally format a range to highlight duplicates

Although the checkbox you added to the worksheet is checked, the cell link in K1 (CheckBoxLink) will read TRUE and all cells with more than two duplicates within the range $A$1:$H$100 will be highlighted. As soon as you deselect the checkbox, its cell link (CheckBoxLink) will return FALSE, and these cells will not be highlighted.

The checkbox gives you a switch so that you can turn conditional formatting on and off from the spreadsheet, with no need to return to the Conditional Formatting dialog box. You can apply the same principle to data validation when using the formula option.

This works because you used the AND function. AND means two things must occur: COUNTIF($A$1:$H$100,A1)>2 must return TRUE, and the cell link for the checkbox (CheckBoxLink) also must be TRUE. In other words, both conditions must be TRUE for the AND function to return TRUE.

HACK #24 Support Multiple Lists in a ComboBox

When working with multiple lists, you can force a list to change by using a combination of option buttons plus a ComboBox.

Excel offers many ways for users to select items from a list, be they names, products, days of the week—whatever the list is composed of. However, to access more than one list of choices simultaneously generally requires that you use three separate controls, such as three ComboBox controls from the Form Controls (pre-2007, the Forms toolbar).

Instead, you can use a ComboBox in combination with option buttons (also called radio buttons and also found on the Form Controls) to have a list change automatically according to which option button you choose. To see how this works, enter the numbers **1** through **7** in the range A1:A7 on a new worksheet. In B1:B7, enter the days of the week starting with **Monday** and ending with **Sunday**. In C1:C7, enter the months **January** through **July**.

> Excel's auto-fill features can make this task much easier. Enter **1** in cell A1, select cell A1, press the Ctrl (⌘ on the Mac) key, and then left-click the fill handle. While holding down the left mouse button and the Ctrl key simultaneously, drag down to row 7. Excel will fill in the numbers for you. Next, enter **Monday** in cell B1 and double-click the fill handle for this cell. Enter **January** in cell C1 and double-click the fill handle for this cell. Excel will fill in the days and months for you!

Select Developer → Controls → Insert → Form Controls (pre-2007, View → Toolbars → Forms) and press Option. Then, click the spreadsheet anywhere in three separate spots to place three option buttons on the spreadsheet.

Now, follow the same process but this time click the ComboBox option under Form Controls and again click somewhere on the spreadsheet to insert a ComboBox on it. Using the drag handles, size the ComboBox to a manageable size and position the option buttons so that they're directly below the ComboBox.

Right-click the first option button, select Edit Text, then replace the words Option Button 1 with the word **Numbers**. Use the same process for Option

Button 2, replacing it with the word **Weekdays**, and for Option Button 3, replacing it with the word **Months**. This is shown in Figure 2-8.

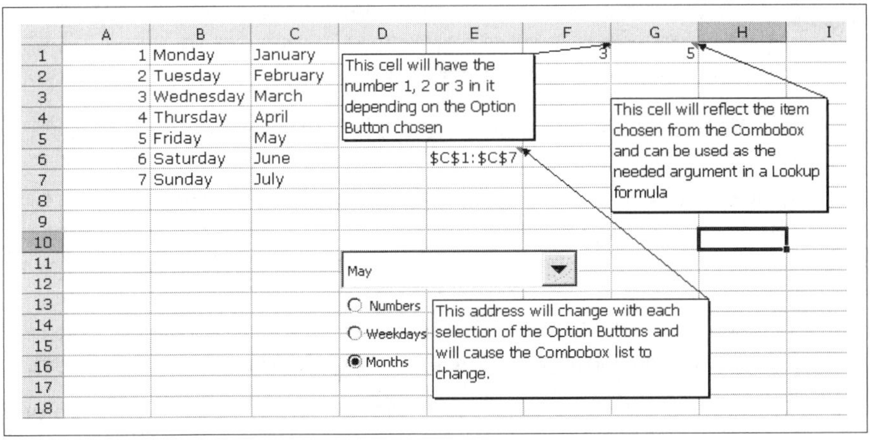

Figure 2-8. A multilist ComboBox controlled by option buttons

While holding down the Ctrl key, click each option button so that all three are highlighted, then right-click and select Format Control → Control (on the Mac, you can select View → Toolbars → Drawing, and use the Select Objects tool to select the group). Specify cell $F$1 as the cell link (make sure it is absolute—use those dollar signs).

In cell E6, enter the following formula:

```
=ADDRESS(1,$F$1) & ":" & ADDRESS(7,$F$1)
```

Select Formulas → Defined Name → Define Name (pre-2007, Insert → Name → Define). Under Name (pre-2007, Names in Workbook), type **MyRange** and in the Refers To: field, type the following:

```
=INDIRECT($E$6)
```

Click OK. Right-click the ComboBox and select Format Control → Control. Make the Input range **MyRange** and the cell link **$G$1**, then click OK. You should be able to select one of the option buttons, and the list within the ComboBox should automatically reflect which option button you chose.

When setting this up for your own spreadsheet, you should use some off-screen cells for the ComboBox links and lists. You might even want to hide these cells from users so that your links stay where they should. Also, you need to modify the two ADDRESS functions to reflect the cell range you are using. In the ADDRESS functions we used in this example, 1 represents the first row number of the lists, while 7 represents the last row number.

HACK #25 Create Validation Lists That Change Based on a Selection from Another List

ALL   Validation needs can vary depending on the context in which the validation is used. However, you can create a spreadsheet in which one validation list changes depending on what you select in another.

To make this hack work, the first thing you need to do is set up a worksheet with some data. On a clean worksheet named Lists and located in cell A1, type the heading **Objects**. In cell B1, type the heading **Corresponding List**. In cells A2:A5, repeat the word **Can**. In cells A6:A9, repeat the word **Sofa**. In cells A10:A13, repeat the word **Shower**. In cells A14:A17, repeat the word **Car**. Then, starting with cell B2 and ending with cell B17, enter the following words (corresponding to the Objects list): **Tin**, **Steel**, **Opener**, **Lid**, **Bed**, **Seat**, **Lounge**, **Cushion**, **Rain**, **Hot**, **Cold**, **Warm**, **Trip**, **Journey**, **Bonnet**, and **Boot**.

In cell C1, enter the heading **Validation List**. Next, to create a list of unique entries, enter the word **Can** in cell C2, the word **Sofa** in cell C3, the word **Shower** in cell C4, and the word **Car** in cell C5.

> You also can use the Advanced Filter to create a list of unique items. Select cells A1:A17, select Data → Sort & Filter → Advanced (pre-2007, Data → Filter → Advanced Filter), and then select Unique Records Only, Filter the List in Place. Click OK, and then select cells A2:A14 (which will include the hidden cells). Copy and paste them to cell A18. Select Data → Filter → Show All, select the list of unique objects, and cut and paste them into cell C2. Now you've got your list!

Select Formulas → Defined Names → Name Manager, click New (pre-2007, Insert → Name → Define) and in the Name: field, type the word **Objects**. In the Refers To: box, type the following formula and click OK (pre-2007, click Add, which will allow you to add another named range as below):

```
=OFFSET($A$2,0,0,COUNTA($A$2:$A$20),1)
```

Now click the New (pre-2007, Add) button. In the Name: box, type the name **ValList**, and in the Refers To: box, enter **$C$2:$C$5**. Click Close. Now insert another worksheet, call it **Sheet1**, and roll up your sleeves as you put this strange data to work.

With Sheet1 still active, on the Formula tab, select Define Names → Name Manager, click New (pre-2007, Insert → Name → Define), enter **CorrespondingList** in the Name: field, and in the Refers To: field, enter this rather lengthy formula and then click OK:

```
=OFFSET(INDIRECT(ADDRESS(MATCH(Val1Cell,Objects,0)+1,2,,,"Lists")),0,0,COUNT
IF(Objects,Val1Cell),1)
```

Now click the New (pre-2007, Add) button and in the Name: box, type the name **Val1Cell**. In the Refers To: box, enter **$D$6** and click OK. Click New again and in the Names: field type **Val2Cell**. In the Refers To: box, enter **$E$6** and again click OK. Click Close (pre-2007, click OK) to take yourself back to Sheet1 and then select $D$6.

This is a long process, but you are nearly done.

Select Data Validation under Data Tools options on the Data tab, and ensure you are on the Settings tab (pre-2007, Data → Validation → Settings). Select List from the Allow: box, and in the Source: box, type **=ValList**. Ensure that the In-Cell drop-down checkbox is selected and click OK.

Select cell E6 and again select Data Validation under Data Tools options on the Data tab (pre-2007, Data → Validation). Select List from the Allow: box, and in the Source: box, type **=CorrespondingList**. Then, ensure that the In-Cell drop-down box is checked, and click OK.

> When applying the data validation to E6, you will get the information message, "The source currently evaluates to an error. Do you want to continue?" Press Yes. This message occurs because D6 is currently blank.

Select one of the objects from the validation list in cell D6, and the validation list in cell E6 will change automatically to reflect the object you selected.

You now have one very user-friendly validation (pick) list, shown in Figure 2-9, whose contents will change automatically based on the item chosen from the other pick list.

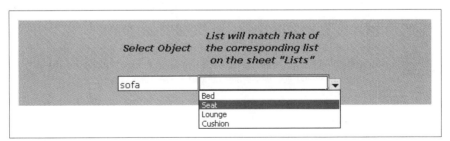

Figure 2-9. Two corresponding validation lists in use

H A C K
#26
ALL

Use Replace... to Remove Unwanted Characters

When importing data or copying and pasting data from other sources into Excel, unwanted characters appear throughout your spreadsheet. Using this hack, you can spare yourself the trouble of removing them by hand.

Excel's Replace... feature can help you remove unwanted characters from your spreadsheet, but it takes a few extra steps. For instance, you can replace cells containing unwanted characters with nothing (effectively deleting them) so that they no longer exist. To do this, you need to know the character code of the characters you want removed. All characters have a character code, and Excel will tell you what it is if you apply the CODE function to them. The CODE function returns a numeric code for the first character in a text string. The returned code corresponds to the character set used by your computer.

To make this work, select one of the cells containing an unwanted character. From the Formula bar, highlight the character and copy it to the clipboard. Then select any unused cell (A1, for example) and paste the character into the cell on its own.

In another cell, enter the following formula:

    =CODE($A$1)

This returns the character code of the unwanted character.

Select all your data, select Home → Editing → Find & Select → Replace (pre-2007, Edit → Replace...), click the Find What: field, press the Alt or ⌘ key, and enter **0** followed by the code number the CODE function returned. If the code number is 163, press the Alt or ⌘ key and type **0163**. Leave the Replace With: field empty and click Replace All. This will very quickly remove all the unwanted characters matching that character code. Repeat these steps for each unwanted character.

Convert Text Numbers to Real Numbers

The contents of a cell might look like numbers, especially in imported data, but it still might be impossible to use these numbers in calculations. Here are a few ways in which you easily can convert these "text" numbers to true numbers.

Remember that numbers in Excel are right-aligned by default, and that text is left-aligned by default. One easy way to identify those problematic text numbers in a column of what you think is composed entirely of true numbers is to select the column, go to the Home tab, launch the Alignment options by clicking the dialog launcher in the bottom right corner of the

Alignment group, select Format Cells → Alignment (pre-2007, Format → Cells → Alignment), ensure that the horizontal alignment is set to Excel's default of General, and click OK. Widen the column to a reasonable width, and all true numbers will be aligned to the right while any problematic text numbers will be aligned to the left. Dates will also be aligned to the right, as a date's true underlying value is nothing more than a number.

Using Paste Special

Now that you know you have numbers that are being seen as text, here is a quick and easy way to convert them all to true numbers, making Excel consider them usable for calculations. Copy any blank cell and then select your list of numbers. Right-click, select Paste Special... and then select Values under the Paste options. Select Add under the Operation options and click OK.

This will change to true numbers any numbers that are being seen as text. This happens because a blank cell has a value of 0, and when you add any number to a number that Excel is treating as text, you will force the text number to become a true number.

Using the TEXT Functions

You can apply this logic to some of Excel's standard functions—in particular, Excel's TEXT functions. Usually, when you use any of Excel's TEXT functions and the result returned is a number, Excel will still return that number as a text value rather than as a numeric value.

Assume you have a range of cells starting from $A$1. Each cell contains a dollar amount, followed by a space, then a person's name. Using the following formula, which combines the two TEXT functions LEFT and FIND, you can extract this dollar value:

```
=LEFT(A1,FIND(" ",A1)-1)
```

If cell A1 contains the data $22.70 Fred, the formula's result will be $22.70. However, this result will be returned as text rather than as a true numeric value; therefore, by default it will be left-aligned within the cell.

You can modify the formula so that the result is no longer a text value, but rather, a true numeric value, by adding **0** to the value:

```
=LEFT(A1,FIND(" ",A1)-1)+0
```

This will force the dollar value returned to become a true number; therefore, it will be right-aligned by default. All you need to do now is format the cell accordingly.

Extract the Numeric Portion of a Cell Entry

HACK #28

Often, you might have entries in your lists that contain both text and numbers within them. Using a custom function, you can easily take care of this problem, regardless of the length of the string.

ALL

Another problem that can arise regarding text and numbers occurs when you mix text and numbers in the same cell, with no real way of extracting the numeric portion only. In this case, you can use a custom function to extract the numeric portion from a text string.

To create this custom function, press Alt/Option-F11, select Insert → Module, and enter the following code:

```
Function ExtractNumber(rCell As Range)
Dim lCount As Long, l As Long
Dim sText As String
Dim lNum As String

sText = rCell

  For lCount = Len(sText) To 1 Step -1
      If IsNumeric(Mid(sText, lCount, 1)) Then
      l = l + 1
      lNum = Mid(sText, lCount, 1) & lNum
  End If

      If l = 1 Then lNum = CInt(Mid(lNum, 1, 1))
  Next lCount


ExtractNumber = CLng(lNum)
End Function
```

Press Alt/⌘-Q to exit and save. The function will appear under User Defined in the Paste function (Shift-F3). Use the function as shown in Figure 2-10.

	A	B	C
1	hjl4566klo59	456659	=ExtractNumber(A1)
2	jkh4025lop596	4025596	=ExtractNumber(A2)
3	hgt548kl92	54892	=ExtractNumber(A3)
4			
5			

Figure 2-10. Extracting the numeric portion from a text string

In Figure 2-10, column A contains a mixture of text and numbers, column B contains the result of using the ExtractNumber function, and column C shows how the formula looks in column B.

Customize Cell Comments

H A C K
#29

ALL

Cell comments enable you to place the electronic equivalent of a sticky note to any specified cell in a worksheet. Although many people use cell comments, many don't know that cell comments are customizable.

When you insert a cell comment via Review → Comments → New Comment button (pre-2007, Insert → Comment), by default Excel will also insert the username for the PC being used. You can change this by selecting the Office button → Excel Options → Popular (pre-2007, Tools → Options → General; on the Mac, Excel → Preferences → General). The username will appear at the bottom of the dialog box that opens, where you can type whatever you want to be shown by default.

Although cell comments serve the simple purpose of displaying a message to either yourself or another user, you can customize the cell comment so that it better reflects your intentions.

To make this hack work, you will need to add the Change Shape button to the Quick Access toolbar. Do this by going to the Office button → Excel Options → Customize. Then, from the Choose Commands From drop-down, select the Smart Art Tools/Format tab. Locate the Change Shape tool, click on it, and then select Add to add to the Quick Access toolbar, followed by OK (pre-2007, you won't be able to add this tool, so ensure that the Drawing toolbar is displayed by selecting View → Toolbars → Drawing).

Insert a cell comment into a cell by selecting the cell, going to the Review tab, and selecting Comments → New Comment (pre-2007, Insert → Comment). This automatically places you in Edit mode, ready to enter text into the comment box.

Left-click the outside border of the cell comment so that you are no longer in Edit mode. With the comment selected, select the Change AutoShape tool from your Quick Access Toolbar (pre-2007, select Draw from the Drawing toolbar, then Change AutoShape). You will be presented with a list of options including Basic Shapes, Block Arrow, Flow Chart, Stars and Banners, and Callouts. Choose an option, and the cell comment will change to the shape selected, as shown in Figure 2-11.

If you are using Excel 2007, you will notice that any shape you choose will have a three-dimensional look. If you want to create this look in pre-2007 versions, ensure that your comment is still selected, but that you are no longer in Edit mode. On the Drawing toolbar, click the Shadow Settings icon shown in Figure 2-12 and choose a shadow setting for the cell comment.

Figure 2-11. A dramatically formatted cell comment

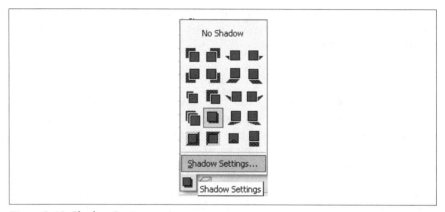

Figure 2-12. Shadow Settings options

Adding a Picture

Another interesting thing you can do with cell comments is use them to display pictures without impinging on any associated data. For instance, you could insert a picture of a chart into a cell comment to better illustrate the data in the chart without having to show the chart all the time.

To add a picture, ensure that the cell comment is selected, but that you are not in Edit mode. Left-click and select Format → Comment, (pre-2007 users can double-click the Comment border). Select Colors and Lines from the Format Comment dialog box. From the Color options, select Fill Effects, and from the Fill Effects dialog, select Picture. Now browse to the picture you want to insert into the cell comment.

Extracting Comment Text

One last thing you can do to cell comments is extract the text that was placed into a cell comment and have it appear in a cell. To do this, you need to place a simple custom function into a standard module. Select Developer → Code → Visual Basic (pre-2007, Tools → Macro → Visual Basic Editor) or select Alt/Option-F11, then select Insert → Module and enter the following code:

```
Function GetCommentText(rCommentCell As Range)
Dim strGotIt As String
    On Error Resume Next
    strGotIt = WorksheetFunction.Clean _
        (rCommentCell.Comment.Text)
    GetCommentText = strGotIt
    On Error GoTo 0
End Function
```

To return to Excel, either click the Close button or press Alt/⌘-Q, then save your workbook. Now, in any cell, enter the following formula:

```
=GetCommentText(A1)
```

where A1 has a cell comment in it. The comment text will appear in the cell.

Sort by More Than Three Columns

Excel's Sort feature is limited in that it enables you to nominate no more than three data fields by which to sort. In most cases, this is enough, but sometimes it can be handy to sort by more than three columns of data. Here is how you can get around this limitation.

For this example, we will assume you have related data in columns A, B, C, D, and E, and you want to sort this data first by column A, then B, then C, then D, and then E. To do this, you need to be able to sort backward—in other words, sort by the last field first, and then work back to the first field.

Select columns A through E and then select Data → Sort. Select the sort order by specifying that column C be sorted first, then D, and then E. Click Sort. Now select columns A through E and select Data → Sort. This time, sort by column A and then by B. Click Sort, and everything will be in order. Excel will have sorted the columns by five fields instead of the usual three.

If you want to automate this task, you can use a macro that will sort the selection and guess whether your data has column headings based on the formatting of the first row in the selection. If headings are in boldface, Excel will know they are column headings and will not sort them. Instead, it will sort by the leftmost column first, through to the rightmost column, for any number of columns up to 256.

The macro code you need to use must be placed into a standard module. To get it there, select Tools → Macro → Visual Basic Editor (Alt/Option-F11), then select Insert → Module and enter this code:

```
Sub SortByX( )
Dim l As Long

For l = Selection.Columns.Count To 1 Step -1
    Selection.Sort Key1:=Selection.Cells(2, 1), _
     Order1:=xlAscending, Header:=xlGuess, Orientation:=xlTopToBottom
Next l
End Sub
```

To return to Excel, either close the window or press Alt/⌘-Q. Once you have the hang of it, you will be able to perform much more complicated sorts than just the standard types on offer.

Random Sorting

You can use Excel to pick three winners—1st, 2nd, and 3rd—chosen at random from a list in your spreadsheet. The easiest and fairest way to do this is to use Excel's RAND function in combination with its sorting capabilities.

Assume you have a three-column table in your spreadsheet, starting from column B and containing Name, Age, and ID No., in that order. You can place the RAND function in cell A2 and copy this down as many rows as needed, all the way to the end of your table. As soon as you do this, each cell in column A containing the RAND function will automatically return a random number by which you can sort the table. In other words, you can sort columns A, B, C, and D by column A in ascending or descending order, and the three winners can be the top three names.

The RAND function is a volatile function that will recalculate automatically whenever an action takes place in Excel—e.g., entering data somewhere else, or forcing a recalculation of the worksheet by pressing F9. You'd better write down your winners quickly.

However, you can use this volatility to your benefit and record a macro that sorts data immediately after you recalculate, and force the RAND function to return another set of random numbers. You then can attach this macro to a button so that each time you want to draw three winners, all you need to do is click the button and use the top three names.

For example, assume you have your data in columns B, C, and D and that row 1 is used for headings. First, place the heading **RAND** in cell A1. Enter **=RAND( )** in cell A2 and copy down as far as needed. Then select any single cell and select Developer → Code → Record Macro (pre-2007, Tools → Macro → Record New Macro...).

Select columns A, B, C, and D and press F9 (to force a recalculation; on the Mac, use ⌘-=). Select Sort & Filter options → Data → Sort and sort the data by column A. Stop recording the macro.

Next, select Controls Options → Developer → Insert (pre-2007, View → Toolbars → Forms). Select a button from the Forms toolbar and place it anywhere on the worksheet. Assign the macro you just recorded to this button and click OK. (Change the text for the button from Button 1 to something more meaningful, if you want.)

You can select column A and hide it completely, as there is no need for a user to see the random numbers generated. Each time you click the button, your data will be sorted randomly, and you can just read off the top three names to be the winners, as shown in Figure 2-13.

	B	C	D	E	F	G
1	Name	Age	ID No.	Place	Pick Winner	
2	Dave	21	11256	1		
3	Paul	19	11257	2		
4	Anne	23	11135	3		
5	Gemma	30	11248			
6	Peter	52	11356			
7	Fred	30	11236			
8	Nigel	36	11237			
9	Bill	25	11234			
10	Jill	52	11245			

Figure 2-13. The end result of a random sort with column A hidden

> The RAND function in Excel 2003 and Excel 2007 has a major flaw. Although the Help file clearly states the random number returned will be between 0 and 1, this is not always the case if the RAND function is used in many cells. Sometimes the RAND function will return a number less than 0. To read Microsoft's take on why they changed the algorithm, visit *http://support.microsoft.com/default.aspx?kbid=828795.*

HACK #32 Manipulate Data with the Advanced Filter

ALL If you are familiar with Excel's AutoFilter tool, you also are familiar with its limitations. If you require extensive data manipulation, using Excel's Advanced Filter tool is the way to go.

Although limited, AutoFilters are a useful way to display only the data that meets particular criteria. Sometimes, however, you cannot glean the information you need using the standard options available in AutoFilters. Excel's versatile Advanced Filter tool enables you to further manipulate your data.

When you use Excel's Advanced Filter tool, your table must be set up in a classic table format as described at the start of Chapter 1.

When using Excel's Advanced Filter tool, you will need a copy of your table's column headings somewhere above your data. You should always leave at least three blank rows above your table of data. To ensure that your headings are exactly the same and will remain so regardless of whether you change your column headings, always reference the column headings with a simple reference formula such as =A4, where A4 contains a column heading. Copy this across for as many column headings as you have in your table. This will ensure that the criteria headings for the Advanced Filter are dynamic. Directly below these copied headings, place the criteria for the Advanced Filter to use. For more details on this process, see the Excel Help under Advanced Filters Criteria.

When using the Advanced Filter, keep in mind that two or more criteria placed directly underneath the applicable heading use an OR statement. If you want to use an AND statement, the column headings and their criteria must appear twice, side by side. Figure 2-14 shows how to use the OR operator to filter your data, and Figure 2-15 shows how to use the AND operator.

Figure 2-14. *Using Advanced Filter with OR to show only those people who have a pay rate greater than $16.00 OR less than $15.00*

Both of the preceding examples show fairly simple uses of the Advanced Filter tool and can be accomplished via AutoFilter if needed. Next we'll provide some examples of the Advanced Filter in which the use of AutoFilter would not be possible.

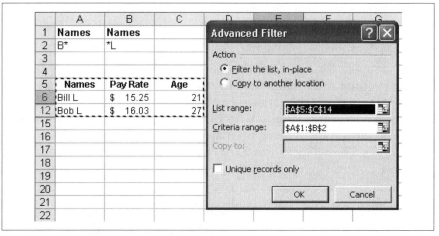

Figure 2-15. *Using Advanced Filter with AND to show only those people who have a name starting with B AND ending with L*

It's important to note that whenever you use a formula for your criteria, you must not use above the criteria a heading that is identical to the one within the table. For example, if you have a list of numeric data in column A and the list begins in cell A5 (with A4 being the heading), and you need to extract all the numbers in that list that are greater than the average, you would use criteria such as these:

```
=A5>AVERAGE($A$5:$A$500)
```

If the criteria were placed in cell A2, the criteria range would be $A$1:$A$2, but $A$1 could not contain the same heading as the one the list uses. It must be either blank or a different heading altogether.

It also is important to note that any formula you use should return either TRUE or FALSE. The range for the Average function is made absolute by the addition of dollar signs, while the reference to cell A5 is a relative reference. This is needed because when you apply the Advanced Filter, Excel will see that A5 is a relative reference and will move down the list one entry at a time and return either TRUE or FALSE. If it returns TRUE, it knows it needs to be extracted. If it returns FALSE, it does not meet the criteria; therefore, it will not be shown.

Assume that many of the names are repeated in the range $A$5:$A$500, with A4 being the headings. Also assume that many of the headings are repeated numerous times. You have been given the task of extracting from

the list all the names that appear more than once. To do this you need to use
the Advanced Filter and the following formula as your criteria:

```
=COUNTIF($A$5:$A$500,A5)>1
```

Once you apply the Advanced Filter to this and use the Copy to Another
Location: option, the newly created list will contain all the names that
appeared more than once in the original list (see Figure 2-16). Many of these
names will be repeated numerous times, but you can easily filter this new list
again with the Advanced Filter, this time selecting Unique Records Only (see
Figure 2-17). This will give you a list of names that appear in the list more
than once.

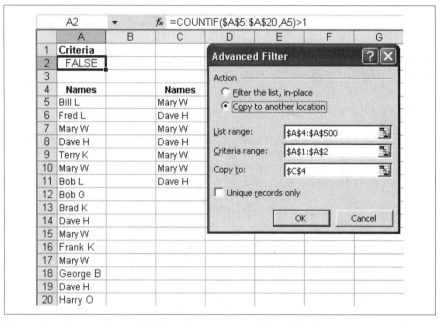

Figure 2-16. *Using Advanced Filter to extract names from a list that appear more than
once*

Advanced Filter users commonly ask how they can force
Excel to filter their data by the exact criteria they have provided. If your criterion is Dave and you perform an
Advanced Filter on a long list of names, Excel would show
not only the name Dave, but also names such as Davey,
Dave J, Dave K, etc. In other words, any name that begins
with the letters Dave, in that order, will be considered a
match for the criteria. To force Excel to find exact
matches—e.g., in this case find only the name Dave—enter
your criteria as **="=Dave"**.

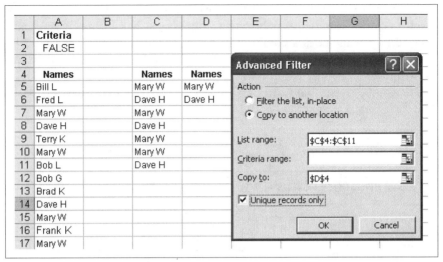

	A	B	C	D	E	F	G	H
1	Criteria							
2	FALSE							
3								
4	**Names**		**Names**	**Names**				
5	Bill L		Mary W	Mary W				
6	Fred L		Dave H	Dave H				
7	Mary W		Mary W					
8	Dave H		Dave H					
9	Terry K		Mary W					
10	Mary W		Mary W					
11	Bob L		Dave H					
12	Bob G							
13	Brad K							
14	Dave H							
15	Mary W							
16	Frank K							
17	Mary W							

Figure 2-17. Using Advanced Filter on the extracted list of names to filter down to show each name only once (Unique Records Only)

HACK #33 Create Custom Number Formats

ALL

Excel comes with built-in number formats, but sometimes you need to use a number format that is not built into Excel. Using the hacks in this section, you can create number formats that you can customize to meet your needs.

Before you try these hacks, it helps if you understand how Excel sees cell formats. Excel sees a cell's format as having the following four sections (from left to right): Positive Numbers, Negative Numbers, Zero Values, and Text Values. Each section is separated by a semicolon (;).

When you create a custom number format, you do not have to specify all four sections. In other words, if you include only two sections, the first section will be used for both positive numbers and zero values, while the second section will be used for negative numbers. If you include only one section, all number types will use that one format. Text is affected by custom formats only when you use all four sections; the text will use the last section.

> Don't interpret the word *number* to mean custom formats applying to numeric data only. Number formats apply to text as well.

The custom number format shown in Figure 2-18 is Excel's standard currency format, which shows negative currencies in red. We modified it by adding a separate format for zero values and another one for text. If you enter a positive number as a currency value, Excel will format it automatically so that it includes a comma for the thousands separator, followed by two decimal places. It will do the same for negative values, except they will show up in red. Any zero value will have no currency symbol and will show two decimal places. If you enter text into a cell, Excel will display the words "No Text Please," regardless of the true underlying text.

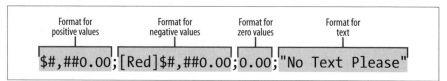

Figure 2-18. Custom number format sections

It is important to note that formatting a cell's value does not affect its underlying true value. For example, type any number into cell A1. Right-click and go to Format Cells → Number → Custom, and using any format as a starting point, type **"Hello"** (with the quotation marks). Then click OK.

Although the cell displays the word Hello, you can see its true value by selecting the cell and looking in the Formula bar, or by pressing F2. If you were to reference this cell in a formula—e.g., =A1+20— the result cell would take on the custom format. If you were to reference cell A1 along with many other cells that have any standard Excel format—e.g., =SUM(A1:A10)—the result cell would still take on the custom format of cell A1. Excel is taking an educated guess that you want the result cell formatted the same way as the referenced cell(s). If the referenced cells contain more than one type of format, any custom format will take precedence.

This means you must always remember that Excel uses a cell's true value for calculations, and not its displayed value. This can create surprises when Excel calculates based on cells that are formatted for no decimal places or for few decimal places, for instance. To see this in action, enter **1.4** in cell A1 and **1.4** in cell A2, format both cells to show zero decimal places, and then place **=A1+A2** into a cell. The result, of course, is 3, as Excel rounds.

> Excel does have an option called "Precision as Displayed," which you can find by selecting the Office button → Excel Options → Advanced (pre-2007, go to Tools → Options → Calculation), but you should be aware that this option will permanently change stored values in cells from full precision (15 digits) to whatever format, including decimal places, is displayed. In other words, once it's been checked and given the okay, there is no turning back. (You can try, but the extra precision information is gone for good.)

The default format for any cell is General. If you enter a number into a cell, Excel often will guess the number format that is most appropriate. For example, if you enter **10%** into a cell, Excel will format the cell as a percentage. Most of the time, Excel guesses correctly, but sometimes you need to change it.

> When using Format Cells, resist the temptation to force a left, right, or center horizontal format! By default, numbers are right-aligned and text is left-aligned. If you leave this alone, you can tell at a glance whether a cell is text or numeric, as in the case of the earlier example in which cell A1 appears to hold text, when in fact, it holds a number.

Each section of a given format uses its own set of formatting codes. These codes force Excel to make data appear how you want it to appear. So, for instance, suppose you want negative numbers to appear inside parentheses, and all numbers, positive, negative, and zero, to show two decimal places. To do this, use this custom format:

```
0.00_ ;(-0.00)
```

If you also want negatives to show up in red, use this custom format:

```
0.00_ ;[Red](-0.00)
```

Note the use of the square brackets in the preceding code. The formatting code tells Excel to make the number red.

You can use many different formatting codes within sections of a custom format. Tables 2-1 through 2-5, derived from Microsoft documentation, explain these codes. Table 2-1 lists formatting codes, Table 2-2 lists text codes, Table 2-3 lists date codes, Table 2-4 lists time codes, and Table 2-5 lists some other miscellaneous codes.

Table 2-1. Formatting codes

Number code	Description
General	General number format.
0 (zero)	A digit placeholder that pads the value with zeros to fill the format.
#	A digit placeholder that does not require extra zeros to be displayed.
?	A digit placeholder that leaves a space for insignificant zeros but does not display them.
%	A percentage. Excel multiplies by 100 and displays the % character after the number.

Table 2-1. Formatting codes (continued)

Number code	Description
, (comma)	A thousands separator. A comma followed by a place-holder scales the number by 1,000.
E+ E- e+ e-	Scientific notation.

Table 2-2. Text codes

Text code	Description
$ - + / ( ) : and blank space	These characters are displayed in the number. To display any other character, enclose the character in quotation marks or precede it with a backslash.
\character	This code displays the character you specify. Note that typing !, ^, &, ' ', ~, {, }, =, <, or > automatically places a backslash in front of the character.
"text"	This code displays the text between the quotes.
*	This code repeats the next character in the format to fill the column width. Only one asterisk per section of a format is allowed.
_ (underscore)	This code skips the width of the next character. This code is commonly used as _) to leave space for a closing parenthesis in a positive number format when the negative number format includes parentheses. This allows both positive and negative values to line up at the decimal point.
@	A placeholder for text.

Table 2-3. Date codes

Date code	Description
M	A month represented as a number without leading zeros (1–12)
Mm	A month represented as a number with leading zeros (01–12)
Mmm	A month given as an abbreviation (Jan–Dec)
Mmmm	An unabbreviated month (January–December)
D	A day represented without leading zeros (1–31)
Dd	A day represented with leading zeros (01–31)
Ddd	A weekday represented as an abbreviation (Sun–Sat)
Dddd	An unabbreviated weekday name (Sunday–Saturday)
Yy	A year given as a two-digit number (for example, 96)
Yyyy	A year given as a four-digit number (for example, 1996)

Table 2-4. Time codes

Time code	Description
H	Hours given as a number with no leading zeros (0–23)
Hh	Hours given as a number with leading zeros (00–23)
m	Minutes given as a number with no leading zeros (0–59)
mm	Minutes given as a number with leading zeros (00–59)
s	Seconds given as a number with no leading zeros (0–59)
ss	Seconds given as a number with leading zeros (00–59)
AM/PM am/pm	Time of day based on a 12-hour clock

Table 2-5. Miscellaneous codes

Miscellaneous code	Description
[BLACK], [BLUE], [CYAN], [GREEN], [MAGENTA], [RED], [WHITE], [YELLOW], [COLOR n]	These codes display characters in the specified colors. Note that n is a value from 1 to 56 and refers to the nth color in the color palette.
[Condition value]	Condition can be <, >, =, >=, <=, or <>, while value can be any number. A number format can contain up to two conditions.

Note in particular the last kind of formatting codes listed in Table 2-5: the comparison operators. Assume you want the custom number format 0.00_ ;[Red](-0.00) to display negative numbers in a red font and in brackets only if the number is less than -100. To do this, use the following:

```
0.00_ ;[Red][<-100](-0.00);0.00
```

The formatting codes [Red][<-100](-0.00) placed in the section for negative numbers make this possible. Using this method in addition to conditional formatting you can double the number of conditional format conditions available from three to six.

Often, users want to display dollar values as words. To do this, use the following custom format:

```
0 "Dollars and" .00 "Cents"
```

This format will force a number entered as 55.25 to be displayed as 55 Dollars and .25 Cents. If you want to convert numbers to dollars and cents, consult these two custom functions from Microsoft: *http://www.ozgrid.com/VBA/ValueToWords.htm* and *http://www.ozgrid.com/VBA/CurrencyToWords.htm*.

You can also use a custom format to display the words Low, Average, or High, along with the number entered. Simply use this formatting code:

```
[<11]"Low"* 0;[>20]"High"* 0;"Average"* 0
```

Note the use of the *. This repeats the next character in the format to fill the column width, meaning that all the Low, Average, or High text will be forced to the right, while the number will be forced to the left.

HACK #34 Add More Levels of Undo to Excel for Windows

<2007

We all are familiar with Excel's fabulous Undo feature, which enables a user to undo his mistakes. Unfortunately, the default level for this is a mere 16 changes. With the hack in this section, you can change the registry so that you can undo up to 100 mistakes.

When you use Excel's Undo feature, and you reach undo number 16, the first undo is replaced by the 17th, and so on. Also, as soon as you save your workbook, the Undo Stack is wiped out, and the Undo History is lost. This is because when you press Save, you're actually telling Excel that you are happy with the changes you made, so it decides for you that your Undo History is no longer required.

You might have discovered that at times having only your last 16 changes retained in the Undo Stack is not enough. Instead of living with this, you can change this by editing the registry, something that works only in Windows. To do this, begin by quitting Excel completely. Select Start → Run, and in the Open box type **Regedit.exe**. Click OK. When Regedit starts, expand the folder for HKEY_CURRENT_USER. Then expand the Software folder underneath it, then the Microsoft folder, the Office folder, and the 10.0 folder. (This last folder varies for different versions. 10.0 is for Excel 2002.) Expand the Excel folder, and finally, open the Options folder.

Select Edit → New → DWORD Value, enter the word **UndoHistory**, and press Enter. Double-click the UndoHistory you just created, and enter a value greater than 16 and less than 100.

Hopefully, 100 undos will be enough for even the most demanding users, though the issue with Save clearing the Undo Stack persists.

HACK #35 Create Custom Lists

ALL

By adding a custom list to Excel, you can type the first item in the list, drag it down using the fill handle, and watch the list fill automatically.

One of Excel's most popular time-saving features is its ability to automatically increment not only numbers, but certain text as well. Excel has a couple of built-in lists, such as days of the week and months of the year. Currently when you use the fill handle, you type the first item, then use the fill handle to fill cells with the next item in the list, and so forth. You can easily create your own custom list for commonly used items.

The most flexible way to create a custom list is to enter the list contents into a range of cells. For example, say you have a list of 100 employee names. Enter each name, starting with cell A1 and ending with cell A100, and sort the list, if needed. Then select the Office button → Excel Options → Popular → Edit Custom Lists (pre-2007, Tools → Options → Custom Lists; on the Mac, Excel → Preferences → Custom Lists). Click the collapse tool to the left of the Import button. Using the mouse pointer, left-click in cell A1 and drag all the way down to A100. Then click the Import button, then OK. From this point on, the custom list will be available to all workbooks on the same computer.

Once you create a custom list, you can turn the list upside down. To do this, return to the column next to the custom list and place the last entry from the list in the top cell. In the cell beneath it, place the second-to-last entry. Select both cells and double-click the fill handle. The list you produced should be reversed. You can sort the original list by going to the Data tab and selecting Sort & Filter → Sort (pre-2007, Data → Sort → Options).

If your list is sorted and you want to turn it upside down, you might find it easier to sort from Z to A if the list originally was sorted from A to Z.

Boldface Excel Subtotals

HACK #36

Wouldn't it be great if you could identify the subtotals in your worksheets so that you can find them easily? With the hacks in this section, you can.

ALL

When you are working with a spreadsheet that has subtotals you created by selecting Data → Subtotals, the subtotals can be very hard to identify, making the spreadsheet hard to read. This is true especially if you applied subtotals to a table of data with many columns.

Typically, the resulting subtotals appear on the right, while their associated headings are often in the first column. As the subtotal values are not in boldface, it can be hard to visually align them with their row headings. You can make these subtotals much easier to read by applying bold formatting to the subtotal values.

To test the problem, set up some data similar to that shown in Figure 2-19.

Now add the subtotals by selecting Data → Outline → SubTotal Button (pre-2007, Data → Subtotals), accepting the defaults in the Subtotals dialog, and clicking OK.

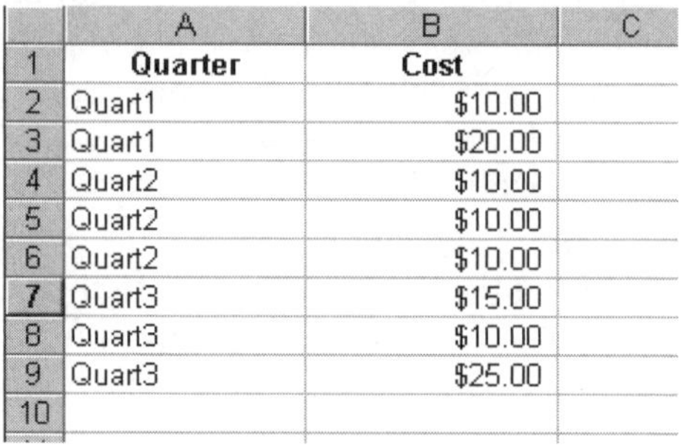

	A	B	C
1	**Quarter**	**Cost**	
2	Quart1	$10.00	
3	Quart1	$20.00	
4	Quart2	$10.00	
5	Quart2	$10.00	
6	Quart2	$10.00	
7	Quart3	$15.00	
8	Quart3	$10.00	
9	Quart3	$25.00	
10			

Figure 2-19. Worksheet data before adding subtotals

In Figure 2-20, the subtotal headings have been boldfaced but their associated results have not. As this table has only two columns, it is not that hard to read and pick out the subtotal amounts.

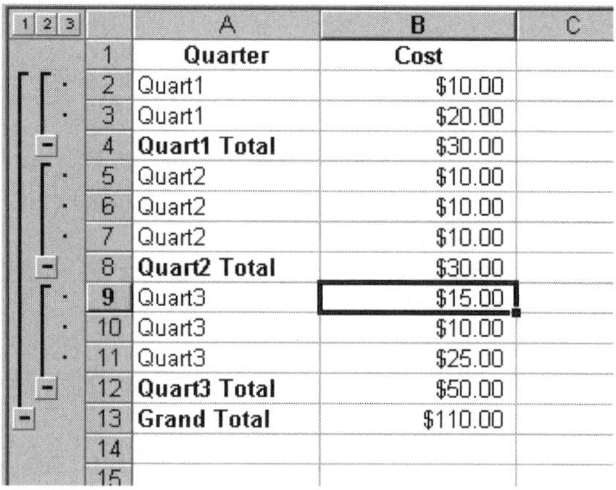

	A	B	C
1	**Quarter**	**Cost**	
2	Quart1	$10.00	
3	Quart1	$20.00	
4	**Quart1 Total**	**$30.00**	
5	Quart2	$10.00	
6	Quart2	$10.00	
7	Quart2	$10.00	
8	**Quart2 Total**	**$30.00**	
9	Quart3	$15.00	
10	Quart3	$10.00	
11	Quart3	$25.00	
12	**Quart3 Total**	**$50.00**	
13	**Grand Total**	**$110.00**	
14			
15			

Figure 2-20. Worksheet data after subtotals have been applied

The more columns a table has, however, the harder it is to visually pick out the subtotals. You can solve this problem by using Excel's conditional formatting. Using the table in Figure 2-19 as an example, try this before adding your subtotals. Select cell A1:B9, ensuring that A1 is the active cell. Select Home → Styles → Conditional Formatting → New Rule → "Use a formula to determine which cells to format" (pre-2007, Format → Conditional Formatting... → Formula Is), and then add the following formula under "Format values where this formula is true":

```
=RIGHT($A1,5)="Total"
```

Now click the Format button and then the Font tab, and select Bold as the Font Style. Click OK, then OK again.

The important part of the formula is the use of an absolute reference of the column ($A) and a relative reference of the row (1). As you started the selection from cell A1, Excel will automatically change the formula for each cell. For example, cells A2 and B2 will have the conditional format formula =RIGHT($A2,5)="Total", and cells A3 and B3 will have the conditional format formula =RIGHT($A3,5)="Total".

Add the subtotals, and they will look like those in Figure 2-21.

1 2 3		A	B	C
	1	Quarter	Cost	
	2	Quart1	$10.00	
	3	Quart1	$20.00	
	4	**Quart1 Total**	**$30.00**	
	5	Quart2	$10.00	
	6	Quart2	$10.00	
	7	Quart2	$10.00	
	8	**Quart2 Total**	**$30.00**	
	9	Quart3	$15.00	
	10	Quart3	$10.00	
	11	Quart3	$25.00	
	12	**Quart3 Total**	**$50.00**	
	13	**Grand Total**	**$110.00**	
	14			

Figure 2-21. Worksheet data after subtotals have been formatted

One last thing to remember is that if you remove the subtotals, the bold-faced font will no longer apply.

Hacking the Hack

The only possible pitfall with this method is that the Grand Total appears in the same style as the Subtotals. It would be nice to see the Grand Total formatted in another way so that it stands outs from the Subtotals and is identified more easily. You can do this using the same example.

Delete the previous conditional formatting rule by going to Conditional Formatting → Manage Rules, clicking on the rule, and selecting Delete Rule (pre-2007, Format → Conditional Formatting → Delete).

Starting with your raw data, select cell A1:B9, ensuring that A1 is the active cell. Now select Conditional Formatting → Manage Rules → New Rule →

"Use a formula to determine which cells to format" (for pre-2007, select Format → Conditional Formatting... → select Formula Is) and add the following
formula under "Format values where this formula is true":

```
=$A1="Grand Total"
```

Click the Format button and then the Font tab, and select Bold as the Font
Style. Click OK, and then click New Rule to add a second format condition
(pre-2007, click Add). Select "Format values where this formula is true"
(Formula Is in older versions) and add the following formula:

```
=RIGHT($A1,5)="Total"
```

Click the Format button and then the Font tab. On this tab, select Bold
Italic as the Font Style. Select Single from Underline, click OK, and then
click OK again.

> For Excel 2007 users, when Rules are added to Conditional
> Formatting, they are added so that the rule you first create is
> at the bottom of the list, then the next rule you create is on
> top of this and so forth. This means that the last rule you
> create will be applied first (the reverse is true for pre-2007
> versions). For this hack you will need to change the order
> that the rules are applied in, so click on the first rule that you
> made (=$A1="Grand Total") and press the "Move up" button.

Next, select the SubTotal Button under Outline options on the Data tab,
(pre-2007, Data → Subtotals) accept the defaults, and click OK.

Your worksheet data should now look like Figure 2-22.

You can use any format you want to make your subtotals easier to read.

1 2 3		A	B	C
	1	**Quarter**	**Cost**	
	2	Quart1	$10.00	
	3	Quart1	$20.00	
	4	***Quart1 Total***	***$30.00***	
	5	Quart2	$10.00	
	6	Quart2	$10.00	
	7	Quart2	$10.00	
	8	***Quart2 Total***	***$30.00***	
	9	Quart3	$15.00	
	10	Quart3	$10.00	
	11	Quart3	$25.00	
	12	***Quart3 Total***	***$50.00***	
	13	**Grand Total**	**$110.00**	
	14			

Figure 2-22. Worksheet data with more prominent grand total

Convert Excel Formulas and Functions to Values

Most Excel spreadsheets contain formulas. Sometimes you may want to force only the result of a formula to occupy a cell, instead of leaving the formula in place, where it will change if/when the data it references changes.

You can do this manually in a couple of ways, or you can use a macro that will make the job a breeze. Let's look at the manual methods first.

Using Paste Special

You can copy the formula results and still leave the original formulas in place using Excel's Paste Special tool. Assume you have formulas residing in cells A1:A100. Select this range, select Copy (you can do this from the Clipboard options on the Home tab or right-click), and then select the starting cell for the mirror results. Select Clipboard → Paste → Paste Values (or right-click and select Paste Special → Values) and click OK.

If you want to override the original formulas with their results, select the formula range and select Copy. With the formula range still selected, select Paste → Paste Values (or right-click and select Paste Special → Values) and then click OK.

Using Copy Here As Values Only

You also can copy formula results and still leave the original formulas in place by using a pop-up menu that many users don't even know exists.

Select the formula range and right-click the right or left border of the selection (in other words, anywhere on the selection border except for the fill handle). While holding down the right mouse button (or Ctrl-clicking on a Macintosh), drag to the destination, release the right mouse button, and click Copy Here as Values Only from the resulting pop-up shortcut menu.

You can also override the original formulas with their results. Select the formula range, then right-click the right or left border of the selection (again, anywhere in the selection except for the fill handle). While pressing the right mouse button (or Ctrl-clicking), drag over one column to the right or left and then back to the starting range, release the right mouse button, and click Copy Here as Values Only from the resulting pop-up shortcut, shown in Figure 2-23.

Using a Macro

If you frequently convert cells containing formulas and functions to their values, you can use this simple macro:

```
Sub ValuesOnly( )
Dim rRange As Range
```

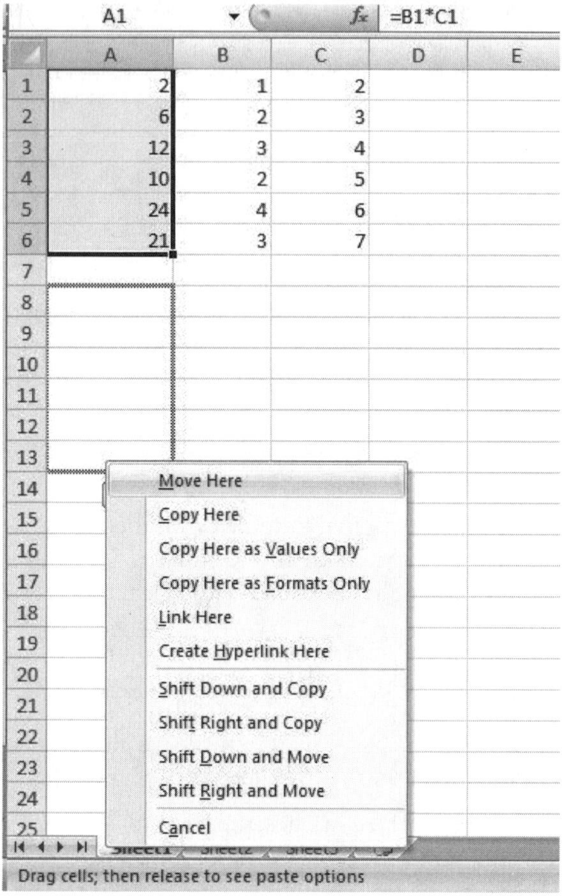

Figure 2-23. Pop-up shortcut menu

```
    On Error Resume Next
        Set rRange = Application.InputBox(Prompt:="Select the formulas", _
                        Title:="VALUES ONLY", Type:=8)
        If rRange Is Nothing Then Exit Sub
    rRange = rRange.Value
End Sub
```

To use this macro, select Developer → Code → Visual Basic (pre-2007, Tools → Macro → Visual Basic Editor) or Alt/Option-F11. While in the VBE, select Insert → Module to insert a standard module. Enter the preceding code directly into the module. Click the window's Close button, or press Alt/⌘-Q to get back to Excel. Select Developer → Code → Macros (pre-2007, Tools → Macro → Macros) or Alt/Option-F8, select **ValuesOnly**, and then click Options to assign a shortcut key to the macro. When you use the macro you will be presented with an InputBox and asked to select a range that contains your formulas. The selected range address will show automatically in the InputBox, and all you need to do to make the conversion is click OK.

Automatically Add Data to a Validation List

HACK #38

ALL

The validation feature in Excel is great, but there is one key thing it cannot do (without the following hack): automatically add a new entry to the list being used as the source for the validation list. This hack allows a user to add to the list, showing a message box and giving the user an option to Add or Cancel. Duplicates are ignored.

If you have used validation, you know it's a neat feature. Perhaps most impressive is its ability to add a list to any cell from which the user can then select. Wouldn't it be nice if, when you enter a new name in a validated cell, Excel automatically adds it to the list? This is possible, thanks to the following hack.

Assume you have a list of names in the range A1:A10, as in Figure 2-24.

	A	B
1	Robyn Fenlon	
2	Joe Smith	
3	Bill Bloggs	
4	Fred Stone	
5	Neil Watts	
6	Judith Thurley	
7	Jacqui Jones	
8	Connie Eldon	
9	Kim Holmes	
10	Andrea Brooks	
11		

Figure 2-24. Workbook set up for validation list

These names represent employees in a company. It is not uncommon for new employees to be added to such a list, but at present, the only way to achieve this is to add the new names to the end of the list and then select the new names from the list in the validated cell.

To overcome this limitation, follow these steps. In cell A11, enter the following formula and copy it down to row 20, as in Figure 2-25 (note the relative reference of A10):

```
=IF(OR($D$1="",COUNTIF($A$1:A10,$D$1)),"x",$D$1)
```

Now, select Formulas → Defined Names → Define Name (pre-2007, Insert → Name → Define), and type **MyNames** in the Names: box. In the Refers To: box, enter the following formula, as shown in Figure 2-26, and then click OK (pre-2007, click Add then click OK):

```
=OFFSET(Sheet1!$A$1,0,0,COUNTA(Sheet1!$A:$A),1)
```

	A	B
1	Robyn Fenlon	
2	Joe Smith	
3	Bill Bloggs	
4	Fred Stone	
5	Neil Watts	
6	Judith Thurley	
7	Jacqui Jones	
8	Connie Eldon	
9	Kim Holmes	
10	Andrea Brooks	
11	x	
12	x	
13	x	
14	x	
15	x	
16	x	
17	x	
18	x	
19	x	
20	x	

Figure 2-25. List with formula added to rows A11:A20

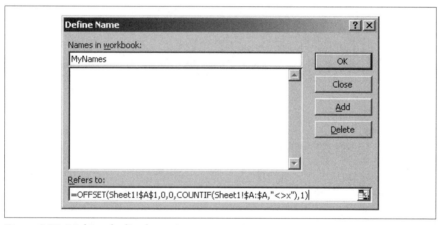

Figure 2-26. Making the list dynamic

Select cell D1, select Data → Data Tools → Data Validation (pre-2007, select
Data → Validation). Choose List from the Allow: box, and in the Source:
box, type **=MyNames**, ensuring that the In-Cell drop-down box is checked.
Click the Error Alert page tab and uncheck the Show error alert after
invalid data is entered box. Now click OK. You'll see the result in
Figure 2-27.

	A	B	C	D	E
1	Robyn Fenlon				
2	Joe Smith				
3	Bill Bloggs				
4	Fred Stone				
5	Neil Watts				
6	Judith Thurley				
7	Jacqui Jones				
8	Connie Eldon				
9	Kim Holmes				
10	Andrea Brooks				
11	x				
12	x				
13	x				

Figure 2-27. The list with validation added to cell D1

Right-click the Sheet Name tab and select View Code. Enter the following code:

```
Private Sub Worksheet_Change(ByVal Target As Range)
Dim lReply As Long
    If Target.Cells.Count > 1 Then Exit Sub

        If Target.Address = "$D$1" Then
            If IsEmpty(Target) Then Exit Sub
            If WorksheetFunction.CountIf(Range("MyNames"), Target) = 0 Then
                lReply = MsgBox("Add " & Target & " to list", vbYesNo +
vbQuestion)
                If lReply = vbYes Then
                    Range("MyNames").Cells(Range("MyNames").Rows.Count + 1,
1) = Target
                End If
            End If
        End If
End Sub
```

Close the window to get back to Excel and save your workbook. Now select cell D1, type in any name that is *not* part of the list, and press Enter. Select cell D1 again and look at the list. The new name should be part of it, as shown in Figure 2-28.

If you want to add more than 10 names to your list, just copy the formula down past row 20.

	A	B	C	D	E
1	Robyn Fenlon			Jim Jones ▼	
2	Joe Smith				
3	Bill Bloggs				
4	Fred Stone				
5	Neil Watts				
6	Judith Thurley				
7	Jacqui Jones				
8	Connie Eldon				
9	Kim Holmes				
10	Andrea Brooks				
11	Jim Jones				
12	x				
13	x				

Figure 2-28. The list after adding a new entry to cell D1

HACK #39   Hack Excel's Date and Time Features

ALL

See #89

Excel's date and time feature is great if you're creating simple spreadsheets, but they can cause problems for more advanced projects. Fortunately, there are ways to get around Excel's assumptions when they don't meet your needs.

Excel (by default) uses the 1900 date system. This means the date 1 Jan 1900 has an underlying numeric value of 1, and that 2 Jan 1900 has a value of 2, and so forth. These values are called *serial values* in Excel, and they enable you to use dates in calculations.

Times are very similar, but Excel treats times as decimal fractions, with 1 being the time 24:00 or 00:00. 18:00 has a numeric value of 0.75 because it is three-quarters of 24 hours.

To see the numeric value of a date and/or a time, format as General the cell containing the value. For example, the date and time 3/May/2007 3:00:00 PM has a numeric value of 39205.625, with the number after the decimal representing the time, and the 39205 representing the serial value for 3/May/2007.

Adding Beyond 24 Hours

You can add times by using the SUM function (or a simple plus sign). Therefore, =SUM(A1:A5) would result in Total Hours if A1:A5 contained valid times. There is, however, a big "Gotcha!" Unless told otherwise, Excel will not add past 24 hours. This is because when a time value exceeds 24 hours (a true value of 1), it rolls into a new day and starts again. To force Excel not to default back to a new day after 24 hours, you can use a cell format of 37:30:55 or a custom format of [h]:mm:ss.

You can use a similar format to get the total minutes or seconds of a time. To get the total minutes of the time 24:00, for instance, format the cell as [m] and you will get 1440. To get the total seconds, use a custom format of [s] and you get 86400.

Time and Date Calculations

If you want to use these real time values in other calculations, keep the "magic" numbers listed in Table 2-6 in mind.

Table 2-6. Magic numbers for time and date calculations

Number	Meaning
60	60 minutes or 60 seconds
3600	60 secs * 60 mins *3600 S/HR*
24	24 hours
1440	60 mins * 24 hours *1440 m/D*
86400	24 hours * 60 mins * 60 secs *86400 S/D*

Once you are armed with these magic numbers and the preceding information, you'll find it's much easier to manipulate times and dates. Take a look at the following examples to see what we mean (assume the time is in cell A1).

If you have the number 5.50 and you really want 5:30 or 5:30 a.m., use this:

    =A1/24

and format as needed.

If it should be 17:30 or 5:30 p.m., use this:

    =(A1/24)+0.5

To achieve the opposite—that is, a decimal time from a true time—use this:

    =A1*24

If a cell contains the true date and the true time (as in 22/May/07 15:36) and you want only the date, use this:

    =INT(A1)

To get only the time, use this:

    =A1-INT(A1)

or:

    =MOD(A1,1)

and format as needed.

To find out the difference between two dates, use this:

```
=DATEDIF(A1,A2,"d")
```

where A1 is the earlier date.

This will produce the number of days between two dates. It will also accept m or y as the result to return—that is, Months or Years. (The DATEDIF function is undocumented in Excel 97 and is really a Lotus 123 function.)

If you do not know in advance which date or time is the earliest, the MIN and MAX functions can help. For example, to be assured of a meaningful result, you can use this:

```
=DATEDIF(MIN(A1,A2),MAX(A1,A2),"d")
```

Also, when working with times, you might need to account for start time and end time, with the start time being 8:50 PM. in cell A1, and the end time being 9:50 AM. in cell A2. If you subtract the start time from the end time (=A2-A1), you get ######, as Excel, by default, cannot work with negative times. See "Display Negative Time Values" [Hack #87] for more on how to work with negative times.

Alternatively, you can work around this in these two ways, ensuring a positive result:

```
=MAX(A1:A2)-MIN(A1:A2)
```

or (you may need to format the cell as a time if it defaults to a numeric format):

```
=A1-A2+IF(A1>A2,1)
```

You can also tell Excel to add any number of days, months, or years to any date:

```
=DATE(YEAR(A1)+value1,MONTH(A1)+value2,DAY(A1)+value3)
```

To add one month to a date in cell A1, use this:

```
=DATE(YEAR(A1),MONTH(A1)+1,DAY(A1))
```

Excel also offers some additional functions that are part of the Analysis ToolPak. Go to the Office button → Excel Options → Add Ins, select the Analysis ToolPak, and click Go. Enable the Analysis ToolPak checkbox, and click OK (pre-2007, select Tools → Add-Ins, enable the Analysis ToolPak checkbox, and then click Yes if you are asked if you want to install it).

You can find all of these functions under the Formula tab in Functions Library → Date & Time (pre-2007, Paste Function dialog in the Function Wizard). The functions are easy to use; the hard part is knowing they're available and turning them on.

By default, this Add-In is not installed in Excel 2007. To install it, go to the Office button → Excel Options → Add Ins, select the Analysis ToolPak, and click Go. Enable the Analysis ToolPak checkbox, and click OK.

Real Dates and Times

Sometimes spreadsheets with imported data (or data that was entered incorrectly) end up with dates and times being seen as text and not real numbers. You can spot this easily in Excel by widening the columns a bit, selecting a column, right-clicking and selecting Format → Cells → Alignment, and then changing the Horizontal alignment to General (the default format for cells). Click OK and examine your dates and times closely. If any are *not* right-aligned, Excel doesn't think they are dates.

To fix this, first copy any empty cell, and then select the column and format as any Date and/or Time format. While the column is still selected, right–click and select Paste Special → Value → Add. This will force Excel to convert any text dates and times to real dates and times. You might need to change the format again. Another simple method is to reference the cell(s) like this:

```
=A1+0 or A1*1
```

A Date Bug?

Excel incorrectly assumes that the year 1900 was a leap year. This means Excel's internal date system believes there was a 29 Feb 1900, when there wasn't! The most surprising part is that Microsoft did this intentionally, or so they say! More information is available at *http://support.microsoft.com/ default.aspx?scid=kb;EN-US;q181370*.

Here are some additional good links to information on dates and times:

HOW TO: Use Dates and Times in Excel 2000
    http://support.microsoft.com/default.aspx?scid=kb;en-us;Q214094#6

Text or Number Converted to Unintended Number Format
    http://support.microsoft.com/default.aspx?scid=kb;en-us;Q214233

Maximum Times in Microsoft Excel
    http://support.microsoft.com/default.aspx?scid=kb;en-us;Q214386

Dates and Times Displayed as Serial Numbers When Viewing Formulas
    http://support.microsoft.com/default.aspx?scid=kb;en-us;Q241072

Controlling and Understanding Settings in the Format Cells Dialog Box
   http://support.microsoft.com/default.aspx?scid=kb;en-us;Q264372

How to Use Dates and Times in Microsoft Excel
   http://support.microsoft.com/default.aspx?scid=kb;en-us;214094

Dates and times are probably one of the most confusing areas within Excel. Armed with this information, hopefully you will understand more about their many quirks and have an easier time dealing with them.

HACK #40 Enable Grouping and Outlining on a Protected Worksheet

ALL

In Excel 2000, Microsoft added many new levels of worksheet protection to Excel. Unfortunately, they neglected to add one that would allow Excel users to use Grouping and Outlining on a protected worksheet.

To enable grouping and outlining on a protected worksheet, you must first set up grouping/outlining on your data. Highlight your data, go to Data → Group → Outline options, and select the drop-down to the right of Group. Click AutoOutline (pre-2007, Data → Group & Outline) to present your data as displayed in Figure 2-29.

	Item	Normal Price per Block 2006	Discount	Total Price	Normal Price per Block 2007	Discount	Total	Grant Total
2	Tooheys New	$30.00	$5.00	$25.00	$29.00	$5.00	$24.00	$49.00
3	Emu Export	$28.00	$4.00	$24.00	$30.00	$4.00	$26.00	$50.00
4	Crown Lager	$36.00	$3.50	$32.50	$38.00	$3.50	$34.50	$67.00
5	Swan Lager	$27.00	$4.00	$23.00	$28.50	$4.00	$24.50	$47.50
6	Matilda Bay Draught	$31.50	$3.00	$28.50	$32.00	$3.00	$29.00	$57.50
7	Heineken Lager	$35.00	$2.80	$32.20	$36.00	$2.80	$33.20	$65.40
8	Swan Gold	$26.00	$3.00	$23.00	$29.00	$3.00	$26.00	$49.00

Figure 2-29. Data with Outline applied

Next, protect your sheet using the password Secret.

To allow the use of Grouping/Outlining on a protected Worksheet, the code in this hack makes use of Excel's UserInterfaceOnly argument of the Protection method (*http://www.ozgrid.com/VBA/excel-macro-protected-sheet.htm*), which is normally used to keep the general Excel interface protected but allow changes from Excel macros. The closing of the workbook, however, will set the UserInterfaceOnly back to False. This is why we need to use the Workbook Open event to set it to True.

The drawback of using the Workbook Open event is that the security settings of your computer might not allow the code to fire on opening. To ensure it does, set your security to Enable All Macros (pre-2007, set it to Low).

 It is imperative to know that by setting your security level to Enable All Macros (pre-2007, Low), you can leave your PC wide open to potentially dangerous code.

To use the macro, right-click on the sheet tab, select View Code, double-click This Workbook (pre-2007, choose the Excel icon in the top left, next to File, and then View Code) and paste the following code:

```
Private Sub Workbook_Open()
    With Sheet1
        .Protect Password:="Secret", UserInterfaceOnly:=True
        .EnableOutlining = True
    End With
End Sub
```

Then, save the Workbook, close it, and reopen it. Even though your workbook is protected and the Group option is grayed out, as shown in Figure 2-30, you should be able to use the Grouping/Outline feature as usual, because it is already applied to your data.

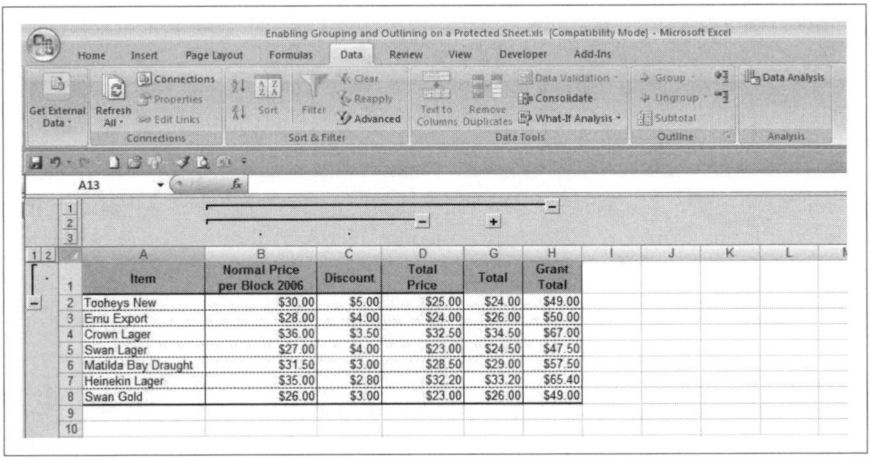

![Screenshot of Excel worksheet showing a protected sheet with beer pricing data and the Group option grayed out on the Data ribbon. Columns include Item, Normal Price per Block 2006, Discount, Total Price, Total, and Grant Total. Rows: Tooheys New $30.00 $5.00 $25.00 $24.00 $49.00; Emu Export $28.00 $4.00 $24.00 $26.00 $50.00; Crown Lager $36.00 $3.50 $32.50 $34.50 $67.00; Swan Lager $27.00 $4.00 $23.00 $24.50 $47.50; Matilda Bay Draught $31.50 $3.00 $28.50 $29.00 $57.50; Heineken Lager $35.00 $2.80 $32.20 $33.20 $65.40; Swan Gold $26.00 $3.00 $23.00 $26.00 $49.00]

Figure 2-30. Protected sheet with Group option grayed out

We have used the worksheets CodeName to reference the correct worksheet, but you can use the tab name, or sheet index number. The use of the worksheets CodeName is a more efficient way. Also note that we have used the password **Secret**.

Prevent Blanks/Missing Fields in a Table

HACK #41

ALL

You can easily manipulate the Data Validation feature of Excel to ensure that you have no blank cells within your list.

With the aid of Data Validation, we can ensure that a table or list cannot have blank/missing entries. For example, let's use a simple two-column table. Suppose you have a heading of Name in A1 and Department in B1. Underneath these headings, you want users to fill out *both* the name and their associated departments leaving neither column blank. (If you're starting with a table that has blank cells that need to be filled, see the "Fill All Blank Cells" sidebar.)

Fill All Blank Cells

As you are no doubt aware, most of Excel's tools, PivotTables, sorting, filters, etc, run into problems when they find a blank cell in a range of cells, so here is a quick way to fill every blank cell with the value of the cell above.

Say you have a list of entries in column A with many blank cells. Select column A, press F5 (on some notebook compputers, such as MacBooks, you will need to hold down the Fn key when you press F5), select Special, check the Blanks option, and click OK. You should now have all blanks selected. Now, press the equals sign (=), followed the Up arrow, and finally, holding down the Ctrl key, press Enter.

Select A3:B100 and ensure that your selection starts from cell A3. Now, select Data → Data Tools → Data Validation (pre-2007, Data → Validation). Select Custom from the Allow: drop-down list, and then add the following formula in the Formula box:

```
=AND(COUNTA($A$2:$A2)=ROW()-2,COUNTA($B$2:$B2)=ROW( )-2)
```

It is very important to note the absolute reference of $A$2 and $B$2 and the relative row/absolute column of $A2 and $B2; otherwise, you will show incorrect results.

Select the Error Alert tab and type an applicable error message that users will see if they leave blanks in the table, as shown in Figure 2-31. Make sure the Error style is set to Stop and click OK.

The validation applied will ensure that all entries (in the table A2:B100) have both a name and a department by not permitting blank cells between the filled-in names and the names being entered.

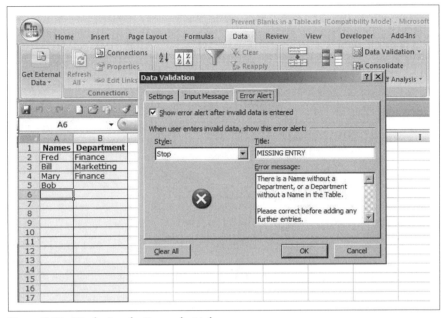

Figure 2-31. Displaying the Error alert tab

HACK #42 Provide Decreasing Data Validation Lists

Wouldn't it be useful if you could give users a list of options to select that decreases as options are used? You can create this nifty feature with the use of Data Validation and some Excel VBA code.

ALL

Say you have one spreadsheet that many users input into. Each of these users needs to select an item from a validation list on the spreadsheet. After each user has selected their items, wouldn't it be great if the validation list only showed what was left (the items that had not yet been selected). This would make data entry easier and more efficient for all, and prevent duplicates of data.

On any worksheet, add your list—say, in A1:A10. Now, select this range and click in the Name box (left of the Formula bar), type the name **MyList**, and press Enter. This will give you a Named Range called MyList.

Now, select the range on another worksheet where you would like the validation list to go. Right-click this sheet name tab, select View Code, and paste the following code:

```
Private Sub Worksheet_Change(ByVal Target As Range)
Dim strVal As String
Dim strEntry As String
    On Error Resume Next
```

```
        strVal = Target.Validation.Formula1
            If Not strVal = vbNullString Then
                strEntry = Target
                Application.EnableEvents = False
                With Sheet1.Range("MyList")
                    .Replace What:=strEntry, _
                        Replacement:="", LookAt:=xlWhole, _
                        SearchOrder:=xlByRows, MatchCase:=False
                    .Sort Key1:=.Range("A1"), Order1:=xlAscending, _
                        Header:=xlNo, OrderCustom:=1, MatchCase:=False, _
                        Orientation:=xlTopToBottom
                    .Range("A1", .Range("A65536").End(xlUp)).Name = "MyList"
                End With
            End If
        Application.EnableEvents = True
    On Error GoTo 0
End Sub
```

Close the window to get back to Excel. Now, select Data → Data Tools → Data Validation (pre-2007, Data → Validation), and choose Allow: → List. Then, under Source:, enter **=MyList** and click OK.

Now, when you select a name from the list, this name no longer appears on the drop-down.

Notice that we have referred to the named range MyList as Sheet1. Range("MyList"), preceding the named range with its sheet codename. We have done so because the reference to the named range (MyList) is in the private module of another Worksheet. Without it, Excel would assume MyList is on the same worksheet as one where the Worksheet_Change code resides.

HACK #43 Add a Custom List to the Fill Handle

Once you have created a few of your own Custom Lists, it can be hard to remember the first item in the list that must be entered in a cell. This hack adds the list to the Fill Handle.

ALL

Creating Excel Custom Lists via the Excel Fill Handle is a great way to quickly get a list of numbers or text onto a worksheet. Excel has built-in Custom Lists for Weekdays (Mon–Fri), Months (Jan–Dec) and numeric sequences, but you can also add your own Custom Lists. With this hack, you can add your own Custom List to the Fill Handle, to remind you which item must be entered first in a cell.

First, you need to create your list by entering it on a worksheet. Let's say you have 10 names in cells A1:A10 on Sheet 1. Sort the list, if necessary. Then, select the Office button → Excel Options → Popular → Edit Custom Lists (pre-2007, Tools → Options → Custom Lists; on the Mac, Excel → Preferences → Custom Lists). Click the collapse tool to the left of the Import button. Using the mouse pointer, left-click in cell A1 and drag down to A10. Then, click the Import button, followed by OK. From this point on, the custom list will be available to all workbooks on the same computer.

To add the list to your fill handle, right-click on your sheet name and select View Code. Go to Insert → Module and paste the following code:

```
Sub AddFirstList()
Dim strList As String
    strList = Application.CommandBars.ActionControl.Caption
    If Not strList Like "*...*" Then Exit Sub
    ActiveCell = Left(strList, InStr(1, strList, ".", vbTextCompare) - 1)
End Sub
```

Now, you need to add the following code to the private module of the workbook object (ThisWorkbook):

```
Private Sub Workbook_SheetBeforeRightClick _
  (ByVal Sh As Object, ByVal Target As Range, Cancel As Boolean)
Dim cBut As CommandBarButton
Dim lListCount As Long
Dim lCount As Long
Dim strList As String
Dim MyList
    On Error Resume Next
        With Application

            lListCount = .CustomListCount
                For lCount = 1 To lListCount
                    MyList = .GetCustomListContents(lCount)
                    strList = .CommandBars("Cell").Controls(MyList(1) & _
                            "..." & MyList(UBound(MyList))).Caption
                        .CommandBars("Cell").Controls(strList).Delete
                        Set cBut = .CommandBars("Cell").Controls. ⏎
Add(Temporary:=True)
                            With cBut
                                .Caption = MyList(1) & "..." & ⏎
MyList(UBound(MyList))
                                .Style = msoButtonCaption
                                .OnAction = "AddFirstList"
                            End With
                Next lCount
        End With
        On Error GoTo 0
End Sub
```

To get there quickly, while in Excel proper, select Developer → Code → Visual Basic and double-click ThisWorkbook (pre-2007, right-click on the Excel icon, in the upper left next to File, and choose View Code). Here's where you need to place the code.

Now, each time you right-click on a cell, you will see the *first...last* items in each Custom List, as shown in Figure 2-32.

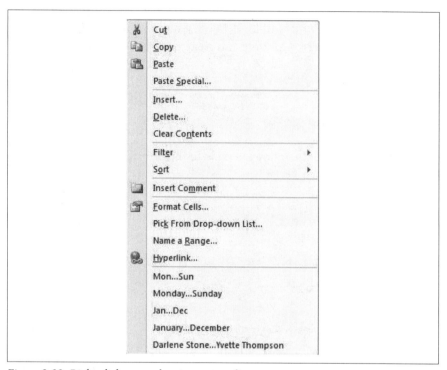

Figure 2-32. Right-click menu showing custom list

When you click the option the first Custom List item goes into the active cell. Then, you simply drag down via the Excel Fill Handle to get the rest of the list.

Naming Hacks
Hacks 44–49

Probably the biggest advantage to using named ranges is that formulas become a lot easier to read and understand, not only to you but also to others who need to work with your spreadsheets. Using named ranges (easily one of Excel's most useful features), you can reference a range of cells and give it a specific name. From that point on, you can reference the range via the name rather than its range address. Although named ranges are powerful, you can go beyond the standard range names in many ways.

HACK #44   Address Data by Name
ALL

Although cell numbers are at the foundation of everything Excel does, it's much easier to remember names, such as Item Number and Quantity, than it is to remember cell numbers, such as A1:A100. Excel makes this easy.

Excel uses the same technique for defining named cells and named ranges: the Name box at the left end of the Formula bar. To name a cell, select it, type the name you want into the Name box, as shown in Figure 3-1, and press Enter. To name a range of cells, select the range, type the name you want for that range in the Name box, and press Enter.

The drop-down list to the right of the Name box enables you to find your named ranges and cells again. (See "Identify Named Ranges on a Worksheet" [Hack #49] at the end of this chapter for more ways to locate ranges.) If you happen to select a range precisely, its name will appear in the Name box instead of the usual cell references.

In formulas, you can use these names in place of cell identifiers or ranges. If you name cell E4 "date," for instance, you could write =date instead of =E4. Similarly, if you create a range called "quantity" in A3:A10 and want a total of the values in it, your formula could say =SUM(quantity) rather than =SUM(A3:A10).

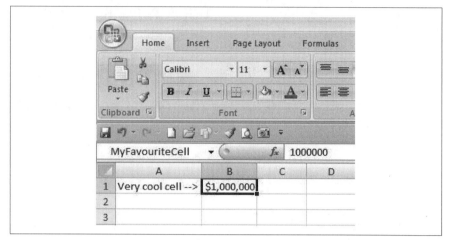

Figure 3-1. Naming a cell MyFavouriteCell

As spreadsheets grow larger and more intricate, named cells and ranges are crucial tools for keeping them manageable.

HACK #45   Use the Same Name for Ranges on Different Worksheets

ALL   Sometimes it would be convenient to use the same name for data in the same place on multiple worksheets within the same workbook. Excel requires a few extra steps to make this work.

Usually when you name a range, the name is at the workbook level, meaning that one name refers to a specified range on a specified worksheet wherever it is used in the workbook. Once the name has been used, it cannot be used again to represent a range on another worksheet. There is a way around this, however.

Assume you have a workbook with three worksheets. These three worksheets are simply named Sheet1, Sheet2, and Sheet3. You want to have a named range called *MyRange* (or some other legitimate name) that will refer to the range Sheet1 A1:A10 when on Sheet1, Sheet2 A1:A10 when on Sheet2, and Sheet3 A1:A10 when on Sheet3.

To do this, activate Sheet1, select the range A1:A10, and then click in the Name box, as you did in "Address Data by Name" **[Hack #44]**. Type **Sheet1!MyRange** and then press Enter. Do the same for Sheet2 and Sheet3, typing **Sheet2!MyRange** and **Sheet3!MyRange**, respectively.

From now on, when you activate any sheet and click the drop arrow on the Name box, you should see only one occurrence of the name MyRange.

Select this and you will be taken directly to the range A1:A10. You can check that it works by activating any other sheet and doing the same. You always will be taken to the range A1:A10 of that sheet.

You can do this because you preceded the name with the sheet name followed by an exclamation mark (!). If you select Formulas → Defined Names → Name Manager, you will see the range names you have created (pre-2007, go to Insert → Name → Define and you will see only one name: the one that refers to the currently active sheet).

If your worksheet name includes spaces (e.g., Class List), you cannot refer to the range Class List A1:A10 as **Class List!MyRange**. Instead, you must call it **'Class List'!MyRange**, putting single apostrophes around the name Class List. In fact, you can also use single apostrophes with a worksheet name with no spaces, so it is a good idea to always use single apostrophes when referring to worksheet names to cover all your bases.

Using Relative References

You can use a relative reference named range as well. By default, named ranges are absolute, but you do not have to leave them this way. Try following these steps:

1. Select cell A11 on any worksheet and then right-click and select Name a Range (pre-2007, select Insert → Name → Define).

2. In the Name: box, type **MyNumbers** (pre-2007, the box is labeled Names in Workbook:).

3. In the Refers To: box, type **=A$1:A$10** and then click OK.

4. Now enter the number **1** in cell A1.

5. Select cell A1, move your cursor to the fill handle, and press the left mouse button. While holding down the Ctrl key, drag down to cell A10. (Holding down the Ctrl key with a single number will cause Excel to create a list incremented by 1.)

6. Enter **1** in cell B1 and drag down to cell B10, without holding down the Ctrl key this time.

7. In cell A11, enter **=SUM(MyNumbers)**.

8. In cell B11, enter **=SUM(MyNumbers)**.

You should get 55 and 10, respectively, because cell A11 was active when you defined the name MyNumbers and referred the range name to A$1:A$10, which is a relative column and absolute row named range.

The dollar sign ($) forces any range to be absolute.

When you use the name MyNumbers in a formula, it always will refer to the 10 cells immediately above the formula. If you use =SUM(MyNumbers) in cell A11 of another worksheet, it still will refer to cells A1:A10 on the sheet that was active when you originally created the range name.

Simplify the summing. If you want to simplify the summing of the 10 cells, try these steps:

1. Select cell A11 on any worksheet.
2. Right–click, select Name a Range (pre-2007, Insert → Name → Define), and type **MySum** in the Name: box.
3. In the Refers To: box, type =SUM(A$1:A$10) and click OK.
4. Now enter the number **1** in cell A1.
5. Select cell A1, move your cursor to the fill handle, and press the left mouse button. Hold down the Ctrl key and drag down to cell A10.
6. Enter **1** in cell B1, and drag down to cell B10 without holding down the Ctrl key.
7. In cell A11, enter =**MySum**.
8. In cell B11, enter =**MySum**.

You will get the same results you got before, but without requiring the SUM function. Mixing up the abgsolute and relative references and nesting a few functions together can be very handy and can save a lot of work.

HACK #46 Create Custom Functions Using Names

Although referencing data by name is convenient, it's sometimes more helpful to store a constant value or even a formula, especially if you've been creating custom functions in VBA.

ALL

Assume you have a tax rate of 10 percent, which you need to use throughout your workbook for various calculations. Instead of entering the value **10%** (**0.1**) into each formula that requires this tax rate, you can enter the word **TaxRate** and Excel will automatically know that TaxRate has a value of 0.1. Here are the steps:

1. Select the Formulas tab and then select Defined Names → Define Name (pre-2007, Insert → Name → Define).
2. Type **TaxRate** in the Names: box.

3. In the Refers To: box, enter **=0.1** and then click Add.

From this point on, you can enter any formula into any cell, and instead of adding 10 percent as part of the calculation, you can use the word TaxRate. Probably one of the biggest advantages to using this method is that if and when your tax rate increases or decreases, and your formulas need to reflect this new percentage, you can select the Formulas tab, choose Defined Names → Define Name (pre-2007, Insert → Name → Define), then select the name TaxRate and just modify it to suit.

To take things a step further with this concept, you can use formulas as your Refers To: range rather than a cell address or constant value. Suppose you want to create a name that, when entered into a cell, automatically returns the SUM of the 10 cells immediately above it. Follow these steps:

1. Select cell A11 on any worksheet, right–click, and go to Name a Range (pre-2007, select Insert → Name → Define).

2. In the Name: box, type the name **Total**, and in the Refers To: box type **=SUM(A1:A10)**. Click OK.

3. Enter any 10 numbers in any column starting from row 1.

4. Now come down to row 11 of the same column and type **=Total**. The name Total automatically will return the SUM of the 10 cells you just entered in A1:A10.

If you want to create a similarly named formula that is not restricted to only 10 cells, but rather, includes all the cells directly above whatever row happens to contain =Total, follow these steps:

1. Select cell B11, go to the Formulas tab, and select Defined Names → Name Manager (pre-2007, select Insert → Name → Define). Click the name Total.

2. Examine the Refers To: box, which will say =SUM(B1:B10). This enables you to create named formulas. In other words, because you did not make the column references absolute for the original name Total, it always will reference the column you use it in.

3. Now, click the Refers To: box and change the formula to =SUM(B$1:B10). Click OK.

From this point on, you can select any row in any column other than row 1 and enter **=Total**, and you automatically will get the SUM of all the cells above where you enter this, regardless of how many rows there are. This is because you anchored the row number 1 by making it an absolute reference, yet left the reference to cell B10 as a relative reference, meaning it always will end up being the cell immediately above where you entered the named formula =Total.

Using Names with Intersect

By combining this hack with the intersect operator (one of Excel's standard, although little known, features), it's possible to create sophisticated lookup functions. If you are not aware of how the intersect method works, here is a small example to get you acquainted:

1. In cell A1, enter the heading **Name**, in cell B1, enter the heading **Pay**, and in cell C1, enter the heading **Title**.
2. Enter **Bill** in cell A2 and **Fred** in cell A3.
3. Enter **10** in cell B2 and **20** in cell B3.
4. Enter **Mr** in cell C2 and **Dr** in cell C3.
5. Now, select the range A1:C3, go to the Formulas tab, and choose Defined Names → Create from Selection (pre-2007, select Insert → Name → Create). Ensure that both the top row and left column checkboxes are checked, then click OK.

At this point, if you select any cell outside your table and enter **=Fred Title**, you should get the correct title for the name Fred.

> The space between the words Fred and Title is important, as this is what Excel understands as the intersect operator.

Building on this concept, you can combine this capability with Excel's named formula capabilities to again make your spreadsheets not only easier to use, but also much easier to read and understand, as the following example will illustrate.

First, assume that you have a table set up on a spreadsheet in a fashion similar to that shown in Figure 3-2, and that you are using this table to create your names in Excel.

Once you create the names for the table, you will see that Excel automatically places an underscore in the spaces between two or more words. This is because the names of named ranges cannot contain a space. Next, follow these steps:

1. Right-click and select Name a Range (pre-2007, Insert → Name → Define).
2. Enter **Select** in the Names: box and **FredsPayRate** in the Names in Workbook: box.
3. In the Refers To: box, type **=Fred_Jones Pay_Rate** and then click OK, as shown in Figure 3-3.

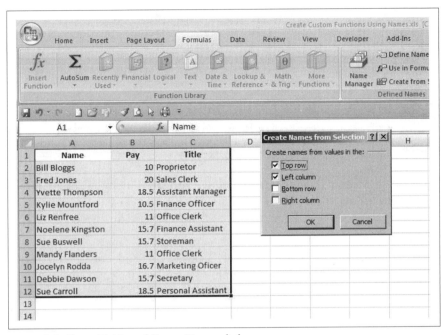

Figure 3-2. Shows Table and Create Names dialog

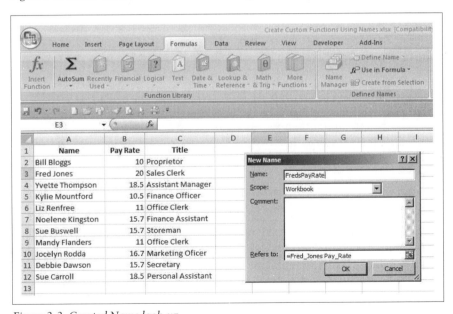

Figure 3-3. Created Name look-up

Now when you enter **=FredsPayRate** in any cell outside your table, the pay rate for Fred will be returned automatically.

You might want to experiment with intersections to see how they work best in your projects.

HACK #47 Create Ranges That Expand and Contract

ALL

If you need to constantly update and add to your data, or if you work with charts and PivotTables, you'll want to create dynamic named ranges, which expand and contract relative to your data.

To understand how dynamic named ranges function, first you should familiarize yourself with Excel's OFFSET function (if you haven't already). The OFFSET function is one of Excel's Lookup and Reference functions.

We'll start off with the simplest of dynamic named ranges, one that will expand down a single column, but only as far as there are entries in that column. For example, if column A contains 10 continuous rows of data, your dynamic named range will incorporate the range A1:A10. Follow these steps to create a basic dynamic named range.

Under the Formulas tab, select Defined Names → Define Name (pre-2007, Insert → Name → Define) and type **MyRange** in the Names: box. In the Refers To: box, type the following:

```
=OFFSET($A$1,0,0,COUNTA($A$1:$A$100),1)
```

Now click Add, then OK.

> When defining the range for COUNTA, resist the temptation to include an entire column of data so that you do not force the COUNTA function to count potentially thousands of unnecessary cells.

Now, provided that you have some data in column A, this named range will incorporate all the data in continuous rows, starting from cell A1. If you want to check a dynamic named range, you can do so in a few ways.

Unfortunately, dynamic named ranges are not available via the standard Name box, immediately to the left of the Formula bar. Despite this, you can click the Name box, type the name **MyRange**, and press Enter. Excel will automatically select the range. Of course, you also can use the Go To... dialog by going to the Home tab and selecting Find & Select → Go To... under Editing options (Ctrl/⌘-G; pre-2007, Edit → Go To...). Enter **MyRange** in the Reference: box and click OK.

The dynamic named range you created in the previous example nests the COUNTA function as the Height argument in the OFFSET function.

> Remember that COUNTA will count all nonblank cells. Be aware that this also will include formulas you have in those cells, which might be returning empty text ("").

If you have a list that contained numeric data only, and at the end of this list you want to store text, but don't want this text included as part of your dynamic named range, you could replace the COUNTA function with Excel's standard COUNT function. COUNT counts only cells containing numeric data.

In this next example, you will use a dynamic named range to define a table of data that you want to be dynamic. To do this, type the following function into the Refers To: box:

```
=OFFSET($A$1,0,0,COUNTA($A$1:$A$100),COUNTA($1:$1))
```

Here, the dynamic named range will expand down as many entries as there are in column A, and across as many rows as there are headings in row 1. If you are sure the number of columns for your table of data will remain stable, you can replace the second COUNTA function with a fixed number such as 10.

The only problem with using a dynamic named range for a table of data is that it assumes column A will set the maximum length for the table. In most cases, this probably will be true; however, sometimes the longest column might be another column on the spreadsheet.

To overcome this potential problem, you can use Excel's MAX function, which returns the highest number in a range of cells. As an example, set up a table in a manner similar to the one shown in Figure 3-4.

Use row 1 to store a number of COUNTA functions that are referencing down the column and, thus, returning the number of entries in each column. Use the MAX function for the Height argument in the OFFSET function. This ensures that the dynamic named range for the table always will expand down as far as the longest column in the table. Of course you can hide row 1, as there is no need for a user to see it.

In all these examples, you assumed your data will always be in continuous rows without blank cells in between. Although this is the correct way to set up a list or a table of data, sometimes you have no control over this.

In the next example, the list of numbers in column A also contains blank cells. This means that if you try to use the COUNT or COUNTA function, the

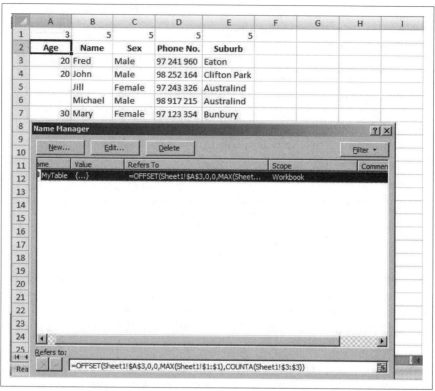

Figure 3-4. Dynamic table of data and the Define Name dialog

dynamic named range will fall short of the real last cell containing any data. For example, consider Figure 3-5.

In this case, although the last number in the range is actually in row 10, the dynamic range is expanding down to row 6. This is because you used the COUNT function to count from A1 to A100. Only six numeric entries are in the list, so the range expands down only six rows.

To overcome this problem, use Excel's MATCH function. The MATCH function is used to return the relative position of an item in an array that matches a specified value in a specified order. For example, if you use this MATCH function:

    =MATCH(6,$A$1:$A$100,0)

on the same set of numbers shown in Figure 3-5, the MATCH function will return the number 10, representing row 10 in column A. It returns 10 because you told the function to find the number 6 in the range A1:A100.

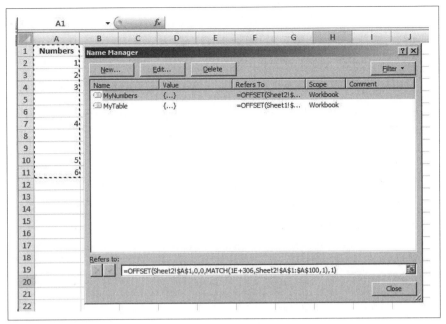

Figure 3-5. Range of numbers and Define Name dialog

Obviously, when using the MATCH function as part of a dynamic named range, the last number in the range probably is not known in advance. Therefore, you need to tell the MATCH function to try and locate a ridiculously high number in the range that would never exist and to swap the last argument for the MATCH function from 0 to 1.

In the previous example, you told MATCH to find the exact number 6, nothing less and nothing more. Replacing 0 with 1 tells MATCH to locate the largest value that is less than or equal to that value.

To do this, use this formula:

```
=MATCH(1E+306,$A$1:$A$100,1)
```

To create a dynamic named range that will expand down to the last row that contains a number (regardless of the blank cells in between), type that formula into the Refers To: box of the Name Manager dialog, as illustrated in Figure 3-6.

```
=OFFSET(Sheet2!$A$1,0,0,MATCH(1E+306,Sheet2!$A$1:$A$100,1),1)
```

The next logical type of dynamic named range that would flow on from this is one that will expand down to the last text entry, regardless of any blank cells in the list or table.

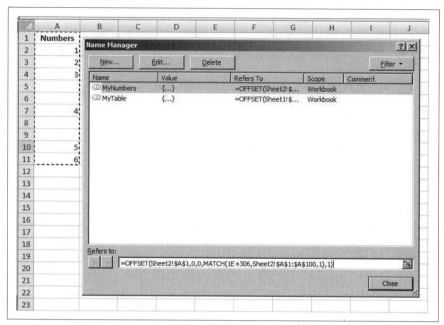

Figure 3-6. A dynamic range extending to the last numeric entry

To do this, replace the MATCH function with the following:

```
MATCH("*",$A$1:$A$100,-1)
```

This always will return the row number for the last text entry in range $A$1:$A$100.

Now that you know how to do this for numeric entries and text entries, it is only logical that you need to somehow define a dynamic named range that will look past blank cells in a list that contains both text and numeric data.

To do this, first insert two blank rows above your list by selecting rows 1 and 2. Then, select Home → Cells → Insert (pre-2007, Insert → Row). In the first row (row 1), add this function:

```
=MAX(MATCH"*",$A$2:$A$100,-1),MATCH(1E+306,$A$2:$A$100,1))
```

In the cell immediately below this, type the number **1**. The cell below this must contain a text heading for your list. You added the number 1 so that the second MATCH function does not return #N/A when or if there are no numbers in A3:A100. The second MATCH function will always find text because you have a heading.

Name cell A1 MaxRow, right-click, and select Name a Range (pre-2007, Insert → Name → Define). Give the dynamic range a name, such as MyList, and type the following function in the Refers To: box, as shown in Figure 3-7:

```
=OFFSET(Sheet1!$A$3,0,0,MaxRow,1)
```

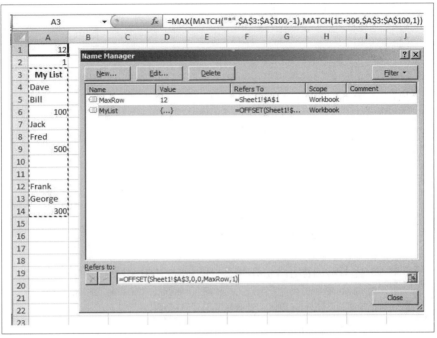

Figure 3-7. Dynamic list for numeric and text entries containing blanks

The following list outlines other types of dynamic named ranges you might find useful. For *all* of these examples, you will need to fill column A with a mix of text and numeric entries. To do this, right-click and select Name a Range (pre-2007, Insert → Name → Define). In the Names: box, type any one-word name (for instance, MyRange). The only part that will change is the formula you place in the Refers To: box:

Expand down as many rows as there are numeric entries
    In the Refers To: box, type the following:

```
=OFFSET($A$1,0,0,COUNT($A:$A),1)
```

Expand down as many rows as there are numeric and text entries
    In the Refers To: box, type the following:

```
=OFFSET($A$1,0,0,COUNTA($A:$A),1)
```

Expand down to the last numeric entry
    In the Refers To: box, type the following:

```
=OFFSET($A$1,0,0,MATCH(1E+306,$A:$A))
```

    If you expect a number larger than 1E+306 (a 1 with 306 zeros), change this to a larger number.

Expand down to the last text entry
    In the Refers To: box, type the following:

```
=OFFSET($A$1,0,0,MATCH("*",$A:$A,-1))
```

Expand down based on another cell value
> Enter the number **10** in cell B1, and then in the Refers To: box, type the following:
>
>   =OFFSET($A$1,0,0,$B$1,1)
>
> Now change the number in cell B1, and the range will change accordingly.

Expand down one row each month
> In the Refers To: box, type the following:
>
>   =OFFSET($A$1,0,0,MONTH(TODAY( )),1)

Expand down one row each week
> In the Refers To: box, type the following:
>
>   =OFFSET($A$1,0,0,WEEKNUM(TODAY( )),1)
>
> This one requires that you have the Analysis ToolPak installed. You can add it by selecting the Office button → Excel options → Add-ins (pre-2007, Tools → Add-Ins).

HACK #48 Nest Dynamic Ranges for Maximum Flexibility

A dynamic named range that resides within another dynamic named range can be very useful for things such as long lists of names.

ALL

For example, it's possible to create a named range called Jnames that refers to all the names in a sorted list beginning with the letter J.

Start with a list of names in column A, such as the ones shown in Figure 3-8, where cell A1 is a heading and the list is sorted. Then follow these steps:

1. Select Home → Defined Names → Name Manager → New (pre-2007, Insert → Name → Define).

2. Enter **Names** in the Names: box and the following formula in the Refers To: box:

       =OFFSET($A$2,0,0,COUNTA($A$2:$A$1000),1)

3. Click OK, then New (pre-2007, click Add, then enter the new name).

4. Now click back into the Names: box and enter the name **Jnames** (J can be any desired letter).

5. In the Refers To: box, enter the following:

       =OFFSET(INDIRECT(ADDRESS(MATCH("J*",Names,0)+1,1)),0 ↵
       ,0,COUNTIF(Names,"J*"), 1)

   where "J*" is a match for the data you want—in this case, names beginning with J).

6. Click OK.

7. In the Name Manager, select **Jnames** and click back into the Refers To: box where the function is. All the names beginning with the letter J will have a marquee around them, as shown in Figure 3-8.

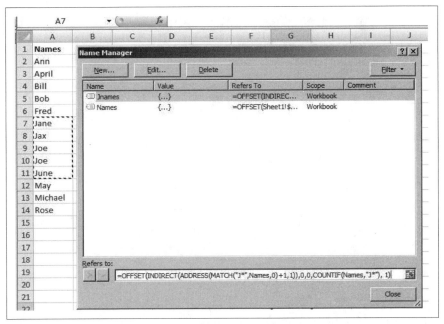

Figure 3-8. A dynamic named range within another dynamic named range

If you want, you can create one named range for each letter of the alphabet, but perhaps a better option is to have the named range change according to a letter that you type into a cell on a worksheet. To do this, follow these steps:

1. Start by simply entering any letter into any unused cell and then name that cell **Letter**.

2. Now, select Data → Data Tools → Data Validation (pre-2007, Data → Validation).

3. Select List from the Allow: box.

4. Click into the Source: box and enter **A*,B*,C*,** etc., until all 26 letters of the alphabet are entered as shown in Figure 3-9. Click OK when you're done.

5. Now, select Formulas → Defined Names → Name Manager → New (pre-2007, Insert → Name → Define).

6. Enter **Names** in the Names: box and the following formula in the Refers To: box:

   ```
   =OFFSET($A$2,0,0,COUNTA($A$2:$A$1000),1)
   ```

7. Click OK, then New.

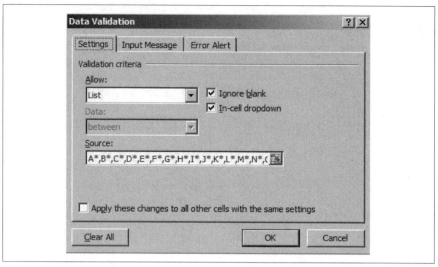

Figure 3-9. A validation list of letters, followed by the wildcard character

8. Click back into the Names: box and type **LetterNames**.

9. Then, in the Refers To: box, enter the following formula:

```
=OFFSET(INDIRECT(ADDRESS(MATCH(Letter,Names,0)+1,1)),0,0,COUNTIF ⏎
(Names, Letter),1)
```

10. When you're done, click OK, then Close.

The result will look like Figure 3-10.

 You don't have to retype the formulas from scratch for the dynamic named ranges. Instead, while working in the Define Name dialog, click an existing dynamic named range, over-type the name that appears in the Names in Workbook: box, then move down to the Refers To: box, modify as needed, and click Add. This will not replace the original dynamic named range, but rather, add a totally new one with the different name you have given it.

To test this, select a letter from the Validation drop–down menu in the cell you named Letter, click into the Name Manager, choose LetterNames, and click the collapse tool to the right of the Refers to: box. You should see any data starting with the letter "L" with a marquee around it.

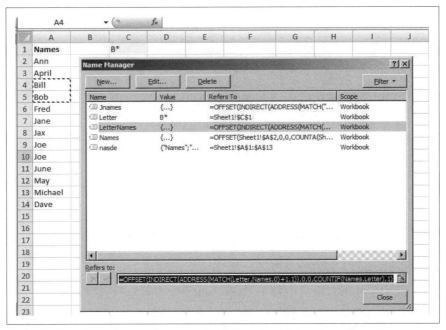

Figure 3-10. A dynamic named range controlled by the content of another cell

Identify Named Ranges on a Worksheet

#49

ALL

Excel enables users to give meaningful names to specific ranges in their worksheets. As the number of different named ranges on a worksheet grows, you will need tools for identifying the areas referenced by your named ranges.

Here are two quick methods you can use to identify the referenced ranges for each named range.

Method 1

One quick way to identify referenced ranges is to select Formula → Defined Names → Use in Formula → Paste Names (pre-2007, Insert → Name → Paste), or press F3. In the Paste Name dialog, click OK, as shown in Figure 3-11, and Excel will list all your names in rows, starting from your active cell, with the names' corresponding references in the opposite column.

This will give you a list of all your names in the active workbook.

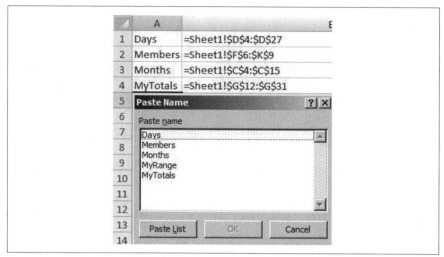

Figure 3-11. The Paste Name dialog

Although this can be handy to help you identify specific ranges, it still requires that you either manually select the specific named range, or perhaps use the Go To... dialog. However, once you have a list of named ranges, you can remove all the referenced cell addresses corresponding to the names and replace them with a simple hyperlink function.

This will enable you to create a list of all named ranges. Clicking any item on the list will take you to the specified range. For instance, assume your list of names resides in column A, starting from cell A1. In cell B1, enter this formula:

```
=HYPERLINK("[Book1.xls]"&A1,A1)
```

Copy this formula down as far as you need to and replace *Book1.xls* with your workbook's name.

Method 2

The second method is simple but not very well known. It was highlighted by one of the OzGrid Excel Forum members in the "Hey! That is Cool!" section of OzGrid.com (*http://www.ozgrid.com/forum/forumdisplay.php?f=13*).

All you need to do is set the zoom on your Excel worksheet to any percentage lower than 40—i.e., 39 percent or less. This will display all your named ranges on the sheet for easy identification, as shown in Figure 3-12.

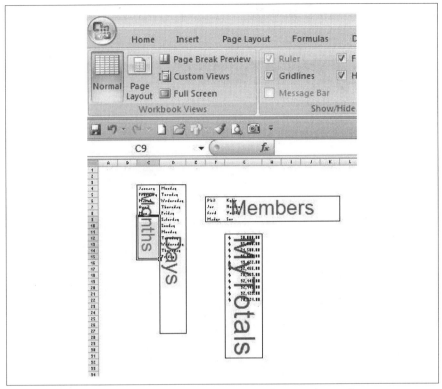

Figure 3-12. Named range zoom providing easy identification of named ranges

This does not work for Dynamic Named Ranges.

CHAPTER FOUR

Hacking PivotTables
Hacks 50–54

PivotTables are one of Excel's most powerful attractions, though many people don't know what they do. PivotTables display and extract a variety of information from a table of data that resides within either Microsoft Excel or another compatible database type. PivotTables are frequently used to extract statistical information from raw data. You can drag around the different fields within a PivotTable to view its data from different perspectives.

> The raw data for a PivotTable must be laid out in a classic table format. Row 1 of the table must be headings, with related data directly underneath. The data should not contain blank columns or blank rows. Even if you aren't planning to use PivotTables, keeping your raw data in this format makes it possible for other people to analyze your data with PivotTables.

If you have not yet delved into the world of PivotTables, you should consider doing so. As a starting point, visit *http://www.ozgrid.com/Excel/default.htm* and work your way through a free online tutorial for Excel PivotTables. To learn more about the benefits of PivotTables as well as how you can create hacks that make PivotTables even more flexible and powerful, read on.

HACK #50

ALL

PivotTables: A Hack in Themselves

PivotTables are one of the wildest but most powerful features of Excel, an ingenious hack themselves that may take some experimentation to figure out.

We use PivotTables a lot when we develop spreadsheets for our clients. Once a client sees a PivotTable, they nearly always ask whether they can create one themselves. Although anyone can create a PivotTable, unfortunately many people tend to shy away from them, as they see them as too complex.

Indeed, when you first use a PivotTable, the process can seem a bit daunting. Some persistence is definitely necessary.

You'll find that persistence will pay off once you experience the best feature of PivotTables: their ability to be manipulated using trial and error and immediately show the result of this manipulation. If the result is not what you expect, you can use Excel's Undo feature and have another go! Whatever you do, you are not changing the structure of your original table in any way, so you can do no harm.

Why Are They Called PivotTables?

PivotTables allow you to pivot data using drag-and-drop techniques and receive results immediately. PivotTables are interactive; once the table is complete, you can easily see how your information will be affected when you move (or pivot) your data. This will become patently clear once you give PivotTables a try.

Even for experienced PivotTable developers, an element of trial and error is always involved in producing desired results. You will find yourself pivoting your table a lot!

What Are PivotTables Good For?

PivotTables can produce summary information from a table of information. Imagine you have a table of data that contains names, addresses, ages, occupations, phone numbers, and zip codes. With a PivotTable, you very easily and quickly can find out:

- How many people have the same name
- How many people share the same zip code
- How many people have the same occupation

You also can receive such information as:

- A list of people with the same occupation
- A list of addresses with the same zip code

If your data needs slicing, dicing, and reporting, PivotTables will be a critical part of your toolkit.

Why Use PivotTables When Spreadsheets Already Offer So Much Analysis Capability?

Perhaps the biggest advantage to using PivotTables is the fact that you can generate and extract meaningful information from a large table of data within a matter of minutes and without using up a lot of computer memory. In many cases, you could get the same results from a table of data by using Excel's built-in functions, but that would take more time and use far more memory.

Another advantage to using PivotTables is that if you want some new information, you can simply drag-and-drop (pivot). In addition, you can opt to have your information update each time you open the workbook or you can right-click and select the Refresh option to refresh at will.

PivotCharts Extend PivotTables

Microsoft introduced PivotCharts in Excel 2000. In an instant, you can create interactive charts that were previously impossible without using either VBA or Excel Controls. PivotCharts are created from PivotTables, so a PivotChart shows graphically a representation of your PivotTable. PivotCharts work very similarly to the standard Excel charts, and most of the features are available. The beauty of PivotCharts and PivotTables is that they are interactive with each other—change something in one, and it will also be reflected in the other.

PivotCharts are not available in Excel for the Macintosh.

Creating Tables and Lists for Use in PivotTables

When you create a PivotTable, you must organize the dataset you're using in a table or in a list. As the PivotTable will base all its data on this table or list, it is vital that you set up your tables and lists in a uniform way.

In this context a *table* is a multi-columned set of data with data laid out directly below the appropriate headings. A *list* (only one column, also with a heading) is often referred to in the context of a table as well. The best practices that apply to setting up a list will help you greatly when you need to apply a PivotTable to your data.

When you extract data via the use of lookup or database functions, you can be a little less stringent in how you set up the table or list. This is because you can always compensate with the aid of a function and probably still get your result. Nonetheless, it's still easiest to set up the list or table as neatly as possible. Excel's built-in features assume a lot about the layout and setup up of your data. Although they offer a degree of flexibility, more often than not you will find it easier to adhere to the following guidelines when setting up your table or list:

- Headings are required, as a PivotTable uses them for field names. Headings should always appear in the row directly above the data. Also, never leave a blank row between the data and the headings. Furthermore, make the headings distinct in some way; for instance, boldface them.

- Leave at least three blank rows above the headings. You can use these for formulas, critical data, etc. You can hide the rows if you want.

- If you have more than one list or table on the same worksheet, leave at least one blank column between each list or table. This will help Excel recognize them as separate entities. However, if the lists and tables are related to each other, combine them into one large table.

- Avoid blank cells within your data. Instead of leaving blank cells for the same data in a column, repeat the data as many times as needed.

- Sort your list or data, preferably by the leftmost column. This will make the data easier to read and interpret.

If you follow these guidelines as closely as possible, using PivotTables will be a relatively easy task.

Figure 4-1 shows a well-laid-out table of data and a PivotTable in progress.

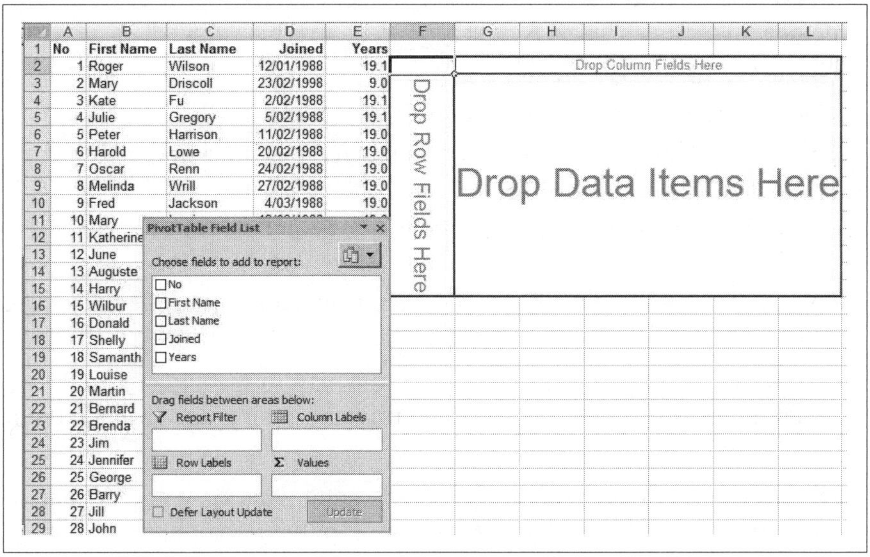

Figure 4-1. PivotTable generated from a well-laid out table of data

Note that many of the same dates are repeated in the Date column. In front of this data is the Pivot Table Field List, showing the field names (or headings) and the optional Areas you can drag them to.

In pre-2007 versions of Excel, the Layout step for the data shows the optional Page, Row, and Column fields, as well as the mandatory Data field.

PivotTable Creation

When you create a PivotTable (by going to the Insert tab and selecting Pivot Table; pre-2007, select Data → Pivot Table Report), a dialog pops up asking you to select either your table or range, or select an external data source. If your table was set up correctly (i.e., headings defined in some way and no blank rows/columns/cells) and you are clicked somewhere inside your data, your range will be selected automatically. You will then be asked if you want your PivotTable created in a new Worksheet or on the Existing Worksheet.

 This is true for a lot of Excel's functions and analysis tools. Your range will be automatically selected if your data is set up correctly—i.e., headings defined in some way and no blank rows/columns/cells.

Users of pre-2007 versions will need to go through the more cumbersome PivotTable and PivotChart Wizard. This Wizard guides you through the creation of a PivotTable using a four-step process, in which you tell Excel:

1. How the data is set up and whether to create an associated PivotChart (if PivotCharts are available in that version of Excel)

2. Where the data is stored—e.g., a range in the same workbook, a database, another workbook, etc.

3. Which column of data is going into which field: the optional Page, Row, and Column fields, as well as the mandatory Data field

4. Where to put your PivotTable (i.e., in a new worksheet or in an existing one)

You also can take many side steps along the way to manipulate the Pivot-Table, but most users find it easier to do this after telling Excel where to put it.

Now that you know more about PivotTables and what they do, it's time to explore some handy hacks that can make this feature even more powerful.

Share PivotTables but Not Their Data

Create a snapshot of your PivotTable that no longer needs the underlying data structures.

You might need to send PivotTables for others to view, but for whatever reason you cannot send the underlying data associated with them. Perhaps you want others to see only certain data for confidentiality reasons, for instance. If this is the case, you can create a static copy of the PivotTable and enable the recipient to see only what he needs to see. Best of all, the file size of the static copy will be only a small percentage of the original file size.

Assuming you have a PivotTable in a workbook, all you need to do is select the entire PivotTable, copy it, right-click on a clean sheet, and select Paste Special... → Values. Now you can move this worksheet to another workbook or perhaps use it as is.

The one drawback to this method is that Excel does not paste the PivotTable's formats along with the values. This can make the static copy harder to read and perhaps less impressive. If you want to include the formatting as well, you can take a static picture (as opposed to a static copy) of your PivotTable and paste this onto a clean worksheet. This will give you a full-color, formatted snapshot of the original PivotTable to which you can apply any type of formatting you want, without having to worry about the formatting being lost when you refresh the original PivotTable. This is because the full-color, formatted snapshot is not linked in any way to the original PivotTable.

To create a static picture, format the PivotTable the way you want it and then highlight the Pivot Table. Select Home → Clipboard → Paste → As Picture → Copy Picture, and make the selections shown in Figure 4-2 in the Copy Picture dialog box that pops up. Then, click OK.

> Pre-2007, hold down the Shift key, select Edit → Copy Picture, click anywhere outside the PivotTable, and select Edit → Paste.

You will end up with a fully colored and formatted snapshot of your PivotTable, as shown in Figure 4-3. This can be very handy, especially if you have to email your PivotTable to other people for viewing. They will have the information they need, including all relevant formatting, but the file size will be small and they won't be able to manipulate your data. Also, they will be able to see only what you want them to see.

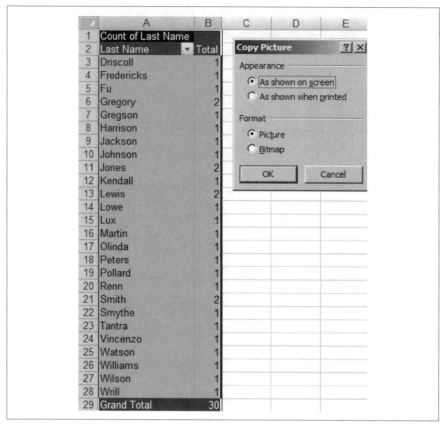

Figure 4-2. Copy Picture dialog in action

You also can use this picture-taking method on a range of cells. You can follow the preceding steps, or you can use the little-noticed Camera icon.

To use this latter method, press the Office button, select Excel Options → Customize, and choose "Commands Not in the Ribbon" from the Choose Commands From: box. Locate the camera, click it, press Add to add it to your Quick Access toolbar, and then click OK.

> In pre-2007 versions, select View → Toolbars → Customize.... From the Customize dialog, click the Commands tab; from the Categories box, select Tools; and from the Commands box on the right side, scroll down until you see Camera. Left-click and drag-and-drop this icon onto your toolbar where you want it to be displayed.

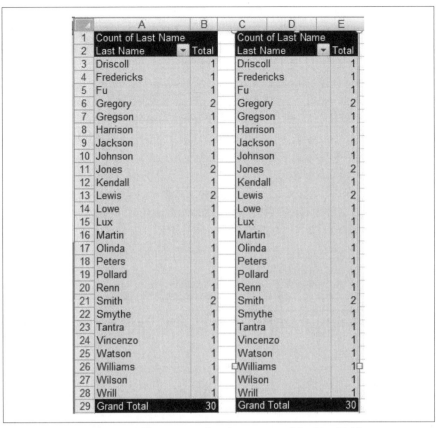

Figure 4-3. Original PivotTable contrasted with a picture of the PivotTable

Now select a range of cells, click the Camera icon, and then click anywhere on the spreadsheet, and you will have a linked picture of the range you just took a picture of. Whatever data or formatting you applied to the original range will automatically be reflected in the picture of the range.

HACK #52 Automate PivotTable Creation

The steps you need to follow to create a PivotTable require some effort, and that effort often is redundant. With a small bit of VBA, you can create simple PivotTables automatically.

ALL

PivotTables are a very clever and potent feature to use on data that is stored in either a list or a table. Unfortunately, the mere thought of creating a PivotTable is enough to prevent some people from even experimenting with them. Although some PivotTable setups can get very complicated, you can create most PivotTables easily and quickly in most situations. For example, two of the most commonly asked questions in Excel concern how to get a count of all items in a list, and how to create a list of unique items from a list that contains many duplicates. In this hack, we'll show you how to create a PivotTable quickly and easily that accomplishes these tasks.

Assume you have a long list of names in column A, with cell A1 as your heading, and the heading of Column A is First Name. To find out how many items are on the list, as well as generate a list of unique items, follow these steps:

1. Select cell A1 (your heading) and select Insert → Pivot Table (pre-2007, Data → Pivot Table Report).

2. Ensure that you have selected New Worksheet as the placement for the Pivot table, and click OK. Your screen should look something like Figure 4-4.

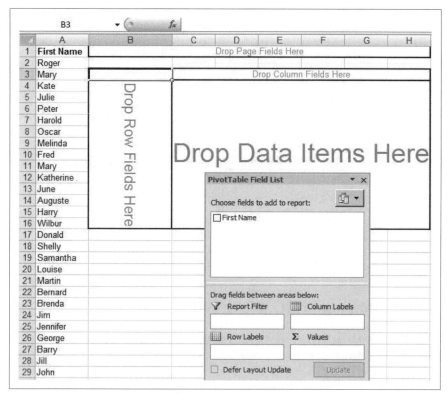

Figure 4-4. PivotTable Field and PivotTable Layout dialogs

3. Now drag the First Name field to the Row labels area.

4. Click on the First Name field again and drag it to the Values area.

5. Click OK.

To create a PivotTable in a pre-2007 version of Excel, follow these steps:

1. For versions of Excel prior to 2007, go to Data → PivotTable and Pivot-Chart Report (or Data → PivotTable Report on Macs) to start the Pivot-Table Wizard.

2. Before you start, make sure that you have selected a single cell within your data. This will allow Excel to automatically detect the underlying data it is to use next.

3. If you're using a Windows PC, select PivotTable under "What kind of report do you want to create?" (This question isn't asked on Macintoshes.)

4. Click the Next button. The PivotTable Wizard should automatically have picked up the correct range for your data in column A and will highlight it in your sheet.

5. If it is highlighted, click the Next button. Otherwise, use your mouse to select the range before clicking the Next button.

6. Click the Layout button and drag to the Data area the Names field.

7. Drag the Names field again, this time into the Row area.

8. Finally, select New Worksheet as the destination of your PivotTable Report and click the Finish button.

 At this stage, you could additionally double-click the button called Count of Product and change the "Summarize value field by:" option to a function of your choice—e.g., Sum, Average, etc. By default, Excel will use the COUNT function if it's working with text and use the SUM function if it's working with numbers.

You should see your PivotTable on a new worksheet containing the unique items from your list along with a count of how many times each item (name) appears in your list.

Save Time with a Macro

What if you want to have a macro perform all those steps for you, creating a PivotTable from any column you feed it? If you simply record a macro, you'll find it often works only if your data has the same heading. To avoid this, you can create a simple macro stored in your workbook or in your personal macro workbook (described in Chapter 7), and use it to create a Pivot-Table on any list of items. This requires that you write some generic VBA code and enter it into a standard module in your personal macro workbook or in any other workbook.

To start, right-click on the sheet tab that contains the data table and select View Code (on Mac, Alt/Option-F11; in pre-2007 versions, Tools → Macro → Visual Basic Editor). Then, choose Insert → Module and enter the following code:

```
Sub GetCount()
Dim Pt As PivotTable
Dim strField As String

    strField = Selection.Cells(1,1).Text
    Range(Selection, Selection.End(xlDown)).Name = "Items"

    ActiveWorkbook.PivotCaches.Add(SourceType:=xlDatabase, _
    SourceData:="=Items").CreatePivotTable TableDestination:="", _
    TableName:="ItemList"

    Set Pt = ActiveSheet.PivotTables("ItemList")
    ActiveSheet.PivotTableWizard TableDestination:=Cells(3, 1)
    Pt.AddFields RowFields:=strField
    Pt.PivotFields(strField).Orientation = xlDataField

End Sub
```

To return to Excel, close the Script window (or press Alt/⌘-Q) and save your workbook.

Before running this code, select the heading of your list and ensure that your list contains no blank cells.

 Sorting your list will remove blank cells quickly, because blank cells are always sorted to the bottom of a list.

The code will automatically create a named range of your list, called Items. It will then create the PivotTable based on this named range on a new worksheet.

The next time you have a long list of data, you can simply select its heading and run this macro. All the PivotTable setup work will be done in the blink of an eye.

Move PivotTable Grand Totals

One of the most annoying things about PivotTables is that the Grand Total that summarizes your data always ends up at the bottom of the table, meaning you have to scroll down just to see the figures. Move your Grand Total up to the top where it's easier to find.

Although PivotTables are a great way to summarize data and extract meaningful information, there is no built-in option to have the Grand Total float to the top for a quick bird's-eye view.

Before we describe a very generic method to move the Grand Total to the top, we'll explain how you can accomplish this with the GETPIVOTDATA function, which is designed specifically to extract data from a PivotTable.

You can use the function like this:

```
=GETPIVOTDATA("Sum of Amount",$B$5)
```

or like this:

```
=GETPIVOTDATA("Amount",$B$5)
```

Either function will extract the data and will track the Grand Total as it moves up, down, left, or right. We used the cell address $B$5, but as long as you use any cell within the PivotTable, you always will pick up the total.

The first function uses the Sum of Amount field, while the second one uses the Number Sold field. If your PivotTable has the Amount field in the Values area (pre-2007, in the Data area), you need to name the field **Amount**. If, however, the Amount field is being used two or more times in the Values area, you must specify the name you gave it, or the name you accepted by default, as shown in Figure 4-5.

You can double-click these fields to change them. This issue can become confusing if you are not up to speed with PivotTables. Luckily in Excel 2002 and later, the process is much easier, as you can have a cell fill in the arguments and give the correct syntax by using the mouse pointer. In any cell, type = (an equals sign) and then use your mouse pointer to click in the cell currently housing the Grand Total. Excel will automatically fill in the arguments for you.

Unfortunately, if you use the Function Wizard, or first type =GETPIVOTDATA( ) and then click in the cell currently housing the Grand Total, Excel makes a mess by trying to nest another GETPIVOTDATA function within that cell.

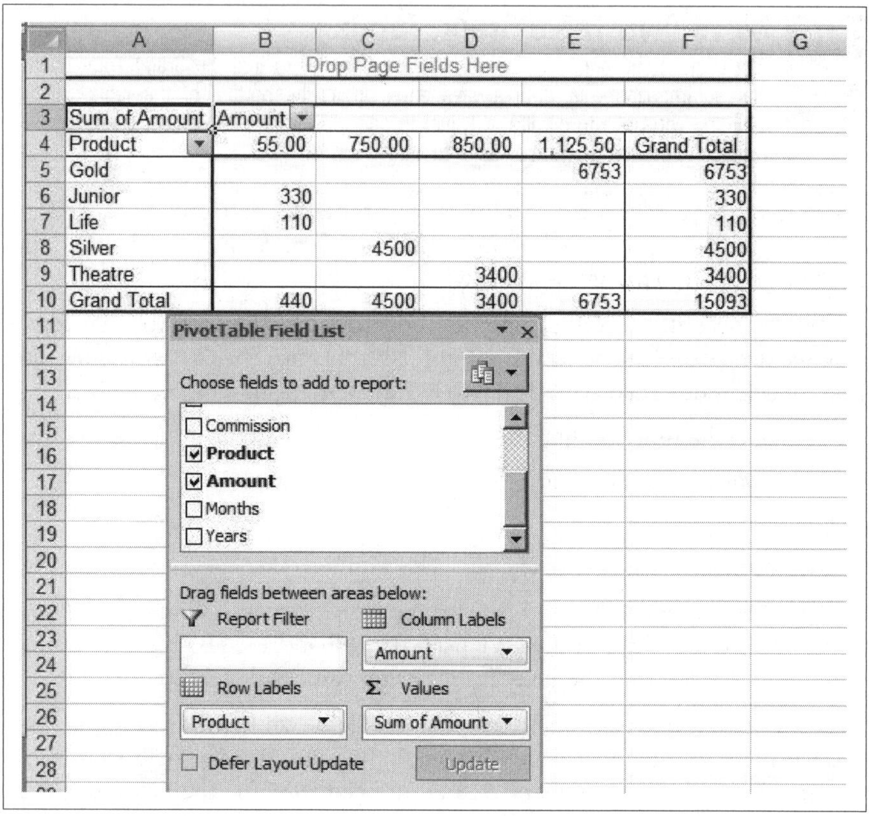

Figure 4-5. The Amount field used twice and named Sum of Amount in one case and Number Sold in the other

Probably the easiest, if least sophisticated, way to extract the Grand Total is to use the following function:

```
=MAX(PivGTCol)
```

where the column currently housing the Grand Total is named `PivGTCol`.

You also can use the `LARGE` and `SMALL` functions to extract from a PivotTable a host of figures according to their size. The following formula, for instance, extracts the second largest figure from a PivotTable:

```
=LARGE(PivGTCol,2)
```

You can add some extra rows immediately above the start of the PivotTable and place these formulas there so that you can see this type of information instantly, without having to scroll to the bottom of your PivotTable.

Efficiently Pivot Another Workbook's Data

Use data residing in another workbook as the source for your PivotTable.

When creating a PivotTable in Excel, you have lots of options for your data source. By far the easiest and most powerful approach is to use data that resides within the same workbook. Unfortunately, for whatever reason, this is not always possible or feasible. Perhaps the data that resides in another workbook is entered daily, for instance, and the users entering the data should not see the PivotTable.

Using a dynamic named range will greatly decrease the refresh time needed for your PivotTable to update. As you cannot reference a dynamic named range from another workbook, this also means you prevented the PivotTable from referencing perhaps thousands of blank rows and causing the file size to increase substantially. This way, you can pull in data from another workbook, and then base your PivotTable on the data in the same workbook rather than referencing it externally. Let's walk through the steps.

1. In the workbook that will contain your PivotTable, insert a new worksheet and call it **Data**.

2. Open the workbook containing the data to be referenced, and ensure that the worksheet containing the data is the active sheet. In any spare cell on this worksheet, enter this formula:

   ```
   =IF(A1="","",A1)
   ```

   where A1 is the very first heading of your data table.

3. Select cell A1. Then cut it, activate your original workbook, and paste cell A1 in cell A1 on the Data sheet. This will give you the reference to the other workbook.

4. Copy this cell across as many columns as there are headings in your data source.

5. Select Formulas → Defined Names → Define Name on (pre-2007, Insert → Name → Define).

6. Type **PivotData** in the Names: field and type the following in the "Refers to:" box:

   ```
   =OFFSET($A$1,0,0,COUNTA($A:$A),COUNTA($1:$1))
   ```

7. Click OK.

8. Next, to insert some code that will run each time the workbook is opened, right-click on the sheet tab and select View Code.

9. Then, double-click This Workbook (pre-2007, go to the Excel icon located at the top left corner of the screen next to the File menu option, right–click, and select View Code) and enter the following code:

```
Private Sub Workbook_Open()
 With Worksheets("Data")
 .Range("2:1000").Clear
 .Range("1:1").AutoFill .Range("1:1000")
 .Range("2:1000") = .Range("2:1000").Value
 End With
End Sub
```

> Right-clicking on the Excel icon isn't available in Excel 2007 or on a Mac. On a Mac, you'll have to open the VBE by pressing Option-F11 or by selecting Tools → Macro → Visual Basic Editor. Then, Ctrl-click This Workbook in the Projects window.

10. Finally, to return to Excel, close the script window or press Alt/⌘-Q, then save your workbook.

The code in Step 9 includes only 1,000 rows of data. The number you specify in the .Range statement should always be greater than the number of rows you believe you will need. In other words, if your table in the other workbook contains 500 rows, specify a few hundred more than that to accommodate any growth in the original table.

> Avoid using an extremely high row number (like 10,000, unless you actually have that much data), as this will greatly impact how quickly the code runs and the data updates.

At this point you are ready to check your macro. Save the workbook, close it, and then reopen it, making certain that you enable macros. The code you added will fire automatically and will copy the formulas in row 1 on the Data sheet, then automatically convert all but row 1 into values only. This will leave you with a copy of your original data source, which will update each time you open the workbook.

If you wanted to, you could hide this sheet by right-clicking and selecting Hide from the shortcut menu, or by using the method described in "Hide Worksheets So That They Cannot Be Unhidden" [Hack #5].

Now, to base a PivotTable on this dynamic named range, select anywhere within the PivotTable, select Pivot Table from the Insert tab, and type **=PivotData** under Select a Table or Range.

In pre-2007 versions, select the Wizard option from the PivotTable toolbar. Click the Back button until you reach Step 1 of the Wizard. Select the first option, Microsoft Excel List or Database, click Next, and in Step 2, type **=PivotData** (the name of the dynamic named range). Then click Finish.

You will not experience the lag that often occurs when a PivotTable is referencing an external data source because now the data itself is stored within the same workbook. As an added bonus, because you can use a dynamic named range, the PivotTable is dynamic without having to reference heaps of blank rows, and the file is kept to a manageable size.

Charting Hacks
Hacks 55–72

Charts are one of Excel's most popular features, giving spreadsheets visual power beyond mere calculations. Although Excel's chart capabilities are impressive, many times you'll want to go beyond the basic functionality provided by the software's built-in Chart Gallery to create charts that are more responsive to changes in data, or you simply will want to go beyond the range of options Excel most obviously provides. The hacks in this chapter enable you to do all of this and more.

HACK #55 Explode a Single Slice from a Pie Chart

Although pie charts are excellent visual aids, sometimes you want to emphasize a particular piece of the pie. Separating it from the rest gives it more attention.

ALL

The default option on an exploded pie chart is to explode all the slices simultaneously and for the same distance. With a couple of mouse clicks, you can explode one slice at a time.

To begin, set up a basic pie chart such as the one shown in Figure 5-1.

Next, click the pie chart once to select it, and then click again on the slice you want to explode. Drag the selected slice of pie away from the center of the chart, and you will see the exploded effect shown in Figure 5-2.

Dragging the single slice will leave the other slices unaffected. You can repeat this for other slices if you want. This technique also works just as well with a 3D pie, although the size of the pie chart shrinks when you drag a slice. To make the pie 3-D, click the chart, go to the Design tab, select

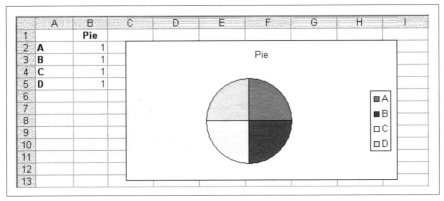

Figure 5-1. Simple pie chart set up from worksheet data

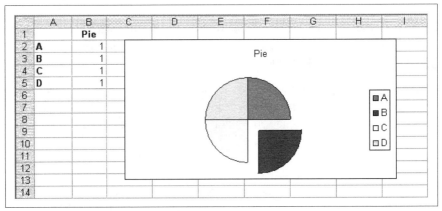

Figure 5-2. Simple pie chart with exploding slice

Change Chart Type under Type options, and click the 3-D pie (pre-2007, right-click on the chart, select Chart Type, and then press the 3-D Pie icon).

If you want to explode all the slices at the same time, simply click the pie to select it and drag away from the center, after which all the slices will have the exploded effect shown in Figure 5-3. The further you drag the slices, the smaller they will get.

The reverse also works if you want to "unexplode" your pie. Simply click a piece of pie and drag toward the middle to put it all back together again.

—Andy Pope

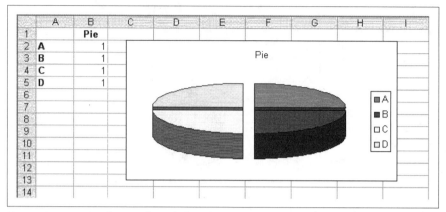

Figure 5-3. 3-D pie chart with exploding slices

Create Two Sets of Slices in One Pie Chart

HACK
#56

ALL

Most people think pie charts are limited to a single set of values, but here is a way to create a pie chart based on two columns of values.

It is a bit tricky to see two series of values charted on separate axes within one chart, but the effect is well worth the effort. To see how this works, first create a basic pie chart. Put some data in the range B1:C5, and then select that range, go to the Insert tab, select Charts → Pie, and click the first pie chart.

> In pre-2007 versions, click the Chart Wizard button in the toolbar. In Step 1 of the Wizard, under Chart Type, select the first pie chart. Now work your way through the Chart Wizard, making any changes you need. When you reach Step 4, make sure you place the chart as an object in the current worksheet.

You'll get the chart shown in Figure 5-4.

Next, select the pie chart, and choose Design → Data → Select Data. Under Legend Entries (Series) click the Add button. Click in Series Name: and select cell C1, and then click in Series Values: and select cells C2:C5. Click OK.

> In pre-2007 versions, right-click the pie chart, and select Format → Source Data → Series. Click Add to add another series. Select cell C1 for the Name and cells C2:C5 for the Values, then click OK.

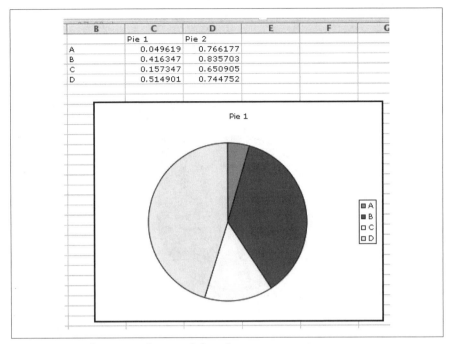

	B	C	D	E	F	G
		Pie 1	Pie 2			
A		0.049619	0.766177			
B		0.416347	0.835703			
C		0.157347	0.650905			
D		0.514901	0.744752			

Figure 5-4. Pie chart set up from worksheet data

Note that, at this stage, your chart looks no different!

OK, now we need to plot onto the secondary axis. To do this, go to the Format tab and on the far left under Current Selection options, click the drop-down menu and select Series 'Pie 1' from the list. Click the Format Selection option immediately below the drop-down and then select the Secondary Axis option and click OK.

In pre-2007 versions, double-click the pie itself again to select it, select Format Data Series, go to the Axis tab, and plot the series on the secondary axis. Click OK.

Again, the pie chart still looks the same on the surface, but it isn't the same underneath.

Select the pie, and while pressing the left mouse button, drag out from the center, then release the left mouse button. This will create the exploded effect you are looking for, as shown in Figure 5-5.

By exploding the pie, you will not only separate the two axes, revealing the second pie chart, but also compress the pie chart plotted on the secondary axis, allowing you to see both charts.

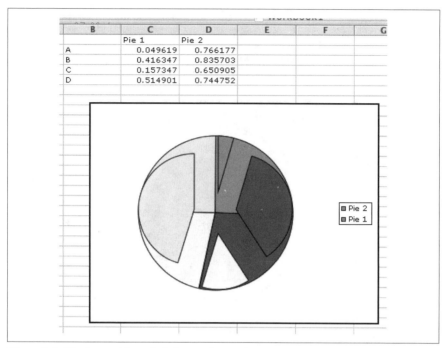

Figure 5-5. Pie chart with exploded secondary axis

Now, select each slice of pie in turn and drag them back to the center of the pie, producing the chart shown in Figure 5-6. Remember that two slow clicks will highlight an individual piece of the pie.

Join all the pieces of the pie again, and you will have a fully functional pie chart plotting two series of data on separate axes. Now you can color and format accordingly.

—Andy Pope

Create Charts That Adjust to Data

HACK **#57**

Your charts can include and plot new data automatically, the moment you add the data to your spreadsheet.

ALL

If you use dynamic named ranges in lieu of range references, your chart will plot any new data the moment you add it to your worksheet. To see how this works, begin with a clean worksheet and set up some data similar to that shown in Figure 5-7.

To create the chart and make it dynamic, you need to add two named ranges. One of the named ranges is for the category labels (Dates) and the other is for the actual data points (Temperature).

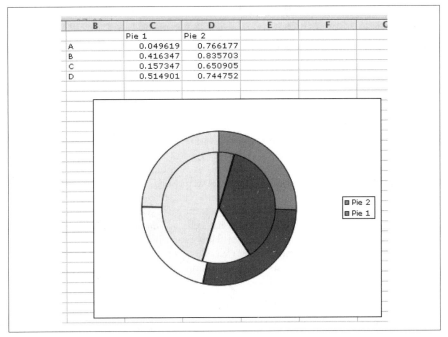

Figure 5-6. Completed pie chart containing two pies

	A	B	C
1	Dates	Temperature	
2	1/10/2003	10	
3	2/10/2003	12	
4	3/10/2003	13	
5	4/10/2003	13	
6	5/10/2003	12	
7	6/10/2003	14	
8	7/10/2003	15	
9	8/10/2003	13	
10	9/10/2003	12	
11	10/10/2003	11	
12			

Figure 5-7. Data to be charted

If you are unsure as to how to insert a dynamic named range, check out "Create Ranges That Expand and Contract" [Hack #47], which discusses this in full.

Create a dynamic named range called `TEMP_DATES` for the dates in column A by selecting Formulas → Defined Names → Define Name (pre-2007, choose Insert → Name → Define). Enter this formula:

```
=OFFSET($A$1,1,0,COUNTA($A:$A)-1,1)
```

Notice the -1 immediately after the `COUNTA` argument. This ensures that the heading is not included in the named range for that particular series.

> This example references the entire column A as the `COUNTA` argument (`$A:$A`). In older versions of Excel, it is often good practice to restrict this range to a much smaller group of cells, so as not to add unnecessary overhead to calculations. In other words, you could be forcing Excel to look in thousands of cells unnecessarily. Some of Excel's functions are smart enough to know which cells are *dirty* (contain data), but some functions are not. However, this is slightly less necessary with more recent versions of Excel, as Excel has improved its handling of large ranges.

Next, for the Temperature readings in column B, set up another dynamic range called `TEMP_READINGS`, using this formula:

```
=OFFSET($B$2,0,0,COUNTA($B:$B)-1,1)
```

Now you can create the chart using the dynamic named ranges you created in lieu of cell references.

Highlight the data (range $A$1:$B$11) select Insert → Charts → Column. Click the first chart sub-type (2D Clustered Column Chart). Now, under Chart Tools, choose Design → Data → Select Data. Under Legend Entries (Series), select Temperature and press the Edit button. Replace the Series Values: with the following formula:

```
=Sheet1!TEMP_READINGS
```

Click OK.

Now, back in the Select Data Source Dialog, press the Edit button under Horizontal (Category) Axis Labels and replace the Axis Label Range: with the following:

```
=Sheet1!TEMP_DATES
```

Click OK and make any further changes you like to your chart.

> In pre-2007 versions, insert these formulas in Step 2 of the Chart Wizard on the Series tab in the "Value:" box (=Sheet1!TEMP_READINGS) and the "Category (X) axis labels:" box (=Sheet1!TEMP_DATES).

The result will look like Figure 5-8.

 It is very important to include the Sheet name of your workbook in your formula references. If you don't, you will not be able to enter the named range in your formula.

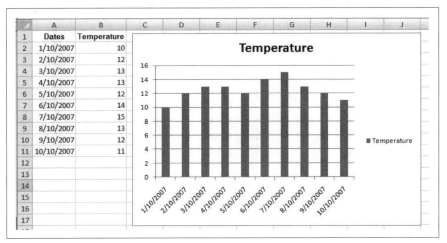

Figure 5-8. Chart created with dynamic named ranges in lieu of static range references

Once this chart is set up, every time you include another entry in either column A (Dates) or column B (Temperature), it will be added to your chart automatically.

Plotting the Last x Number of Readings

Another type of named range that you can use with charts is one that picks up only the last 10 readings (or whatever number you nominate) in a series of data. Try this using the same data you used in the first part of this hack.

For the dates in column A, set up a dynamic named range called TEMP_DATES_ 10DAYS that references the following:

```
=OFFSET($A$1,COUNTA($A:$A)-10,0,10,1)
```

For readings in column B, set up another dynamic named range called TEMP_ READINGS_10DAYS and enter the following:

```
=OFFSET(Sheet1!$A$1,COUNTA(Sheet1!$A:$A)-10,1,10,1)
```

If you want to vary the number of readings (e.g., to 20), change the last part of the formula so that it reads as follows:

```
=OFFSET(Sheet1!$A$1,COUNTA(Sheet1!$A:$A)-20,1,20,1)
```

Using dynamic named ranges with your charts gives you enormous flexibility and will save you loads of time tweaking your charts whenever you make an additional entry to your source data.

—Andy Pope

HACK #58   Interact with Your Charts Using Custom Controls

ALL

To make your chart truly interactive, you can use one or more dynamic ranges in your chart and then use either a scrollbar or a drop-down menu to reveal the figures your readers want to peruse.

As you saw in the previous hack, you can use dynamic named ranges to add flexibility to your charts. But you also can use dynamic named ranges to create interfaces controlling which data the chart plots. By linking dynamic named ranges to custom controls, you enable users to change the chart data by using the control, which simultaneously will update the data in the worksheet or vice versa.

Using a Dynamic Named Range Linked to a Scrollbar

In this example, you will use a scrollbar to reveal monthly figures over a 12-month period. The scrollbar is used to alter the number of months reported. The scrollbar's value also is used in a dynamic range, which in turn is used as the data source of the chart.

To begin, set up some data similar to that shown in Figure 5-9.

	Month	Product XYZ Sales for 2007
4		
5	JAN	505
6	FEB	943
7	MAR	500
8	APR	624
9	MAY	894
10	JUN	612
11	JUL	526
12	AUG	629
13	SEP	665
14	OCT	954
15	NOV	893
16	DEC	954
17		

Figure 5-9. Worksheet data for dynamic chart linked to scrollbar

Create a dynamic named range by selecting Formulas → Defined Names → Define Name (pre-2007, Insert → Name → Define). Type **SALES_PERIOD** in the Name: box. In the Refers To: box, type the following:

```
=OFFSET($B$5,0,0,$C$5,1)
```

By using the OFFSET function, you can use cell $C$5 to force the referenced range for SALES_PERIOD to expand both up and down as the number in $C$5 changes. In other words, changing the number in $C$5 to the number 5 would force the range to incorporate B5:B10.

> If you do not want the user to see cell C5, you can take this a step further and hide the contents of $C$5 by right-clicking it and selecting Format Cells → Custom. Enter the format ;;;, and then click OK. In Figure 5-9, the contents of cell C5 are hidden.

Create a chart (a line chart or a column chart works best). Now go to the Design tab, choose Data → Select Data, choose Product XYZ Sales for 2007, and press Edit. Change the Series Values to read:

```
='<Your workbook name here>'!SALES_PERIOD
```

Doing this will make your chart dynamic.

> In pre-2007 versions, do this in Step 2 of the Chart Wizard. Select the Series tab by changing the Formula Reference in the Values: box.

Once you have created your chart, you will need to insert a scrollbar. Go to the Developer tab and choose Controls → Insert (pre-2007, select View → Toolbars → Forms, which will bring the Forms toolbar onto the screen).

Click the scrollbar icon to select it. Once you have inserted a scrollbar, select it and move it over your chart. Now right-click it and select Format Control, change the minimum value to 1, change the maximum value to 12, and set the cell link to $C$5. The resulting chart will look like that shown in Figure 5-10.

To alter the chart, use the arrows on the scroll bar, drag the slide bar (grey button) on the scrollbar, or enter a number directly into cell C5 (e.g., entering 5 in C5 will show the data in the chart of January–May).

Using a Dynamic Named Range Linked to a Drop-Down List

Another variation is to link to a drop-down list. Starting with some data such as that shown in Figure 5-11, you will add a dynamic range that will be

Interact with Your Charts Using Custom Controls

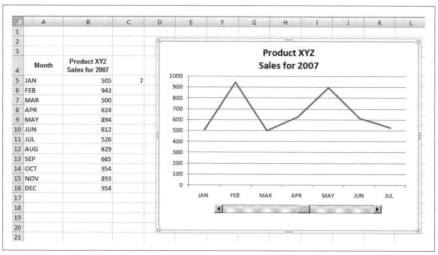

Figure 5-10. Dynamic chart linked to scrollbar

used as a data source for the chart. The dynamic range will be linked to a
drop-down list you can use to view one student's test results from those of a
group of students. You will use the drop-down list to select the name of the
student whose results you want to view.

Set up some data as in Figure 5-11, then type the formula =AVERAGE(B6:B11)
in cell B12 and copy it across to cell F12, as shown in the figure.

	A	B	C	D	E	F
1						
2						
3						
4						
5		Exam A	Exam B	Exam C	Exam D	Exam E
6	Andy	20	89	90	74	56
7	Bernard	48	72	67	85	47
8	Charlie	44	39	43	68	45
9	Dave	81	93	42	47	64
10	Edward	37	58	62	67	72
11	Frank	46	69	55	41	57
12	Average	46	70	60	64	57
13						

Figure 5-11. Worksheet data for dynamic chart linked to a drop-down list

Create a dynamic range by selecting Formulas → Defined Names → Define Name (pre-2007, Insert → Name → Define), and typing **STUDENTS** in the Name: field. In the Refers To: box, type the following:

```
=OFFSET($A$5,$G$6,1,1,5)
```

Create another dynamic range called **STUDENT_NAME**, and in the Refers To: box, type the following:

```
=OFFSET($A$5,$G$6,0,1,1)
```

The use of the cell reference $G$6 in the OFFSET formula forces the referenced ranges for STUDENTS and STUDENT_NAME to expand both up and down as the number in $G$6 changes.

Now, create a clustered column chart using the range A11:F12. Go to the Design tab, select Data → Select Data → Frank, and press Edit. Change the Series Name to read:

```
='<enter in your workbook name here>'!STUDENT_NAME
```

Click in Series Values: and change it to read:

```
='<enter in your workbook name here>'!STUDENTS
```

> In pre-2007 versions, make theses changes in Step 2 of the Chart Wizard.

At this point, you need to insert a ComboBox, so select Developer → Controls → Insert. Select the ComboBox, right-click it, enter **$A$6:A:11** for the input range and enter **$G$6** for the cell link (pre-2007, first display Forms Toolbar View → Toolbars).

To finish, place the CONCATENATE function in an empty cell, such as cell B4, like this:

```
=CONCATENATE("Test Result for ",INDEX(A6:A11,G6))
```

Clicking the downward-pointing arrow on the ComboBox shown in Figure 5-12 will change the name of the student and show his test results.

In our example file, the control is floating over the chart, If you move the chart, the control stays put. In Excel 2007, the control does not disappear behind the chart when the chart has focus, which is what happens in Excel 2003.

—Andy Pope

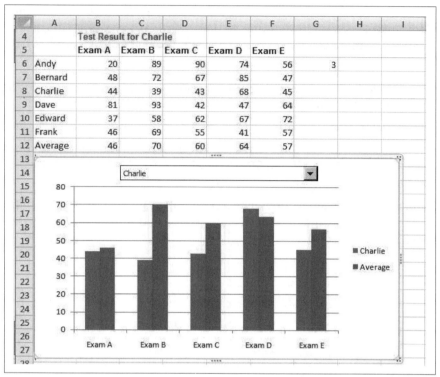

Figure 5-12. A completed dynamic chart linked to a drop-down list

Four Quick Ways to Update Your Charts

HACK #59

Although creating new charts is wonderful, updating them to reflect new circumstances can take a lot of effort. You can reduce the amount of work needed to change the data used by a chart in a number of ways.

Using Drag-and-Drop `<2007`

You can add data to an existing series or create a completely new data series by simply dragging and dropping data onto a chart. Excel will try to decide how to treat the data, which might mean adding to any existing data series when you really wanted a new series. You can, however, get Excel to display a dialog box, which lets you to determine which action you want to use.

Try setting up some data such as that shown in Figure 5-13.

Using the Chart Wizard, create a clustered column chart for the range $A$1:$D$5 only, producing the result shown in Figure 5-14.

🔺	A	B	C	D
1		2006	2007	2008
2	January	7.43	7	3
3	February	1	3	10
4	March	21.3	2	4
5	April	11.6	1	9
6	May	10	3	4

Figure 5-13. Data for clustered column chart

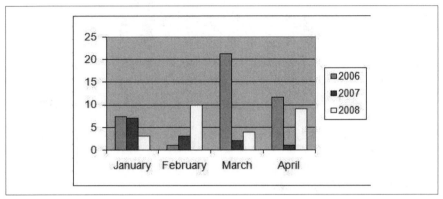

Figure 5-14. Clustered column chart created with range A1:D5 only

Highlight the range A6:D6, right-click the selection border, press the right mouse button, and drag onto the chart. When you release the mouse button, the Paste Special menu will pop up, as shown in Figure 5-15.

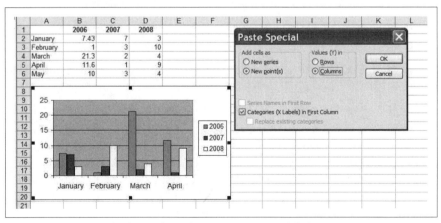

Figure 5-15. Clustered column chart showing Paste Special dialog

Select the Columns option and then click OK. This will add the May data series to the chart, as shown in Figure 5-16.

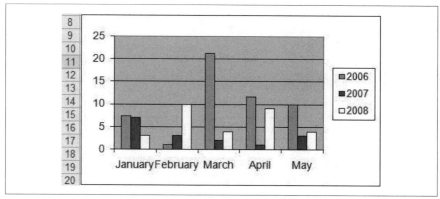

Figure 5-16. Clustered column chart with May data series added

The Paste Special dialog takes care of most of the actions you need in order to use this nifty trick.

Using the Formula Bar   ◄ALL►

You also can update your chart by using the Formula bar. When you select a chart and click a data series within it, look at the Formula bar and you will see the formula Excel uses for the data series.

Called a SERIES function, the formula generally uses four arguments, although a bubble chart requires an additional fifth argument for [Size].

The syntax (or order of structure) of the SERIES function is as follows:

```
=SERIES( [Name] , [X Values] , [Y Values] , [Plot Order] )
```

So, a valid SERIES function could appear as follows, and as shown in Figure 5-17:

```
=SERIES(Sheet1!$B$1,Sheet1!$A$2:$A$5,Sheet1!$B$2:$B$5,1)
```

In Figure 5-17 the first part of the reference, Sheet1!$B$1, refers to the name, or the chart title, which is "2007." The second part of the reference, Sheet1!$A$2:$A$5, refers to the X values, which in this case are the months. The third part of the reference, Sheet1!$B$2:$B$5, refers to the Y values, which are the values 7.43, 15, 21.3, and 11.6. Finally, the last part of the formula, the 1, refers to the plot order, or the order of the series. In this case, there is only one series, so this series can only take the value 1. If there were more than one series, the first series would take the number 1, the second series would take the number 2, and so forth.

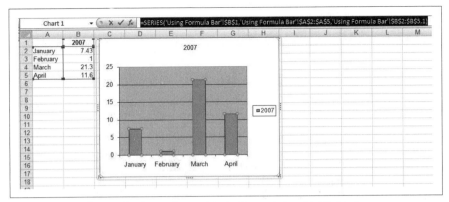

Figure 5-17. A clustered column chart with the Formula bar highlighted

To make changes to the chart, simply alter the cell references in the Formula bar.

Besides using cell references, you can enter explicit values, known as *array constants*, into your charts (see Excel Help for full details). To achieve this, add curly brackets ({}) around the X and Y values, as shown in the following formula:

```
=SERIES("My Bar",{"A","B","C","D"},{1,2,3,4},1)
```

In the previous SERIES formula, A, B, C, and D would be the X values, while 1, 2, 3, and 4 would be their corresponding Y values.

By using this method, you can create or update a chart without having to store data in cells.

Dragging the Bounding Area <2007

If your chart data contains continuous cell references, you can easily extend or reduce the data in the series by dragging the bounding area to a desired point. Slowly click the data series you want to either extend or reduce. After two slow clicks, black square(s) or *handles* will appear around the outside of the series (or in the middle if you're using a line chart). All you need to do is click a square and drag the bounding area in the direction required, as shown in Figure 5-18.

If you either extend or reduce the series data, as shown in Figure 5-19, the original source data as well as the axis labels (if set to Auto) also will alter to reflect the changes you made.

This is great for testing scenarios, when you want to explore what the results of different data sets will be.

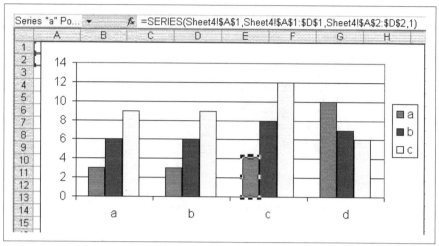

Figure 5-18. A highlighted bounding area for a chart series

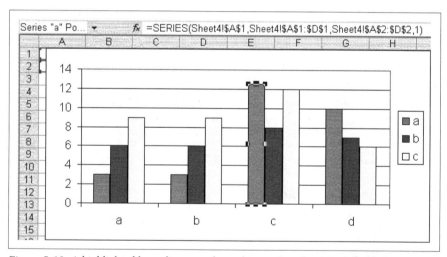

Figure 5-19. A highlighted bounding area for a chart series after it is expanded

Using Paste Special ⟨ALL⟩

If you want to add extra data to a chart, you can copy the data and, using the Paste Special Function, you can decide whether to view the series as a new series, new point, or in columns or rows, as shown in Figure 5-20.

Note that Paste Special is not available from the right-click menu when using this method.

—Andy Pope

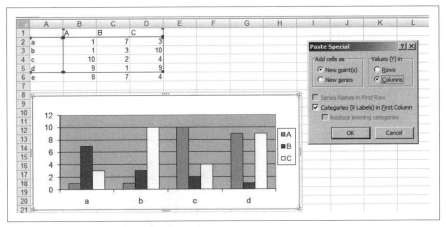

Figure 5-20. Copying additional data into a chart using Paste Special

Hack Together a Simple Thermometer Chart

#60

Excel doesn't provide a thermometer chart. If you want one, you'll have to construct it.

By creating a basic clustered column chart that compares values across categories, and then manipulating the various chart elements, you can create a visual, workable thermometer chart with little effort.

Set up some data, such as that shown in Figure 5-21, and then create a basic clustered column chart, charting the data in rows. We used the range B3:C4.

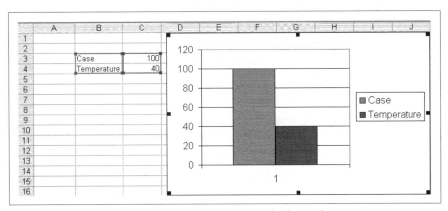

Figure 5-21. Series data and creation of basic clustered column chart

Remove the legend and the gridlines (click them to highlight them, then press Delete), and format the Temperature Data Series to the Secondary axis. To do this, select the series and choose Chart Tools → Format → Current Selection → Format Selection → Secondary Axis (pre-2007, right-click on the temperature bar, select Format Data Series → Axis, and choose the Secondary Axis option). Your chart should look like the chart in Figure 5-22.

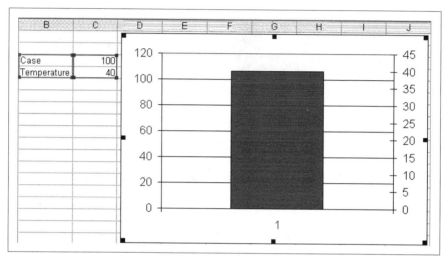

Figure 5-22. Two series plotted on the Y2 axis

Format both the Primary (on the left) and Secondary (on the right) axes by highlighting each axis in turn, right-clicking, and selecting Format Axis (pre-2007, select the Scale tab). Set the Minimum to 0, the Maximum to 100, the Major Unit to 10, and the Minor Unit to 5. You'll see the chart shown in Figure 5-23.

Format the Case data series to white, format the Temperature series to red, and format the Plot Area to white. At this point, the thermometer chart should be taking shape.

Reduce the Gap Width property for both columns by right-clicking and selecting Format Data Series → Series Options. Finally, remove the X axis (highlight the axis and click Delete) and then size and position to suit.

As Figure 5-24 demonstrates, by fiddling around a bit with Excel's existing chart features, you can come up with a thermometer chart that looks great and works well.

—Andy Pope

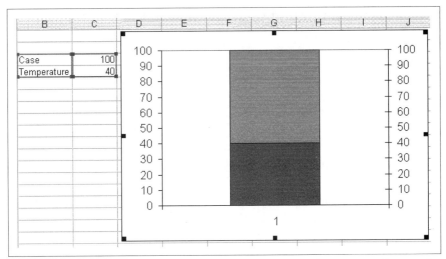

Figure 5-23. Case series on Y1 axis, temperature series on Y2 axis, both axes formatted identically

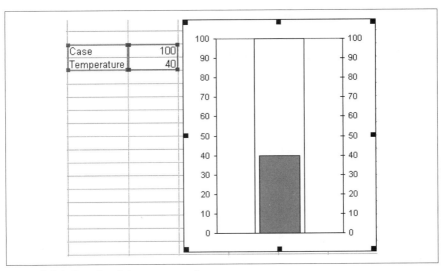

Figure 5-24. Completed thermometer chart

Create a Column Chart with Variable Widths and Heights

#61

ALL

Wouldn't it be nice to create a column chart whose columns can vary in width and height? Then, as you plot your data into the columns, the columns' width and height cleverly adjust themselves simultaneously.

Excel doesn't provide this feature directly, but by hacking an XY scatter chart you can create a very effective variable width column chart. XY scatter charts are used to compare values; therefore, they provide a perfect base on which to start creating a variable width column chart.

Figure 5-25 shows a variable width column chart that charts the percent share versus cost for the following expenses: gas, electricity, water, food, travel, and other. The X axis (the axis along the bottom of the chart) shows the percentages (%), while the Y axis (the axis on the left-hand side) shows the cost ($).

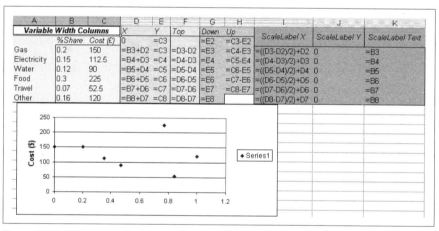

Figure 5-25. XY scatter chart set up from range D2:E8

To create this chart, set up some data such as that in Figure 5-25, select Insert → Charts → Scatter. Select the first chart subtype: the Scatter with only markers. Insert an Axis label for the Primary Vertical Axis (Value (Y) axis), by selecting Chart Tools → Layout → Labels → Axis Titles → Primary Vertical Axis Title. When the Axis Title box appears, type **Cost ($)**. (In pre-2007 versions, use the Chart Wizard to create the Scatter chart, and ensure the chart is created with the columns option selected and is set as an object.)

You can use Ctrl-~ (which is the same on the Mac) to show you the correct formulas to place in the cells. You also could select the Office button → Excel Options → Advanced, and choose "Show formulas in cells instead of their calculated result." Pre-2007 users should choose Tools → Options... → View (Views under Excel → Preferences on Mac OS X) and check Formulas under Window options.

Now it's time to play around with the chart to create columns. First, remove the legend and gridlines (highlight them, then click Delete) and ensure your plot area has no fill.

 A plot area with no fill is the default for Excel 2007, but users of earlier versions must format the plot area to no fill by clicking the gray background, right-clicking, and selecting Format Plot Area. Under Area, select None.

Highlight the X axis and right-click to get to the Format Axis dialog (pre-2007, press Scale). Under Axis Options (Scale on the Mac), set the Minimum to 0 and the Maximum to 1. Also make sure to change the Major Tick Mark type to None and the Axis Labels to None (pre-2007, Tick Mark options are found on the Patterns tab ["Colors and Lines" on the Mac]), then click OK.

The scatter chart will look something like that shown in Figure 5-26.

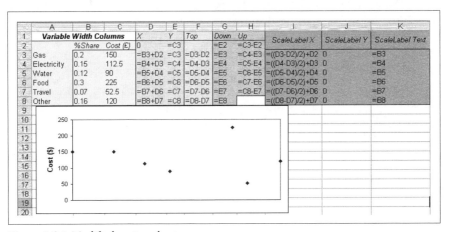

Figure 5-26. Modified scatter chart

The next step is to create the lines for the columns so click on the chart and under Chart Tools, select the Layout tab. Then choose the Error Bars option, followed by More Error Bars. Under Display, select Both. Choose Custom → Specify Value and set the Positive Error Value to H2:H7 and the Negative Error Value to G2:G8. Click OK, then Close.

In pre-2007 versions, you make changes to the Error bars by double-clicking on the data points to bring up the Format Data Series dialog. Under both the X and Y Error Bars, set the "custom - range" to:

=Sheet1!$F$2:$F$8=Sheet1!$F$2:$F$8

Under the Y Error Bars, set the "custom + range" to:

=Sheet1!$H$2:$H$7

(Replace Sheet1 with the name of your sheet if it's different.) You must also set the X Error Bars to "Minus" under the Display section, and the Y Error Bars to "Both."

This will give you the vertical sides of the column, and yes, your chart looks a bit weird at the moment and has horizontal lines on it as well. Let's change that. Click on one of the horizontal lines and select Chart Tools → Layout → Analysis → Error Bars → More Error Bars. This time, select Display → Minus. Select Custom → Specify Value and set the Negative Error Value to F2:F8. Click OK, then Close.

Now that all the hard work is done, it's time to tidy up a bit and add some labels. First, under the Format Data Series dialog, choose Marker → None (pre-2007, select Patterns) to display the results shown in Figure 5-27.

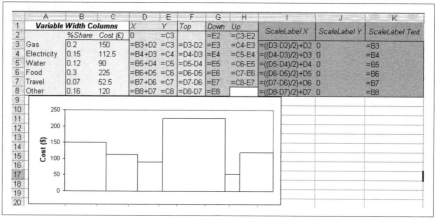

Figure 5-27. XY scatter chart manipulated to produce variable width column chart

If you want to use labels, you need to download John Walkenbach's Chart Tools, available from *http://j-walk.com/ss/excel/files/charttools.htm*. Part of this add-in is designed specifically for data labels. It enables you to specify a worksheet range for the data labels for a chart series.

 Unfortunately, Walkenbach's Chart Tools add-in doesn't seem to work on Excel for the Macintosh, even after extraction from its EXE distribution.

Before you use Chart Tools, you must add a new data series to provide X-axis labels for the chart. So, highlight the chart and choose Design → Data → Add to add another series. Under "Series X values," highlight the range I3: I8; under "Series Y values," select J3:J8. Again, format the series to have no marker.

 To add a new series in pre-2007 versions, right-click and select Source Data → Series. Press Add to add a new series.

Now it's time to use Walkenbach's add-in. Make sure you have highlighted your chart, and then select AdIns → JWalk Chart Tools AddIn (pre-2007, Chart → JWalk Chart Tools). When the dialog box pops up, type **K3:K8** for the data label range. Ensure that you have the Create Links to the Label Cells box checked and click OK.

To add yet another new data series to provide column labels for the chart, select Data → Design → Select Data → Add. Under "Series X values," highlight the range I3:I8; under "Series Y values," select J3:J8. Again, format the series to have no marker.

 To add a new series in pre-2007 versions, highlight the chart, right-click, and select Source Data → Series. Press Add to add a new series.

Again, use Walkenbach's add-in. This time, highlight Series 3 and link the data labels to A3:A8. The result will look like Figure 5-28.

The fantastic thing about this type of chart is that the bars will either expand or contract up the Y axis and along the X axis when the entries in the % Share or the Cost ($) columns change. Pretty nifty.

—*Andy Pope*

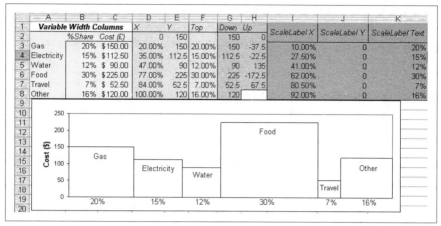

Figure 5-28. Completed variable width column chart

HACK #62 Create a Speedometer Chart

ALL

You can create a really impressive, workable speedometer (or "speedo") chart, complete with moving needle, by using a combination of doughnuts and pie charts. The added touch is that you can control the speedometer via a scrollbar.

Excel's Charts offers many different designs, but not, unfortunately, a *speedometer chart*. A speedometer chart provides a slick way to represent data. With the tools in this hack, you can create a speedometer chart and add a scrollbar that will alter the chart and change the data in the worksheet simultaneously.

The first thing you need to do is to set up some data, such as that shown in Figure 5-29, and create a doughnut chart. Doughnut charts work a bit like pie charts, but they can contain multiple series, whereas a pie chart cannot.

Press Alt/Control-~ to show the actual formulas on the worksheet. You also can select the Office button → Excel Options → Advanced and check the "Show formulas in cells instead of their calculated result" option under "Display options for this Workbook" (pre-2007, select Tools → Options...; on a Mac, use Excel → Preferences...) to see the formulas, though that's a longer process.

Now, highlight the range B2:B5, go to the Insert tab, and select Charts → Other Charts. Under Doughnut, select the first chart subtype to create your chart. As in Figure 5-30, your chart will be placed as an *object* in the worksheet in which it is created, which is Excel's default. Ensuring your chart is an object will make it easier to work with as you are setting up the speedometer.

	A	B	C	D	E	F
1	Bands	Dial	Dial Labels	Labels	Needle	
2	25	180	180	=$F$3 & "% Share"	200	Share
3	75	=(180/100)*A2	9	0	=((180/100)*F3)-1	0
4		=(180/100)*(A3-A2)	18	10	2	
5		=360-SUM(B2:B4)	18	20	=360-SUM(E2:E4)	
6			18	30		
7			18	40		
8			18	50		
9			18	60		
10			18	70		
11			18	80		
12			18	90		
13			9	100		
14						
15				Low		
16				Normal		
17				High		
18						

Figure 5-29. Data set up for speedometer chart

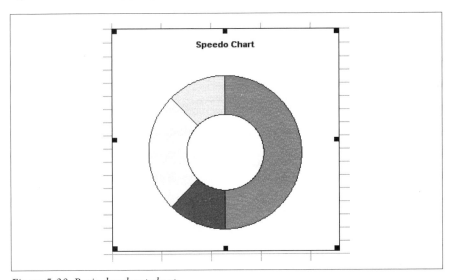

Figure 5-30. Basic doughnut chart

In pre-2007 versions, create the doughnut chart by using the Chart Wizard. In Step 1 of the Wizard, select the Standard Types tab (this should be the default anyway). Then, under Chart Type, select the first doughnut. Click the Next button to go to Step 2 of the Wizard, and make sure your data is charted in columns. Click the Next button to proceed to Step 3. You can make changes in Step 3 if you need to, but they aren't necessary for this hack. Click Next to go to Step 4, and make sure the chart ends up as an object in the current worksheet (again, this is the default).

Highlight the doughnut chart, slowly double-click the largest slice to select it, and then right-click and select Format Data Point (pre-2007, then click Options). Set the angle of this slice to 90 degrees.

Now, click to highlight each of the other slices in turn, then right-click your right mouse button to get back to the Format Data Point dialog and color the other three bands as required. The doughnut chart should look like the one in Figure 5-31.

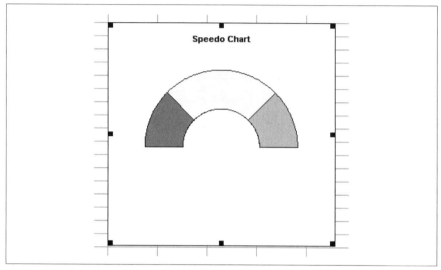

Figure 5-31. Doughnut chart with 90% angle and no color or border on the first slice

You need to add another series (Series 2) of values to form the slots for the dial labels, so again highlight the chart and select Design → Data → Select Data → Add. Then, under Series values, select the range C2:C13 and click OK.

> To add a new series in pre-2007 versions, right-click, select Source Data, and then select the Series tab. Click the Add button to create a new series.

Click the Add button again to add a third series (Series 3) to create the needle, and under Series values, select the range E2:E5. Your result should look like Figure 5-32.

At this point, the speedometer is starting to take shape. If you want to add labels to the speedometer, you can download a tool for adding them for free from John Walkenbach's Chart Tools site, at *http://j-walk.com/ss/excel/files/charttools.htm*.

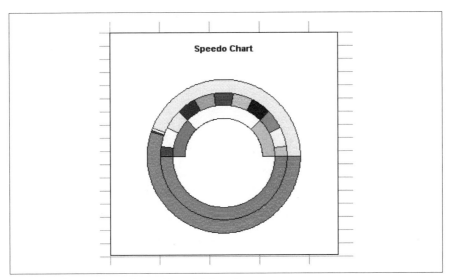

Figure 5-32. Doughnut chart with multiple series

Part of this add-in, which unfortunately works only on Windows, is designed specifically for data labels. It enables you to specify a worksheet range for the data labels for a chart series. Walkenbach's add-in also contains the features described in the following list:

Chart Size
Enables you to specify an exact size for a chart, or enables you to make all charts the same size.

Export
Enables you to save charts as *.gif*, *.jpg*, *.tif*, or *.png* files.

Picture
Converts a chart to a picture (color or grayscale).

Text Size
Freezes the size of all text items in a chart. When the chart is resized, the text elements will not change size.

Chart Report
Generates a summary report for all charts, or a detailed report for a single chart.

Use the add-in to format Series 2 to display data labels using the range D2: D13. Again, highlight Series 2, and then right-click to bring up the Format Data Series dialog. Press Fill and check No Fill; then press Border Color and check No Line (pre-2007, click the Patterns tab, set the area and border of this slice to None, and then click OK).

Your chart should look like that shown in Figure 5-33.

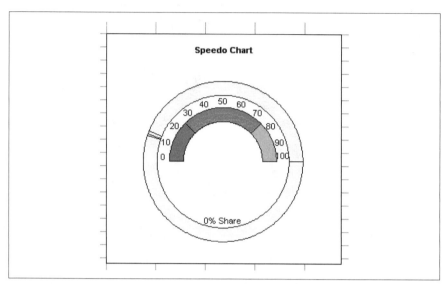

Figure 5-33. Improved speedometer chart, with labels added

Highlight Series 3, and select Design → Type → Change Chart Type. Select the first Pie chart and click OK (pre-2007, right-click your mouse button and select Chart Type).

Yes, it looks strange when you see it in Figure 5-34. But rest assured, if the pie chart overlays the doughnut chart, you have done this correctly.

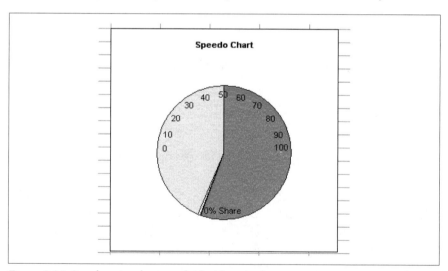

Figure 5-34. Speedometer chart overlaid with a pie chart

Next you need to reduce the size of the pie chart you just laid over the doughnut. To do this, explode it and reassemble the smaller slices. Click on Series 3 and, holding the left mouse button down, drag outwards; this will explode the pie and make it smaller. Resize the slices (remember, two slow clicks to select an individual slice), to make your chart look like Figure 5-35.

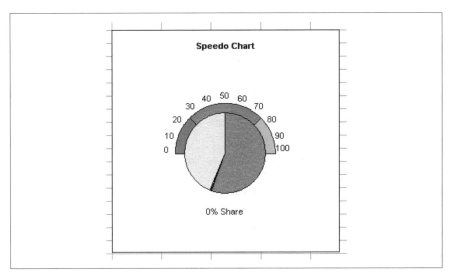

Figure 5-35. Pie chart exploded and resized

Now, select the whole pie, right-click it, and choose Format Data Series (pre-2007, click the Options tab). Change the Angle of the first slice to 90 degrees.

Change the Border and the Area to none for all slices except the third slice, which needs to have a fill of Black. This will produce the chart shown in Figure 5-36.

If you want to add a legend, highlight the chart, double-click it, and select Layout → Labels → Legend (pre-2007, right-click and select Chart → Data Labels → Legend Key).

This produces the speedometer in Figure 5-37. Now move, size, and edit the chart as required.

Now that the speedometer chart is built, you need to create a scrollbar and make the scrollbar and chart talk to each other. Choose Developer → Controls → Insert.

In pre-2007 versions, right-click the gray area at the top of the screen and select Forms, bringing the Forms toolbar onto the screen. Then, right-click the toolbar area of the screen and select Control Toolbox.

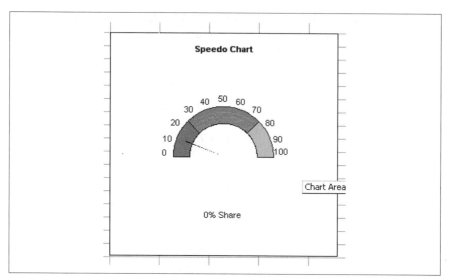

Figure 5-36. Speedometer chart with only the third series of pie chart showing color

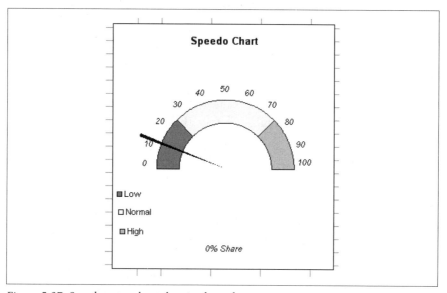

Figure 5-37. Speedometer chart showing legend

Click the scrollbar icon to select it, and draw the scrollbar on your worksheet. Once you have inserted and sized your scrollbar, select it and move it onto your chart. Right-click it, and select Format Control to display the Format Control dialog. Click the Control tab and choose cell F3 as the linked cell, and set the Maximum value to 100 and the Minimum value to 0. When you close the Properties dialog and move the scrollbar onto the chart, you'll see something that looks like Figure 5-38.

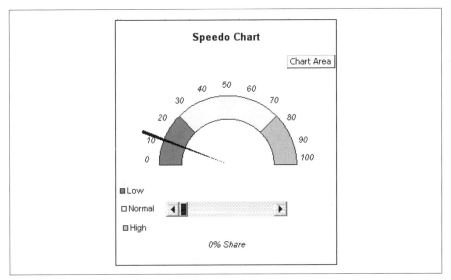

Figure 5-38. Final speedometer chart

Clicking the arrows or dragging the slide bar will alter the speedometer, but remember this also will change the data on the worksheet to which it is linked.

—Andy Pope

Link Chart Text Elements to a Cell

HACK #63

ALL

When creating and using charts repeatedly, it is handy to know how to link some of a chart's text elements (e.g., titles and labels) directly to a cell. This means that if and when your underlying data changes, your chart data and its text elements will always be in harmony.

The chart text elements you can link to a cell are the chart title, the primary and secondary X-axis titles, the primary and secondary Y-axis titles, and the series data labels.

To see how this is done, you will link the title of a chart to a cell. To begin, set up some data such as that shown in Figure 5-39. Go to the Insert tab, and select the first chart (2D clustered column) under Columns (pre-2007, use the Chart Wizard). Now, click cell A17 and type **Age of Employees**.

The next step is to establish a link between the chart title and the cell. So, select the chart title (Age, in this case), then go to the Formula bar, type **=**

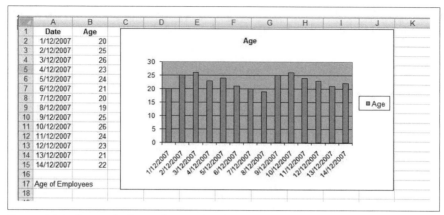

Figure 5-39. Clustered column chart with title created automatically

(an equals sign), click cell A17, and press Enter. Note that if you are referencing a cell on another sheet, you will have to type the sheet name followed by an exclamation mark (!), then the cell reference.

The same process works for data labels, but you need to select an individual data label before linking it to a cell. Your results should look like Figure 5-40.

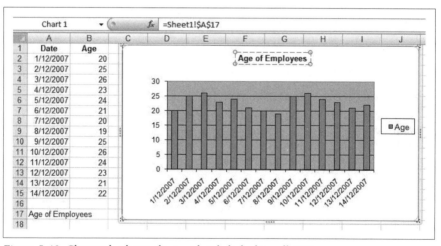

Figure 5-40. Clustered column chart with title linked to cell A17

This smart hack will make your chart text elements and chart data stay in harmony. Plus, it can save you time when creating charts.

—*Andy Pope*

Hack Chart Data So That Empty or FALSE Formula Cells Are Not Plotted

ALL When plotting data that results from a formula, Excel treats cells with formulas that return nothing ("") or FALSE as though they have a value of 0, which can result in some ugly charts. Your chart can suddenly drop off, leaving you with a chart that no longer accurately paints the picture you are trying to convey. These hacks keep these cells from being plotted.

You can prevent empty ("") and FALSE formula cells from being plotted in two very easy ways: by hiding rows or columns, and by having cells return a value of #N/A.

Hiding Rows or Columns

Set up some data as shown in Figure 5-41, create a line chart highlighting the range A1:B12, and see what it looks like with a mixture of FALSE and empty ("") results from your formula.

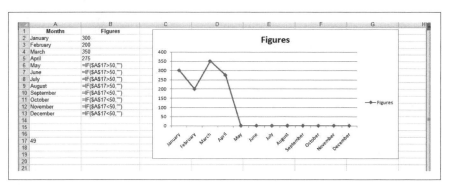

Figure 5-41. Data with line chart plotting empty or FALSE values

The chart in Figure 5-41 is plotting Sales Figures by Month. This means that if the current month is April, the chart will plot eight months of data as 0. To avoid this, simply hide rows 5:12 (May:Dec). Excel will not plot hidden rows, and thereby will produce the result shown in Figure 5-42. To hide these rows, select them, and then right-click and select Hide.

Using #N/A to Plot Blank Cells

Using the previous method works if you are trying to hide rows in a sequence. However, if you have a gap or a 0 value in your data range, as shown in Figure 5-43, your data will either show the gap or show 0, making your chart look odd.

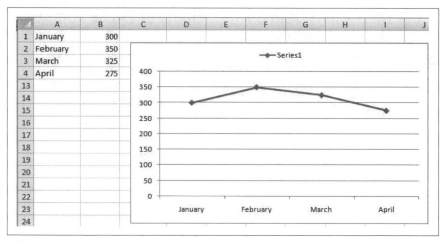

Figure 5-42. Data with rows 5 through 12 hidden, and a chart plotting January through April figures only

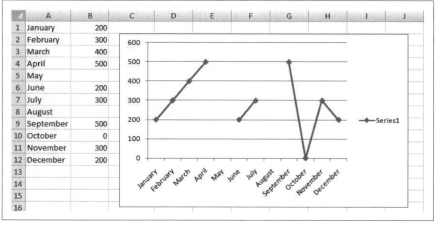

Figure 5-43. Data with B5and B8 showing no value and B10 showing a zero value

In this case, hiding rows will also result in hiding the row label, further skewing your data, as shown in Figure 5-44.

An easy way around this is to type =NA( ) in the blank cells, or, if you are using a formula, try using #N/A instead of using "" or 0 if the formula is FALSE.

Using one of these methods to show the error message #N/A as in Figure 5-45 will force Excel to ignore the cell, thereby making your chart much more user-friendly and easier to understand and ensuring your trend is not adversely affected.

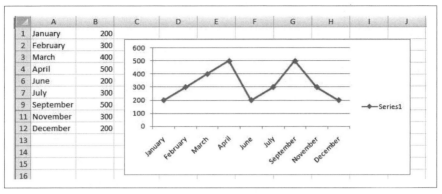

Figure 5-44. Chart with rows 5, 8 and 10 hidden

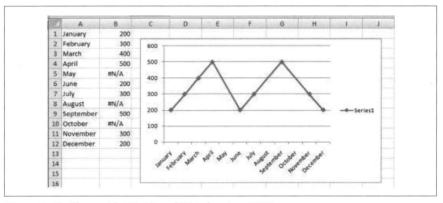

Figure 5-45. Chart with B5, B8 and B10 showing #N/A,

—Andy Pope

HACK #65 Add a Directional Arrow to the End of a Line Series

Create an arrow that automatically adjusts to point in the direction suggested by the last two points in the data series, making it easy to visualize which way you are going.

When you create a line chart in Excel, you can easily change the data point markers to suit your purpose. However, if you want to place a directional arrow at the end of your line chart, the steps are slightly more involved.

First, set up some data, as shown in Figure 5-46, and create a normal line chart on the data in range A1:B9.

Select the data points once, to highlight all the points. We only want to highlight the last data point, so click on this point once more to remove highlighting from the rest of the points, as shown in Figure 5-47.

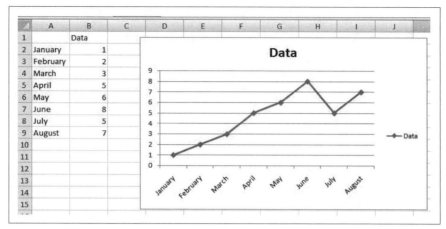

Figure 5-46. Standard Line Chart

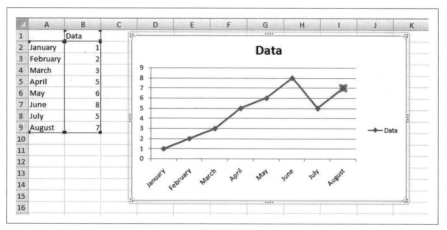

Figure 5-47. Last data point in the line series is selected

Right-click on the data point and select Format Data Point → Line Style. Then, under Arrow Settings, select the drop–down menu for End Type, choose the second arrow, and press Close. The finished chart should look like Figure 5-48.

> If you use a line chart with data points identified, you can remove the data point formatting by highlighting the last point, right-clicking, selecting Format Data Point → Marker Fill, and setting it to No Fill, then selecting Marker Line Color and setting it to No Line.

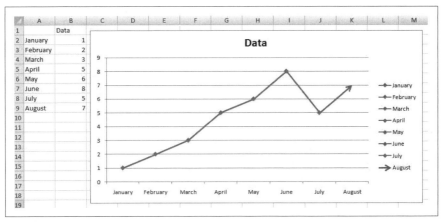

Figure 5-48. Finished chart with arrow styling

The chart will automatically update if the data changes. Try clicking in cell B9 and changing the contents from 7 to 2. Notice that your arrow will change direction from pointing upward to pointing downward.

—Andy Pope

Place an Arrow on the End of a Horizontal (X) Axis

HACK #66

As a variation on the previous hack, you can also place an arrow on the end of a horizontal (X) or vertical (Y) axis.

ALL

To place an arrow on the end of an axis, you first need to create a dummy data point. Set up some data as shown in Figure 5-49. The actual chart data is in the range A1:B6. The values in A10:B10 are for positioning the dummy data point.

	A	B
1		My Data
2	Jan	2
3	Feb	3.5
4	Mar	4
5	Apr	5.5
6	May	8
7		
8		
9	X	Y
10	5.5	0
11		

Figure 5-49. Data to be used in the chart

Although this hack works for all versions of Excel, the instructions are much simpler in Excel 2007.

In Excel 2007

To continue in Excel 2007, you can ignore the values in A10:B10. All you need to do is right-click on the Horizontal (X) axis and select Format Axis. Then, under Line Style, select the drop-down arrow for End Type under Arrow Settings and choose the desired arrow. Figure 5-50 shows the results of selecting the stealth arrow.

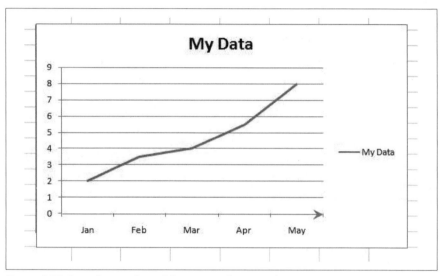

Figure 5-50. Line chart with stealth arrow on horizontal (x) axis

In Older Excel Versions

Accomplishing the same effect in versions of Excel prior to 2007 is much more of a hack. Follow these steps.

1. Highlight the range A1:B6, select the Chart Wizard, and create a Line chart using the first chart subtype.

2. Right-click and select Source Data → Series → Add. Give the series the name Axis Arrow.

3. Set the range of the Series X Values to $A$10 and the Series Y Values to $B$10, and press OK.

4. Now, we need to change the Chart Type of the Axis Arrow data series to XY Scatter, markers only. Select the Axis Arrow series, right-click,

select Chart Type, and choose the first subtype under (XY) Scatter. Your chart should now look like Figure 5-51.

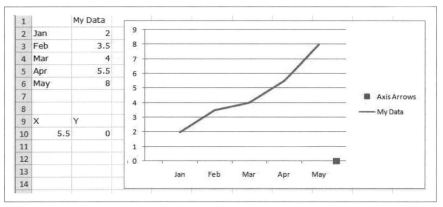

Figure 5-51. Created line chart with Axis Arrow series plotted as a scatter chart

5. To format the chart to display Value data labels, right-click and select Chart options → Data Labels.

6. Check the Value box, and click OK.

7. Edit the data label for the Axis Arrow (scatter) series, replacing the number 1 with the number 4.

8. Keep the data label selected and change the font to Marlett via the Formatting toolbar. When you do this, you will get a right arrowhead, as shown in the completed chart shown in Figure 5-52.

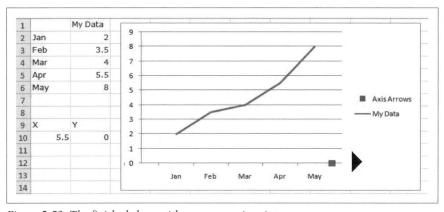

Figure 5-52. The finished chart with arrow as axis pointer

Increase the font size to suit your chart (the one in Figure 5-52 is 40 points). Also, adjust the label position to center it over the data point if necessary.

You can adapt the same technique for the Y axis by making the Y Value $B$10 and the X value $A$10 in the first step, but you will substitute the number 4 for the lowercase letter *t*.

—Andy Pope

HACK #67 — ALL

Correct Narrow Columns When Using Dates

When you create a chart, Excel will attempt to interpret your data. This usually works great. However, sometimes the result is not the desired one, especially if the category labels are dates. If Excel gets it wrong, this can result in columns that are very narrow and look rather odd.

The reason for this is that Excel is treating the X-axis as a Time series rather than categorical data. Therefore each column only occupies the space for a single day, which results in narrow columns.

To see what we mean, set up some data as in Figure 5-53, and create a simple column chart of the data range A1:B9.

	A	B	C	D	E	F	G	H	I	J	K
1		Data									
2	1/01/2007	2									
3	22/01/2007	3									
4	10/02/2007	4									
5	2/03/2007	3									
6	22/03/2007	2									
7	11/04/2007	3									
8	1/05/2007	4									
9	21/05/2007	3									
10											
11											
12											
13											
14											
15											
16											
17											

Figure 5-53. Simple column chart created using range A1:B9

To fix the columns, follow these steps:

1. Select the horizontal (X) axis.
2. Click either the Layout or Format tab on the Chart Tools contextual tab.
3. Click the Format Selection item on the Current Selection group. This will display the Format dialog.
4. Select Axis Options from the list.

5. Check the Text axis option under Axis Type (pre-2007, right-click the chart and select Chart Options → Axes, then check the Category option). Figure 5-54 shows the results.

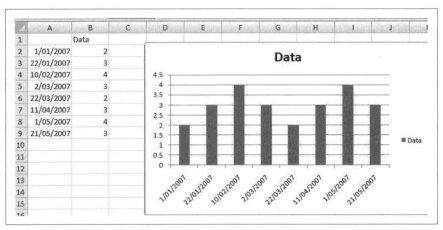

Figure 5-54. Simple column chart with Axis changed to Text

By changing the Axis option to Text, the columns return to their normal thickness.

—Andy Pope

HACK
#68
ALL

Position Axis Labels

Change how or where your axis labels are displayed by moving their position from the default.

When you create a bar chart, the position of your axis labels is automatically determined. However, depending on your chart requirements, you might want to change how or where your labels are displayed. To make your chart more professional, here are two methods you can use to change how your labels are set. The second method also reverses a series.

Changing Label Position

When you create a bar chart with both positive and negative values, the bars are formed to the left or to the right of the axis. Because negative value series created in a bar chart will be colored and formed to the left of your X axis, they will hide the axis labels. Using this method, you can reformat where your labels are positioned.

Set up some data as shown in Figure 5-55, and create a basic bar chart on the range A1:B6.

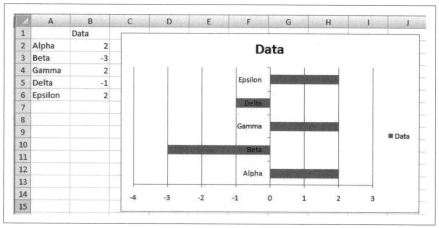

Figure 5-55. Basic bar chart created on range A1:B6

As you can see, the negative value columns obscure the axis labels. Let's change this.

Select the horizontal (X) axis, right-click, and select Format Axis (or press Ctrl-1 to display the Format Axis dialog). Select Axis Options from the list, and choose Low from the Axis labels drop-down menu (pre-2007, select the axis, right-click, choose Format Axis → Colors and Lines, and check Low under Tick mark labels).

Your labels should now be set to the left of all the bars in your chart, as shown in Figure 5-56.

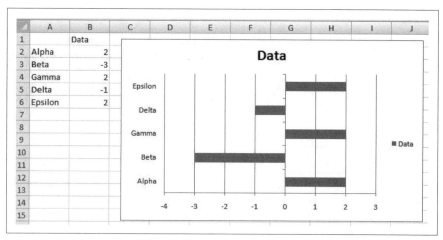

Figure 5-56. Basic bar chart with Axis labels set to Low

Reversing Label Order

When creating a bar chart, sometimes you'll want to reverse the order in which both the series and the labels are displayed. Using this simple method, you can reorder the series ensuring the corresponding labels move with the series.

Create a bar chart using some data, as shown in Figure 5-57.

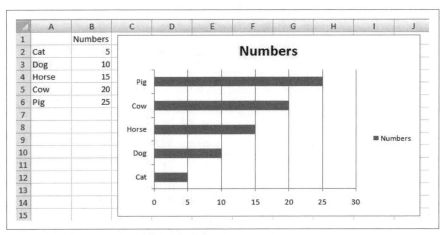

Figure 5-57. Data and basic bar chart formed automatically

Select the (X) axis and press Ctrl-1 to display the Format Axis dialog (or right-click to get there). Under Axis Options, select "Categories in reverse order" and "At maximum category" and click Close (pre-2007, select "At maximum category" and "Value (y) axis crosses at maximum category" and click OK). Your chart should now be reversed, labels and all, as shown in Figure 5-58.

—Andy Pope

HACK #69   Tornado Chart

A tornado chart (also known as a population pyramid) is not standard in Excel 2007, but you can easily create one by manipulating a simple bar chart.

ALL

A *tornado chart* displays two sets of data in a bar chart, with the two series emanating from a shared vertical axis. One of the series goes to the left, the other to the right.

First, set up some data as shown in Figure 5-59, and then follow these steps.

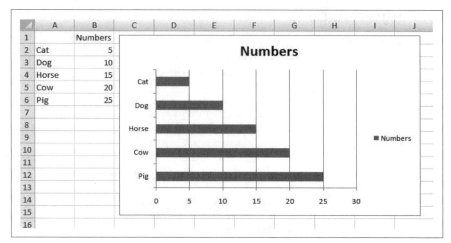

Figure 5-58. Bar chart with labels and series reversed

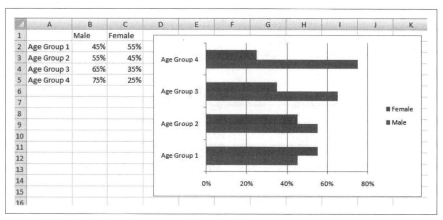

Figure 5-59. Simple bar chart created from A1:C5

Create a basic bar chart by selecting the data in A1:C5, choosing Insert → Charts → Bar, and clicking the first chart sub-type—the clustered 2D bar (pre-2007, use the Chart Wizard).

Select the Male series and move it to the secondary axis by right-clicking, and selecting Format Data Series → Series Options → Secondary Axis (pre-2007, double-click the Male series, select the Axis tab, and check Secondary axis).

Now, highlight the primary horizontal axis (the one at the bottom), right-click, select Format Axis → Axis Options (pre-2007, select Scale), and format as follows:

- Fixed Minimum value of −1

- Fixed Maximum value of 1
- Fixed Major Unit of 0.25

Your chart should look like Figure 5-60.

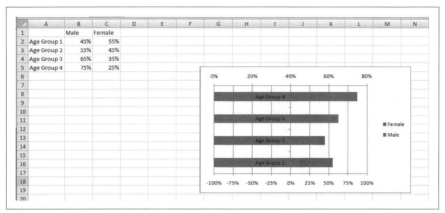

Figure 5-60. Tornado chart taking shape

Highlight the secondary horizontal axis, right-click, select Format Axis → Axis Options (pre-2007, select Scale), and format as follows:

- Fixed Minimum value of −1
- Fixed Maximum value of 1
- Fixed Major Unit of 0.25
- Values in reverse order
- Major Tick Marks type is None
- Axis Labels is None

Finally, to remove the negative horizontal axis labels, we can apply a custom number format to the axis. Highlight the axis, right-click and select format Axis. Select Number → Custom under the category menu. Enter the number format **0%;0%**.

The end product will be a completed tornado chart that cleverly displays your charted data, as shown in Figure 5-61.

—Andy Pope

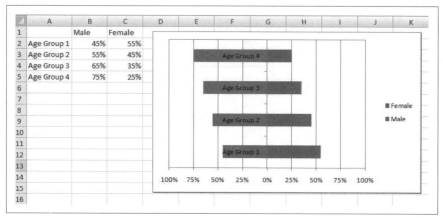

Figure 5-61. Completed tornado chart

Gauge Chart

Wouldn't it be nice if you could create a chart with a custom marker that you could use to display data in a smart, visually appealing way?

This hack creates a line chart with a custom marker using the pentagon shape, flipped horizontally.

Click in cell A2 and enter the word **Gauge**. Then, click in B2 and enter the number **3**. Select cells A2:B2 and choose Insert → Chart → Line. Click on the first chart with visual data points; i.e., the 2-D line with markers (pre-2007, use the Chart Wizard). Your chart should look similar to Figure 5-62.

Now, we need to add a shape to the sheet that we want to use for the gauges pointer. For this hack, we'll use the pentagon shape, flipped horizontally.

Select Insert → Illustrations → Insert → Shapes → Block Arrows (pre-2007, Insert → Picture → AutoShapes → Block Arrows), choose the pentagon shape, and draw a pentagon on your worksheet somewhere. Now, flip the pentagon on its side so the arrow is facing left, as shown in Figure 5-63. Do this by selecting the green circle (rotate tool) and dragging in the required direction.

Select the shape and copy it using Ctrl-C. Select the line series and paste the shape from the clipboard using Ctrl-V. As shown in Figure 5-64, the data series marker will take on the shape of the flipped pentagon and will move up and down in relation to the value in B2.

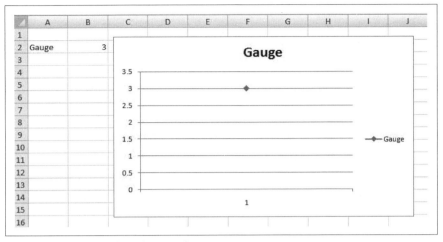

Figure 5-62. Created chart showing data point

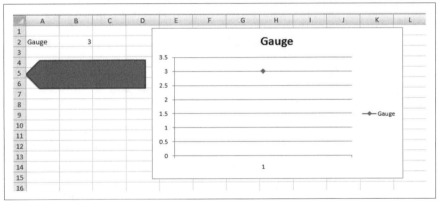

Figure 5-63. Pentagon shape created and rotated to point left

 You might want to change the vertical (Y) axis options Maximum and Minimum to get a better look, because the axis is created automatically.

—Andy Pope

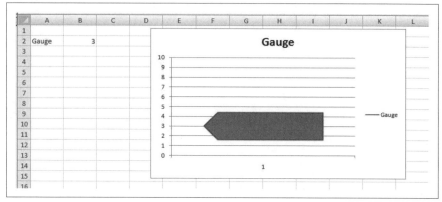

Figure 5-64. Completed chart with pentagon as marker

Conditional Highlighting Axis Labels

A snazzy trick would be to highlight X-axis category labels in a certain color when the data drops below a certain range. You can do this by creating a clustered column, then adding the data labels of two extra data series and plotting these extra series as lines.

Let's say you've created a chart and you want to show horizontal (X) axis value labels in red when your data drops below 25 and in blue when the data is above 25. Here is how you can do this.

Set up a spreadsheet like in Figure 5-65, which shows the data and formulas used to build the chart. The actual data for the column chart is in the range C3:C14. The formula in columns D and E test the data value and either output a zero or #N/A depending on the value typed in column C, and therefore determining whether a red or blue label should be displayed. Then complete the following steps.

Using this data will highlight horizontal (X) axis labels in red when the monthly data drops below 25.

1. First we need to create the basic chart, so highlight the data in C3:C14 and go to the Insert tab.
2. Under Chart options, select Columns and choose the first column chart (pre-2007, use the Chart Wizard; Insert → Chart).
3. Go to the Layout tab and choose Series Red Label from the drop-down menu under the current selection.

	A	B	C	D	E	F
1						
2			Data	Red Labels	Blue Labels	
3	Jan	82	=IF(C3<25,0,NA())	=IF(C3>=25,0,NA())	
4	Feb	99	=IF(C4<25,0,NA())	=IF(C4>=25,0,NA())	
5	Mar	81	=IF(C5<25,0,NA())	=IF(C5>=25,0,NA())	
6	Apr	50	=IF(C6<25,0,NA())	=IF(C6>=25,0,NA())	
7	May	4	=IF(C7<25,0,NA())	=IF(C7>=25,0,NA())	
8	Jun	35	=IF(C8<25,0,NA())	=IF(C8>=25,0,NA())	
9	Jul	76	=IF(C9<25,0,NA())	=IF(C9>=25,0,NA())	
10	Aug	67	=IF(C10<25,0,NA())	=IF(C10>=25,0,NA())	
11	Sep	15	=IF(C11<25,0,NA())	=IF(C11>=25,0,NA())	
12	Oct	18	=IF(C12<25,0,NA())	=IF(C12>=25,0,NA())	
13	Nov	63	=IF(C13<25,0,NA())	=IF(C13>=25,0,NA())	
14	Dec	16	=IF(C14<25,0,NA())	=IF(C14>=25,0,NA())	
15						
16						

Figure 5-65. Data and formulas used to build chart

4. Select Design → Type → Change Chart Type (pre-2007, right-click on the Red Label series and select Chart Type).

5. Select a Line chart from the menu presented.

6. Repeat Steps 1–5 for the Blue Label series.

> In pre-2007 versions, highlight the series, right-click, and select Chart Type.

7. Once again, go to the Layout tab, and select Series Red Label from the drop-down menu.

8. Choose Labels → Data Labels → More Data Label Options (pre-2007, double-click on the series and select Data Labels).

9. Check Category under Label Options.

10. Repeat Steps 7–9 for the Blue Label series.

> In Step 9, make sure that Value is *not* selected under Category name.

11. Yet again, go to the Layout tab, and select Series Red Label from the drop-down menu.

12. Select Data Labels → Below (pre-2007, right-click on the data series, select the Alignment tab, and change the Label Position to Below).

13. Repeat Steps 11 and 12 for the Blue Label series.

14. Highlight your original horizontal (X) axis, right-click your mouse, and select Format Axis (pre-2007, double-click the horizontal axis and select the Patterns tab).

15. Under Axis Options, set the Major tick mark style to None and the Axis Labels to None. This will clear the original axis.

16. Highlight the Red Labels data labels and go to the Home tab (pre-2007, use the Formatting toolbar).

17. Under Font, change the Font color to Red

18. Repeat Steps 16 and 17 with the Blue Labels, formatting the font color to blue.

Your final chart, with conditional highlighting, should look like Figure 5-66.

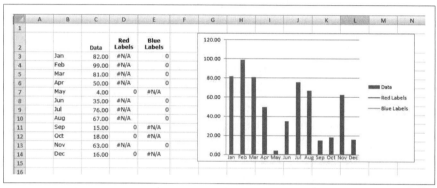

Figure 5-66. Chart with labels highlighted

—*Andy Pope*

Create Totals on a Stacked Column Chart
#72
Display the totals of stacked categories above the columns in a chart.

ALL

When you create a stacked chart, you can't normally show the total of each category in an easily distinguishable way. This hack allows you to show the totals of each category above the stacked columns of a chart.

Before you begin, you'll need to set up some data to work with, as shown in Figure 5-67.

Create a stacked column chart on the range A1:E7 by highlighting the range and selecting Insert → Charts → Columns (pre-2007, select the Chart Wizard tool from the standard toolbar and in Step 1 of the Wizard under Chart

	A	B	C	D	E
1		X	Y	Z	Total
2	a	7	6	4	17
3	b	2	2	2	6
4	c	3	3	3	9
5	d	4	4	4	12
6	e	5	5	5	15
7	f	6	6	6	18
8					

Figure 5-67. Data used to create the stacked column chart

Type). Choose Column, then select the second chart subtype (the stacked column chart). Your chart will appear as an object in your worksheet.

Select the Total series and then select Type → Change Chart Type (pre-2007, click the chart to select it, then go to Chart → Chart Type), choose Line, and click on a line chart with no markers. Click OK. Your chart should look like Figure 5-68.

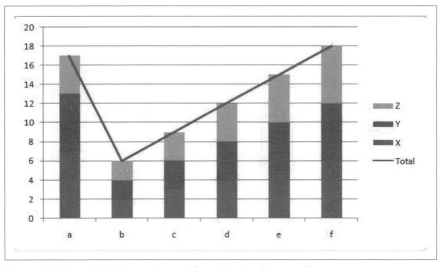

Figure 5-68. Stacked Column chart with total series shown as line

Now, you need to place some labels in your chart, so select the line series, right-click, and select Add Data Labels (pre-2007, right-click, choose Format Data Series → Labels → Show Value, and click OK). You should now have labels for your series, probably to the right, which is not the clean finish we are looking for.

Select the data labels again, right-click and select Format Data Labels →
Label Options → Label Position → Above, and then click Close (pre-2007,
right-click on one of the total numbers, and select Format Data Labels →
Alignment and set the Label Position to Outside End; on the Mac, set the
Label Position to Above).

Now we will get rid of the line and leave only the value labels showing.
Select the line again, right–click, and select Format Data Series → Line Color
→ No Line → Close (pre-2007, right-click and select Format Data Series,
select Patterns → Line → None → OK; on the Mac, go to "Colors and Lines"
and under "Line color," select "No line" and click OK).

Finally, remove the legend entry for the Total series. Two slow clicks on the
legend border will enable you to click inside the Legend. Delete the Total
series. Your chart should now look like the one in Figure 5-69.

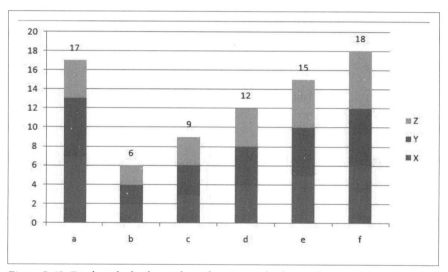

Figure 5-69. Final stacked column chart showing totals above columns

This enables you to now show your totals as well as your data without causing confusion.

—Andy Pope

Hacking Formulas and Functions

Hacks 73–105

Formulas and functions provide the logic that powers spreadsheets. Managing programming logic is always a challenge, but keeping track of programming logic across multiple cells, sheets, and workbooks can be particularly difficult, especially as spreadsheets grow and are reused. What's more, the formula and function capabilities built into Excel might not always be what you want, further complicating the situation. Fortunately, there are a lot of ways you can keep your formulas and functions sane.

Add Descriptive Text to Your Formulas

HACK #73
ALL

Excel's named ranges and cell comments can help clarify formulas, but sometimes you want to put documentation into the formula itself. With the hacks in this section, you can add descriptive text to your formulas quickly and easily.

Even when you have written various formulas and functions yourself, coming back to them at a later date often requires that you follow cell references to try to figure out what the formulas are doing. It would be great if you could simply add to the end of your formula some text that wouldn't interfere with the result, but would give you the information you require at a later stage.

The problem, of course, is that the moment you add or incorporate text into part of a formula, the result will no longer be numeric and cannot be used in further calculations. Excel does, however, provide one often-overlooked function that you can use to add descriptive text to formulas or functions.

Say you have the following formula in cell A11:

```
=SUM($A$1:$A$10)*$B$1
```

Assume $A$1:$A$10 houses various numeric results that represent totals for a particular month, and $B$1 contains a percentage value that represents a tax rate. You could add some descriptive text to the formula using Excel's N function:

```
=SUM($A$1:$A$10,N("Values for April"))*$B$1+N("Tax Rate for April")
```

Now you can determine what the formula is being used for simply by selecting this cell and looking in the Formula bar. The N function always will return a value of 0 for any text, and so does not interfere with the formula's result in any way.

HACK #74 Move Relative Formulas Without Changing References

In Excel, a formula reference can be either relative or absolute. Sometimes, however, you might want to reproduce the same formulas somewhere else in your worksheet or workbook, or on another sheet.

When a formula needs to be made absolute, type $ (a dollar sign) in front of the column letter and/or row number of the cell reference, as in $A$1 (or you can use the F4 key (⌘-T on the Mac) to toggle through the different types of reference style). Once you do this, no matter where you copy your formula, it will reference the same cells.

Sometimes, however, you might set up a lot of formulas that contain not absolute references, but relative references. You would usually do this so that when you copy the original cell formula down or across, the row and column references change accordingly.

Yet other times you might set up your formulas using a mix of relative and absolute references, and you want to reproduce the same formulas in another range on the same worksheet, another sheet in the same workbook, or perhaps another sheet in another workbook.

You can do all these things without changing any range references inside the formulas by following these steps:

1. Select the range of cells you want to copy.
2. Go to the Home tab and choose Editing → Find & Select → Replace (pre-2007, Edit → Replace...).
3. In the Find What: box, type = (an equals sign).
4. In the Replace With: box, type & (an ampersand), or any other symbol you are sure is not being used in any of the formulas.
5. Make sure the "Match Entire cell contents" option is not enabled, and click Replace All.
6. All the formulas will appear on your worksheet with an & in place of an =, so you can now copy your cells to any locations you wish.

7. After moving the cells, select Home → Editing → Find & Select → Replace (pre-2007, Edit → Replace...). This time, replace the & with an =.

When you're done, your formulas will reference the same cell references as the originals.

HACK
#75

ALL

Compare Two Excel Ranges

Spotting the differences between two large tables of data can be a very time-consuming task. Fortunately, there are at least two ways in which you can automate what would otherwise be a very tedious manual process.

The two methods you will use are methods we have used in the past when we received an updated copy of a spreadsheet and we needed to identify which cells in the updated copy differed from the ones in the original copy. Both methods save hours of tedious manual checking and, more importantly, eliminate the possibility of mistakes.

For the following examples, we copied the newer data onto the same sheet as the older data beforehand. Figure 6-1 shows how the data is presented as two ranges. Note that for easier viewing, we boldfaced the cells in Table 2 that are not the same as their counterparts in Table 1.

	A	B	C
1	**Name**	**Age**	**Area**
2	Bill	22	1a
3	Joe	33	1a
4	Frank	55	2c
5	Brad	48	3d
6	Mary	29	3d
7	Anne	45	4a
8			
9	**Name**	**Age**	**Area**
10	Bill	22	**2c**
11	Joe	33	1a
12	Frank	55	**2d**
13	Brad	**43**	3d
14	**Dave**	29	3d
15	Anne	45	4a

Figure 6-1. Two ranges to be compared

Method 1: Using True or False

The first method involves entering a simple formula into another range of the same size and shape. The best part about this method is that you can add the formula in one step without having to copy and paste.

To compare the ranges shown in Figure 6-1 we will array-enter a formula. First, select the range E1:G7, starting from cell E1 (which ensures that E1 is the active cell in the selection). With this range selected, click in the Formula bar and type the following and then press Ctrl-Enter:

```
=A1=A9
```

By pressing Ctrl and Enter at the same time, you are entering the relative reference formula into each cell of the selection. This is the standard method of entering a formula into an array of cells and having their references change appropriately, and is referred to as *array-entering* a formula.

The range E1:G7 should be filled with True (the same) and False (not the same) values.

If your two sets of data reside on different worksheets, you can use a third worksheet to store the True/False values simply by array-entering the formula. For example, assuming the second table of data is on Sheet2 and starts in cell A9, and the original table of data is on Sheet1 and starts in cell A1, on a third worksheet you can array-enter this formula:

```
=Sheet1!A1=Sheet2!A9
```

You might find it useful to adjust your zoom downward when working with large amounts of data.

Method 2: Using Conditional Formatting

Using conditional formatting is often preferred, as it is easier to make any needed changes once the comparison is made. However, with this method, both sets of data must reside on the same worksheet, which should entail only a simple copy and paste.

Again, assuming we're comparing the two ranges from Figure 6-1, select the range A1:C7, starting from cell A1. This ensures that A1 is the active cell in the selection.

With this range selected, select Home → Styles → Conditional Formatting → New Rule, choose "Use a formula to determine which cells to format" (pre-2007, Format → Conditional Formatting... → Select Formula Is), and under "Format values where this formula is true:" type the following formula:

```
=NOT(A1=A9)
```

Click the Format button, shown in Figure 6-2, and choose the format with which you want to highlight the differences.

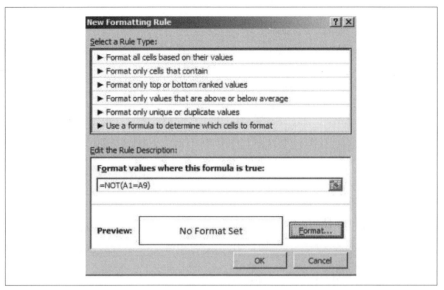

Figure 6-2. Conditional formatting dialog

Click OK and all the differences will be formatted according to the format you chose.

When or if you make any changes to your data, the cells' format will automatically revert back to normal if the cell content is the same as the cell in the other table.

HACK #76 Fill All Blank Cells in a List

Often, many people will leave a blank cell if the data for that cell is the same as the cell above it. Visually this makes lists easy to read, but structurally it is not a good idea. With the hacks in this section, you can fill all blank cells in a list quickly and easily.

Many of Excel's functions are designed to be used on lists. For most of these functions to work correctly, lists should not contain any blank cells, and column headings should be formatted differently from the data in the list.

When setting up data in Excel, it is good practice to ensure that all cells within a list are occupied. However, many lists are set up in a similar manner to the one shown in Figure 6-3.

Whereas prices are repeated in the Cost column, the types of fruits in the Fruits column are not. As discussed at the beginning of Chapter 1, this will create many problems when using features such as Subtotals and PivotTables. In most cases, Excel expects your related data will be set up in a continuous list or table, with no blank cells.

	A	B
1	Fruits	Cost
2	Apple	$1.25
3		$1.25
4	Banana	$2.55
5		$2.55
6		$2.55
7	Orange	$1.55
8		$1.55
9		$1.55
10	Strawberry	$4.55
11		

Figure 6-3. Worksheet list set up with blank cells

You can fill blank cells in a list by using a formula or by using a macro.

Method 1: Filling Blanks via a Formula

Say you have a list of entries in column A similar to Figure 6-3, and within the list you have many blank cells. Here is a quick and easy way to fill those blanks with the values of the cells above them.

Select all the data in column A, and then select Home → Editing → Find & Select → Go To Special (pre-2007, Edit → Go To...or hit Ctrl-G and choose Special). Check the Blanks option and click OK. At this point, you have selected only the empty cells within the list. Press the equals key (=), then the up arrow key. Holding down the Ctrl key, press Enter.

You can quickly convert formulas to values only by selecting column A in its entirety. Right-click and select Copy (Ctrl-C), right-click again and select Paste Special..., check the Values checkbox, and then click OK.

Method 2: Filling Blanks via a Macro

If you will be filling in blank cells frequently, you should consider handling this via a macro. The following macro makes this a breeze. To use it, select Alt/Option-F11, then select Insert → Module and enter the following code:

```
Sub FillBlanks()
Dim rRange1 As Range, rRange2 As Range
Dim lReply As Integer

 If Selection.Cells.Count = 1 Then
 MsgBox "You must select your list and include the blank cells", _
 vbInformation, "OzGrid.com"
 Exit Sub
 ElseIf Selection.Columns.Count > 1 Then
 MsgBox "You must select only one column", _
 vbInformation, "OzGrid.com"
 Exit Sub
 End If
```

```
Set rRange1 = Selection

On Error Resume Next
Set rRange2 = rRange1.SpecialCells(xlCellTypeBlanks)
On Error GoTo 0

If rRange2 Is Nothing Then
MsgBox "No blank cells Found", _
vbInformation, "OzGrid.com"
Exit Sub
End If

rRange2.FormulaR1C1 = "=R[-1]C"

lReply = MsgBox("Convert to Values", vbYesNo + vbQuestion, "OzGrid.com")
If lReply = vbYes Then rRange1 = rRange1.Value
End Sub
```

After entering this code, close the window to get back to Excel, and then save your workbook. Now go to the Developer tab and select Code → Macros or Alt/Option-F8 (pre-2007, Tools → Macro → Macros → FillBlanks → Run) or use Options to assign a shortcut key.

HACK #77 Make Your Formulas Increment by Rows When You Copy Across Columns

ALL Excel's automatic incrementing of cell references works well most of the time, but sometimes you might want to override how it works.

You might want to reference a single cell, such as cell A1, and then copy this reference across columns to the right. Naturally, this results in the formula reference changing to =B1, =C1, =D1, etc, which is not the desired result. You want the formula to increment by rows rather than columns—that is, =A1, =A2, =A3, etc.

Unfortunately, there is no option in Excel that lets you do this. However, you can get around this by using the INDIRECT function with the ADDRESS function nested inside.

Perhaps the best way to explain how to create the required function is to use an example with predictable results. In cells A1:A10, enter the numbers **1** through **10** in numerical order. Select cell D1, and in this cell enter the following:

```
=INDIRECT(ADDRESS(COLUMN(A:A),1))
```

As soon as you enter this, the number 1 should appear in cell D1. This is because the formula references cell A1.

If you copy this formula across the column to the right, cell E1 will contain the number 2. In other words, although you are copying across columns, the formula reference is incrementing by rows, as shown in Figure 6-4.

> This method is especially useful when a spreadsheet has headings going down rows in one column, and you want to create a dynamic reference to these row headings across other columns.

	D1	▾		fx	=INDIRECT(ADDRESS(COLUMN(A:A),1))			
	A	B	C	D	E	F	G	H
1	1			1	2	3	4	
2	2							
3	3							
4	4							
5	5							
6	6							
7	7							
8	8							
9	9							
10	10							
11								

Figure 6-4. The result of copying cell D1 to cell E1

If you keep copying this to the right, cell F1 will contain the number 3, cell G1 will contain the number 4, etc. This is a fairly straightforward process if you are referencing only a single cell. Many times, however, you will need to reference a range of cells that is being used in the argument for a function.

We'll use the ever-popular SUM function to demonstrate what we mean. Assume you receive a long list of numbers, and your job is to sum the column of numbers in a running total fashion, like this:

    =SUM($A$1:$A$2), =SUM($A$1:$A$3), =SUM($A$1:$A$4)

The problem occurs because the results need to be dynamic and to span across 100 columns on row 1 only, not down 100 rows in another column (as often would be the case).

Naturally, you could manually type such functions into each individual cell, but this would be very time-consuming. Instead, you can use the same principle as the one that you used when referencing a single cell.

Fill the range A1:A100 with the numbers **1** through **100** in numeric order. Enter **1** into cell A1, select cell A1, hold down the Ctrl key, left-click, and drag down 100 rows with the fill handle.

Select cell D1 and enter this formula:

```
=SUM(INDIRECT("A1:" &ADDRESS(COLUMN(A:A),1)))
```

This will give you a result of 1, which is the sum of cells A1:A1. Copy this formula across to cell E1 and you will get a result of 3, which is the sum of cells A1:A2. Copy to cell F1 and you will get a result of 6, which is the sum of cells A1:A3, and so forth, as shown in Figure 6-5.

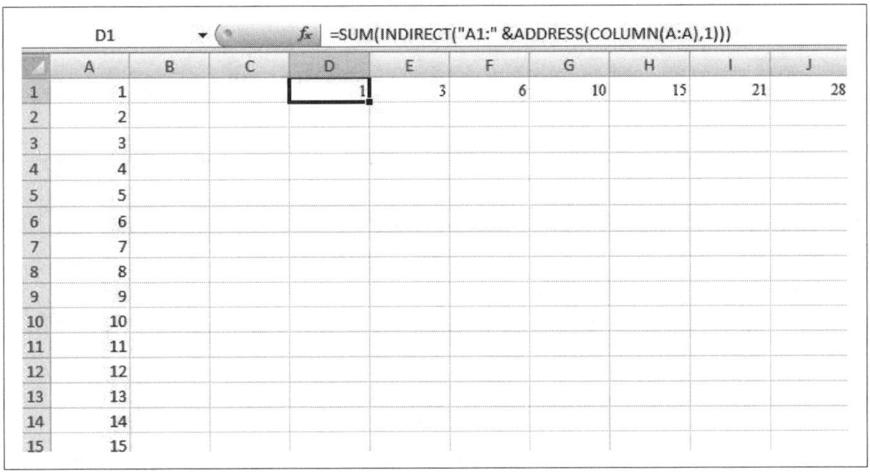

	D1		▼	*fx*	=SUM(INDIRECT("A1:" &ADDRESS(COLUMN(A:A),1)))					
	A	B	C	D	E	F	G	H	I	J
1	1			1	3	6	10	15	21	28
2	2									
3	3									
4	4									
5	5									
6	6									
7	7									
8	8									
9	9									
10	10									
11	11									
12	12									
13	13									
14	14									
15	15									

Figure 6-5. The result of copying cell D1 to cell F1

The volatile COLUMN function caused the last cell reference to increment by 1 each time you copied it across to a new column. This is because the COLUMN function always returns the column number (not letter) of the cell that houses it unless you reference a different cell.

Alternatively, you can use the Paste Special... → Transpose feature in Excel. Add the formula **=SUM($A$1:$A2)** to cell B1 (note the relative row absolute column reference to $A2), and then copy this formula down to cell B100 (a double-click on your fill handle will do this). With B1:B100 selected, copy, select cell D1 (or any cell that has 100 or more columns to the right), and then right-click and select Paste Special... → Transpose. If you like, you can delete the formulas in B2:B100.

Convert Dates to Excel Formatted Dates

#78

ALL

Dates imported from other programs frequently cause problems in Excel. Many people manually retype them, but there are easier ways to solve the problem.

Let's look at some of the date formats you might encounter and how to convert them to standard Excel dates.

As Figure 6-6 shows, the formulas in column B convert the data in column A to three results in column C, all of which follow the U.S. date format of *mm/dd/yy*.

> The format of the data in column A must be text and your PC must be set to American dates for this to work.

	A	B	C
1	Old Date	Formula Used	New Date
2	112307	=VALUE(MID(A2,3,2)&"/"&LEFT(A2,2)&"/"&RIGHT(A2,2))	11-23-07
3	071123	=VALUE(RIGHT(A3,2)&"/"&MID(A3,3,2)&"/"&LEFT(A3,2))	11-23-07
4	231107	=VALUE(LEFT(A4,2)&"/"&MID(A4,3,2)&"/"&RIGHT(A4,2))	11-23-07
5			

Figure 6-6. Date formats converted to valid dates (U.S. format)

Figure 6-7 shows the same approach at work, except that the cells in column C were formatted with the European date format of dd/mm/yy, so use this if your PC is set to European dates.

	A	B	C
1	Old Date	Formula Used	New Date
2	112307	=VALUE(MID(A2,3,2)&"/"&LEFT(A2,2)&"/"&RIGHT(A2,2))	23-11-07
3	071123	=VALUE(RIGHT(A3,2)&"/"&MID(A3,3,2)&"/"&LEFT(A3,2))	23-11-07
4	231107	=VALUE(LEFT(A4,2)&"/"&MID(A4,3,2)&"/"&RIGHT(A4,2))	23-11-07
5			

Figure 6-7. Date formats converted to valid dates (European format)

Hopefully, these nifty formulas will take some of the stress out of working with imported dates.

Sum or Count Cells While Avoiding Error Values

#79

Error values are useful warnings, but sometimes you need to do calculations despite the errors. Choosing functions that tolerate errors will let you do this.

ALL

When a range of cells contains one or more error values, most formulas that reference that range of cells also will return an error. You can overcome this frustration by using the DSUM function.

Assume you have a long list of numbers for which you need to get the sum total. However, one of the cells, for whatever reason, is returning the #N/A error.

Set up some data such as that shown in Figure 6-8.

	A	B
1	**Numbers1**	**Numbers2**
2	#N/A	#N/A
3	1	1
4	2	2
5	3	3
6	4	4
7	5	5
8	6	6
9	7	7
10	8	8
11	9	9
12		

Figure 6-8. Data set up to generate #N/A error message

To generate the #N/A error, enter the formula =**NA( )** in cells A2 and B2. Cell A12 uses a standard SUM function that sums cells A2:A11, and because cell A2 has the #N/A error, the SUM function also returns #N/A. The range D1: D2 has been named Criteria and is used as the last argument in the DSUM function, which resides in cell B12.

The syntax for the DSUM function (and all the database functions) is as follows:

```
=DSUM(database,field,criteria)
```

The *database* argument identifies the range of cells that comprise the list or database. Within the database range, rows of related information are treated as records, while columns of data are treated as fields. The first row contains labels for all the columns.

The *field* argument indicates which column is used in the function. The column can be identified by name using the labels at the top of the column, or it can be identified by position. The first column is 1, the fourth column is 4, and so on.

The *criteria* argument identifies a range of cells containing conditions. The range used for the criteria must include at least one column label plus at least one cell below the column label that specifies a condition for the column.

So, in cell B12, enter the following formula:

```
=DSUM($B$1:$B$11,$B$1,Criteria)
```

You should get the result of 45, which is the sum of cells B3 to B11. B1 and B2 are ignored, even though they are included in the range, as shown in Figure 6-9.

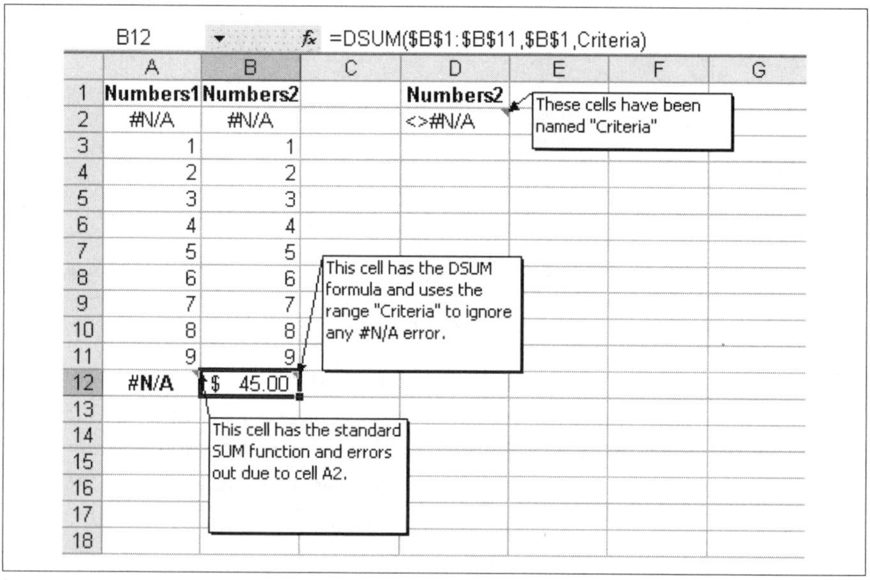

	A	B	C	D	E	F	G
	B12		fx	=DSUM($B$1:$B$11,$B$1,Criteria)			
1	Numbers1	Numbers2		Numbers2	These cells have been		
2	#N/A	#N/A		<>#N/A	named "Criteria"		
3		1	1				
4		2	2				
5		3	3				
6		4	4				
7		5	5	This cell has the DSUM			
8		6	6	formula and uses the			
9		7	7	range "Criteria" to ignore			
10		8	8	any #N/A error.			
11		9	9				
12	#N/A	$ 45.00					
13							
14		This cell has the standard					
15		SUM function and errors					
16		out due to cell A2.					
17							
18							

Figure 6-9. Using the DSUM function to ignore a number of different errors

If the data you want to sum will likely contain a variety of different kinds of errors, you might need to consider using the DSUM function with a wide range of criteria to accommodate the possible errors. However, it is always best to address the error at the source and eliminate it whenever possible rather than work around it.

Excel has a rich set of database functions, and you can use any one of them in the same way. Consider using the same method for DCOUNT, DCOUNTA, DMAX, DMIN, DPRODUCT, etc.

HACK #80 Reduce the Impact of Volatile Functions on Recalculation

ALL

Volatile functions, which must be recalculated almost every time the user performs an action in Excel, can waste an enormous amount of time. Although volatile functions are too useful to discard entirely, there are ways to reduce the delays they create.

A *volatile function* is simply a function that will recalculate each time any action is performed in Excel, such as entering data, changing column widths, etc. (One of the few actions that will not trigger a recalculation of a volatile function is changing a cell's formatting, unless you do this via Paste Special... → Formats.)

Probably the most well-known of all volatile functions are the TODAY and the NOW functions. Because the TODAY function returns the current date, and the NOW function returns the current date and time, it is vital that both of them recalculate often. If you have a worksheet that contains many volatile functions, however, you could be forcing Excel to perform many unnecessary recalculations on a continuous basis. This problem can worsen when you have volatile functions nested within nonvolatile functions, as the formula as a whole will become volatile.

To see what we mean, assume you have a worksheet that is using the TODAY function in a 20-column-by-500-row table. This will mean you have 10,000 volatile functions in your workbook when a single one could accomplish the same job.

Rather than nesting 10,000 TODAY functions within each cell of your table, in most cases you can simply enter the TODAY function into an out-of-the-way cell, name it TodaysDate (or just use the cell identifier) or another applicable name, and then reference TodaysDate in all your functions.

> A quick and easy way to do this is to select the entire table and then select Find & Select → Replace..... under Editing options on the Home tab (pre-2007, go to Edit → Replace...) and replace TODAY( ) with TodaysDate in all your formulas.

You will now have one TODAY function in place of the 10,000 you would have had otherwise.

As another example, say the first 500 rows of column B are filled with a relative formula such as =TODAY( )-A1, and the first 500 rows of column A have different dates that are less than today's date. You are forcing Excel to recalculate the volatile TODAY function 499 times more than necessary each time you do something in Excel! By placing the TODAY function in any cell and naming the cell TodaysDate (or something similar), you can use = TodaysDate-A1. Now Excel needs to recalculate only the one occurrence of the TODAY function, resulting in a much lower performance hit.

HACK #81 Count Only One Instance of Each Entry in a List

When you have a large list of items, you might want to perform a count on the items without counting entries that appear multiple times. With this hack, you can count each unique entry only once.

ALL

There are a few different ways to make this hack work, depending on which version of Excel you're using and how you want to go about it. First we discuss a method for pre-2007 versions of Excel, followed by an alternative that works in Excel 2007 as well as older versions, and finally a method that uses a pivot table.

Before Excel 2007

Consider the list in Figure 6-10, which has been sorted so that you can see multiple entries easily.

	A
1	**Names**
2	Bill W
3	Bill W
4	Bob G
5	Dave H
6	Dave H
7	Fran T
8	Fran T
9	Frank W
10	Frank W
11	George H
12	Harry O
13	Mark W
14	Mary O
15	Mary O
16	Peter G
17	Raina H

Figure 6-10. Range of sorted names

A normal count on this list (using COUNTA) would result in the names Bill W, Dave H, Fran T, Frank W, and Mary O being counted more that once. The DCOUNTA function offers an alternative that is very efficient and easy to modify.

The syntax of the DCOUNTA function is as follows:

```
DCOUNTA(database,field,criteria),
```

 The arguments for this function are the same as those for the DSUM function described in "Convert Dates to Excel Formatted Dates" [Hack #78].

Building on the preceding list, in cell D1 enter the word **Criteria** (or any heading that is *not* the same as the field or column heading). Below this, in cell D2, enter this formula:

```
=COUNTIF($A$2:A2,A2)=1
```

Note the combination of relative (A2) references and absolute ($A$2) references! These are vital to the criteria working.

Now, in the cell where you want your result shown, enter this function:

```
=DCOUNTA($A$1:$A$100,1,$D$1:$D$2)
```

This will use the criteria to exclude duplicates and give you the result you need, which is 11, as there are 11 unique names.

Excel 2007

If you tried the previous steps in Excel 2007, you would get the answer of 2, which is incorrect. Try this, which also works in pre-2007 versions.

In any cell to the right of your list, place the following array formula:

```
=SUM(1/COUNTIF(A2:A17,A2:A17))
```

Press Ctrl-Shift-Enter to enter this formula as an array. This will return the correct results from the range A2:A17.

Using a Pivot Table

To use a pivot table to glean the same results, select Insert → Pivot Table and drag the word Names down to the row labels area (this is called Data Items in older versions). This will produce a list of unique names from the list. You could then use a formula like this:

```
=COUNTA(A3:A15)-2
```

The -2 takes care of the two labels that the pivot table produces.

You could also drag the Names field to the Values area of the Pivot Table Field list, thereby creating a count of the names in the range A2:A17.

Sum Every Second, Third, or Nth Row or Cell

HACK
#82

ALL

Every now and then you might want to sum every second, third, fourth, etc., cell in a spreadsheet. Now you can, with the following hack.

Excel has no standard function that will sum every *n*th cell or row. However, you can accomplish this in a number of different ways. All these approaches use the ROW function and the MOD function.

The ROW function returns the row number of a single cell reference:

    ROW(*reference*)

The MOD function returns the remainder after *number* is divided by *divisor*:

    MOD(*number*,*divisor*)

Nest the ROW function within the MOD function (to supply the number argument), divide it by 2 (to sum every second cell), and check to see whether the result is 0 (zero). If it is, the cell is summed.

You can use these functions in numerous ways—some of them producing better results than others.

Using an Array Formula

You could use an array formula to SUM every second cell in the range $A$1:$A$10; for example:

    =SUM(IF(MOD(ROW($A$1:$A$10),2)=0,$A$1:$A$10,0))

Because this is an array formula, you must enter it by pressing Ctrl-Shift-Enter. Excel will add the curly brackets so that it looks like this:

    {=SUM(IF(MOD(ROW($A$1:$A$10),2)=0,$A$1:$A$10,0))}

You must let Excel add the curly brackets, as adding them yourself will cause the array formula to fail.

Although this will do the job, it is not good spreadsheet design to use this method. It is an unnecessary use of an array formula. To make matters worse, it has the volatile ROW function nested within it, making the whole array formula volatile. This means the formula would constantly recalculate whenever you are working in the workbook. This is a bad way to go!

Using SUMPRODUCT

Here's another formula you can use, which is a slightly better choice:

```
=SUMPRODUCT(((MOD(ROW($A$1:$A$10),2)=0)*($A$1:$A$10)))
```

You should, however, be aware that this formula will return #VALUE! if any cells in the range contain text rather than numbers. This formula, although not a true array, also will slow down Excel if too many instances of it are used, or if those instances reference a large range.

Fortunately, there is a much better way that is not only more efficient, but also far more flexible.

Using DSUM

Using the DSUM function is perhaps the best choice. For this example, we used the range A1:A10 as the range for which we need to sum every nth cell.

Enter the word **Criteria** in cell E1. In cell E2, enter this formula:

```
=MOD(ROW(A2)-$C$2,$C$2)=0
```

Select cell C2 and then select Data → Data Tools → Data Validation (pre-2007, Data → Validation). Select List from the Allow: box, and in the Source: box, type: **2,3,4,5,6,7,8,9,10**. Ensure that the In-Cell drop-down box is checked and click OK.

> Using the MOD function will omit row 1, hence the validation list starts from 2.

In cell C1, enter **SUM every...**. In any cell after row 1, enter this formula:

```
=DSUM($A:$A,1,$E$1:$E$2)
```

In the cell directly above where you entered the DSUM function, enter this:

```
="Summing Every " & $C$2 &
CHOOSE($C$2,"st","nd","rd","th","th","th","th","th","th","th") & " Cell"
```

Now all you need to do is choose the desired number from cell C2 and the DSUM function will do the rest.

As you can see from Figure 6-11, you can use one DSUM function to sum each cell at the interval you specify. The DSUM function is a far more efficient formula than an array formula or the SUMPRODUCT function. Although setup can take a little more time, it's really a case of a little pain for a lot of gain.

	A	B	C	D	E	F	G
1	**Numbers**		SUM every....		**Criteria**	This cell **cannot** have
2	$ 5.00				FALSE	the same heading as our
3	$ 7.50		**Summing Every 3rd Cell**			numbers.
4	$ 23.45		$ 35.46			
5	$ 10.00					
6	$ 9.96					
7	$ 6.00					

Figure 6-11. Possible end result with formatting

Find the Nth Occurrence of a Value

#83 Excel's built-in lookup functions can do some pretty clever stuff, but unfortunately Excel has no single function that will return the nth occurrence
ALL of specified data. Fortunately, there are ways to make Excel do this.

You can use Excel's lookup and reference functions on a table of data to extract details corresponding to a specified value. Perhaps the most popular of these Excel functions is VLOOKUP. Although VLOOKUP is great for finding a specified value in the leftmost column of a table, you cannot use it to find the *n*th occurrence in the leftmost column.

You can, however, use a very simple method to find any specified occurrence you choose when using VLOOKUP, or one of the other lookup functions.

For this example, we will assume you have a two-column table of data, with column A housing first names and column B their corresponding ages, as shown in Figure 6-12.

You can use a VLOOKUP function to extract a person's age based on his name. Unfortunately, some names occur more than once. You want to be able to look up the name Dave and have the VLOOKUP function find not the first occurrence, but rather, subsequent occurrences of the name. Here is how you can do this (remember, in this example, data is in columns A and B).

First, select column A in its entirety by clicking the letter A at the column head. Then, right-click and select Insert to insert a blank column (which will become column A). Click in cell A2 (skipping A1 because B1 is a heading), and enter this formula:

```
=B2&COUNTIF($B$2:B2,B2)
```

Copy this down as many rows as you have data in column B (click back in cell A2 and double-click the fill handle). You will end up with names such as Dave1, Dave2, Dave3, etc., as shown in Figure 6-13. Note the absolute reference to $B$2 in the COUNTIF function and the use of a relative reference for all references. This is vital to the function working correctly.

	A	B
1	**Names**	**Ages**
2	Fred	20
3	Joe	25
4	Dave	18
5	James	22
6	Dave	13
7	Reece	15
8	Jill	19
9	Robyn	18
10	Marlene	17
11	Dave	25
12	Tania	23
13	Bob	24
14	Wendy	22
15	Aleisha	20
16	Kate	18
17	Dave	19
18	Jack	21
19	Bill	23

Figure 6-12. Data setup for VLOOKUP

	A	B	C
1		**Names**	**Ages**
2	Fred1	Fred	20
3	Joe1	Joe	25
4	Dave1	Dave	18
5	James1	James	22
6	Dave2	Dave	13
7	Reece1	Reece	15
8	Jill1	Jill	19
9	Robyn1	Robyn	18
10	Marlene1	Marlene	17
11	Dave3	Dave	25
12	Tania1	Tania	23
13	Bob1	Bob	24
14	Wendy1	Wendy	22
15	Aleisha1	Aleisha	20
16	Kate1	Kate	18
17	Dave4	Dave	19
18	Jack1	Jack	21
19	Bill1	Bill	23

Figure 6-13. Data with VLOOKUP formula added to column A

If you haven't guessed already, now you can use column A as the column to find the *n*th occurrence of any name.

Click in cell D2 and enter in the following formula:

```
=VLOOKUP("Dave3",$A$1:$C$100,3,FALSE)
```

The formula will return the age for the third occurrence of the name Dave, as shown in Figure 6-14.

	A	B	C	D
1		**Names**	**Ages**	
2	Fred1	Fred	20	25
3	Joe1	Joe	25	
4	Dave1	Dave	18	
5	James1	James	22	
6	Dave2	Dave	13	
7	Reece1	Reece	15	
8	Jill1	Jill	19	
9	Robyn1	Robyn	18	
10	Marlene1	Marlene	17	
11	Dave3	Dave	25	
12	Tania1	Tania	23	
13	Bob1	Bob	24	
14	Wendy1	Wendy	22	
15	Aleisha1	Aleisha	20	
16	Kate1	Kate	18	
17	Dave4	Dave	19	
18	Jack1	Jack	21	
19	Bill1	Bill	23	

Figure 6-14. Data with second VLOOKUP formula added to column D

You can, of course, hide column A from view, as you do not need to see it.

You also can use the names in column A as the Source range for a list in another cell by selecting Data → Data Tools (pre-2007, Data → Validation → List). Then reference the cell housing this list in your VLOOKUP function.

Make the Excel Subtotal Function Dynamic
HACK #84

ALL

Although SUBTOTAL is one of Excel's most convenient functions, you sometimes want to choose the function it uses, or apply it to data that can expand and contract.

You use the SUBTOTAL function in Excel to perform a specified function on a range of cells that have had AutoFilters applied to them. When the AutoFilter has been applied, the SUBTOTAL function will use only the visible cells; all hidden rows are ignored. The operation it performs depends solely on the number (between 1 and 11) that you supply to its first argument, Function_num. For example:

    =SUBTOTAL(1,A1:A100)

will average all visible cells in the range A1:A100 after AutoFilters have been applied. If all rows in A1:A100 are visible, it will simply average them all and give the same result as:

```
=AVERAGE(A1:A100)
```

The number for the first SUBTOTAL argument, Function_num, and its corresponding functions are as shown in Table 6-1.

Table 6-1. SUBTOTAL function numbers and their corresponding functions

Function_Num	Function
1	AVERAGE
2	COUNT
3	COUNTA
4	MAX
5	MIN
6	PRODUCT
7	STDEV
8	STDEVP
9	SUM
10	VAR
11	VARP

Because you need to use only a number between 1 and 11, you can have one SUBTOTAL function perform whatever function you choose. You even can choose from a drop-down list that resides in any cell. Here is how to do this.

Add all the function names, in the same order as in Table 6-1, to a range of cells. For this example, we will use D1:D11. With this range selected, click the Name box (the white box on the left of the Formula bar) and type the name **Subs**. Then click Enter.

Select column D in its entirety and then right-click and select Hide. Now, select Developer → Controls → Insert → Form Controls (pre-2007, View → Toolbars → Forms), click the ComboBox control, and then click cell C2.

Use the size handles to size the ComboBox so that it can display the longest function name—i.e., AVERAGE.

> To have your ComboBox automatically snap to the size of the column and row it resides in, hold down your Alt key at the same time as you size the ComboBox.

Right-click the ComboBox and choose Format Control, then the Control tab. In the Input range, type **Subs**. In the Cell-Link box, type **$C$2**. Now change the drop-down lines to **11**. In cell G1, enter this formula:

```
=IF($C$2="","","Result of "&INDEX(Subs,$C$2))
```

In cell G2, enter this formula:

```
=IF($C$2="","",SUBTOTAL($C$2,$A$4:$A$100))
```

where $A$4:$A$100 is the range on which the SUBTOTAL should act.

Now all you need to do is select the required SUBTOTAL function from the ComboBox and the correct result will be displayed, as shown in Figure 6-15.

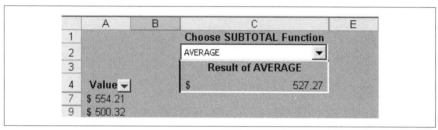

Figure 6-15. An adjustable SUBTOTAL

Add Date Extensions

#85

Excel's date formats consist of many different formats that you can use to display a date. However, one format that has always been lacking in Excel— and still does not exist—is the ability to display a date as 15th October 2007. You can make Excel do this if you need it.

The use of the "th" after the digits 15 is the one format Excel does not have. To make matters even worse, as far as we are aware, it is not possible to set a custom format to display the date in this manner. Although most people simply accept that this is not possible, here is a way you can accomplish it.

On a clean worksheet, starting in cell A1, make the following entries: A1=**st**, A2=**nd**, A3=**rd**, A4:A20=**th**, A21=**st**, A22=**nd**, A23=**rd**, A24:A30=**th**, A31=**st**.

Name this range Extensions and then right-click and select Name a Range (pre-2007, users Insert → Name → Define), and in the Names in Workbook: box, type **MyToday**. In the "Refers to": box, enter the following formula:

```
=TEXT(TODAY(),"dddd d")&INDEX(Extensions,DAY(TODAY()),1) & TEXT(TODAY(),"
mmmm yyyy")
```

Click Add, then OK.

Now, in any cell, simply enter **=MyToday**, and the current date always will display with the format Thursday 16th October 2007, or whatever date it happens to be.

If you would rather not use cells on a worksheet to store date extensions (th, st, rd, nd), you can use the CHOOSE function to house them. To do this, right-click, go to Names in Workbook (pre-2007, Insert → Name → Define), and enter the word **TheDay** in the Names in Workbook: box.

In the "Refers to:" box, enter this formula:

```
=THEDAY(TODAY())
```

Click OK. Right-click again, go back to the Names in Workbook: box and enter the word **MyToday2**.

In the "Refers to:" box, enter the following formula, and click Add:

```
=TEXT(TODAY(),"dddd
d")&IF(TheDay=31,"st",IF(TheDay=30,"th",CHOOSE(TheDay,"st","nd","rd","th",
"th","th","th","th","th","th","th","th","th","th","th","th","th","th","th",
"th","st","nd","rd","th","th","th","th","th","th")))&TEXT(TODAY()," mmmm
yyyy").
```

After you click OK, you can enter **=MyToday2** into any cell in which you want to display this format of date.

> The date returned by the use of either of these functions will not be a true numeric date as far as Excel is concerned; it will simply be a text entry, meaning you will not be able to reference the cell housing it in any formula that expects numeric data.

HACK #86 Convert Numbers with the Negative Sign on the Right to Excel Numbers

ALL

Have you ever had to work with imported negative numbers that have the negative sign on the right? SAP is one such program that does this with negative numbers—e.g., 200- instead of -200. Changing these by hand so that Excel understands them can be a hassle, but it doesn't need to be.

Say you have a long list of numbers you just imported and some of them are those so-called negative numbers. Your job is to convert these to valid negatives that Excel will recognize. For the purposes of this exercise, you will use the range A1:A100. In cell B1, enter this formula:

```
=SUBSTITUTE(IF(RIGHT(TRIM(A1))="-",RIGHT(TRIM(A1))&A1,A1),"-","",2)+0
```

Enter this as many cells down the column as needed and then copy them and select cell A1. Right-click and select Paste Special... → Values to remove the formula and retain the values only. Figure 6-16 shows a before-and-after example (A1:A7 represents before).

	A	B
1	200-	-200
2	150	150
3	356-	-356
4	200	200
5	526	526
6	301-	-301
7	258	258

Figure 6-16. Before and after moving the negative sign

To give you an idea of how the formula works, enter the following formula in any cell where A1 has the text 200-:

```
=RIGHT(TRIM(A1),1)&A1
```

You will end up with -200-.

The TRIM function simply ensures that there are no space characters in the cell. As you end up with -200-, you need to remove the second occurrence of the negative sign. This is what the SUBSTITUTE function is doing. You told it to substitute the second occurrence of - with "" (empty text). The result returned is actually text (as that is what the SUBSTITUTE function returns), so you simply use +0, and Excel will convert it to a number.

If you need to do this frequently, you should consider a macro to make the job easier. Here is one that will do the task at hand. It has been optimized for speed:

```
Sub ConvertMirrorNegatives()
Dim rCell As Range
Dim rRange As Range
Dim lCount As Long
Dim lLoop As Long

'Ensure they have the data selected and display a message if they _
 don't, then exit the macro.
If Selection.Cells.Count = 1 Then
 MsgBox "Please select the range to convert", vbInformation
 Exit Sub
End If

'Set a variable to ONLY text cells, e.g., 200-
On Error Resume Next
Set rRange = Selection.SpecialCells(xlCellTypeConstants, xlTextValues)

'If our variable returns Nothing, there are no incorrect negatives _
 so display a message, then exit the macro
```

```
If rRange Is Nothing Then
 MsgBox "No mirror negatives found", vbInformation
 On Error GoTo 0
 Exit Sub
End If

'Count just how many cells are like 200- and pass this number _
 to a variable to control how many loops are needed.
 lCount = WorksheetFunction.CountIf(Selection, "*-")
 'Set a variable to the first cell in the selection
Set rCell = Selection.Cells(1, 1)

 'Loop only as many times as there are incorrect negatives
 For lLoop = 1 To lCount
 'At each loop set a variable to the cell housing *-
 'The asterisk is a wildcard character
 Set rCell = rRange.Find(What:="*-", After:=rCell, _
 LookIn:=xlValues, LookAt:=xlPart, _
 SearchOrder:=xlByRows, SearchDirection:= _
 xlNext, MatchCase:=False)
 'Use the standard Replace feature to replace the negative sign _
 with nothing. In other words, we remove it.
 rCell.Replace What:="-", Replacement:=""
 'Multiply the cell by -1 to convert it to a negative number
 rCell = rCell * -1
 Next lLoop

 On Error GoTo 0
 End Sub
```

To use this macro, press Alt/Option-F11 or right-click the sheet tab and select View Code (pre-2007, go to Tools → Macro → Visual Basic Editor). Now, select Insert → Module and paste in the preceding code. Close the window to return to Excel, save your workbook, press Alt-F8, and then select ConvertMirrorNegatives. Click Options and assign a shortcut key. Now when you have to convert those imported negatives to true negatives that Excel will recognize, simply select the figures and use your shortcut key.

HACK #87 Display Negative Time Values

Sometimes you want to display negative time values, but Excel will only display ######. There are several ways to escape this problem.

ALL

If you enter the time **12:00:00** (midday) into any cell and then format it as General, you will see that it has a numeric value of 0.5. Similarly, enter the time **24:00:00** in any cell. Look in the Formula bar and you will see that Excel shows 1/1/1900 12:00:00 AM.

Excel sees dates and times as nothing more than numbers. In the case of a date, by default Excel considers 1 January 1900 to have a numeric value of

1; 2 January 1900 a numeric value of 2; and so forth. Times are seen as decimals, with the exception of midnight, which has a numeric value of 1 (see "Hack Excel's Date and Time Features" **[Hack #39]** for full details). Because of this, Excel has real trouble coping with the notion of negative time.

Here are three methods to get Excel to display negative time values.

Method 1: Changing Excel's Default Date System

One quick and easy way to display negative values is to simply press the Office button, go to Advanced (pre-2007, Tools → Options → Calculation; on the Mac, Excel → Preferences... → Calculation), and check the "Use 1904 date system" checkbox. Enter **5:00:00 AM** in cell A2. In cell A3, enter **6:00:00 AM**. In cell A4, type **=A2-A3**.

You will get the result of -1:00, but only if you checked the 1904 date system checkbox as described.

> The 1904 date system is also called Macintosh dates and times.

Now you will be able to subtract times from each other and have the result displayed as a negative time value.

> Be aware that doing this will cause Excel to change the starting dates from which all cells are calculated from 1 January 1900 to 2 January 1904. Changing this option will affect only the workbook in which you make the change.

If changing Excel's default date system to the 1904 date system is likely to cause problems within the workbook for other time calculations, you need to use another method that will change the appearance of a cell housing a negative value.

Method 2: Using the TEXT Function

The second method requires the use of the TEXT function. To begin, enter **5:00:00 AM** in cell A2. In cell A3, enter **6:00:00 AM**. In cell A4, type the following:

```
=TEXT(MAX($A$2:$A$3)-MIN($A$2:$A$3),"-H::MM")
```

With this nested formula, you are subtracting A3 from A2 to give a positive time value. Then you are formatting the cell using the TEXT function so that it shows a negative time. Using the combination of the MAX and MIN functions ensures that you are always subtracting the earlier time from the later time.

You need to be aware that the result returned is actually a text value, not a numeric value, in case you intend to use the result in another formula.

Method 3: Using a Custom Format

One final way you can display negative times, without changing to the 1904 date system and still returning a true numeric value, is to select Home → Cells → Format Cells tab, or right-click and go to Format Cells (pre-2007, Format → Cells). Select the Custom option under Category and use a Custom format of -h:mm.

This method works *only* if you always want a negative time value displayed. It also requires that you always subtract the earlier time from the later time. This means *all* times returned really will be positive and will only appear negative.

So, by using any one of these three methods, you will be able to display negative times. Just remember that there are pitfalls to each of them, so always use them with these pitfalls in mind.

Use the VLOOKUP Function Across Multiple Tables

HACK #88

ALL

Although VLOOKUP itself is very handy, it is restricted to looking in a specified table to return a result, which sometimes is not enough. You can escape this limitation with the INDIRECT function.

Sometimes you might need to use a single VLOOKUP formula to look in different tables of data in a spreadsheet. One way in which you can do this is to nest several VLOOKUP functions together, telling them to look into a specified table depending on a number that you enter into another cell. For instance:

```
=IF(A1=1,VLOOKUP(B1,Table1,2,FALSE),IF(A1=2,VLOOKUP(B1,Table2,2,FALSE),""))
```

In this formula, you tell the VLOOKUP function to look in the named range Table1 if A1 contains the number 1 (IF(A1=1, VLOOKUP(B1,Table1,2,FALSE)), and to look in the named range Table2 if A1 contains the number 2 (IF(A1=2,VLOOKUP(B1,Table2,2,FALSE)).

As you can imagine, the formula will become very large and unwieldy if you use more than two nested IF functions. The following formula, for instance, uses only five nested functions, but it is very daunting!

```
=IF(A1=1,VLOOKUP(B1,Table1,2,FALSE),IF(A1=2,VLOOKUP(B1,Table2,2,FALSE),
IF(A1=3,VLOOKUP(B1,Table2,3,FALSE),IF(A1=4,VLOOKUP(B1,Table4,2,FALSE),
IF(A1=5,VLOOKUP(B1,Table5,2,FALSE),"")))))
```

Use the VLOOKUP Function Across Multiple Tables

Although the formula will return the desired results, you can make the formula a lot shorter, add more than five conditions, and end up with a formula that is very easy to manage.

Assume you have 12 different tables set up on a spreadsheet, each representing a different month of the year. Each table is two columns wide and contains the names of five employees and five corresponding amounts. Each table has been named according to the month that it represents—i.e., January's data has a named range of January, February's data has a named range of February, and so on, as shown in Figure 6-17.

C	D	E	F	G	H	I	J
January		**February**		**March**		**April**	
Name	Amount	Name	Amount	Name	Amount	Name	Amount
Fred	20	Fred	35	Fred	35	Fred	19
Bill	21	Bill	32	Bill	32	Bill	15
Jack	22	Jack	36	Jack	36	Jack	22
Joe	23	Joe	31	Joe	31	Joe	23
Phil	20	Phil	35	Phil	35	Phil	25
May		**June**		**July**		**August**	
Name	Amount	Name	Amount	Name	Amount	Name	Amount
Fred	25	Fred	28	Fred	15	Fred	56
Bill	26	Bill	13	Bill	22	Bill	84
Jack	28	Jack	22	Jack	33	Jack	52
Joe	27	Joe	45	Joe	65	Joe	31
Phil	31	Phil	85	Phil	98	Phil	31
September		**October**		**November**		**December**	
Name	Amount	Name	Amount	Name	Amount	Name	Amount
Fred	25	Fred	25	Fred	25	Fred	25
Bill	26	Bill	26	Bill	26	Bill	26
Jack	28	Jack	28	Jack	28	Jack	28
Joe	27	Joe	27	Joe	27	Joe	27
Phil	31	Phil	31	Phil	31	Phil	31

Figure 6-17. Twelve tables, each representing a month of the year

Once your data tables are set up, follow these steps:

1. Select cell A1.

2. Select Data → Data Tools → Data Validation (pre-2007, Data → Validation).

3. Ensure you are on the Settings tab, and select List from the Allow: box.

4. In the Source: box, type each month of the year, separating each with a comma.

5. It is vital that your named ranges for each table are the same as the month names you used in the validation list. Click OK.

6. Select cell B1 and set up a validation list as explained earlier, this time using the names of each employee (if the employee names are too large to type, simply reference a range of cells containing them for the source). Click OK.

7. In cell A2, enter this formula:

```
=VLOOKUP($B$1,INDIRECT($A$1),2,FALSE)
```

At this point, if you select the required month from the list in cell A1 and the required employee name from the list in cell B1, then the formula in cell A2 will return the corresponding amount for that person for that month.

> There are a few advantages to using this approach. If you are not familiar with the INDIRECT function, it is used to read the contents of a cell as a range address rather than as text. As you named 12 different ranges, each representing a month of the year, the formula using the INDIRECT function reads the word January as a range reference rather than as a text string.
>
> If you use a pre-2007 version of Excel, another advantage to using a formula with the INDIRECT function is that you can escape Excel's restriction of having only seven levels of nested functions.

HACK #89 Show Total Time As Days, Hours, and Minutes

When you add hours in Excel, you can have the result return as total hours and minutes, but unfortunately, not as days, hours, and minutes. Displaying that will take some extra work.

ALL

For example, if the total time was equal to 75 hours, 45 minutes, and 00 seconds, the total generally would be displayed as 75:45:00, proving the result cell is custom-formatted as [h]:mm:ss, which then allows for hours greater than 24. Although this is certainly the correct result, it means you must manually calculate how many days, hours, and minutes the total represents. This can be time-consuming and error-prone.

Assume you have a list of valid times in cells A1:A10. In cell A11, you have a regular SUM function that is summing up the total hours—i.e., =SUM($A$1:$A$10). If the total of this sum is to exceed 24 hours, the result cell housing the SUM function should be formatted as [h]:mm. Assume the result of this total is 306:26:00, which, of course, represents 306 hours and 26 minutes. However, this does not tell you how many days/hours/minutes this total represents.

To have the result shown in days, hours, and minutes, use this formula:

```
=INT(A11) &" Days " & INT(MOD(A11,INT(A11))*24) & " Hours and " &
MINUTE(A11) & " Minutes"
```

Provided that cell A11 has the value of 306:26:00, the result of this formula is 12 days, 18 hours, and 26 minutes.

Let's look at how this works. If you are not familiar with how Excel stores and uses dates and time, you should first read and understand "Hack Excel's Date and Time Features" [Hack #39]✓

Select the formula result cell and then click the fx sign to the left of the Formula bar (pre-2007 and Mac, click the equals sign). Click the first occurrence of INT from the Formula bar. This function will return the whole number 12 from the value 12.76805556. This is how many days there are.

Next you need to determine how many hours remain after taking off 12 days. Click the second INT function from the Formula bar. Here you are using MOD(A11,INT(A11)) to return the remainder of 12.76805556 divided by 12, which is 0.76805556 (the number of minutes represented as a decimal number). Now you need to multiply that by 24 (which is 18.433333) to return a number that will represent the minutes. As you want only the whole number (18), we have nested the formula MOD(A11,INT(A11))*24 into the INT function.

Click the MINUTE function from within the Formula bar. The function will return 26 from the serial number 12.76805556.

As the result returned from the MINUTE function will never be a numeric value, it is wise to at least keep the original SUM function, which returns the total as hours in a cell, so that it can be referenced and used in further calculations if needed. The row that houses the total as hours can, of course, be hidden.

HACK #90 Determine the Number of Specified Days in Any Month

ALL When you're creating calendar-related applications, especially payroll applications, you sometimes need to know how many times a given day of the week appears in a particular month.

Although Excel has many date and time functions, at the time of this writing, it does not have a date and time function that will, for example, tell you how many Mondays are in the month of January in the year 2007. You could use a very deeply nested set of Excel's date and time functions to figure this out, but unfortunately, as you can imagine, this would be very cumbersome and awkward to reproduce.

This is a case in which VBA can simplify a complicated task. Instead of fumbling with complex functions, you can write a custom function that will do the same thing, and all you need to do is input the day and date for which you want a count.

You can use the following function to determine how many days are in any specified month. For example:

```
=HowManyDaysInMonth("1/12/07","wed")
```

will return 4, as there were four Wednesdays in the month of December in 2007. (Note that the date format should match your local settings—12/1/07 in the United States, for instance. The date format in the example is from Australia.)

Similarly, the following function:

```
=HowManyDaysInMonth("1/12/07","thu")
```

will return 4, as there were four Thursdays in the month of December in 2007.

To use this custom function in a workbook, you must first place the following code into a standard module, so open the workbook into which you want to place the code and press Alt/Option-F11, or else right-click on the Sheet tab and select View Code (pre-2007, Tools → Macro → Visual Basic Editor). Then select Insert → Module and paste in the following code:

```
'The Code
Function HowManyDaysInMonth(FullDate As String, sDay As String) As Integer
Dim i As Integer
Dim iDay As Integer, iMatchDay As Integer
Dim iDaysInMonth As Integer
Dim FullDateNew As Date

iMatchDay = Weekday(FullDate)
 Select Case UCase(sDay)
 Case "SUN"
 iDay = 1
 Case "MON"
 iDay = 2
 Case "TUE"
 iDay = 3
 Case "WED"
 iDay = 4
 Case "THU"
 iDay = 5
 Case "FRI"
 iDay = 6
 Case "SAT"
 iDay = 7
 End Select
```

```
iDaysInMonth = Day(DateAdd("d", -1, DateSerial _
(Year(FullDate), Month(FullDate) + 1, 1)))
FullDateNew = DateSerial(Year(FullDate), Month(FullDate), iDaysInMonth)
For i = iDaysInMonth - 1 To 0 Step -1
If Weekday(FullDateNew - i) = iDay Then
HowManyDaysInMonth = HowManyDaysInMonth + 1
End If
Next i
End Function
```

Close the window to return to Excel, then save your workbook.

Now simply enter the function into any cell as shown earlier, and Excel will return a number that represents how many times the specified day occurred in the specified month.

HACK #91 Construct Mega-Formulas

ALL

Mega-formulas—a formula within a formula, within a formula—are enough to send even the most seasoned Excel veteran running for the hills. With a little forethought and by working step by step toward the formula you need, however, you can tame those complex mega-formulas without fear.

Does the very thought of having to make sense of, let alone construct, nested formulas fill you with dread? Some of those cells, so chock-full of complex functional gobbledygook, make us feel a little faint too. But with a little forethought and a step-by-step approach, you'll be creating mega-formulas without fear. And maybe, just maybe, you'll even be able to read and understand them again later.

The trick is to build up your formulas, bit by bit, using Excel's standard functions. Use one function per cell, obtaining individually manageable results, and then nest them together to yield the result you need. Here's an example of such a process in action.

Say you've been given a long list of people's names, each consisting of first, middle, and last names—one full name per cell. Your job is to write a formula in the adjacent column to extract only the person's last name.

What you're after, then, is the start of the last name—the third word—in the cell. Actually, what you'll be looking for is the position of the second space character in the cell. Excel has no standard built-in function to automatically locate the second space character in a cell, but you can bring the FIND function to bear in such a way that it does what you need it to do.

Type the name **David John Hawley** (or any three-word name) into cell A1. In cell C1, enter this function:

```
=FIND(" ",A1)
```

The FIND function finds one text string (find_text) within another text string (within_text), and returns the number of the starting position of find_text from the first character of within_text.

Here is the syntax:

```
=find(find_text, within_text, start_num)
```

This will find the starting position of the first space character in cell A1 as you have told it to find " " (a space) in cell A1. In the case of David John Hawley, it will return a value of 6. But it's the second space you're after, not the first. What you'll do is use the number returned by the formula in C1 as the starting point for another FIND function in search for the second space character. So, in cell C2, enter the following:

```
=FIND(" ",A1,C1+1)
```

Notice you've passed the FIND function a third argument this time, the initial position found by C1 (6, in this example), plus 1; this will serve as the starting point for the FIND function to find a space. The value returned will be the position of the second space character.

With that in hand, you want the next function to grab all characters thereafter until the end of the string of text. Use the MID function, which is designed to extract a range of characters from a string. In cell C3, enter the following:

```
=MID(A1,C2+1,256)
```

The MID function returns a specific number of characters from a text string, starting at the position you specify, based on the number of characters you specify. Here is its syntax:

```
MID(text, start_num, num_chars)
```

This tells the MID function to extract 256 characters from cell A1, starting with the first character after the second space in the string of text. You used 256 simply to ensure that regardless of the length (assuming it's less than 256 characters), you get the person's entire last name.

With all the parts in hand, it's time to build out the whole thing: a nested formula you'd have cringed at just a few minutes ago. Basically, you simply replace all cell references (except A1) within the functions with the formula in those cells. You do this via the use of cut and paste working within the Formula bar.

Click cell C2, and in the Formula bar, highlight the function and copy the entire FIND function except for the =, like this:

```
FIND(" ",A1,C1+1)
```

Press Enter to leave the cell, which will place you into cell C3. With cell C3 selected, in the Formula bar, highlight the reference to cell C2 and paste the FIND function (Ctrl-V) that you just copied in its place. Press Enter. Your function in cell C3 should now be as follows:

```
=MID(A1,FIND(" ",A1,C1+1)+1,256)
```

Now you need to replace the reference to cell C1 with the function that resides in cell C1. Select cell C1, highlight the formula from the Formula bar, omitting the =, click Copy, then press Enter twice to get back to cell C3. While in cell C3, highlight C1 in the Formula bar and paste the FIND function you just copied. Press Enter.

Now all you need to do is cut cell C3 and paste it into cell B1, then delete the formulas left over in cells C1 and C2. You should now end up with a final formula like this:

```
=MID(A1,FIND(" ",A1,FIND(" ",A1)+1)+1,256)
```

Following this concept, you should be able to see how you can build mega-formulas using a variety of Excel's functions. All you need to do is first plan a way that you will achieve it and then use individual cells to obtain the results needed. Finally, replace all cell references with the functions that are housed within them.

> In pre-2007 versions, if you have more than seven levels of nested functions, you'll also want to use the INDIRECT function, described in "Display Negative Time Values" **[Hack #87]**. Excel 2007 allows up to 64 levels of nested functions.

HACK #92 Hack Mega-Formulas that Reference Other Workbooks

ALL Excel formulas get pretty complicated when a mega-formula references another workbook. Not only do you need to include cell references, but also you must include workbook names or sheet names, and even the full path if the referenced workbook is closed. There are several ways to simplify what can be a complex process.

Writing such formulas from scratch can become unwieldy quickly. In this hack, we will show you a quick and easy way that enables you to construct these formulas without the need for workbook names and file paths. The method is so simple it is often overlooked.

Let's first ensure that you use the correct means to reference cells and worksheets. When writing a formula, it is always a good idea to never type cell references, sheet names, or workbook names because this can introduce incorrect syntax and/or typos. Most people at an intermediate level should be using only their mouse pointer to reference cells, sheets, and workbooks. This certainly goes a long way toward preventing syntax errors and typos, but if you have ever done this with a nested function, you know the formula quickly becomes unwieldy and is very difficult to follow.

For instance, take a look at this formula:

```
=INT(SUM('C:\Ozgrid Likom\Finance\SoftwareSales\[Regnow.xls]Product
Sales'!C2:C2924))
```

It is a pretty straightforward SUM function nested with the INT function. As it references cells from a closed workbook, the entire path is included along with the cell references, worksheet name, and workbook name. However, if you need to nest some additional functions within this one, it will soon become very difficult to write.

Here is a quick way to write mega functions that reference external workbooks. The trick is to simply write the function in the workbook that you will be referencing in any spare cell. If you are going to be referencing only one worksheet in this workbook, it is best to use a cell on this worksheet.

First, using the method shown in "Determine the Number of Specified Days in Any Month" **[Hack #90]** that explained an easy way to nest functions, simply develop the formula in any spare cell in the workbook that it will end up referencing. Once you have the desired result, cut the formula from the cell, activate the workbook in which the result should reside, select the appropriate cell, and paste.

Excel does all the hard work for you by including the workbook names and any sheet names. When/if you need to add or modify the formula, simply open the referenced workbook, cut the formula from the original workbook, and paste it into the referenced workbook. Then make your changes and cut and paste back to where it came from.

HACK #93 Hack One of Excel's Database Functions to Take the Place of Many Functions

ALL Excel's database functions (e.g., DSUM, DCOUNT) can take the place of potentially thousands of functions, thereby reducing both recalculation time and workbook space.

When using Excel's database functions, you can specify many different criteria. You might, for example, want to sum amounts in column A where the corresponding amount in column B is greater than 100 and the corresponding value in column C is less than 40. If, however, you want to sum amounts where corresponding values in column B are less than 50, you need to use another function and a different range of criteria. It would be much easier if you had a single function and could easily and quickly change the criteria! If you have never used Excel's database functions before, we strongly recommend that you familiarize yourself with them, as they are very good for extracting statistical information from an Excel database or table.

To see how this works, set up your data as shown in Figure 6-18. Keep the column headings the same, but the data that resides in it can be any fictitious data. Name this table of data, including all column headings, **AllData**. Name the sheet **Data**.

	A	B	C	D	E	F	G
1	**Name**	**Dates**	**Full Cost**	**Amount Paid**	**Percent Paid**	**Cost Remaining**	
2	Bill J	1/03/2007	$25.00	$10.00	40%	$15.00	
3	John J	19/03/2007	$35.00	$12.00	34%	$23.00	
4	Fred B	18/03/2007	$25.00	$20.00	80%	$5.00	
5	Joe H	4/03/2007	$65.00	$65.00	100%	-	
6	Mary K	3/03/2007	$88.00	$80.00	91%	$8.00	
7	Lisa G	20/03/2007	$45.00	$25.00	56%	$20.00	
8	Dave H	23/03/2007	$61.00	$55.00	92%	$5.00	
9	Edward F	8/03/2007	$21.00	$21.00	100%	-	
10	Keith B	30/03/2007	$33.00	$10.00	30%	$23.00	
11	Aleisha H	2/03/2007	$22.00	$22.00	100%	-	
12	Kylie M	11/02/2007	$25.00	$20.00	80%	$5.00	
13	John D	19/02/2007	$44.00	$15.00	4%	$29.00	
14	Bill W	13/02/2007	$88.00	$45.00	51%	$43.00	
15	Harry B	14/02/2007	$77.00	$28.00	36%	$49.00	
16							

Figure 6-18. Proposed data

Insert another worksheet and call this worksheet **Results**. In cell A2, enter the following formula:

```
=Data!A1
```

Copy this across to cell F2 so that you have a mirror image of your table headings. In cell A3, enter any name that exists in your table on the data sheet, such as **John D**. Then, in cell B3, enter the following formula:

```
=DGET(AllData,B2,$A$2:$A$3)
```

Copy this formula across to cell F3 and format cells C3:F3 in the required format.

> To quickly copy cells such as this without formatting, select the cell, right-click the fill handle, and drag across as far as needed while holding down the right mouse button. Then select Fill Without Formatting.

The corresponding data should be extracted out of the table for the name you entered into cell A3. This is just a simple example of how you can use the DGET function to extract relevant information.

> If you get the #NUM! error, it means you have two or more identical names in your Name column.

At this point, most people would follow the same concept for all names for which they need information extracted from the table. However, this effort is unnecessary.

As you are always referencing cell A3 for the name, it would make a lot more sense in most cases if you could simply have a drop-down list in cell A3 containing all the names that are in the table. You can use Excel's standard validation feature to create such a list. However, as the original list of names resides on another worksheet, you cannot reference the list in the same way as you would a list residing on the same sheet—i.e., a standard range reference. You can overcome this easily by naming the Name column in the original table, then using that name as the list source for the validation.

> As most tables are not static—in other words, data is usually continuously added and removed—you should consider using a dynamic named range for the Names column. See "Create Ranges That Expand and Contract" [Hack #47] for more details on this.

Click back onto the Data sheet and, with any cell selected, select Formulas → Defined Names → Define Name (pre-2007, Insert → Name → Define). In the Names: box, enter **Names**. In the Refers To: box, type the following formula, and click Add:

```
=OFFSET($A$2,0,0,COUNTA($A$2:$A$1000),1)
```

Click the Results worksheet, select cell A3, and then select Data → Data Tools → Data Validation (pre-2007, Data → Validation). Select List from the Allow: box, and in the Source: box, type the following:

```
=Names
```

Ensure that the In-Cell drop-down checkbox is checked and then click OK. Now you can select any name from the list in cell A3, and your data to the right will display the appropriate information automatically.

Using DCOUNT to Filter on Two Criteria

You can take this to another level and use the DCOUNT function to extract a count of people that have a full cost greater than a number you specify, and a percent paid less than a number you specify.

To do this, first you need to create a dynamic named range for both the Full Cost column and the Percent Paid column. Click back on the Data sheet and go to the Formulas tab. Select Defined Names → Define Name (pre-2007, Insert → Name → Define) and enter **FullCost** in the Names: box. In the Refers To: box, type the following formula, and click OK:

```
=OFFSET($C$2,0,0,COUNTA($C$2:$C$1000),1)
```

Repeat for the Percent Paid column by going back to the Define Name dialog and in the Names: box entering **PercentPaid**. In the Refers To: box, type the following formula and click OK:

```
=OFFSET($E$2,0,0,COUNTA($E$2:$E$1000),1)
```

Activate the Results sheet, select cell A11, and then select Data → Data Tools → Data Validation (pre-2007, Data → Validation). Select List from the Allow: box and enter **=FullCost** in the Source: box. Click OK.

Select cell B11, and then select Data → Data Tools → Data Validation (pre-2007, Data → Validation). Select List from the Allow: box and enter **=PercentPaid** in the Source: box. Click OK.

In cell A12, enter the following:

```
=Data!C1
```

Select cell B12, and enter the following:

```
=Data!E1
```

Select cell A13, and enter the following:

```
=">"&A11
```

Select cell B13, and enter the following:

```
="<"&TEXT(B11,"0%")
```

In cell A15, enter the following:

```
=DCOUNT(AllData,$A$12,$A$12:$B$13)
```

Select any Full Cost amount from cell A11 and any percent paid amount from cell B11, and the DCOUNT function will give you a count of all the people who meet those criteria. For instance, if you select 65 and 100 percent, you will be extracting a count of people that have a Full Cost greater than 65 and a Percent Paid less than 100.

As you can see, you can use this one DCOUNT function to extract any combination of criteria for the Full Cost and Percent Paid columns. With a little more work, you can take this to yet another level and make the comparison operators used in the criteria interchangeable.

Making the Comparison Operators Interchangeable

To make the comparison operators used in the criteria interchangeable, follow these steps:

1. First, create a list of comparison operators that you can use in a validation list. Scroll across to an out-of-the-way column on the Results sheet, and on any row in that column, enter the heading **Operators**.

2. Below the heading and moving down one cell at a time, enter =, >=, >, <, and <=, as shown in Figure 6-19.

Figure 6-19. Comparison operators

3. To name this range, select the heading and all operators below it and then select Formulas → Defined Names → Create from Selection (pre-2007, Insert → Name → Create).

4. Ensure that Top Row Only is selected, and click OK. Excel automatically will name the range based on the heading— in this case, Operators.

5. Select cell G7 and enter the heading **Select a Criteria**.

6. With cells G7 and H7 selected, center this across by right-clicking and selecting Format Cells, clicking the Alignment tab, and from the Horizontal Text Alignment box, selecting Center Across Selection.

7. Select cells G8 and H8, select Data → Data Tools → Data Validation (pre-2007, Data → Validation).

8. Select List from the Allow: box.

9. In the Source: box, type **=Operators**.

10. Ensure that the In-Cell drop-down box is checked and click OK.

11. Click back on the Data sheet and select Formulas → Defined Names → Define name.

12. In the Names: box, type **Dates**.

13. In the Refers To: box, type the following formula and click OK:

    ```
    =OFFSET($B$2,0,0,COUNTA($B$2:$B$1000),1)
    ```

14. Select cell G7, copy it, and paste it into cell G9.

15. Change the word Criteria to **Date**.

16. Select cells G10:H10 and then select Data → Data Tools → Data Validation (pre-2007, Data → Validation).

17. Select List from the Allow: box.

18. In the Source: box, enter **=Dates**.

19. Ensure that the In-Cell drop-down box is checked and click OK.

20. Select cell G11, and enter the following:

    ```
    =Data!$B$1
    ```

21. Copy that formula across to cell H11.

22. Select cell G12, enter the following formula, and copy it across to cell H12:

    ```
    =G8&TEXT(G10,"dd/mm/yy")
    ```

 You should use the date format applicable to your particular region.

23. In cell F13, enter the word **Result** and center it across the selection, with F13 and G13 selected.

24. In cell H13, enter the following function:

    ```
    =DSUM(AllData,Data!$C$1,$G$11:$H$12)
    ```

The end result should look like Figure 6-20, which, for the sake of demonstration, has all formulas displayed.

Select a criteria		
>	<	
Select a Date		
1/3/2007	3/3/2007	
Dates	Dates	
=G8&TEXT(G10,"dd/mm/yy")	=H8&TEXT(H10,"dd/mm/yy")	
Result	=DSUM(AllData,Data!$C$1,$G$11:$H$12)	

Figure 6-20. Worksheet showing correct formulas and headings

At this point you can hide rows 11 and 12, as you do not need to see them. You will end up with a simple-to-use table that looks like Figure 6-21, which has had formatting applied for ease of reading.

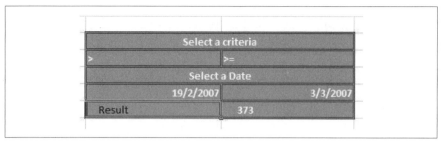

Select a criteria		
>	>=	
Select a Date		
19/2/2007		3/3/2007
Result	373	

Figure 6-21. Worksheet with final interface

By using this principle, you can easily have either one or a few database functions doing the work of what usually would require hundreds.

For a working example of this exercise, as well as similar examples, visit *http://www.ozgrid.com/download/default.htm* and click the heading DFunctionsWithValidation.zip.

HACK #94 Extract Specified Words from a Text String

ALL

Even though Excel is not specifically designed for text, you still might often have many words as data in your spreadsheets. Excel has a powerful and useful Text formula/function that we can use to extract words from a string of words or, put another way, parse out specific words from a text string of words.

In this hack, we'll show how to extract the last word, the first word, and the *n*th word from a string of text.

Getting the Last Word

To return the last word in a string of text, try this. In cell A2, type in the text **Our main business focus is Excel spreadsheets**. Now, click in cell B2 and type the following function:

```
=MID(SUBSTITUTE(A2," ","^",LEN(A2)-LEN(SUBSTITUTE(A2,"
 ",""))),FIND("^",SUBSTITUTE(A2," ","^",LEN(A2)-LEN(SUBSTITUTE(A2,"
 ",""))))+1,256)
```

This formula uses a combination of the MID function (to return a specific number of characters from a text string, starting at the position you specify, based on the number of characters you specify), the SUBSTITUTE function (to replace specific text in a text string), and the LEN function (to return the actual number of characters in the text string) to get the result, spreadsheets, in cell B2.

Note the use of ^. This is used to replace the necessary space character of the text string in A2. If your text includes ^, then choose another character that is *not* part of the text string.

Getting the First Word

If you want to return the *first* word from a text string, still using the text Our main business focus is Excel spreadsheets in cell A2, enter in the following function in cell B3:

```
=LEFT(A2,FIND(" ",A2)-1)
```

This formula will display the word Our in cell B3, by using a combination of the LEFT function (to return the first character or characters in a text string, based on the number of characters you specify) and the FIND function to locate one text string within a second text string, and return the number of the starting position of the first text string from the first character of the second text string.

Get the Nth Word

To take this a step further, you can use a formula to extract the exact word that you want from a text string. We will extract the fourth word. Again using the previous example, click in cell B3 and enter in the following formula:

```
=MID(MID(MID(SUBSTITUTE(A2," ","^",3),1,256),FIND("^",SUBSTITUTE(A2,"
 ","^",3)),256),2,FIND(" ",MID(MID(SUBSTITUTE(A2,"
 ","^",3),1,256),FIND("^",SUBSTITUTE(A2," ","^",3)),256))-2)
```

This last one can seem a bit overwhelming. The four occurrences of the number 3 determine that we parse out the fourth word. In other words, to get the fifth word, all occurrences of the number 3 would need to be changed to the number 4. If we wanted the second word, we would change all occurrences of the number 3 to the number 1.

This formula should display the word is in cell B3.

HACK #95 Count Words in a Cell or Range of Cells

ALL Unlike the Word Count feature in Microsoft Word, Excel does not give us a readymade way to find out the number of words in a cell or a range of cells containing text. However, with the help of the SUBSTITUTE function/formula and the LEN function/formula we can easily work this out.

To get a word count of any cell or range of cells, we'll use a combination of SUBSTITUTE and LEN function/formulas.

SUBSTITUTE

The SUBSTITUTE function is used to replace specific text in a text string with a different string of text. The syntax for the SUBSTITUTE function is as follows:

```
=SUBSTITUTE(text,old_text,new_text,instance_num)
```

where *new_text* replaces *old_text* in a text string.

To see it in action, type the text **Sales Data** in cell A1. In cell B1, type the following function:

```
=SUBSTITUTE(A1, "Sales", "Cost")
```

Cell B1 will display the result Cost Data, replacing the old text, Sales, with the new text, Cost.

LEN

The LEN function is used to return the number of characters in a text string. The syntax for LEN is:

```
=LEN(text)
```

To see how this works, we will continue with the previous example, with the words **Sales Data** in cell A1. In cell B2, enter the following function:

```
=LEN(A1)
```

You will get the result of 10, because the text entry Sales Data in cell A1 has nine text characters and one space contained in it.

Putting It Together

Now, to find out the number of words in the cell, we can use a combination of the LEN and SUBSTITUTE functions.

Again, using the previous example, with the text Sales Data in cell A1, click in cell B3 and enter the following function:

```
=LEN(A1)-LEN(SUBSTITUTE(A1," ",""))+1
```

The LEN function will return the number of characters within the text Sales Data (10) and the SUBSTITUTE function substitutes the spaces between words with nonspaces, and so would return 9. The number of spaces (0) will always be 1 less than the number of words. The use of +1 takes care of this. Using this function will display the result of 2, because there are two words in cell A1.

Hacking the Hack

Be aware that, when using the previous method, superfluous spaces are also counted and may give misleading results. To ensure accuracy, we can simply nest the TRIM function/formula in the first LEN.

To take this a step further, if you had text entries in a range of cells, you could use a combination of the LEN, TRIM, SUBSTITUTE, and ROWS functions to work this out. In cells F1:F5 place a mixture of text entries, with differing amounts of words in the cells, as in Figure 6-22.

f_x	=LEN(TRIM(F1&F2&F3&F4&F5))-LEN(SUBSTITUTE(F1&F2&F3&F4&F5," ",""))+ROWS(F1:F5)							
D	E	F	G	H	I	J	K	L
		It is wise to set	23	Returns the number of words in the range F1:F5				
		up your spreadsheets						
		with no blank cells						
		to ensure that Excels						
		built in features work to their optimum						

Figure 6-22. Spreadsheet showing LEN, TRIM, SUBSTITUTE, and ROWS functions

In cell G2, enter the following formula:

```
=LEN(TRIM(F1&F2&F3&F4&F5))-LEN(SUBSTITUTE(F1&F2&F3&F4&F5," ",""))+ROWS(F1:F5)
```

Using the previous example, this nested function will return 23, because there are 23 words in the range F1:F5. Again, the LEN function will return the number of characters within the text, the SUBSTITUE function substitutes spaces between words with nonspaces, and the ROW function returns the number of the row in a specified range. Using the TRIM function nested within the LEN function ensures all spaces are removed from our text except for single spaces between words.

H A C K   Return a Worksheet Name to a Cell
#96

ALL

Sometimes, you might want to use a worksheet name in a cell as a variable and also use that worksheet name in a formula. This would enable you to switch worksheet names and have one single formula able to return results from all worksheets.

This hack shows how you can display the entire path of your worksheet in a cell using the CELL function. Then, a combination of the MID and FIND functions extracts only the worksheet name from the full pathname, allowing you to use it in formulas.

Create a List of Worksheet Names

Creating a list of worksheet names is relatively easy using the CELL function/ formula. In any existing *saved workbook* already loaded with data, create a new worksheet named **Worksheets**, and add the heading **Names** to A1. Now, in cell A2 enter the following formula:

```
=CELL("filename",Sheet1!$A$1)
```

where Sheet1 is the name of the first worksheet in your workbook (excluding the one we just added and named Worksheets).

This formula will return the file path, workbook name, and worksheet name. We will pull out what we need (the worksheet name) soon.

Now, copy this formula down as many rows as you have worksheets. Change each occurrence of Sheet1 to the names of your other worksheets. Leave !$A$1 as is.

We referenced A1 (can be any cell) on each specific sheet, so that our CELL formulas/functions change when/if the worksheet name changes. Also, if no worksheet is specified (e.g., =CELL("filename",A1)), the worksheet name will *always* be the current active worksheet. This will be an issue when we reference the list from another worksheet, because the CELL function will return the worksheet name of the worksheet housing the formula unless a cell reference is supplied.

Extract Worksheet Names Only

Now we have found out what the file and path of our worksheet is we can extract the actual worksheet name.

In B2, enter the following formula:

```
="'"&MID(A2,FIND("]",A2)+1,256)&"'!"
```

In the previous example, this formula returns 'Sheet1'!.

Note the use of the two single apostrophes in the result. This allows for worksheet names that have spaces in their name. It's unnecessary for worksheet names without spaces, but it doesn't do any harm to cover your bases—that is, should you change the worksheet name to include a space.

Copy the previous formula down to reference all the data in Column A. In B1, enter the heading **Worksheet Names**. Highlight/select B1 down until the last formula row in Column B. Now, select Formulas → Defined Names → Create from Selection (pre-2007, Insert → Name → Create). Ensure only Top Row is checked and click OK. Excel will create the named range **Worksheet_Names**, omitting cell B1.

Use the List in Formulas

Add another new worksheet, named Formulas, to use for the formulas we will add. Let's say you are doing a VLOOKUP and/or SUM on a worksheet (any worksheet except the one housing the formulas and worksheet names) and you need variable worksheet names. Select A1 (any cell) and go to Data → Data Options → Data Validation (pre-2007, Data → Validation). Select List from the Allow: box, type **=Worksheet_Names** in the Source: box, and click OK. With this cell still selected, click in the Name Box (left of formula bar), type **SheetNames**, and press Enter.

Now, add the following VLOOKUP and INDIRECT function in cell A4:

```
=VLOOKUP("Sales",INDIRECT(SheetNames&"A1:G7"),2,FALSE)
```

> Make sure you have chosen a worksheet name from the list in the named range SheetNames.

In cell A7, enter the following SUM and INDIRECT function:

```
=SUM(INDIRECT(SheetNames&"B1:B7"))
```

Make the Range Address Variable

You might want to make the range references in the formulas variable, depending on which worksheet is chosen from your list in the named range SheetNames.

Go back to the Worksheets worksheet you added, and enter the name Range in C1. In C2 downward, add range references that you want to correspond to each worksheet name. For example, A1:G7 might correspond to Sheet1 in B2 and so would go in C2, G9:M15 might correspond to Sheet2 in B3 and so would go in C3, and so on, as shown in Figure 6-23.

	A	B	C
1	Names	Worksheet Names	Range
2	C:\Documents and Settings\RAINA\My Documents\OzGrid\HACKS BOOK #2\Chapter 6\[102 Return WorksheetNames to Cells_2.xls]Sheet1	'Sheet1'!	A1:G7
3	C:\Documents and Settings\RAINA\My Documents\OzGrid\HACKS BOOK #2\Chapter 6\[102 Return WorksheetNames to Cells_2.xls]Sheet2	'Sheet2'!	G9:M15
4	C:\Documents and Settings\RAINA\My Documents\OzGrid\HACKS BOOK #2\Chapter 6\[102 Return WorksheetNames to Cells_2.xls]Sheet3	'Sheet3'!	D5:J11
5			

Figure 6-23. Spreadsheet showing names, worksheet names, and ranges

> You can use range names in place of cell addresses.

Select C1 and highlight down until the last formula row in Column C. Now, select Formulas → Defined Names → Create from Selection (pre-2007, Insert → Name → Create). Ensure that only Top Row is checked and click OK. Excel will create the named range Range, omitting C1. Select B1:C*<last row>*

(don't start from A1), click in the Name Box (left of formula bar), type **MyTable**, and press Enter.

Come back to the worksheet (Formulas) you added the range name SheetNames to, and delete the formulas you created in cells A4 and A7.

In the cell next to this (B1), add the following formula:

```
=VLOOKUP(SheetNames,MyTable,2,FALSE)
```

Click back in this formula cell, and name it **RangeLook**. Use the two formulas that follow in place of the previous VLOOKUP and SUM formulas.

In cell A4 type the following formula:

```
=VLOOKUP("Sales",INDIRECT(SheetNames&RangeLook),2,FALSE)
```

In cell A7, type the following formula:

```
=SUM(INDIRECT(SheetNames&RangeLook))
```

Now, depending on which worksheet is selected from your list in the named range SheetNames, the corresponding range on the worksheet selected will be displayed in cell B1, and therefore the displayed range will be used in the calculations in A4 and A7.

Should you wish, you can use Data Validation to list the range name **=Range** and change ranges at will.

Sum Cells with Multiple Criteria

HACK #97

ALL

The most efficient method to sum cells based on multiple criteria is to use a PivotTable. However, if you are not familiar with PivotTables (check out Chapter 4 to see how they can make your spreadsheet life much easier), or your data is not set up in a contiguous list (which is required to create a PivotTable), as an alternative you could use either of these three methods to get the same results.

There are many times you might need to sum cells based on multiple criteria. If you are not already aware, the Excel SUMIF formula/function can only check to see if specified cells meet one condition. This means that if we wish to sum multiple criteria, we will need to use another method.

SUMIF

Let's first have a look at how the SUMIF function works to meet one condition. Here's the syntax for the SUMIF function:

```
=SUMIF(range,criteria,sum_range)
```

Let's say you have a spreadsheet with two columns of numbers in cells A1: A10 and B1:B10. Click in cell C1 and enter in the following formula:

```
=SUMIF(A1:A10,">20",B1:B10)
```

In this example, the range to be examined is A1:A10. The criterion used is >20 (greater than 20) and the *sum_range* is B1:B10. So, using this method will sum all numeric cells in the range B1:B20 for which the corresponding row in A1:A10 is greater than 20.

If you omit the last optional argument (*sum_range*) the SUMIF function sums all cells in the range A1:A10 that are greater than 20. Click in cell D1 and enter in the following formula:

```
=SUMIF(A1:A10,">20")
```

> The criteria argument is in the form of a number, expression, or text that defines which cells will be summed. For example, criteria can be expressed as 20, "20", "=20", ">20", "North", or "N*".

So, if you need to sum a range of cells where corresponding cells (on the same row) meet two or more conditions, you can no longer use SUMIF. Instead, you can use, in order of their efficiency:

1. DSUM

2. SUMPRODUCT

3. SUM with an IF function nested and entered as an array formula

DSUM

For these examples, we have used the named range DataTable, which refers to the range A2:E25 in Figure 6-24.

DSUM adds the numbers in a column of a list, or database, that match criteria you specify. For example, the following formula sums all cells in B2:B25 that meet the criteria in the named range Criteria, as shown in Figure 6-25:

```
=DSUM(DataTable,B2,Criteria)
```

The top row of the Criteria range has exact copies of the headings in the DataTable range. The reference to cell B2 tells the DSUM formula to sum the numbers in B2:B25 that meet the criteria. We could replace the reference to B2 with the text Quantity or the number 2, because the Quantity column is the second column in the table.

The criteria text Bourbon and Vodka, under the criteria table heading Description, tells DSUM that either Bourbon or Vodka is a match. The same principle is used for Alcohol Content—i.e., High or Low. The DSUM formula sees this as an OR condition.

	A	B	C	D	E
1			Hawleys Brewery		
2	Description	Quantity	Use By Date	Location	Alcohol Content
3	Vodka	20	7/04/2007	Warehouse 1	High
4	Bourbon	30	1/07/2007	BottleShop	Low
5	Crown Lager	45	12/01/2007	BottleShop	Medium
6	Scotch	25	1/06/2007	Warehouse 3	Low
7	Mailbu	28	1/09/2007	Front Bar	High
8	Baileys Irish Cream	30	1/05/2007	BottleShop	High
9	Galliano	45	1/01/2007	Warehouse 3	High
10	Kaluha	32	1/02/2007	BottleShop	High
11	Crown Lager	21	3/05/2007	Warehouse 3	Low
12	Emu Export	45	5/03/2007	BottleShop	High
13	Baileys Irish Cream	28	1/10/2007	Front Bar	High
14	Swan Lager	3	4/02/2007	Warehouse 1	Low
15	Swan Lager	20	1/11/2007	Warehouse 1	High
16	Heinekin Lager	15	1/07/2007	BottleShop	High
17	Swan Gold	31	2/07/2007	Front Bar	High
18	Bourbon	25	19/04/2007	Front Bar	Low
19	Galliano	32	14/08/2007	Warehouse 1	High
20	Crown Lager	15	29/10/2007	Warehouse 1	Medium
21	Vodka	30	1/03/2007	Front Bar	Low
22	Vodka	28	14/03/2007	Warehouse 3	High
23	Crown Lager	45	16/11/2007	BottleShop	High
24	Mailbu	30	7/09/2007	Warehouse 1	Low
25	Crown Lager	20	5/10/2007	Bottleshop	High
26					
27					

Figure 6-24. DataTable named range

G	H	I	J	K
Description	Quantity	Use By Date	Location	Alcohol Content
Vodka		>07/04/2007		High
Bourbon		>07/04/2007		Low

Figure 6-25. Criteria named range

Note the repetition of the date under Use By Date. This is necessary when using more than two rows, because DSUM sees a blank cell as a wildcard character and could throw out erroneous results. If we wanted to sum only data that lies between two dates, we would need have two Use By Date headings in our Criteria range and use >7-Apr-2007 below one of these headings and <7-Jun-2007 under another. DSUM sees this as an AND condition.

SUMPRODUCT

An alternative to DSUM would be to use the SUMPRODUCT function. This function multiplies corresponding values in the given ranges and returns the sum of those products.

As with the first DSUM example, this formula sums all Quantity values for which the corresponding Use By Date is greater than 7-Apr-2007, the Description is either Vodka or Bourbon, and the Alcohol Content is High or Low:

```
=SUMPRODUCT((A3:A25="Vodka")*(C3:C25>VALUE("7-Apr-2007")))*(E3:
E25="High")*(B3:B25))+SUMPRODUCT((A3:A25="Bourbon")*(C3:C25>VALUE("7-Apr-
2007")))*(E3:E25="Low")*(B3:B25))
```

Note how the range for each column of the table starts at row 3 and not row 2. This is because SUMPRODUCT returns the result of each criteria check as TRUE (has a value of 1) or FALSE (has a value of 0). So, in the first row check (if we used row 2), the formula would look like this:

```
=SUMPRODUCT((0)*(0)*(0)*("Quantity"))+SUMPRODUCT((0)*(0)*(0)*("Quantity"))
```

The result of multiplying a text string is always an error. This formula would cause the result of the SUMPRODUCT to return #VALUE!

SUM and IF

Now try this one. The following formula does the same thing as the preceding two examples. However, this is an array formula and must be entered by pressing Ctrl-Shift-Enter:

```
=SUM(IF(A2:A25="Bourbon",IF(C2:C25>VALUE("7-Apr-2007"),IF(E2:E25="Low",B2:
B25)))+SUM(IF(A2:A25="Vodka",IF(C2:C25>VALUE("7-Apr-2007"),IF(E2:
E25="High",B2:B25)))))
```

 You *must* enter array formulas by pressing Ctrl-Shift-Enter. Excel will add curly brackets at the start and end of your formula. If you try to insert them yourself, your array formula will not work correctly.

It is important to know that using SUM and IF or SUMPRODUCT over a large number of cells will cause a noticeable slowdown in Excel's recalculation time.

The DSUM is far more efficient in this regard and, as mentioned at the beginning of this hack, a pivot table would be even more efficient, and take up virtually no recalculation time at all. Pivot tables require your data to be set up in a certain way (no gaps, field names highlighted in some way).

However, if your data is not set up in a list, or you are unfamiliar with pivot tables, or can't get your head around them, these are great alternatives.

Count Cells with Multiple Criteria

PivotTables are ideal for counting cells with multiple criteria (check out Chapter 4 to see how powerful and easy to use they can be), but if PivotTables aren't your thing, or your data is not set up in the format a PivotTable requires, here are a two alternatives, the second more efficient than the first.

Counting cells with multiple criteria can also be achieved in a few different ways. Let's start with array formulas, which are the least efficient but the easiest to do.

Array Formulas

Excel array formulas are powerful and useful formulas that allow more complex calculations than standard formulas. You can tell an array formula at a glance because it is encased in braces ({}). The one drawback is that they take up more memory than traditional formulas. Excel's Help defines them like this:

> An array formula can perform multiple calculations and then return either a single result or multiple results. Array formulas act on two or more sets of values known as array arguments.

Before we look at a few examples of array formulas, we need to bear in mind three fundamentally important rules:

- Each argument within an array must have the same number of rows and/or columns.
- You cannot add the braces ({}) that surround an array yourself; pressing the key combination of Ctrl-Shift-Enter will do this for you.
- You cannot use an array formula on an entire column.

Let's assume you have a set of data, set up as shown in Figure 6-26.

You have data in columns A:D down to row 20, with the first row of all columns a heading. Column A is Name, B is Age, C is Male/Female (M/F), and D is Wage.

Let's say you want to count the occurrences of people with the name Dave, who are older than 20, male, and earn more than $500. Click in cell F2 and enter the following formula:

```
=SUM(((A2:A20="Dave")*(B2:B20>20)*(C2:C20="M")*(D2:D20>500)))
```

	A	B	C	D
1	Names	Ages	Male/Fema	Wage
2	Dave	22	M	$ 550.00
3	Liz	29	F	$ 350.00
4	Yvette	32	F	$ 450.00
5	Jocelyn	37	F	$ 300.00
6	Mandy	36	F	$ 600.00
7	Liz	25	F	$ 650.00
8	Dave	25	M	$ 380.00
9	Dave	37	M	$ 650.00
10	Kylie	41	F	$ 450.00
11	Liz	40	F	$ 550.00
12	Dave	21	M	$ 600.00
13	Fred	23	M	$ 400.00
14	Joe	35	M	$ 300.00
15	Jocelyn	46	F	$ 700.00
16	Mandy	52	F	$ 550.00
17	Dave	36	M	$ 300.00
18	Frank	45	M	$ 630.00
19	Joe	23	M	$ 480.00
20	Kylie	31	F	$ 550.00
21				

Figure 6-26. Data set

Press Ctrl-Shift-Enter to enter as an array formula. You should get the result of 3, because there are three people named Dave in the list that are older than 20, male, and earn more than $500.

Now, let's say you want to count the number of people who are between 21 and 29 years old and who have a wage between $301 and $399.

You can use a formula like this:

```
=SUM((B2:B20>20)*(B2:B20<30)*(D2:D20>300)*(D2:D20<400))
```

 Again, remember to press Ctrl-Shift-Enter to enter as an array formula.

You should get a result of 2, because there are two people between 21 and 29 years old who have a wage between $301 and $399.

Although these examples use the SUM function, the results are counted and not summed. This is because the SUM function sums the results of the multiplication of TRUE (has a value of 1) and FALSE (has a value of 0). So, any row that has a FALSE value will result in the value of 0. Since including 0 in the multiplication always yields a result of 0, one FALSE means a result of 0. If all are TRUE, then the formula ends up being SUM(1*1*1*1), which of course always equals 1.

SUMPRODUCT

The more efficient way to gain the same result is by using the SUMPRODUCT function. It uses the same principle described in the previous section for arrays, but you *do not* need to enter SUMPRODUCT via Ctrl-Shift-Enter.

Using the same criteria we used for the previous array formula, let's again count the occurrences of people with the name Dave, who are older than 20, male, and earn more than $500.

Click in an empty cell and enter the following formula:

```
=SUMPRODUCT((A2:A100="Dave")*(B2:B100>20)*(C2:C100="M")*(D2:D100>500))
```

And again you will get the result of 3.

To find the number of people between 21 and 29 years old, with a wage between $301 and $399, use this formula:

```
=SUMPRODUCT((B2:B100>20)*(B2:B100<30)*(D2:D100>300)*(D2:D100<400))
```

And you will again get the result of 2.

To use the same data to sum values based on multiple criteria, you can use the SUM function with the IF function nested within it. Since we have meaningful numbers only in column D (Wage), this will be the column we sum.

The criteria we will use to sum values in column D will be the occurrences of people with the name Dave who are older than 20, male, and earn more than $200 and less than $400. Click in any cell and enter the following formula:

```
=SUM(IF(A2:A100="Dave",IF(B2:B100>20,IF(C2:C100="M",IF(D2:D100>200,IF(D2:
D100<400,D2:D100))))))
```

Again, you can use SUMPRODUCT to do the same thing like this:

```
=SUMPRODUCT((A2:A100="Dave")*(B2:B100>20)*(C2:C100="M")*(D2:D100>200)*(D2:
D100<400)*(D2:D100))
```

Using the SUMPRODUCT function is more efficient.

Important Warning

The overuse of either array formulas or SUMPRODUCT with multiple criteria will result in a dramatic slowdown in Excel's calculation and recalculation. Basically, it comes down to the total number of cells being used in the arrays and/or SUMPRODUCTs.

If you are going to be counting or summing a large number of cells, we would advise strongly to use the appropriate Dfunction (database function), which are designed specifically for the job of using multiple criteria when you have an overly large number of cells.

H·A·C·K #99 Calculate a Sliding Tax Scale

ALL

Here are four solutions for the difficult problem of calculating tax payable or commission earned on a sliding scale.

Trying to calculate tax payable or commission earned on a sliding scale can be quite complicated. This hack provides four ways to make the process a little easier. The first uses the IF function/formula and the SUM function/formula and the second uses a Vlookup function to derive results. The last two alternatives use custom functions.

> The formula for the custom function uses named ranges to make the formula easier to read and modify if necessary.

Using IF/SUM

The first approach we will look at uses a combination of the IF and SUM functions. To make the hack easier to read and understand, Figure 6-27 shows a table with cell names next to their named cells. The formula that follows will use only the grey cells in the table. The columns to the left of the grey columns merely provide descriptions of those cells.

Each cell in column F (Taxable Amount) is the result of subtracting the tax scale in column B from the previous tax scale above. For example, the $13,000.00 total in row 15 (Level1TaxAmount) is derived by subtracting Level2Tax in row 16 ($25,000) from Level1Tax in row 15 ($12,000). That is:

```
=Level2Tax-Level1Tax
```

Here's the formula used in cell B3 and copied down to B11 to work out tax payable:

	A	B	C	D	E	F
1		Tax Payable				
2	Gross Pay	Built in Functions				
3	$ 50,000.00	$ 12,150.00				
4	$ 45,000.00	$ 9,900.00				
5	$ 40,000.00	$ 8,000.00				
6	$ 35,000.00	$ 6,100.00				
7	$ 30,000.00	$ 4,360.00				
8	$ 25,000.00	$ 2,860.00				
9	$ 20,000.00	$ 1,760.00				
10	$ 15,000.00	$ 660.00				
11	$ 10,000.00	$ -				
12						
13	Name of "Scale"	Scale	Name of "Tax Rate"	Tax Rate	Name of "Amount of Tax Payable on"	Amount of Tax Payable on
14	TaxFree	0	TaxFreeRate	0%	TaxFreeAmount	$ 12,000.00
15	Level1Tax	12000	Level1TaxRate	22%	Level1TaxAmount	$ 13,000.00
16	Level2Tax	25000	Level2TaxRate	30%	Level2TaxAmount	$ 7,000.00
17	Level3Tax	32000	Level3TaxRate	38%	Level3TaxAmount	$ 13,000.00
18	Level4Tax	45000	Level4TaxRate	45%	Level4TaxAmount	$ 5,000.00
19						
20	Gross Pay	Named Formulas				
21	$ 50,000.00	$ 12,150.00				
22	$ 45,000.00	$ 9,900.00				
23	$ 40,000.00	$ 8,000.00				
24	$ 35,000.00	$ 6,100.00				
25	$ 30,000.00	$ 4,360.00				
26	$ 25,000.00	$ 2,860.00				
27	$ 20,000.00	$ 1,760.00				
28	$ 15,000.00	$ 660.00				
29	$ 10,000.00	$ -				

Figure 6-27. Table of information used to calculate sliding tax scale

```
=IF(A3>Level4Tax,SUM((A3-
Level4Tax)*Level4TaxRate,Level3TaxAmount*Level3TaxRate,Level2TaxAmount*Level
2TaxRate,Level1TaxAmount*Level1TaxRate),IF(A3>Level3Tax,SUM((A3-
Level3Tax)*Level3TaxRate,Level2TaxAmount*Level2TaxRate,Level1TaxAmount*Level
1TaxRate),IF(A3>Level2Tax,SUM((A3-
Level2Tax)*Level2TaxRate,Level1TaxAmount*Level1TaxRate),IF(A3>
Level1Tax,SUM((A3-Level1Tax)*Level1TaxRate),0))))
```

As we have done in this formula, if you prefer, the key numbers in your data (such as the Scales in column B) can become *named constants* (a named constant is a value that is given a user-friendly name) as opposed to *named ranges* (a block of cells that is given a user-friendly name). For example, to create the named constant Level1Tax, select Formulas → Defined Names → Define Name (pre-2007, Insert → Name → Define). Type **Level1Tax** in the Name: box type and **=12000** in the Refers to: box, and click OK.

The beauty of using a named constant is twofold: it makes your formulas more friendly, and if you want to change the constant you only need to change it in one place, rather than wherever it occurs throughout your workbook.

Using a VLOOKUP Formula

There is another method you could use to get the same results: by using the VLOOKUP function/formula. Some users, if they are familiar with VLOOKUP, may find this method easier to maintain, because it doesn't use as many nested functions as the previous formula. However this method relies on precalculating *quick deductions*, shown in G14:G18 in Figure 6-28, and placing them at the end of the white and grey table used in the previous section.

	A	B	C	D	E	F	G
1		Tax Payable					Tax Payable
2	Gross Pay	Built in Functions					Built in Functions
3	$ 50,000.00	$ 12,150.00					$ 12,150.00
4	$ 45,000.00	$ 9,900.00					$ 9,900.00
5	$ 40,000.00	$ 8,000.00					$ 8,000.00
6	$ 35,000.00	$ 6,100.00					$ 6,100.00
7	$ 30,000.00	$ 4,360.00					$ 4,360.00
8	$ 25,000.00	$ 2,860.00					$ 2,860.00
9	$ 20,000.00	$ 1,760.00					$ 1,760.00
10	$ 15,000.00	$ 660.00					$ 660.00
11	$ 10,000.00	$ -					$ -
12							
13	Name of "Scale"	Scale	Name of "Tax Rate"	Tax Rate	Name of "Amount of Tax Payable on"	Amount of Tax Payable on	Quick deduction
14	TaxFree	0	TaxFreeRate	0%	TaxFreeAmount	$ 12,000.00	$ -
15	Level1Tax	12000	Level1TaxRate	22%	Level1TaxAmount	$ 13,000.00	$ 2,640.00
16	Level2Tax	25000	Level2TaxRate	30%	Level2TaxAmount	$ 7,000.00	$ 4,640.00
17	Level3Tax	32000	Level3TaxRate	38%	Level3TaxAmount	$ 13,000.00	$ 7,200.00
18	Level4Tax	45000	Level4TaxRate	45%	Level4TaxAmount	$ 5,000.00	$ 10,350.00
19							
20	Gross Pay	Named Formulas					
21	$ 50,000.00	$ 12,150.00					
22	$ 45,000.00	$ 9,900.00					
23	$ 40,000.00	$ 8,000.00					
24	$ 35,000.00	$ 6,100.00					
25	$ 30,000.00	$ 4,360.00					
26	$ 25,000.00	$ 2,860.00					
27	$ 20,000.00	$ 1,760.00					
28	$ 15,000.00	$ 660.00					
29	$ 10,000.00	$ -					
30							

Figure 6-28. Table of information showing quick deductions in G14:G18

In this table, we've placed the following VLOOKUP formula in cell G3 to calculate the "Quick deductions."

```
=A3*VLOOKUP(A3,$B$14:$G$18,3)-VLOOKUP(A3,$B$14:$G$18,6)
```

Next we create the actual function to work out the tax payable. We can go one step further toward simplifying this function by using *named formulas* (a named formula is a formula/function that has been given a user-friendly name, which can be then be used to nest within other formulas or on its own) for each tax level calculation. We have done this in the following calculation.

> Not only does this formula simplify the calculation, but again, if you want to alter your named formula you only need to change it in one area (i.e., the Name Manager).

Here is the formula used in cell B21 and below:

```
=IF(A1>Level4Tax,Level4TaxCalc,IF(A1>Level3Tax,Level3TaxCalc,IF(A1>
Level2Tax,Level2TaxCalc,IF(A1>Level1Tax,Level1TaxCalc,0))))
```

Here are the steps to create this function and the *named formulas* contained within it. Create named ranges, or named constants that will hold the figures needed. Place your Gross pay in cell A1 and below.

Select cell B1 and go to Formulas → Defined Names → Name Manager (pre-2007, Insert → Name → Define). Select New and in the Names: box type **Level1TaxCalc**. Then, in the Refers to: box type **=SUM((A1-Level1Tax)*Level1TaxRate)** and click OK.

Note how we have referred to cell A1. This now makes the named formula (Level1TaxCalc) always look on the same row in the immediate column to the left for the gross pay.

We need to create three more named formulas. From the Name Manager, select New and in the Names: box type **Level2TaxCalc**. Then, in the Refers to: box, type **=SUM((A1-Level2Tax)*Level2TaxRate,Level1TaxAmount*Level1TaxRate)** and click OK.

Select New, and In the Names: box type **Level3TaxCalc** Then, type **=SUM((A1-Level3Tax)*Level3TaxRate,Level2TaxAmount*Level2TaxRate,Level1TaxAmount *Level1TaxRate)** in the Refers to: box and click OK.

Finally, for the last time, again select New. In the Names: box type **Level4TaxCalc**. Then, in the Refers to: box, type **=SUM((A1-Level4Tax)*Level4TaxRate,Level3TaxAmount*Level3TaxRate,Level2TaxAmount *Level2TaxRate,Level1TaxAmount*Level1TaxRate)**. Click OK → Close to close the Name Manager.

Using a Custom Function

The two previous methods get their results from deeply nested formulas using a combination of standard functions, named ranges, named constants and named formulas. As an alternative, you could use either one of the following custom Excel functions—or *user-defined functions* (UDF)—that have been written to calculate tax based on a sliding scale. The first one is based entirely on the built-in method (shown first in this hack) and requires named ranges, or constants. The second is more self-contained and requires no named ranges or constants.

Method 1. The first UDF contains named ranges and named constants, which house the information required to make the UDF work.

To insert the code, right-click on the sheet name and select View Code, or press Alt-F11 (pre-2007, Tools → Macro → Visual Basic Editor), and then select Insert → Module and paste the following code:

```
Function TaxPayable(Amount As Currency) As Currency

Select Case Amount
    Case Is > Range("Level4Tax")
        TaxPayable = ((Amount - Range("Level4Tax")) * Range("Level4TaxRate")) + _
                     Range("Level3TaxAmount") * Range("Level3TaxRate") + _
                     Range("Level2TaxAmount") * Range("Level2TaxRate") + _
                     Range("Level1TaxAmount") * Range("Level1TaxRate")
```

```
        Case Is > Range("Level3Tax")
          TaxPayable = ((Amount - Range("Level3Tax")) * Range("Level3TaxRate")) + _
                            Range("Level2TaxAmount") * Range("Level2TaxRate") + _
                            Range("Level1TaxAmount") * Range("Level1TaxRate")


        Case Is > Range("Level2Tax")
          TaxPayable = ((Amount - Range("Level2Tax")) * Range("Level2TaxRate")) + _
                            Range("Level1TaxAmount") * Range("Level1TaxRate")

        Case Is > Range("LowTax")
            TaxPayable = ((Amount - Range("Level1Tax")) * Range("Level1TaxRate"))

        Case Else
            TaxPayable = 0
    End Select

  End Function
```

Now click in any cell and type:

```
=TaxPayable(A2)
```

Where TaxPayable is the name of the UDF and cell A2 contains the gross amount that you want to work out the tax payable on.

Method 2. The second UDF contains its information hardcoded into the UDF rather than relying on the information being contained in named ranges or constants.

To insert the code, right-click on the sheet name and select View Code, or press Alt-F11 (pre-2007, Tools → Macro → Visual Basic Editor), and then select Insert → Module and paste the following code:

```
Function Tax_Payable(Amount As Currency, L1_Tax As Currency, _
L1_Tax_Rate As Currency, L1_Taxable_Amount As Currency, _
Optional L2_Tax As Currency, Optional L2_Tax_Rate As Currency, _
Optional L2_Taxable_Amount As Currency, Optional L3_Tax As Currency, _
Optional L3_Tax_Rate As Currency, Optional L3_Taxable_Amount As Currency, _
Optional L4_Tax As Currency, Optional L4_Tax_Rate As Currency) As Currency

Select Case Amount
    Case Is > L4_Tax
        Tax_Payable = (Amount - L4_Tax) * L4_Tax_Rate + L3_Taxable_Amount * ↵
L3_Tax_Rate + _
            L2_Taxable_Amount * L2_Tax_Rate + L1_Taxable_Amount * L1_Tax_Rate

    Case Is > L3_Tax
        Tax_Payable = (Amount - L3_Tax) * L3_Tax_Rate + L2_Taxable_Amount * ↵
L2_Tax_Rate + _
            L1_Taxable_Amount * L1_Tax_Rate
```

```
        Case Is > L2_Tax
            Tax_Payable = (Amount - L2_Tax) * L2_Tax_Rate + L1_Taxable_Amount * ↵
    L1_Tax_Rate


        Case Is > L1_Tax
            Tax_Payable = (Amount - L1_Tax) * L1_Tax_Rate


        Case Else
            Tax_Payable = 0
        End Select

    End Function
```

Now click in any cell and type:

```
=Tax_Payable(A2,12000,22%,13000,25000,30%,7000,32000,38%,13000,45000,45%)
```

Where Tax_Payable is the name of the UDF and cell A2 contains the gross amount that you want to work out the tax payable on.

Armed with this information, you can use one of these four methods to calculate tax payable or commission earned on a sliding scale.

HACK 100 — Add/Subtract Months from a Date

ALL

Excel is well suited to work with dates, but adding and subtracting months from specific dates can be a problem, since months have different numbers of days. Thankfully, Excel provides a couple solutions to this problem.

It's common to want to use Excel to add an arbitrary number of months to a specific date. For example, if cell A1 houses the date 31-Aug-2007, you might want to add (or subtract) one month to that date. Because not all months have the same number of days, there will always be dispute over the number of days to use to represent a month. This hack presents two ways that take care of that problem.

EDATE

The first method we'll use requires the EDATE function/formula, which is a standard function in Excel 2007.

> In previous versions of Excel, EDATE is a part of the Excel Analysis Toolpak. To make sure the Analysis Toolpak is installed, select Tools → Add-ins and check Analysis Toolpak).

Here's how to can use the EDATE function to add one month to the date in A1 (31-Aug-2007).

First, click in cell A1 and type in the date **31-Aug-2007**. Then, click in B1 and enter in the following formula:

    =EDATE(A1,1)

This formula yields a result of 30-Sep-2007, rather than 31-Sep-2007, because there are only 30 days in September.

To subtract month from the same date, you can use this formula:

    =EDATE(A1,-1)

This yields the result 31-Jul-2007. This means that by using EDATE you are adding or subtracting a calendar month to your date. This may or may not be what you'd expect, depending on how many days you define a month as having.

Without EDATE

The other method you could use will sometimes yield a result that's different from the result EDATE provides. Again, ensure you have the date 31-Aug-2007 in cell A1. Click in B2 and enter in the following formula:

    =DATE(YEAR(A1),MONTH(A1)+1,DAY(A1))

Using this formula returns the result of 1-Oct-2007, even though A1 houses the date 31-Aug-2007, because of the syntax of the DATE function:

    DATEDIF(Year,Month,Day)

This function contains the following variables:

Year

> Microsoft Excel interprets the year argument according to the date system you are using. By default, Excel for Windows uses the 1900 date system; Excel for the Macintosh uses the 1904 date system. Our formula has returned 2007.

Month

> A positive or negative integer representing the month of the year from 1 to 12 (January to December). Our formula has returned September, which is the month from cell A1, plus 1.

Day

> A positive or negative integer representing the day of the month from 1 to 31. If *Day* is greater than the number of days in the month specified, that number of days is added to the first day in the month. Our formula has returned 31.

Because no date of 31 September 2007 exists, Excel has returned 1-Oct-2007.

Remember, EDATE gave the result as 30-Sep-2007.

As you can see, there are differences between the two methods you can use when adding or subtracting months from a date. Choose which one suits your needs best but be aware both methods will not always yield the same result. It depends on how you determine a "month."

HACK 101 Find the Last Day of Any Given Month

Dates can tricky to work with, and finding the last day of a given month can be a challenge.

ALL

Like adding or subtracting months from a specific date **[Hack #100]**, another common request Excel users have is to work out the last day of any given month. This hack provides a few ways to do this. The first two use standard formulas, the third uses a function contained in the Analysis Toolpak, and the last one uses code.

Using Formulas

Let's suppose A1 houses the date 23-Jun-2007 and you want to have Excel reference this cell and return the date of the last day of June 2007. This following function returns 30-Jun-2007:

```
=DATE(YEAR(A1),MONTH(A1)+1,0)
```

This is because the function adds one month to the date in A1 (June becomes July) and uses 0 for the day, which forces Excel to return the last day of the previous month.

Or, you can hardcode the date as shown here:

```
=DATE(YEAR("22-Jun-2007"),MONTH("22-Jun-2007")+1,0)
```

Again you will get the result 30 June 2007.

Using EOMONTH

There is a slightly shorter method, but it requires the Analysis Toolpak. To install it, select the Office button → Excel Options → Add-Ins, ensure that the Manage box displays Excel Add-Ins, and press Go button (pre-2007, select Tools → Add-Ins and check Analysis Toolpak).

Then, you can use the EOMONTH function as shown here:

```
=EOMONTH(A1,0)
```

EODATE returns the last serial number of the last day of the month before or after a specified number of months, so in this case it will return 30 June 2007.

 EODATE will only work if the Analysis Toolpak is installed on your PC, so if you email a spreadsheet to someone who does not have the Analysis Toolpak installed, EODATE will return #NAME.

Using a Custom Function

The following custom function will return the last specified day of any given month (for example, the last Monday of the month). To use it, right-click on your sheet name and select View Code (or Alt-F11). Then, select Insert → Module and paste the following code:

```
Function LastDayOfMonth(Which_Day As String, Which_Date As String) As Date
Dim i As Integer
Dim iDay As Integer
Dim iDaysInMonth As Integer
Dim FullDateNew As Date

Which_Date = CDate(Which_Date)

        Select Case UCase(Which_Day)
            Case "SUN"
                iDay = 1
            Case "MON"
                iDay = 2
            Case "TUE"
                iDay = 3
            Case "WED"
                iDay = 4
            Case "THU"
                iDay = 5
            Case "FRI"
                iDay = 6
            Case "SAT"
                iDay = 7
            End Select

    iDaysInMonth = Day(DateAdd("d", -1, DateSerial _
        (Year(Which_Date), Month(Which_Date) + 1, 1)))

    FullDateNew = DateSerial(Year(Which_Date), Month(Which_Date), iDaysInMonth)

    For i = 0 To iDaysInMonth
```

```
        If Weekday(FullDateNew - i) = iDay Then
            LastDayOfMonth = FullDateNew - i
            Exit For
        End If
    Next i

End Function
```

Press the Close button to return to Excel proper, then save your workbook.

Then, click in cell C6 and enter the following formula:

```
=LastDayOfMonth(Which_Day,Which_Date)
```

where Which_Day is a text abbreviation of any day (e.g., Sat) and Which_Date is a text representation of any valid date (e.g., 10-Oct-2007, 10-10-2007, etc).

For example, use the following formula to calculate the last Monday in October 2007:

```
=LastDayOfMonth("Mon","10/10/2007")
```

This function will return 29-Oct-2007.

Calculate a Person's Age

HACK #102

A little-known function can return the age of any person in years, months, and days.

ALL

This nifty hack makes life a little easier for anyone who wants to calculate a person's exact age, and all it takes is the DATEDIF function.

Here's the syntax:

```
DATEDIF(Start_Date,End_Date,Unit)
```

Valid Units are "M" (returns months), "D" (returns days), "Y" (returns years), "YM" (returns number of months in year), "YD" (returns the number of days in the year), and "MD" (returns the number of days in the month).

To use the function, click in cell A1 and type your birthday in a true Excel date format. Then, click in cell B1 and enter the following formula:

```
=DATEDIF(A1,TODAY(),"Y") & " Years, " & DATEDIF(A5,TODAY( ),"YM") & " Months,
" & DATEDIF(A1,TODAY( ),"MD") & " Days"
```

If you had the date 31-Dec-65 in cell A1, and today's date were 31 October 2007, your formula would return 41 years, 10 months, and 0 days. The Start_Date is the birthday in A1, the End_Date is TODAY( ) (or 31 October 2007 in this case). The units pull out the portion of the date that we are looking for.

Now, although this works, it is good spreadsheet design to have only one occurrence of any volatile function in a spreadsheet (in this case, the volatile function is TODAY( )) and to reference it as needed.

So, instead of calling this function within the formula itself, place the formula =TODAY( ) in any cell and press Enter. Then, name this cell Today by clicking in the Name box above column A, typing in **Today**, and pressing Enter.

Now, whenever you need today's date, simply reference it by calling on the named cell Today, as in the following formula:

```
=DATEDIF(A1,TODAY,"Y") & " Years, " & DATEDIF(A1,TODAY,"YM") & " Months, " &
DATEDIF(A1,TODAY,"MD") & " Days"
```

> Remember, using names makes your formulas easier to read and understand, both for you and for other people that might use them.

Return the Weekday of a Date

When finding the weekday associated with any date, most of us would rather see it returned as a name of the day, rather than as a number (the default).

This hack shows how to extract the weekday of any date by using the WEEKDAY function. By default, the day is given as a whole number, ranging from 1 (Sunday) to 7 (Saturday). However, this is often meaningless, and we usually would rather see the weekday returned as a name, such as Monday/Mon, Tuesday/Tue, and so on.

Get the Weekday as a Number

Before getting to the name of the day, we'll need to begin by extracting the number of the weekday. Here's the syntax for the WEEKDAY function:

```
WEEKDAY(serial_number,return_type)
```

Let's say you want to return the weekday number of 31-Jul-2007. The serial_num is any valid date (in this case 31-Jul-2007) and the return_type is a number that refers to the type of return value. The result you are looking for will determine the return_type that you will use; refer to Table 6-2.

Table 6-2. WEEKDAY function's return type and result

return_type	Day of week
1 or omitted	Numbers 1 (Sunday) through to 7 (Saturday)
2	Numbers 1 (Monday) through 7 (Sunday)
3	Numbers 0 (Monday) through 6 (Sunday)

We will use the default function by omitting the *return_type*. Click in cell A1 and type in a valid Excel date, such as 31-Jul-2007 (which is a Tuesday). Then, click in cell B1 and enter the following formula:

```
=WEEKDAY(A1)
```

This formula will return the number 3, which equates to Tuesday, which is the day of the week that 31 July 2007 is.

An alternative would be to hardcode the date like this:

```
=WEEKDAY("31 Jul 2007")
```

Return the Weekday as Weekday Name

Remember, the WEEKDAY formula shown in the previous section only returns the weekday as a number. There are at least two ways we can use formulas to force Excel to show the actual name of the weekday.

The first method is perhaps the simplest, and all you need to do is apply a custom number format of DDD or DDDD. Again using 31-Jul-2007 as an example, select the date cell, right-click, go to Format Cells, and then choose Number tab → Custom. Enter the custom format DDD under Type and click OK. You will get Tue in your cell.

Another, probably safer way is to reference the date cell (e.g., =A1) and format this cell with a custom number format of DDD or DDDD. The big advantage to this method is that it leaves our true underlying date as a valid Excel date.

Return the Weekday as Weekday Text

If you won't be using the weekday that is returned in any further calculations, you can use either of the formulas that follow (TEXT or WEEKDAY with CHOOSE) to return the weekday of a date as text.

The first formula uses TEXT and assumes you have a valid date, such as 31-Jul-2007, in cell A1:

```
=TEXT(A1,"DDDD")
```

Given 31-Jul-2007 in cell A1 it will return Tuesday. Or you could hardcode the date like this:

```
=TEXT("31 Jul 2007","DDDD")
```

Alternatively, you could use a combination of the WEEKDAY and CHOOSE functions to get the same result:

```
=CHOOSE(WEEKDAY(A1),"Sunday","Monday","Tuesday","Wednesday","Thursday",
"Friday","Saturday")
```

Again, you could also hardcode the date like this:

```
=CHOOSE(WEEKDAY("31 July 2007"),"Sunday","Monday","Tuesday",
"Wednesday","Thursday","Friday","Saturday")
```

All of these formulas will return the same result: Tuesday. But remember that the underlying value of your cell will still be 31-Jul-2007, even though your cell reads Tuesday.

HACK 104   Evaluate a Text Equation

ALL   By using an old Excel4 macro function called EVALUATE in a special way, you can easily evaluate text equations (an equation formatted as text and interpreted as such by Excel) as actual calculations.

Sometimes you might want to evaluate an equation that is formatted and interpreted as text by Excel, such as 21+69+89+25+31. If these numbers were typed into a cell with no equals (=) sign, Excel would read them as text and they would be treated as such with regards to calculation. But with this hack, we can get Excel to evaluate the equation anyway.

Set up your spreadsheet like the one shown in Figure 6-29, ensuring that none of your formulas have an equals sign (=). This will ensure that Excel treats them as text.

	A
1	21+69+89+25+31
2	21*25
3	100/10
4	100/10*(10*10+10)
5	100/10*10*10+10
6	

Figure 6-29. Mixture of text equations

In our example, we want to leave the original cell contents intact and use Column B to return the result of the equations.

Click in cell B1 and try the usual suspect of = "="&A1. You will see that the results in B1 only show =21+69+89+25+31, rather than evaluating the formula. We need to apply the EVALUATE function to get the results we want.

Again, click in cell B1 and enter the following formula:

```
=EVALUATE(A1)
```

Excel won't like this and will return the error message "That function is not valid." But we can force it to be valid. Click in cell B1 and select Formulas → Defined Names → Define Name (pre-2007, Insert → Name → Define). In the Names: box, type **Result** (or any valid range name), and type **=EVALUATE($A1)** in the Refers to: box. Click OK.

> You must select cell B1 and used a relative row reference for $A1.

Now click in cell B1, enter **=Result**, and copy down to B5.

You will get the results shown in Figure 6-30.

	A	B	C	D
	B1	▼	f_x	=Result
	A	**B**	**C**	**D**
1	21+69+89+25+31	235		
2	21*25	525		
3	100/10	10		
4	100/10*(10*10+10)	1100		
5	100/10*10*10+10	1010		

Figure 6-30. Results of using EVALUATE function as a named range

EVALUATE even follows the rules of parentheses.

Lookup from Within a Cell

HACK 105

ALL

Usually, in order to use one of Excel's lookup functions, you are required to lookup from within a table of cells in a worksheet. This hack shows how to perform a lookup on a small number of items, without leaving the cell.

Let's assume you have a changing value in A1 and want to return a result to B1 that varies based on the value in A1. For example, keeping it simple, say you have a validation list in cell A1 that a user can choose from any one of either Cat, Dog, Mouse, Horse or Rabbit. Based on their choice, we want to display a different result in B1.

First, set up a validation list. In cell G1, type in the word Cat, type Dog in G2, Mouse in G3, Horse in G4, and Rabbit in G5. Then, click in cell A1 and select Data → Data Tools → Data Validation (pre-2007, Data → Validation). Select List from the Allow: box, highlight G1:G5 in the Source: box, and click OK.

CHOOSE and MATCH

Now, to perform a lookup from within a cell, we'll use a combination of the CHOOSE function nested with the MATCH function. In B1, enter the following formula:

```
=CHOOSE(MATCH(A1,{"Cat","Dog","Mouse","Horse","Rabbit"},0),"Cat Food","Dog
Food","Mouse Food","Horse Food","Rabbit Food")
```

Click back in cell A1 and make a selection from the validation list. Once you have chosen a value from Cat, Dog, Mouse, Horse, or Rabbit, you will see the results, shown in Figure 6-31. The use of {"Cat","Dog","Mouse","Horse","Rabbit"} in the MATCH formula is know as an *array constant*, not be confused with *array formulas*.

Figure 6-31. Result of picking dog from validation list in A1

Keeping It Clean and Global

The main problems with the formula in the previous section are its length and, most importantly, the fact that editing the lookup values or the array constant would require doing each cell individually, or using the Find and Replace option, if possible. This is where we can use range names or, specifically *named constants* (key values we have given friendly names to). However, once we've done that, we can no longer use the CHOOSE Function. We'll then need to use the INDEX function instead.

Try this. First, select Formulas → Defined Names → Define Name (pre-2007, Insert → Name → Define). Enter the word **Pet** in the Names: box and ={"Cat","Dog","Mouse","Horse","Rabbit"} in the "Refers to:" box, and click OK. Now, create another defined name using **PetFood** in the "Names:" box, ={"Cat Food","Dog Food","Mouse Food","Horse Food","Rabbit Food"} in the "Refers to:" box, and click OK.

Now, click in cell B2 and enter the following formula:

```
=INDEX(PetFood,MATCH(A1,Pet,0))
```

If you need to edit the named constants PetFood or Pet, you can now do so in one location and the result will flow through the entire workbook.

Lookup Scale

So far, we have only looked up text values. However, you'll often need to lookup numbers that match a scale. That is, all results between 0 and 99.99 should return one result, while those between 100 and 199.99 another, and so on. Let's say you need to match the sales amount by person to determine their commission percentage.

Set up some data in cells A1:A12, as shown in Figure 6-32.

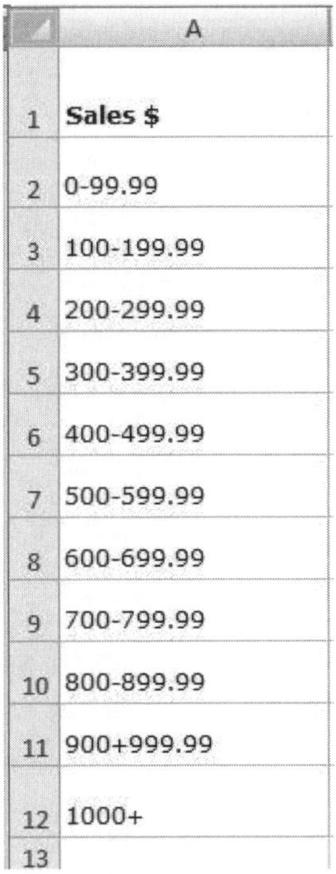

	A
1	Sales $
2	0-99.99
3	100-199.99
4	200-299.99
5	300-399.99
6	400-499.99
7	500-599.99
8	600-699.99
9	700-799.99
10	800-899.99
11	900+999.99
12	1000+
13	

Figure 6-32. Data showing sales amounts

Select Formulas → Defined Names → Define Name (pre-2007, Insert → Name → Define). Type **Commission** in the Names: box and **={0,0.1,0.2,0. 3,0.4,0.5,0.6,0.7,0.8,0.9,1}** in the Refers to: box, and click OK.

Now, create another named range called Sales, enter **={0,100,200,300,400,500,600,700,800,900,1000}** in the Refers to: box and click OK. Click in cell B2 and enter in the following formula:

```
=INDEX(Commission,MATCH(A1,Sales,1))
```

Press Enter and copy down to cell A12. This will return a percentage between 0 and 100, based on the Sales $ value in A1. Your results will look like those shown in Figure 6-33.

	A	B
1	Sales $	% Commission
2	0-99.99	0%
3	100-199.99	10%
4	200-299.99	20%
5	300-399.99	30%
6	400-499.99	40%
7	500-599.99	50%
8	600-699.99	60%
9	700-799.99	70%
10	800-899.99	80%
11	900+999.99	90%
12	1000+	100%

Figure 6-33. Results of using formula

In this hack's example, both of the array constants (entered in the Refers to: box) are in ascending order and we have used 1 for the optional Match_type argument for the MATCH function. If you use descending order, Match_type must be -1.

Macro Hacks
Hacks 106–134

Macros make it wonderfully easy to automate repetitive tasks in Excel, but the way they're created and the facilities for using them are sometimes problematic. Fortunately, Excel is flexible enough that you can fix those problems and create new features with a minimum of effort.

Speed Up Code While Halting Screen Flicker

HACK 106

ALL

When you record macros from within Excel, the code it generates often produces screen flicker, which not only slows down your macro, but also makes the macro's activity look very disorganized. Fortunately, you can eliminate screen flicker while at the same time speeding up your code.

One drawback with recorded macros in Excel is that the code produced is often very inefficient. This can mean macros that should take a matter of seconds to complete often take a lot longer and look very unsightly. Also, when you write macros using the macro recorder, all keystrokes are recorded, whether they are meant to be or not. This means that if you make an error and then correct it, the keystrokes required to complete those actions also will be recorded in your macro code.

If you have played around a bit with macros or dabbled in VBA code, you might have heard of the `Application.ScreenUpdating` property. By setting `ScreenUpdating` to False at the start of a macro, you will not only stop the constant screen flicker associated with a recorded macro, but also speed up the macro's execution. The reason this method speeds up code is because Excel no longer needs to repaint the screen whenever it encounters commands such as `Select`, `Activate`, `LargeScroll`, `SmallScroll`, and many others.

To include `Application.ScreenUpdating = False` at the beginning of your existing macro, select Developer → Code → Macros (pre-2007, Tools →

Macro → Macros) or press Alt/Option-F8. Select your macro, click the Edit button, and enter the following code:

```
'
' a Macro
' Macro recorded 1/01/2007 by OzGrid.com
'


'
Application.ScreenUpdating = False
'YOUR CODE
Application.ScreenUpdating = True
End Sub
```

Note how you set ScreenUpdating back to True on completion. Although Excel will set this back to True whenever focus is passed back to Excel (in other words, when your macro finishes), in most cases it pays to play it safe and include the code at the end.

In some cases, you might find that ScreenUpdating is set back to True before your recorded macro completes. This can happen with recorded macros that use the Select command frequently. If this does happen, you might need to repeat the line Application.ScreenUpdating = False in other parts of your macro.

HACK 107 Run a Macro at a Set Time

ALL

Many times it would be great to run a macro at a predetermined time or at specified intervals. Fortunately, Excel provides a VBA method that makes this possible.

The Application.OnTime method can make macros run automatically, once you've done some setup. Suppose you have a macro that you want to run each day at 15:00 (3:00 p.m.). First you need to determine how to kick off the OnTime method. You can do this using the Workbook_Open event in the private module of the Workbook object.

In Windows, the fastest way to get to the private module of the Workbook object is to press Alt/Option-F11 and double-click **ThisWorkbook** (pre-2007, right-click the Excel icon next to File and select View Code). On a Macintosh, open the VBE and then open the module for the Workbook object from the Project window. Enter the following code:

```
Private Sub Workbook_Open( )
 Application.OnTime TimeValue("15:00:00"), "MyMacro"
End Sub
```

MyMacro should be the name of the macro you want to run. It should reside in a standard module and contain the OnTime method, as follows:

```
Sub MyMacro( )
 Application.OnTime TimeValue("15:00:00"), "MyMacro"
'YOUR CODE

End Sub
```

This will run the procedure MyMacro at 15:00 each day, so long as Excel is open.

Now suppose you want to run MyMacro at 15-minute intervals after opening your workbook. Again you will kick it off as soon as the workbook opens, so press Alt/Option-F11 and double-click ThisWorkbook (pre-2007, right-click the Excel icon next to File and select View Code). Enter the following code:

```
Private Sub Workbook_BeforeClose(Cancel As Boolean)
 Application.OnTime dTime, "MyMacro", , False
End Sub

Private Sub Workbook_Open( )
 Application.OnTime Now + TimeValue("00:15:00"), "MyMacro"
End Sub
```

In any standard module (accessed by selecting Insert → Module), enter the following code:

```
Public dTime As Date
Sub MyMacro( )
dTime = Now + TimeValue("00:15:00")
Application.OnTime dTime, "MyMacro"

'YOUR CODE
End Sub
```

Note how you pass the time of 15 minutes to the public variable dTime. This is so that you can have the OnTime method cancelled in the Workbook_ BeforeClose event by setting the optional Schedule argument to False. The Schedule argument is True by default, so by setting it to False, you are telling Excel to cancel the OnTime method that is set to run at a specified time.

If you didn't pass the time to a variable, Excel would not know which OnTime method to cancel, as Now + TimeValue("00:15:00") is *not* static, but becomes static when passed to a variable. If you didn't set the optional Schedule argument to False, the workbook would open automatically every 15 minutes after you close it and run MyMacro.

HACK 108 Use CodeNames to Reference Sheets in Excel Workbooks

ALL   Sometimes you need to create a macro that will work even if the sheet names that it references change.

If you have recorded a macro in Excel that references a specific sheet in your workbook, you know the code will continue to work only if the sheet name remains the same. For example, if your worksheet is named Budget, and the code in your macro reads Sheets("Budget").Select and then you change the worksheet name, the macro will no longer work. This is because the macro recorder generates code based on the sheet's tab name or on the name you see when working in Excel.

To overcome this limitation, you have two options, the first of which is to use index numbers. A sheet's index number is determined by its position in the workbook. The leftmost sheet will always have an index number of 1, the next worksheet immediately to the right will always have an index number of 2, and so on. Excel VBA enables you to specify any sheet by using its index number, but unfortunately Excel does not use this method when you record a macro.

Also, although using an index number such as Sheets(3).Select is a better option than using Sheets("Budget").Select, the sheet's position in the workbook could change if you add, remove, or move sheets.

Instead of using index numbers, savvy VBA coders use CodeNames. Each sheet in a workbook is given a unique CodeName that does not change even when that sheet is moved or renamed, or when any other sheets are added. You can see a sheet's CodeName only by going into the VBE (press Alt/Option-F11) and then displaying the Project window if necessary (select View → Project Explorer or press Ctrl-R).

In Figure 7-1, the CodeName for the sheet with a tab name of Budget is Sheet3. A sheet's CodeName is always the name that appears outside the parentheses when you look in the Project Explorer. You can reference this sheet with VBA code in the workbook by using Sheet3.Select, as opposed to Sheets("Budget").Select or Sheets(3).Select.

If your workbook is already full of VBA code (recorded or written) that does not use CodeNames, you can change the code at the project level (all code in all modules in the workbook) by selecting Edit → Replace... while in the VBE.

The only time you *cannot* use a sheet's CodeName is when you reference a sheet that is in a workbook different from the one in which the code resides.

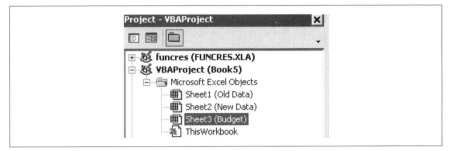

Figure 7-1. CodeNames and sheet names in the VBE Project window

HACK 109 Connect Buttons to Macros Easily

ALL

Instead of giving every button its own macro, it's sometimes more convenient to create a single macro that manages all the buttons.

Users generally prefer to run macros via either a shortcut key or a button they can simply click, instead of having to hunt through menus and dialog boxes. The most popular way to access a button is from the Forms toolbar, available by selecting Developer → Controls → Insert (pre-2007, View → Toolbars → Forms). These buttons, in our opinion, are the best choice for running macros, especially recorded macros, because recorded macros often require the user to be on a specific worksheet when the macro is run. Simply put, recorded macros always use ActiveSheet if you recorded the macro without changing sheets. This means that if the user is not on the required worksheet (in other words, the same one you were on when recording), the recorded macro will often "bug out" and/or make changes on the wrong sheet. By using a button on a worksheet, you can force the user to navigate to that worksheet button to set the right conditions for the macro before clicking it.

> Why a button from the Forms toolbar and not the Control Toolbox toolbar? Buttons are almost always used to detect a mouse click and then run a specified macro. You should use a command button from the Control Toolbox toolbar only when you need to determine other events such as double-clicks, right-clicks, and so on. The controls on the Control Toolbox toolbar are known as ActiveX controls, and using them to only run a macro adds unnecessary overhead to Excel, especially if you use a lot of buttons. It is akin to using a sledgehammer to bang in a nail.

When you have a lot of buttons in a workbook and each button is used to run a specified macro, you can attach the macros to the buttons by right-clicking the button border and choosing Assign Macro. Then find the correct macro in the Assign Macro dialog, as shown in Figure 7-2.

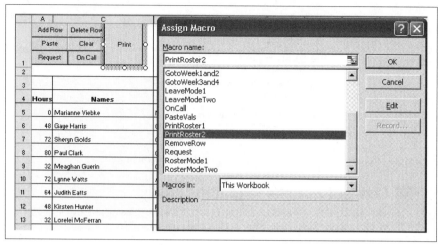

Figure 7-2. *Print button highlighted and Assign Macro dialog active, with macro highlighted*

Because each button is usually used to run a different macro, often you must scroll through the entire macro list to find the correct one. There is a really simple way you can assign all the buttons to the same macro but still have each button run a different macro.

Place the following code into any standard module. Press Alt/Option-F11 and create a new module by selecting Insert → Module and then entering the following code:

```
Sub WhichButton( )
  Run Application.Caller
End Sub
```

Now you need to give each button the same name as the macro it should run. To name a button from the Forms toolbar, simply left-click it, then replace the name shown in the Name box (at the left of the Formula bar) with the name of the macro the button should run. Do the same for all buttons. Now, if you named a button Macro1 and then assigned it to the macro WhichButton, when clicked it will run the macro Macro1.

Create a Workbook Splash Screen

HACK
110

ALL

Splash screens provide that extra bit of polish to an application—not to mention that they keep you entertained while the application loads. Why shouldn't a spreadsheet do the same?

You can use Excel's VBA capabilities to create a splash screen for any workbook; you'll find the process is easier than you might imagine it would be.

To create a splash screen that shows for 5 to 10 seconds when a workbook opens, then closes itself automatically, start by pressing Alt/Option-F11, to open the VBE. Then select Insert → UserForm. If the Control toolbox is not showing, select View → Toolbox to view it.

From the toolbox, left-click the Label control (you can hover your mouse pointer over each control to display its name). Left-click anywhere on the UserForm to insert the label. Using the size handles, drag out the label so that you can type some brief text into it. With the label still selected, left-click again. If the label is not selected, slowly double-click it. You should now be in Edit mode and should be able to highlight the default caption Label1.

Within that label, enter the text **My Splash Screen**. To change other properties of the label (e.g., font size, color), ensure that the label is selected and then press F4 or select View → Properties Window. Then change the required property in the Label Controls Property window. Now double-click the UserForm (not the label) and then select **Initialize** from the Procedure box at the top right of the screen, as shown in Figure 7-3.

Figure 7-3. Procedure drop-down box for the various events of the UserForm object

Within this procedure, enter the following:

```
Application.OnTime Now + TimeValue("00:00:05"), "KillForm"
```

Your code for the UserForm should look like this:

```
Private Sub UserForm_Initialize( )
  Application.OnTime Now + TimeValue("00:00:05"), "KillForm"
End Sub
```

Next, select Insert → Module, and enter the following code.

```
Sub KillForm( )
Unload UserForm1
End Sub
```

Note that UserForm1 is the default name of the newly inserted UserForm; if your UserForm has another name, you will need to substitute in the code.

Now all you need is some code in the private module of the Workbook object (ThisWorkbook). In the Project Explorer, you should see the name of your workbook. Expand the folders branching off the bottom of the workbook until you see ThisWorkbook. Double-click ThisWorkbook to expose its private module.

In the private module of the ThisWorkbook object, enter the following:

```
Private Sub Workbook_Open( )
  UserForm1.Show
End Sub
```

Close the window to get back to Excel. Save and close the workbook, and reopen it to see your splash screen in action. Figure 7-4 shows an example.

Figure 7-4. Example splash screen in action

Just remember that the splash screen should show for only a short period of time and should contain brief but relevant text. Showing it for longer than 10 seconds might annoy users.

Display a "Please Wait" Message

HACK
111
ALL

Have you ever had one of those macros that seem to take forever to complete? If this is a problem with your macro, you can have Excel display a "Please Wait" message to the user.

Most users expect code to run and complete almost instantaneously. Sadly, this doesn't always happen. Recorded macros in particular generally take much longer to complete than well-written VBA code. To add to the problem, Excel VBA code is generally slower than a lot of other types of code.

Fortunately, you can use a bit of extra code to create a "Please Wait" message so that users know the code is running and Excel has not locked up on them! Unfortunately, one of the more popular ways to let users know code is running is via the use of an Excel progress meter.

There are two problems with this method. First, the progress meter can slow down your code even more, compounding the issue. Second, your slow code must be caused by a loop, and you cannot use the macro recorder to create a loop.

We prefer using VBA code, such as the following DoIt macro, which uses a rectangle found in Insert → Illustration → Shapes:

```
Sub DoIt( )
Application.ScreenUpdating = True
    With Sheet1.Shapes("Rectangle 1")
        .Visible = msoTrue = (Not .Visible)
    End With
    'Forces TextBox to show while code is running
    Sheet2.Select
    Sheet1.Select
End Sub
```

To use this code, add a rectangle from the Drawing toolbar to any sheet in the appropriate workbook. While the rectangle is selected, click in the Name box and name the rectangle **Rectangle1** (if it's not already called that).

Enter the text you want displayed while your code is running, and format, position, and size the rectangle as desired. Enter the preceding DoIt macro into a standard module of your workbook. If necessary, change Sheet1 in the code to the CodeName of the sheet on which you placed Rectangle1. (For more information on CodeNames, see "Use CodeNames to Reference Sheets in Excel Workbooks" [Hack #108].) Then select Developer → Code → Macros or Alt/Option-F8 (pre-2007, Tools → Macro → Macros) and run DoIt from within Excel. This will hide Rectangle1 completely.

At the very start of the slow code, place the following:

```
Run "DoIt"
Application.ScreenUpdating = False
```

The use of Application.ScreenUpdating = False stops screen flicker and speeds up macros. At the very end of the slow code, simply place the code Run "DoIt". Then run your macro as usual.

Have a Cell Ticked or Unticked upon Selection

Sometimes it's difficult to make choices with checkboxes. Fortunately, you can simplify this process using a basic bit of code.

You can use Excel workbooks to collect data for surveys. Usually you do this by offering users a number of answers to choose from and placing a checkbox next to each choice. Users then check the appropriate checkboxes. The problem with using this method, though, is that your workbook soon can end up with hundreds of checkboxes.

Instead, you can use some very simple VBA code to tick any cell within a specified range as soon as it's selected. If the cell within the specified range is ticked already, the code will remove it. The trick to the code is the use of the letter "a" in a cell whose font is set to Marlett. When it's time to add up the results, simply use the COUNTIF function to count the occurrences of the letter "a", like this:

```
=COUNITIF($A$1:A$100,"a")
```

The following code examples work only on the range A1:A100, but you can modify them easily to suit any range. To use the code, activate the worksheet on which the ticks should be displayed, right-click the Sheet Name tab, and select View Code. Paste in either CODE 1 (if you want the cell ticked when it's selected) or CODE 2 (if you want the cell ticked when it's double-clicked):

```
'CODE 1 - tick cell with selection

Private Sub Worksheet_SelectionChange(ByVal Target As Range)
 If Target.Cells.Count > 1 Then Exit Sub
 If Not Intersect(Target, Range("A1:A100")) Is Nothing Then
 Target.Font.Name = "Marlett"
 If Target = vbNullString Then
 Target = "a"
 Else
 Target = vbNullString
 End If
 End If
End Sub


'CODE 2 - tick cell with double-click

Private Sub Worksheet_BeforeDoubleClick(ByVal Target As Range, Cancel As
Boolean)
 If Not Intersect(Target, Range("A1:A100")) Is Nothing Then
 Cancel = True 'Prevent going into Edit Mode
 Target.Font.Name = "Marlett"
 If Target = vbNullString Then
 Target = "a"
 Else
 Target = vbNullString
 End If
 End If
End Sub
```

Once the desired code is in place, simply close the window to get back to Excel and save your workbook. If you need to see whether the cell is checked, just examine its contents.

Count or Sum Cells That Have a Specified Fill Color

HACK 113

ALL

Using a bit of code, you can easily SUM or COUNT cells whose fill color was specified manually.

Every now and then, it's convenient to SUM or COUNT cells that have a specified fill color that you or another user have set manually, as users often understand paint colors more readily than named ranges. To do this, first open the workbook where you want to COUNT or SUM cells by a fill color. Go into the VBE by selecting Alt/Option-F11 and then select Insert → Module to insert a standard module. In this module, type the following code:

```
Function ColorFunction(rColor As Range, rRange As Range, Optional SUM As
Boolean)
Dim rCell As Range
Dim lCol As Long
Dim vResult

lCol = rColor.Interior.ColorIndex

  If SUM = True Then
  For Each rCell In rRange
  If rCell.Interior.ColorIndex = lCol Then
  vResult = WorksheetFunction.SUM(rCell) + vResult
  End If
  Next rCell
  Else
  For Each rCell In rRange
  If rCell.Interior.ColorIndex = lCol Then
  vResult = 1 + vResult
  End If
  Next rCell
  End If

  ColorFunction = vResult
  End Function
```

Close the window to get back to your worksheet, and save your workbook.

Now you can use the custom function ColorFunction in formulas such as this:

```
=ColorFunction($C$1,$A$1:$A$12,TRUE)
```

to sum the values in the range of cells $A$1:$A$12 that have the same fill color as cell $C$1. The function will sum in this example because you used TRUE as the last argument for the custom function.

To count the cells that have the same fill color as cell $C$1, you can use this:

```
=ColorFunction($C$1,$A$1:$A$12,FALSE)
```

or:

```
=ColorFunction($C$1,$A$1:$A$12)
```

By omitting the last argument, the function automatically defaults to using FALSE as the last argument. Now you easily can SUM or COUNT cells that have a specified fill color, as shown in Figure 7-5.

	A	B	C	D	E
1	20				
2	22				
3	23				
4	25				
5	26				
6	27				
7	29				
8	30				
9	31				
10	32				
11	54				
12	21				
13	78	=ColorFunction($C$1,$A$1:$A$12,TRUE)			
14	3	=ColorFunction($C$1,$A$1:$A$12)			
15					

Figure 7-5. Using the custom ColorFunction to count by fill color

HACK 114   Add the Microsoft Excel Calendar Control to Any Excel Workbook

ALL   If you want to ensure that users enter dates correctly, the Excel Calendar Control can make things easier for both you and the users of the spreadsheet. With this hack, you can add the Calendar Control to any Excel workbook.

Unless a date is entered correctly, Excel won't recognize it as valid. This sometimes means you cannot perform calculations with figures that look like dates but aren't. It also means any charts or PivotTables based on these dates will not be valid. Although the use of Excel's very versatile validation feature (described in Chapter 2) can help with this, it is far from bulletproof.

With this hack, you can add the Calendar Control to any Excel workbook:

1. To start, open the workbook for the calendar.

2. It is a good idea to use your *Personal.xls* file for this, in which case you should first select View → Window → Unhide (pre-2007, Window → Unhide). If this option is grayed out, it means you do not have a *Personal.xls* file yet. You can create one easily by recording a dummy macro:

a. Select Developer → Code → Record Macro (pre-2007, Tools → Macro → Record New Macro).

b. Choose Personal Macro Workbook from the Store Macro In: box.

c. Then click OK, select any cell, and stop recording. Excel will create your *Personal.xls* file automatically.

3. Next, press Alt/Option-F11 and then select Insert → UserForm from within the VBE. This should display the Control toolbox (if it doesn't, select View → Toolbox).

4. Right-click the Control toolbox and select Additional Controls. Scroll through the list until you see the Calendar Control 12.0 checkbox (the number will differ depending on the version of Excel you are using). Check the checkbox and click OK.

5. Click the calendar that is now part of the toolbox and then click the UserForm you inserted earlier.

6. Using the size handles on both the UserForm and the Calendar Control, size the UserForm and Calendar Control to a reasonable size, as shown in Figure 7-6.

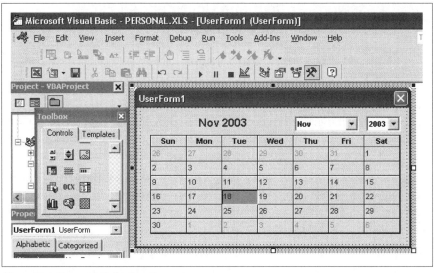

Figure 7-6. Inserted Calendar Control

7. Make sure the UserForm is selected (as shown in Figure 7-6) and then select View → Properties Window (F4).

8. Select Caption from the Properties window and replace UserForm1 with the word **Calendar**.

9. Now select View → Code (F7), and in the private module, add the following code:

```
Private Sub Calendar1_Click()
  ActiveCell = Calendar1.Value
End Sub

Private Sub UserForm_Activate()
  Me.Calendar1.Value = Date
End Sub
```

10. Select Insert → Module, and in the public module, place this code:

```
Sub ShowIt()
  UserForm1.Show
End Sub
```

11. Close the window to return to Excel, then save your workbook.

12. Press Alt/Option-F8 and then select ShowIt.

13. Click Options, assign a shortcut key, and you're done.

Just press your shortcut key, and the calendar will show with today's date as the default. Click any date and it will be inserted into the active cell.

HACK 115 Password-Protect and Unprotect All Excel Worksheets in One Fell Swoop

ALL

Sadly, there is no standard feature in Excel that will enable you to protect and unprotect all worksheets in one go; however, some simple code can make it happen.

Excel provides protection that you can add to an Excel worksheet by selecting Review → Changes → Protect Sheet (pre-2007, Tools → Protection → Protect Sheet). You can also supply a password so that another user cannot unprotect the worksheet and gain access unless he knows the password.

Sometimes, though, you want to password-protect and unprotect all worksheets in a workbook in one step, because protecting and unprotecting each worksheet individually is a huge nuisance. Here is how you can simplify this task.

1. Open the workbook to which you want to apply the code.

   Alternatively, select Windows → View → Unhide to unhide your *Personal.xls* file and make it available to any workbook. If this option is grayed out, it means you do not have a *Personal.xls* file yet. You can create one easily by recording a dummy macro:

   a. Select Developer → Code → Record Macro (pre-2007, Tools → Macro → Record New Macro).

   b. Choose Personal Macro Workbook from the Store Macro In: box.

   c. Click OK, select any cell, and stop recording. Excel will create your *Personal.xls* file automatically.

2. Next, press Alt/Option-F11 and select Insert → UserForm. This should display the Control toolbox. If it doesn't, select View → Toolbox.

3. From the toolbox, select a TextBox (indicated as ab|). Click onto the UserForm to add the TextBox to the UserForm. Position it in the top left of your form and size it to your preference.

4. Ensure that the textbox is still selected and then select View → Properties (F4). From the Properties window of the textbox, scroll down until you see PasswordChar, and in the white box on the right, enter an asterisk (*).

5. From the toolbox, select a CommandButton and then click the UserForm and position it in the top right of your form.

6. With the CommandButton still selected, select View → Properties (F4). From the Properties window of the CommandButton, scroll down until you see Caption, and in the white box on the right, enter the caption OK. If you are using Excel 97, also scroll down until you see TakeFocusOn-Click, and set this to False.

7. Now select the UserForm and, from its Properties window, find Caption and change it to Protect/Unprotect all sheets. Your form should look like that shown in Figure 7-7.

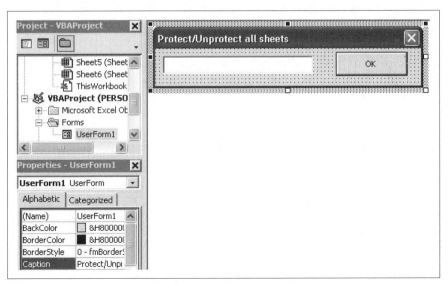

Figure 7-7. UserForm inserted in the VBE

8. Select View → Code (F7) and enter the following code exactly as shown:

```
Private Sub CommandButton1_Click( )
Dim wSheet As Worksheet
  For Each wSheet In Worksheets
  If wSheet.ProtectContents = True Then
  wSheet.Unprotect Password:=TextBox1.Text
  Else
  wSheet.Protect Password:=TextBox1.Text
  End If
  Next wSheet
  Unload me
End Sub
```

The code loops through all worksheets in the active workbook. If one is protected, it unprotects it using the password entered into the text box. If the worksheet is already unprotected, it protects it using the password entered into the text box.

9. Now select Insert → Module and enter this code, which is used to launch the UserForm:

```
Sub ShowPass( )
  UserForm1.Show
End Sub
```

10. Close the window to get back to Excel, then save your workbook.

11. Press Alt/Option-F8, select ShowPass, and then click Options and assign a shortcut key. This will unprotect all worksheets that are protected and protect all worksheets that are unprotected.

12. Remember to save your workbook.

 As this macro does not ask you to confirm your password, you should be very sure of what you type. Otherwise, you may find that typos lock you out of your spreadsheets.

If you're protecting the contents only from yourself, the following macro lets you perform the same tasks with a blank password instead:

```
Option Explicit

Sub Protect_Unprotect( )
Dim wSheet As Worksheet

For Each wSheet In Worksheets
 With wSheet
 If .ProtectContents = True Then
 .Unprotect Password:=""
 Else
 .Protect Password:=""
 End If
```

```
End With
Next wSheet

End Sub
```

Although it's not very secure, it's definitely convenient.

HACK Retrieve a Workbook's Name and Path
116

ALL

Every now and then you might want a cell to return the name of a workbook, or even the workbook's filename and path. With this hack, it's easy to retrieve a workbook's name and path.

The three user-defined functions we explain in this section place the name of a workbook into a cell, or the workbook's filename and path into a cell. The first two examples, MyName and MyFullName, do not take any arguments. The last one, SheetName, is used in place of nesting the MID and other functions inside the CELL function to get the sheet name, a process that commonly would require the following unwieldy formula:

```
=MID(CELL("filename",$A$1),FIND("]",CELL("filename",$A$1))+1,255)
```

As you can see, this requires quite a bit of typing for such a simple result, which is why we initially developed the SheetName custom function.

To use this user-defined function, press Alt/Option-F11, select Insert → Module, and paste in the following code:

```
Function MyName( ) As String
 MyName = ThisWorkbook.Name
End Function
Function MyFullName( ) As String
 MyFullName = ThisWorkbook.FullName
End Function
Function SheetName(rAnyCell)
 Application.Volatile
 SheetName = rAnyCell.Parent.Name
End Function
```

Save the function and close the window. The function will appear under User Defined in the Insert Function dialog (Shift-F3).

You can use the functions as shown in Figure 7-8. They take no arguments. The formulas in column A are shown for demonstration purposes only and have no effect on the result.

In cell A4 in Figure 7-8, we also placed the standard CELL function that returns a workbook's name, file path, and active sheet name. The CELL function is a standard function that will return information about the current operating system—in other words, information on formatting, location, and contents of a workbook.

	A	B
	Formula	Result
1		
2	=MyName()	Workbook Path.xls
3	=MyFullName()	C:\OzGrid\Learning\Workbook Path.xls
4	=CELL("filename")	C:\OzGrid\Learning\[Workbook Path.xls]Sheet1
5	=sheetname(A1)	Sheet1

Figure 7-8. Functions and their result

HACK 117
Get Around Excel's Three-Criteria Limit for Conditional Formatting

<2007> You can use VBA to hack conditional formatting to use more than three criteria on your data. In fact, you can use the code to apply virtually an unlimited number of criteria.

Excel has a useful feature named conditional formatting (described in Chapter 2). You can find it by selecting Format → Conditional Formatting... on the worksheet menu bar. Conditional formatting enables you to format a cell based on its content. For example, you can change to a red background all cells whose value is greater than 5 but less than 10. Although this is handy, Excel supports only up to three conditions, which sometimes is not enough.

If you want to set more than three conditions, you can use Excel VBA code that is fired automatically whenever a user changes a specified range. To see how this works, say you want to have six separate conditions in the range A1:A10 on a particular worksheet. Set up some data such as that shown in Figure 7-9.

	A
	Numbers
1	
2	3
3	
4	8
5	
6	13
7	
8	18
9	23
10	28
11	3
12	7
13	12
14	17
15	23
16	28

Figure 7-9. Data setup for conditional formatting experiment

Save your workbook, then activate the worksheet, right-click its Sheet Name tab, select View Code, and enter the following code:

```
Private Sub Worksheet_Change(ByVal Target As Range)

Dim icolor As Integer
If Not Intersect(Target, Range("A1:A10")) is Nothing Then
 Select Case Target
 Case 1 To 5
 icolor = 6
 Case 6 To 10
 icolor = 12
 Case 11 To 15
 icolor = 7
 Case 16 To 20
 icolor = 53
 Case 21 To 25
 icolor = 15
 Case 26 To 30
 icolor = 42
 Case Else
 'Whatever
 End Select
 Target.Interior.ColorIndex = icolor
 End If

End Sub
```

Close the window to get back to your worksheet, then save your workbook. Your results should look like Figure 7-10.

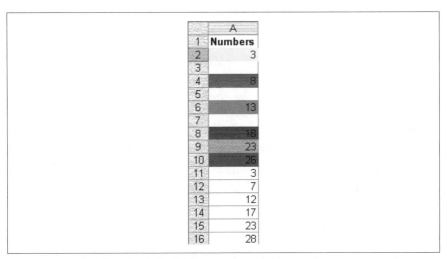

Figure 7-10. What data should look like once the code is entered

The background color of each cell should have changed based on the number passed to the variable `icolor`, which in turn passes this number to `Target.Interior.ColorIndex`. The number that is passed is determined by the line `Case x To x`. For example, if you enter the number 22 in any cell within the range A1:A10, the number 15 is passed to `icolor`, and then `icolor` (now having a value of 15) is passed to `Target.Interior.ColorIndex`, making the cell gray. `Target` is always the cell that changed and, thus, fired the code.

Run Procedures on Protected Worksheets

HACK 118

ALL

Excel macros are a great way to save time and eliminate errors. However, sooner or later you might try to run your favorite Excel macro on a worksheet that has been protected, with or without a password, resulting in a runtime error. Avoid that problem with the following hack.

If you have ever tried to run an Excel macro on a worksheet that's been protected, you know that as soon as the worksheet is encountered, your macro probably won't work and instead will display a runtime error.

One way to get around this is to use some code such as the following to unprotect and then protect your worksheet:

```
Sub MyMacro( )

Sheet1.Unprotect Password:="Secret"

'YOUR CODE

Sheet1.Protect Password:="Secret"
End Sub
```

As you can see, the code unprotects `Sheet1` with the password `Secret`, runs the code, and then password-protects it again. This will work, but it has a number of drawbacks. For one, the code could bug out and stop before it encounters the `Sheet1.Protect Password:="Secret"` line of code. This, of course, would leave your worksheet fully unprotected. Another drawback is that you will need similar code for all macros and all worksheets.

Another way to avoid this problem is to use `UserInterFaceOnly`, which is an optional argument of the `Protect` method that you can set to `True`. (The default is `False`.) By setting this argument to `True`, Excel will allow all Excel VBA macros to run on the worksheets that are protected with or without a password.

However, if you use the `Protect` method with the `UserInterfaceOnly` argument set to `True` on a worksheet and then save the workbook, the entire worksheet (not just the interface) will be fully protected when you reopen the workbook. To set the `UserInterfaceOnly` argument back to `True` after the workbook is opened, you must again apply the Protect method with UserInterfaceOnly set to True.

To avoid this hassle, you need to use the Workbook_Open event, which is fired as soon as the workbook is opened. Because this is an event of the Workbook object ThisWorkbook, you must place the following code in the private module of ThisWorkbook. To do this, press Alt/Option-F8 and double-click on ThisWorkbook (on Macs, open the Workbook object from the Projects window of the VBE). Then enter the following code:

```
Private Sub Workbook_Open( )
'If you have different passwords
'for each worksheet.

Sheets(1).Protect Password:="Secret", UserInterFaceOnly:=True
Sheets(2).Protect Password:="Carrot", UserInterFaceOnly:=True

'Repeat as needed.
End Sub
```

Close the window to get back to your worksheet, and save your workbook. The preceding code is good if each worksheet on which you want your macros to operate has a different password, or if you do not want to protect all worksheets. You can set the UserInterfaceOnly argument to True without having to unprotect first.

If you want to set the UserInterfaceOnly argument to True on all worksheets and they have the same password, you can use the following code, which must be placed in the same place as the preceding code:

```
Private Sub Workbook_Open( )
Dim wSheet As Worksheet

For Each wSheet In Worksheets
wSheet.Protect Password:="Secret", _
UserInterFaceOnly:=True
Next wSheet
End Sub
```

Now, each time you open the workbook, the code will run and will set the UserInterfaceOnly property to True, allowing your macros to operate while still preventing any user changes.

Distribute Macros

HACK #119

Although you can distribute a macro along with a workbook, if you want to distribute only the macro's functionality, an Excel add-in is the way to go.

An Excel add-in is nothing more than an Excel workbook that was saved as an add-in by selecting the Office button → Save As... → Microsoft Excel

Add-in (*.xlam*); however, in pre-2007 versions, select File → Save As... → Microsoft Excel Add-in (*.xla*).

Once it's saved and reopened, the workbook will be hidden and can be seen only in the Project Explorer via the VBE. It is not hidden in the same way as the *Personal.xls* file, as this can be seen (and made visible) via View → Unhide (pre-2007, Windows → Unhide).

Once you have completed the workbook you want to use as an add-in, you need to save a copy of it. You can save it to any location you want, but make sure to note where you placed it.

Open any workbook, and on the Office button, select Excel Options → Add-Ins (pre-2007, Tools → Add-Ins), make sure Add-Ins is showing in the Manage: box, and press Go. Click Browse, locate your add-in from where you saved it, select it, and then click OK.

Ensure that your add-in is in the Add-Ins Available: box and that the box is checked. Then click OK to install the add-in. You can save most code to an Excel add-in without too many changes. There are a few issues worth considering, however:

- The ThisWorkbook object will always refer to the add-in, not to the user's workbook. Use the ActiveWorkbook object instead.

- You cannot refer to sheets in the ActiveWorkbook with CodeNames.

- You should always put ribbons, etc, back to the way the user had them originally. There is nothing worse than an add-in that changes all your Excel settings without your knowledge.

- Always include some sort of error handling (yes, most add-ins will cause errors at some time).

- Be very aware that the user might have many sorts of protection applied. *Never* use code to unprotect any part of the user's workbook. Simply display a message asking the user to unprotect.

- Make full and good use of the worksheet you have in the add-in. We use the worksheet(s) to store user settings.

- Holding down the Shift key will *not* prevent add-in workbook events from running (holding down the Shift key will prevent a normal Excel file from running, however).

- If you need to look at or work with the add-in workbook again (e.g., to incorporate updates or modifications), go into the VBE while the add-in is installed and, from the Properties window, select the IsAddin property and set it to False. Saving the workbook as an add-in sets this property to True.

- Apply protection to the modules of your add-in by selecting Tools → VBAProject Properties → Protection.

Once you have installed an add-in in Excel 2007, you can select the Add-Ins tab, then right-click on your add-in and select Add to Quick Access Toolbar. This will add an icon to the toolbar, which when clicked will display the add-in name for selection.

Add a Menu Item <2007

If you aren't using Excel 2007, you won't have the Quick Access Toolbar option, so once you have created your add-in, you will need to make the macros within it easy for the user to run. This is best achieved by using the Workbook_AddinInstall and Workbook_AddinUnInstall events in the private module of the ThisWorkbook object. Simply double-click ThisWorkbook for the *.xla* file, and Excel will take you into the private module where the code is placed, as shown in Figure 7-11.

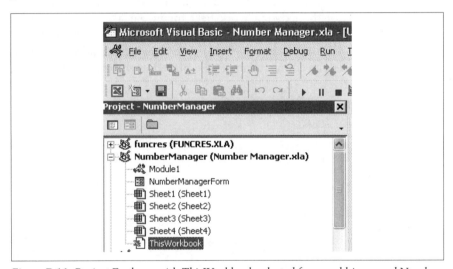

Figure 7-11. Project Explorer with ThisWorkbook selected for an add-in named Number Manager.xla

Here is a simple example of the code:

```
Option Explicit
Dim cControl As CommandBarButton
Private Sub Workbook_AddinInstall( )

On Error Resume Next 'Just in case
  'Delete any existing menu item that may have been left.
  Application.CommandBars("Worksheet Menu Bar").Controls("Super Code").Delete
  'Add the new menu item and set a CommandBarButton variable to it
```

```
Set cControl = Application.CommandBars("Worksheet Menu Bar").Controls.Add
'Work with the Variable
With cControl
.Caption = "Super Code"
.Style = msoButtonCaption
.OnAction = "MyGreatMacro" 'Macro stored in a Standard Module
End With
On Error GoTo 0

End Sub


Private Sub Workbook_AddinUninstall()

On Error Resume Next 'In case it has already gone.
Application.CommandBars("Worksheet Menu Bar").Controls("Super Code").Delete
On Error GoTo 0

End Sub
```

This is all the code you'll need to add a single menu item (called Super Code) to the end of the existing worksheet menu bar as soon as the user installs the add-in via Tools → Add-Ins. When the Super Code menu item is clicked, a macro (that is within a standard module of the add-in) is run. Remember that the preceding code *must* be placed in the private module of ThisWorkbook for the add-in.

If you want the Super Code menu item added, say, before the format menu item, you can use this code:

```
Option Explicit
Dim cControl As CommandBarButton

Private Sub Workbook_AddinInstall()

Dim iContIndex As Integer
 On Error Resume Next 'Just in case
 'Delete any existing menu item that may have been left.
 Application.CommandBars("Worksheet Menu Bar").Controls("Super Code").Delete
 'Pass the index of the "Format" menu item number to a variable.
 'Use the FindControl method to find its Index number. ID number _
 is used in case of customization
 iContIndex = Application.CommandBars.FindControl(ID:=30006).Index
 'Add the new menu item and set a CommandBarButton variable to it.
 'Use the number passed to our Integer variable to position it.
 Set cControl = Application.CommandBars("Worksheet Menu Bar") _
 .Controls.Add(Before:=iContIndex)
 'Work with the Variable
 With cControl
 .Caption = "Super Code"
 .Style = msoButtonCaption
 .OnAction = "MyGreatMacro" 'Macro stored in a standard module
```

```
End With
 On Error GoTo 0
End Sub
```

You would not have to change the `Workbook_AddinUninstall( )` code in this case.

In these examples, all the menu item code is in `Workbook_AddinInstall` and `Workbook_AddinUnInstall`. This is not a problem when the code is adding only one menu item. However, if you will be adding more than one item (and perhaps even submenus), you should place the menu item code in a procedure (or two) inside a standard module. Use some code such as this:

```
Private Sub Workbook_AddinInstall( )
 Run "AddMenus"
End Sub

Private Sub Workbook_AddinUninstall( )
 Run "DeleteMenu"
End Sub
```

In the standard module, put some code such as this:

```
Sub AddMenus( )
Dim cMenu1 As CommandBarControl
Dim cbMainMenuBar As CommandBar
Dim iHelpMenu As Integer
Dim cbcCutomMenu As CommandBarControl

 '(1)Delete any existing one. We must use On Error Resume next _
 in case it does not exist.
 On Error Resume Next
 Application.CommandBars("Worksheet Menu Bar").Controls("&New Menu").Delete


 '(2)Set a CommandBar variable to the worksheet menu bar
 Set cbMainMenuBar = _
 Application.CommandBars("Worksheet Menu Bar")

 '(3)Return the index number of the Help menu. We can then use _
 this to place a custom menu before it.
 iHelpMenu = _
 cbMainMenuBar.Controls("Help").Index

 '(4)Add a control to the "Worksheet Menu Bar" before Help.
 'Set a CommandBarControl variable to it
 Set cbcCutomMenu = _
 cbMainMenuBar.Controls.Add(Type:=msoControlPopup, _
 Before:=iHelpMenu)

 '(5)Give the control a caption
 cbcCutomMenu.Caption = "&New Menu"
```

```
'(6)Working with our new control, add a sub control and _
give it a caption and tell it which macro to run (OnAction).
With cbcCutomMenu.Controls.Add(Type:=msoControlButton)
.Caption = "Menu 1"
.OnAction = "MyMacro1"
End With

'(6a)Add another sub control and give it a caption _
and tell it which macro to run (OnAction)
With cbcCutomMenu.Controls.Add(Type:=msoControlButton)
.Caption = "Menu 2"
.OnAction = "MyMacro2"
End With
'Repeat step "6a" for each menu item you want to add.


'Add another menu that will lead off to another menu
'Set a CommandBarControl variable to it
Set cbcCutomMenu = cbcCutomMenu.Controls.Add(Type:=msoControlPopup)
' Give the control a caption
cbcCutomMenu.Caption = "Ne&xt Menu"

'Add a control to the sub menu just created above
With cbcCutomMenu.Controls.Add(Type:=msoControlButton)
.Caption = "&Charts"
.FaceId = 420
.OnAction = "MyMacro2"
End With


 On Error GoTo 0
End Sub

Sub DeleteMenu( )
 On Error Resume Next
 Application.CommandBars("Worksheet Menu Bar").Controls("&New Menu").Delete
 On Error GoTo 0
End Sub
```

When using the OnAction property, it is possible that you may encounter problems if there is a macro in the user's workbook that has the exact same name as a macro that resides in your add-in. To play it safe, it is often a good idea to use a method like this:

```
With cbcCutomMenu.Controls.Add(Type:=msoControlButton)
.Caption = "&Charts"
.FaceId = 420
.OnAction = ThisWorkbook.Name & "!MyMacro2"
End With
```

By doing this, you ensure that Excel knows which macro you want run when the user clicks the button. With these snippets of code, you'll find it easy to distribute and use macros to their fullest potential.

Delete Rows Based on a Condition

Use specific criteria to delete rows from your worksheet, with or without the AutoFilter feature.

ALL

One question we are often asked is: "How can I delete rows from my Excel worksheet based on a specified criteria or condition?" There are a number of ways you can do this, and this hack presents the two fastest. The first (using the AutoFilter) is the fastest by far.

Both examples are based on your data being in a contiguous range with the criteria/condition you're looking for in the relative column of the table you specify. The first row of your table should be headings.

With AutoFilter

Let's assume you have some data in a table, set up like Figure 7-12, and you have applied an AutoFilter in column E to show Administration, Finance, and Maintenance Departments only.

	A	B	C	D	E	F	G	H
1	Staff Payroll N	Title	First Name	Last Name	Department	Role	Date of Bir	
2	31256	Ms	Aleisha	Fenlon	Administration	Secretary	7/04/1963	
5	31267	Ms	Ashley	Fresh	Finance	Personal Assistant	9/03/1971	
6	31267	Miss	Jemma	Roberts	Maintenance	Clerk	5/12/1961	
8	31589	Ms	Maddison	Dawson	Finance	Supervisor	2/06/1970	
9	31658	Mr	Fred	Oates	Finance	Accountant	19/12/1982	
11	31687	Mr	Michael	Thurley	Maintenance	Leading Hand	15/04/1979	
12	31689	Miss	Patricia	Smith	Administration	Supervisor	11/07/1979	
13	31854	Mr	Jack	Blythe	Administration	Assistant	7/04/1964	
15	34589	Ms	Jennifer	Briggs	Maintenance	Storeman	30/01/1968	
16	34895	Ms	Angela	Morris	Maintenance	Clerk	21/06/1983	
17	37896	Ms	Kirstyn	McGinley	Administration	Receptionist	29/09/1974	
18	38976	Ms	Katelyn	Chell	Administration	Personal Assistant	3/02/1964	
19	40056	Ms	Aleisha	Fenlon	Administration	Secretary	7/04/1963	
22	43296	Ms	Ashley	Hammer	Finance	Personal Assistant	9/03/1971	
23	44376	Miss	Jemma	Roberts	Maintenance	Clerk	5/12/1961	
25	46536	Ms	Maddison	Dawson	Finance	Supervisor	2/06/1970	
26	48696	Mr	Fred	Oates	Finance	Accountant	19/12/1982	
28	50856	Mr	Michael	Thurley	Maintenance	Leading Hand	15/04/1979	
29	51936	Miss	Patricia	Smith	Administration	Supervisor	11/07/1979	
30	53016	Mr	Jack	Blythe	Administration	Assistant	7/04/1964	
32	55176	Ms	Jennifer	Briggs	Maintenance	Storeman	30/01/1968	
33	56256	Ms	Angela	Morris	Maintenance	Clerk	21/06/1983	
34	57336	Ms	Kirstyn	McGinley	Administration	Receptionist	29/09/1974	
35	58416	Ms	Katelyn	Chell	Administration	Personal Assistant	3/02/1964	
36	59496	Ms	Aleisha	Fenlon	Administration	Secretary	7/04/1963	
39	62736	Ms	Ashley	Hammer	Finance	Personal Assistant	9/03/1971	

Data

Figure 7-12. Table set up with Auofilter applied in column E

Delete Rows Based on a Condition

Now, let's say you want to delete all rows with the word Finance in the Department column (Column E). Right-click on the sheet tab, select View Code, and enter in the following code:

```
Sub DeleteRowsFastest( )
Dim rTable As Range
Dim lCol As long
Dim vCriteria

On Error Resume Next
    'Determine the table range
    With Selection
        If .Cells.Count > 1 Then
            Set rTable = Selection
        Else

            Set rTable = .CurrentRegion
            On Error GoTo 0
        End If
    End With

    'Determine if table range is valid
    If rTable Is Nothing Or rTable.Cells.Count = 1 Or WorksheetFunction. ↵
CountA(rTable) < 2 Then
        MsgBox "Could not determine you table range.", vbCritical, "Ozgrid.com"
        Exit Sub
    End If

    'Get the criteria in the form of text or number.
    vCriteria = Application.InputBox(Prompt:="Type in the criteria that ↵
matching rows should be deleted. " _
    & "If the criteria is in a cell, point to the cell with your mouse ↵
pointer", _
        Title:="CONDITIONAL ROW DELETION CRITERIA", Type:=1 + 2)

    'Go no further if they Cancel.
    If vCriteria = "False" Then Exit Sub

    'Get the relative column number where the criteria should be found
    lCol = Application.InputBox(Prompt:="Type in the relative number of the ↵
column where " _
    & "the criteria can be found.", Title:="CONDITIONAL ROW DELETION COLUMN ↵
NUMBER", Type:=1)

    'Cancelled
    If lCol = 0 Then Exit Sub

    'Remove any existing AutoFilters
    ActiveSheet.AutoFilterMode = False

    'Filter table based on vCriteria using the relative column position ↵
stored in lCol.
```

```
        rTable.AutoFilter Field:=lCol, Criteria1:=vCriteria

        'Delete all rows that are NOT hidden by AutoFilter.
        rTable.Offset(1, 0).SpecialCells(xlCellTypeVisible).EntireRow.Delete

        'Remove AutoFilters
        ActiveSheet.AutoFilterMode = False
    On Error GoTo 0
End Sub
```

Close the window to get back to your worksheet, and then save your workbook. Now, select any single cell in your table and select Developer → Code options → Macros (pre-2007, Tools → Macros) or press Alt/Option-F8.

To run the code, select the macro name `DeleteRowsFastest( )` and press Run. You will be asked to select your criteria by clicking a cell within your table, so select a cell in column E (Departments) containing the word Finance and click OK. Then, you will be asked which column in the table your criteria resides in. Enter the number 5 as the criteria, because Finance resides in the fifth column of the table. Click OK. Once you have made both selections, the code will run and will remove all rows with the desired criteria in them.

> The code will remove the AutoFilters after deleting the required rows.

Without AutoFilter

Using the previous code is the fastest and cleanest way to delete rows based on criteria. It is also the most useful way, because most times you would want to remove data after an AutoFilter has been applied.

But if you don't have AutoFilters applied to your table, you can use the following code to do the same thing.

Right-click on the sheet tab, select View Code, and enter the following code:

```
Sub DeleteRowsSecondFastest( )
Dim rTable As Range
Dim rCol As Range, rCell As Range
Dim lCol As Long
Dim xlCalc As XlCalculation
Dim vCriteria

On Error Resume Next
    'Determine the table range
    With Selection
        If .Cells.Count > 1 Then
            Set rTable = Selection
        Else
```

```
                Set rTable = .CurrentRegion
                On Error GoTo 0
            End If
        End With

        'Determine if table range is valid
        If rTable Is Nothing Or rTable.Cells.Count = 1 Or WorksheetFunction. ↵
    CountA(rTable) < 2 Then
            MsgBox "Could not determine you table range.", vbCritical, "Ozgrid.com"
            Exit Sub
        End If

        'Get the criteria in the form of text or number.
        vCriteria = Application.InputBox(Prompt:="Type in the criteria that ↵
    matching rows should be deleted. " _
        & "If the criteria is in a cell, point to the cell with your mouse ↵
    pointer", _
        Title:="CONDITIONAL ROW DELETION CRITERIA", Type:=1 + 2)

        'Go no further if they Cancel.
        If vCriteria = "False" Then Exit Sub

        'Get the relative column number where the criteria should be found
        lCol = Application.InputBox(Prompt:="Type in the relative number of the ↵
    column where " _
        & "the criteria can be found.", Title:="CONDITIONAL ROW DELETION COLUMN ↵
    NUMBER", Type:=1)

        'Cancelled
        If lCol = 0 Then Exit Sub

        'Set rCol to the column where criteria should be found
        Set rCol = rTable.Columns(lCol)
        'Set rCell to the first data cell in rCol
        Set rCell = rCol.Cells(2, 1)

        'Store current Calculation then switch to manual.
        xlCalc = Application.Calculation
        Application.Calculation = xlCalculationManual

        'Loop and delete as many times as vCriteria exists in rCol
        For lCol = 1 To WorksheetFunction.CountIf(rCol, vCriteria)
            Set rCell = rCol.Find(What:=vCriteria, After:=rCell, LookIn: ↵
    =xlValues, _
                LookAt:=xlWhole, SearchOrder:=xlByRows, SearchDirection:=xlNext, _
                MatchCase:=False).Offset(-1, 0)
                rCell.Offset(1, 0).EntireRow.Delete
        Next lCol

        'Put back calculation to how it was.
        Application.Calculation = xlCalc
        On Error GoTo 0
    End Sub
```

Close the window to get back to your worksheet, and then save your workbook.

Now, select any single cell in your table and select Developer → Code → Macros (pre-2007, Tools → Macros) or press Alt/Option-F8. To run the code, select the macro name DeleteRowsSecondFastest( ) and press Run.

Track and Report Changes in Excel

To overcome the limitations of the Track Changes feature, you can employ some help from Excel VBA and Excel's Change Events feature.

If you want to track any changes that either you or someone else has made to your data, you can use Excel's Track Changes feature, under Review → Changes (pre-2007, Tools → Track Changes). However, by doing it this way this function has a couple of drawbacks. When Track Changes is enabled, you are forced to share the workbook, whether you want to or not. Also, Track Changes makes many standard Excel features unavailable. We can easily conquer this problem with some code.

> Be aware that this code is designed to track and record user changes only *one cell at a time*.

Track Changes on a Particular Worksheet

For this to work, you need to have a workbook with two worksheets. Sheet1 contains the data to which you want to track and record any changes made, such as in Figure 7-13. Sheet 2 will contain a list of the tracked changes when we run the code.

To track user changes on a single worksheet, place the following code in the Private module of the worksheet where you would like changes tracked and logged (remember, we have used Sheet1). To get there easily, right-click on the sheet name tab, choose View Code, and paste the following code:

```
Dim vOldVal 'Must be at top of module
Private Sub Worksheet_Change(ByVal Target As Range)
Dim bBold As Boolean

If Target.Cells.Count > 1 Then Exit Sub
On Error Resume Next

    With Application
        .ScreenUpdating = False
        .EnableEvents = False
    End With
```

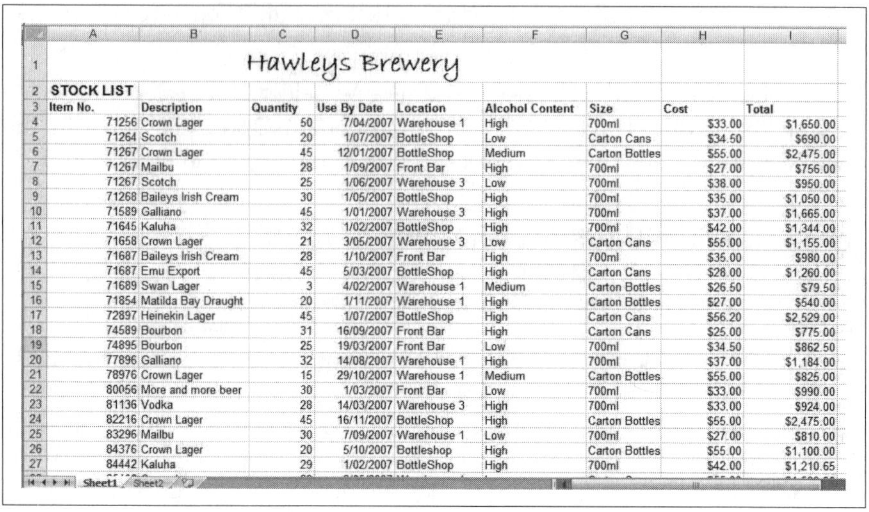

	A	B	C	D	E	F	G	H	I
1	Hawleys Brewery								
2	STOCK LIST								
3	Item No.	Description	Quantity	Use By Date	Location	Alcohol Content	Size	Cost	Total
4	71256	Crown Lager	50	7/04/2007	Warehouse 1	High	700ml	$33.00	$1,650.00
5	71264	Scotch	20	1/07/2007	BottleShop	Low	Carton Cans	$34.50	$690.00
6	71267	Crown Lager	45	12/01/2007	BottleShop	Medium	Carton Bottles	$55.00	$2,475.00
7	71267	Mailbu	28	1/09/2007	Front Bar	High	700ml	$27.00	$756.00
8	71267	Scotch	25	1/06/2007	Warehouse 3	Low	700ml	$38.00	$950.00
9	71268	Baileys Irish Cream	30	1/05/2007	BottleShop	High	700ml	$35.00	$1,050.00
10	71589	Galliano	45	1/01/2007	Warehouse 3	High	700ml	$37.00	$1,665.00
11	71645	Kaluha	32	1/02/2007	BottleShop	High	700ml	$42.00	$1,344.00
12	71658	Crown Lager	21	3/05/2007	Warehouse 3	Low	Carton Cans	$55.00	$1,155.00
13	71687	Baileys Irish Cream	28	1/10/2007	Front Bar	High	700ml	$35.00	$980.00
14	71687	Emu Export	45	5/03/2007	BottleShop	High	Carton Cans	$28.00	$1,260.00
15	71689	Swan Lager	3	4/02/2007	Warehouse 1	Medium	Carton Bottles	$26.50	$79.50
16	71854	Matilda Bay Draught	20	1/11/2007	Warehouse 1	High	Carton Bottles	$27.00	$540.00
17	72897	Heinekin Lager	45	1/07/2007	BottleShop	High	Carton Cans	$56.20	$2,529.00
18	74589	Bourbon	31	16/09/2007	Front Bar	High	Carton Cans	$25.00	$775.00
19	74895	Bourbon	25	19/03/2007	Front Bar	Low	700ml	$34.50	$862.50
20	77896	Galliano	32	14/08/2007	Warehouse 1	High	700ml	$37.00	$1,184.00
21	78976	Crown Lager	15	29/10/2007	Warehouse 1	Medium	Carton Bottles	$55.00	$825.00
22	80056	More and more beer	30	1/03/2007	Front Bar	Low	700ml	$33.00	$990.00
23	81136	Vodka	28	14/03/2007	Warehouse 3	High	700ml	$33.00	$924.00
24	82216	Crown Lager	45	16/11/2007	BottleShop	High	Carton Bottles	$55.00	$2,475.00
25	83296	Mailbu	30	7/09/2007	Warehouse 1	Low	700ml	$27.00	$810.00
26	84376	Crown Lager	20	5/10/2007	Bottleshop	High	Carton Bottles	$55.00	$1,100.00
27	84442	Kaluha	29	1/02/2007	BottleShop	High	700ml	$42.00	$1,210.65

Sheet1 Sheet2

Figure 7-13. Data to be tracked

```
        If IsEmpty(vOldVal) Then vOldVal = "Empty Cell"
        bBold = Target.HasFormula
            With Sheet2
                .Unprotect Password:="Secret"
                    If .Range("A1") = vbNullString Then
                        .Range("A1:E1") = Array("CELL CHANGED", "OLD VALUE", _
                            "NEW VALUE", "TIME OF CHANGE", "DATE OF CHANGE")
                    End If


                With .Cells(.Rows.Count, 1).End(xlUp)(2, 1)
                      .Value = Target.Address
                      .Offset(0, 1) = vOldVal
                          With .Offset(0, 2)
                            If bBold = True Then
                              .ClearComments
                              .AddComment.Text Text:= _
                                   "OzGrid.com:" & Chr(10) & "" & Chr(10) & _
                                      "Bold values are the results of formulas"
                            End If
                              .Value = Target
                              .Font.Bold = bBold
                          End With

                    .Offset(0, 3) = Time
                    .Offset(0, 4) = Date
                End With
                .Cells.Columns.AutoFit
                .Protect Password:="Secret"
            End With
        vOldVal = vbNullString
```

```
With Application
    .ScreenUpdating = True
    .EnableEvents = True
End With

On Error GoTo 0
End Sub

Private Sub Worksheet_SelectionChange(ByVal Target As Range)
    vOldVal = Target
End Sub
```

Now double-click on Sheet2 in the VBA Project window. Ensure Sheet2 has a Sheet CodeName of Sheet2, which will be shown next to Name in the Properties window of the VBE. This worksheet should also be set to xlVeryHidden by selecting it from the drop-down menu next to Visible in the Properties window of the VBE. This will make sure that other users are not able to modify the report.

The code also protects Sheet2 with the password Secret. While worksheet protection is applied to Sheet2, Excel's worksheet protection is rather weak, so hiding of the sheet is an added measure, especially if you lock the Visual Basic Editor, which will ensure macro code is not visible to end users and to a point protects your intellectual property.

Exit the VBE and save your workbook.

Next time you open your workbook and make any changes to Sheet1, the changes will be recorded in Sheet2, in the format shown in Figure 7-14. Remember, though, you can only unhide Sheet2 by setting the Visible property of Sheet2 to xlSheetVisible.

	A	B	C	D	E
1	CELL CHANGED	OLD VALUE	NEW VALUE	TIME OF CHANGE	DATE OF CHANGE
2	$B$4	Crown Lager	Vodka	12:50:05 PM	9/04/2007
3	$C$4	50	30	12:50:07 PM	9/04/2007
4	$F$4	High	Medium	12:50:14 PM	9/04/2007
5	$H$4	$33.00	38	12:50:17 PM	9/04/2007
6					

Figure 7-14. Sheet2 showing record of changes to Sheet1

Track Changes on All Worksheets in One Workbook

Using similar code, you can also track changes on all worksheets in a given workbook. Like the previous example, this code places the tracked changes on Sheet2 of the workbook. Sheet2 must therefore have a codename of Sheet2 and should be set to xlVeryHidden.

However, this code must be placed in the Workbook module (ThisWorkbook) of the workbook. Right-click on the sheet name tab, choose View Code, double-click on ThisWorkbook in the Project window of the VBE, and paste the following code:

```
Dim vOldVal 'Must be at top of module

Private Sub Workbook_SheetChange(ByVal Sh As Object, ByVal Target As Range)
Dim bBold As Boolean

If Target.Cells.Count > 1 Then Exit Sub
On Error Resume Next

    With Application
        .ScreenUpdating = False
        .EnableEvents = False
    End With

    If IsEmpty(vOldVal) Then vOldVal = "Empty Cell"
    bBold = Target.HasFormula
        With Sheet2
            .Unprotect Password:="Secret"
                If .Range("A1") = vbNullString Then
                    .Range("A1:E1") = Array("CELL CHANGED", "OLD VALUE", _
                        "NEW VALUE", "TIME OF CHANGE", "DATE OF CHANGE")
                End If


            With .Cells(.Rows.Count, 1).End(xlUp)(2, 1)

                .Value = "'" & Sh.Name & "'!" & Target.Address
                .Offset(0, 1) = vOldVal
                    With .Offset(0, 2)
                        If bBold = True Then
                          .ClearComments
                          .AddComment.Text Text:= _
                              "OzGrid.com:" & Chr(10) & "" & Chr(10) & _
                                  "Bold values are the results of formulas"
                        End If
                        .Value = Target
                        .Font.Bold = bBold
                    End With

                .Offset(0, 3) = Time
                .Offset(0, 4) = Date
            End With
            .Cells.Columns.AutoFit
            .Protect Password:="Secret"
        End With
    vOldVal = vbNullString

    With Application
```

```
        .ScreenUpdating = True
        .EnableEvents = True
    End With

On Error GoTo 0

End Sub

Private Sub Workbook_SheetSelectionChange(ByVal Sh As Object, ByVal Target
As Range)
    vOldVal = Target
End Sub
```

Again, exit the VBE and save and close your workbook.

When you open your workbook, make sure you enable macros to run the code, and any changes you make to any of the worksheets in the workbook will be tracked and recorded on Sheet2 in the same format as Figure 7-14, except that this code will also record the sheet name as well as the cell reference in column A.

HACK 122 Automatically Add Date/Time to a Cell upon Entry

Enter a static date, or date and time, into a corresponding cell after data is entered into other cells.

ALL

You can easily automate the insertion of date/time information into a cell by using the TODAY( ) or NOW( ) function, but if the date entered must be static, you'll need this hack.

Let's suppose you've set up some data and you want the current date entered into column B when data is entered in column A in the same row.

Add the following code to the Private module of the worksheet that will store the data and corresponding date. To quickly get there from Excel, right-click on the sheet name tab, choose View Code, and paste the following code:

```
Private Sub Worksheet_Change(ByVal Target As Range)
    If Target.Cells.Count > 1 Then Exit Sub
        If Not Intersect(Target, Range("A2:A100")) Is Nothing Then
            With Target(1, 2)
                .Value = Date
                .EntireColumn.AutoFit
            End With
        End If
End Sub
```

Exit the VBE and save your workbook.

Now, test it by adding any data to any cell in the range A2:A100. You will see the current date appear in the corresponding cell of B2:B100, as shown in Figure 7-15.

	A	B	C
1			
2	1	19/03/2007	
3	cat	19/03/2007	
4	3	19/03/2007	
5	$500	19/03/2007	
6	elephant	19/03/2007	
7	####	19/03/2007	
8	asdfasdf	19/03/2007	
9			

Figure 7-15. All entries in column A result in today's date being shown in column B

To get both the current date and time use .Value = Now as opposed to .Value = Date. For only the time, use .Value = Time. If you want to hardcode the date in only a few instances, you can use the Ctrl-: shortcut (hold down the Ctrl key and press the colon key).

HACK
123 Create a List of Workbook Hyperlinks

2003
2000

Use a bit of Excel VBA macro code to create a list of hyperlinked Excel workbook names on any Excel worksheet.

Using the code in this hack, you can get Excel to create a list of all hyperlinked files in an Excel workbook, which is a great tool if you have a large workbook with many hyperlinks in it and you want to see at a glance where the hyperlinks go. If you prefer, you can even restrict the list of hyperlinks to a specific workbook by specifying the workbook name in the part of the code that reads .Filename = "Book*.xls".

This hack also works with Excel versions 2000–2003.

The code uses the MsoFileType constant msoFileTypeExcelWorkbooks and is therefore restricted to Excel workbooks only (a *.MSO* file is a Microsoft Office file type), but you could adapt the code to record any of the following MsoFileType constants:

```
msoFileTypeAllFiles
msoFileTypeBinders
```

```
msoFileTypeCalendarItem
msoFileTypeContactItem
msoFileTypeCustom
msoFileTypeDatabases
msoFileTypeDataConnectionFiles
msoFileTypeDesignerFiles
msoFileTypeDocumentImagingFiles
msoFileTypeExcelWorkbooks
msoFileTypeJournalItem
msoFileTypeMailItem
msoFileTypeNoteItem
msoFileTypeOfficeFiles
msoFileTypeOutlookItems
msoFileTypePhotoDrawFiles
msoFileTypePowerPointPresentations
msoFileTypeProjectFiles
msoFileTypePublisherFiles
msoFileTypeTaskItem
msoFileTypeTemplates
msoFileTypeVisioFiles
msoFileTypeWebPages
msoFileTypeWordDocuments
```

The Code

To insert the code, right-click on your worksheet name, select View Code, go to Insert → Module, and paste the following:

 Remember to change the file paths to suit your own environment.

```
Sub HyperlinkXLSFiles()

Dim lCount As Long

Application.ScreenUpdating = False
Application.DisplayAlerts = False
Application.EnableEvents = False

'On Error Resume Next
    With Application.FileSearch
        .NewSearch

        'Change path to suit
```

```
                .LookIn = "C:\OzGrid Likom\Testings\"
                .FileType = msoFileTypeExcelWorkbooks

         ' .Filename = "Book*.xls"
                If .Execute > 0 Then 'Workbooks in folder
                    For lCount = 1 To .FoundFiles.Count 'Loop through all.
                        ActiveSheet.Hyperlinks.Add Anchor:=Cells(lCount, 1), ⅃
Address:= _
                            .FoundFiles(lCount), TextToDisplay:= _
                            Replace(.FoundFiles(lCount), "C:\OzGrid Likom\ ⅃
Testings\", "")
'Change path to suit
                    Next lCount
                End If
        End With

        On Error GoTo 0

        Application.ScreenUpdating = True
        Application.DisplayAlerts = True
        Application.EnableEvents = True

    End Sub
```

Exit and return to Excel proper, and save your workbook.

Running the Hack

To run the code, make sure you have a clean worksheet. Then, select Tools
→ Macros or press Alt/Option-F8, select the macro, and press Run.

> Ensure the active worksheet at the time of running the code
> is clean, to avoid overwriting existing data.

As shown in Figure 7-16, a list of hyperlinks will be created for you to copy,
paste, change, or do whatever you like with!

HACK
124   Advanced Find
ALL

Allow a user to specify more than one item to locate with the Find feature by
using some code and a UserForm.

The standard Excel Find feature is great for locating matching cells. However, by default, it cannot be used to locate, say, three matching cells on the
same row within a table. This hack removes this limitation of the Find feature, allowing the user to specify more than one item to locate.

	A	B	C	D	E	F	G	H	I
1	C:\Ozgrid Likom\Testings\#12-Gregs-Budget-Spreadsheet-2006-PART-1-of-2-vADDINS.xls								
2	C:\Ozgrid Likom\Testings\[savefile]060808105710_Xpto.xls								
3	C:\Ozgrid Likom\Testings\+Macro for combining multiple trades for each date.xls								
4	C:\Ozgrid Likom\Testings\+Macros for 2000-2004 dates.xls								
5	C:\Ozgrid Likom\Testings\010203_0907_AM.xls								
6	C:\Ozgrid Likom\Testings\010203-0906-AM.xls								
7	C:\Ozgrid Likom\Testings\02-08.xls								
8	C:\Ozgrid Likom\Testings\040404.xls								
9	C:\Ozgrid Likom\Testings\050828 TLS Time Sheet.xls								
10	C:\Ozgrid Likom\Testings\08- 205 August Daily Numbers.xls								
11	C:\Ozgrid Likom\Testings\09-Feb-04 TO 22-Feb-04.xls								
12	C:\Ozgrid Likom\Testings\10012004.xls								
13	C:\Ozgrid Likom\Testings\100-150.xls								
14	C:\Ozgrid Likom\Testings\1006.xls								
15	C:\Ozgrid Likom\Testings\10-2-03 All Plans- Sorted and Duplicates removed.xls								
16	C:\Ozgrid Likom\Testings\123.xlt								
17	C:\Ozgrid Likom\Testings\1Km Run Times.xls								
18	C:\Ozgrid Likom\Testings\1MacroRanges.xls								
19	C:\Ozgrid Likom\Testings\2004_07_26.xls								
20	C:\Ozgrid Likom\Testings\2004_full day.xls								
21	C:\Ozgrid Likom\Testings\21863.xls								
22	C:\Ozgrid Likom\Testings\21GR.xls								
23	C:\Ozgrid Likom\Testings\23rd June 03.xls								
24	C:\Ozgrid Likom\Testings\25586.xls								
25	C:\Ozgrid Likom\Testings\25801.xls								
26	C:\Ozgrid Likom\Testings\26_11_04.xls								
27	C:\Ozgrid Likom\Testings\28072006.xls								
28	C:\Ozgrid Likom\Testings\28072006plus.xls								
29	C:\Ozgrid Likom\Testings\280K@5% DN.xls								

Sheet2 / Sheet1

Figure 7-16. List of created hyperlinks

If you have a large table of data (say, A1:H1000), you might want to find a
specific row in that table where three or more items exist.

> The number of items can be greater or smaller than three,
> but we'll use three for this example.

The UserForm

To begin, you'll need to create a UserForm. Right-click on the sheet tab and
select View Code, or press Alt/Option-F11. Then, select Insert → UserForm
and insert three ComboBoxes (named ComboBox1, ComboBox2, and
ComboBox3) from the Controls toolbox that pops up (select View → Tools
if it doesn't). Place them vertically on the left side of UserForm with
ComboBox1 at the top and ComboBox3 at the bottom. Set the Enabled
property of ComboBox2 and ComboBox3 to False.

Now for some labels. Insert five labels, again from the Controls toolbox, named Label1 (positioned above ComboBox1), Label2 (positioned above ComboBox2), Label3 (positioned above ComboBox3), Label4 (positioned above Label1), and Label5 (anywhere for now). Change the Caption property of Label4 to read "Select up to 3 fields" and "Matching Rows. Double click to go there" for Label5.

From the Controls toolbox, insert two CommandButtons: CommandButton1 and CommandButton2. Change the Caption property to "Find" for CommandButton1 and "Close" for CommandButton2. Position both of these at the top right of the UserForm.

Now, underneath the Find and Close buttons, insert a ListBox (named ListBox1) and place Label5 above it. Make the ListBox1 the same width as Label5, but make it as long as your UserForm will allow.

Your form should look like Figure 7-17.

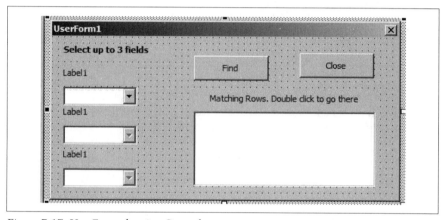

Figure 7-17. UserForm showing Controls

The Code

That's all you need to create the form. Now, it's time to add the all-important code. Double-click the UserForm and add this code:

```
Option Explicit

'Module Level Variables
Dim rRange As Range
Dim strFind1 As String
Dim strFind2 As String
Dim strFind3 As String
```

```vba
Private Sub ComboBox1_Change( )
    'Pass chosen value to String variable strFind1
    strFind1 = ComboBox1
    'Enable ComboBox2 only if value is chosen
    ComboBox2.Enabled = Not strFind1 = vbNullString
End Sub


Private Sub ComboBox2_Change( )
    'Pass chosen value to String variable strFind1
    strFind2 = ComboBox2
    'Enable ComboBox3 only if value is chosen
    ComboBox3.Enabled = Not strFind2 = vbNullString
End Sub


Private Sub ComboBox3_Change( )
    'Pass chosen value to String variable strFind1
    strFind3 = ComboBox3
End Sub

Private Sub CommandButton1_Click( )
'Procedure level variables
Dim lCount As Long
Dim lOccur As Long
Dim rCell As Range
Dim rCell2 As Range
Dim rCell3 As Range
Dim bFound As Boolean

    'At least one value, from ComboBox1 must be chosen
    If strFind1 & strFind2 & strFind3 = vbNullString Then
        MsgBox "No items to find chosen", vbCritical
            Exit Sub 'Go no further
    ElseIf strFind1 = vbNullString Then
        MsgBox "A value from " & Label1.Caption _
            & " must be chosen", vbCritical
        Exit Sub 'Go no further
    End If

'Clear any old entries
On Error Resume Next
ListBox1.Clear
On Error GoTo 0

'If String variable are empty pass the wildcard character
If strFind2 = vbNullString Then strFind2 = "*"
If strFind3 = vbNullString Then strFind3 = "*"

'Set range variable to first cell in table.
Set rCell = rRange.Cells(1, 1)
'Pass the number of times strFind1 occurs
lOccur = WorksheetFunction.CountIf(rRange.Columns(1), strFind1)
```

```
        'Loop only as many times as strFind1 occurs
        For lCount = 1 To lOccur
            'Set the range variable to the found cell. This is then also _
            used to start the next Find from (After:=rCell)
                Set rCell = rRange.Columns(1).Find(What:=strFind1, After:=rCell, _
                    LookIn:=xlValues, LookAt:=xlWhole, SearchOrder:=xlByRows, _
                    SearchDirection:=xlNext, MatchCase:=False)
            'Check each find to see if strFind2 and strFind3 occur _
            on the same row.
            If rCell(1, 2) Like strFind2 And rCell(1, 3) Like strFind3 Then
                bFound = True 'Used to not show message box for no value found.
                'Add the address of the found cell and the cell on the _
                same row but 2 columns to the right.
                ListBox1.AddItem rCell.Address & ":" & rCell(1, 3).Address
            End If
        Next lCount

If bFound = False Then 'No match
    MsgBox "Sorry, no matches", vbOKOnly
End If
End Sub

Private Sub CommandButton2_Click( )
'Close UserForm
Unload Me
End Sub


Private Sub ListBox1_DblClick(ByVal Cancel As MSForms.ReturnBoolean)
'Check for range addresses
If ListBox1.ListCount = 0 Then Exit Sub
'GoTo doubled clicked address
Application.Goto Range(ListBox1.Text), True
End Sub

Private Sub UserForm_Initialize( )
'Procedure level module
Dim lRows As Long

'Set Module level range variable to CurrentRegion _
of the Selection
Set rRange = Selection.CurrentRegion
    If rRange.Rows.Count < 2 Then ' Only 1 row
        MsgBox "Please select any cell in your table first", vbCritical
        Unload Me 'Close Userform
        Exit Sub
    Else

        With rRange
            'Set Label Captions to the Table headings
            Label1.Caption = .Cells(1, 1)
            Label2.Caption = .Cells(1, 2)
            Label3.Caption = .Cells(1, 3)
```

```
                    'Set RowSource of ComboBoxes to the appropriate columns _
                    inside the table
                    ComboBox1.RowSource = .Columns(1).Offset(1, 0).Address
                    ComboBox2.RowSource = .Columns(2).Offset(1, 0).Address
                    ComboBox3.RowSource = .Columns(3).Offset(1, 0).Address
                End With
            End If
        End Sub

        Private Sub UserForm_Terminate( )
        'Destroy Module level variables
        Set rRange = Nothing
        strFind1 = vbNullString
        strFind2 = vbNullString
        strFind3 = vbNullString
        End Sub
```

Finally, insert a Module (Insert → Module) and paste the following code:

```
Sub ShowForm( )
On Error Resume Next
UserForm1.Show
On Error GoTo 0
End Sub
```

Exit from the VBE and save your workbook.

Running the Hack

To test the code, click inside your table of data and run the code, or you can attach it to a shortcut key, a button, or assign it to a toolbar.

Shortcut key. Attaching the code to a shortcut key is easily done by selecting Developer → Macros (pre-2007, Tools → Macros → Macros…) → Options.

Button. If you prefer, you can attach the macro to a button. To add to a button, just insert a button onto your worksheet, right-click it, select Assign Macro, and then double-click on your macro name to attach it to the button.

Toolbar. To add a macro to the Quick Access Toolbar, select the drop-down menu to the right of the Quick Access Toolbar, and choose More Commands. Under Choose Commands From, select Macros, click on your macro name (in this case, ShowForm), and select Add. The Modify button at the bottom of the Quick Access Toolbar pane allows you to change the button if you like. Click OK when you've finished.

In pre-2007 versions, right-click your toolbar, select Customize → Commands → Macros → Custom Button and drag to
your toolbar. When you do this, the Modify Selection button will become active, allowing you to change button style
if desired. Click Close when finished.

In Figure 7-18, we have attached the ShowForm macro to a button and called
it Find.

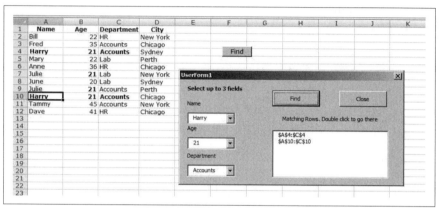

Figure 7-18. Advanced Find in action

Try it and you will see how easy and useful it can be to identify your specified criteria.

Find a Number Between Two Numbers

125

Enhance Excel's Find feature to search for the first occurrence of a number
that falls between two specified numbers.

ALL

Like all Microsoft Office applications, Excel has a Find feature to help locate
a specified value or text string in a range, worksheet, or workbook. However, no such feature exists to find the first occurrence of a number that is
between an arbitrary minimum and a maximum number. This hack provides some Excel VBA macro code to do just that.

Many people would go with a *loop* to get a number between
a nominated range, but that can be extremely slow and hor-
ribly inefficient if the worksheet contain thousands of used
cells. The method in this hack makes use of the SpecialCells
method to check numeric cells only.

The code works in the same way as the standard Find feature does. That is, it searches *all* cells on the worksheet if only a single cell is selected or *only* the selected cells if more than one cell is selected.

It searches by rows, locating and selecting the *first cell* that has a value between (not equal to) the specified minimum and maximum.

For this example, let's begin with some data, as shown in Figure 7-19.

	A	B	C	D	E	F	G	H	I	J
1	1	2	3	4	5	6	7	8	9	10
2	7	8	9	10	11	12	13	14	15	16
3	9	10	11	12	13	14	15	16	17	18
4	4	5	6	7	8	9	10	11	12	13
5	15	16	17	18	19	20	21	22	23	24
6	15	16	17	18	19	20	21	22	23	24
7	17	18	19	20	21	22	23	24	25	26
8	20	21	22	23	24	25	26	27	28	29
9	22	23	24	25	26	27	28	29	30	31
10	25	26	27	28	29	30	31	32	33	34
11	27	28	29	30	31	32	33	34	35	36
12	30	31	32	33	34	35	36	37	38	39
13	32	33	34	35	36	37	38	39	40	41
14	35	36	37	38	39	40	41	42	43	44
15	37	38	39	40	41	42	43	44	45	46
16	40	41	42	43	44	45	46	47	48	49
17	42	43	44	45	46	47	48	49	50	51
18										

Figure 7-19. Data of mixed numbers in range A1:J17

The Code

Right-click on the sheet tab of the worksheet and select View Code → Insert → Module. In the new module, paste the following code:

```
Sub GetBetween()
Dim strNum As String
Dim lMin As Long, lMax As Long
Dim rFound As Range, rLookin As Range
Dim lFound As Long, rStart As Range
Dim rCcells As Range, rFcells As Range
Dim lCellCount As Long, lcount As Long
Dim bNoFind As Boolean

    strNum = InputBox("Please enter the lowest value, then a comma, " _
        & "followed by the highest value" & vbNewLine & _
        vbNewLine & "E.g. 1,10", "GET BETWEEN")

        If strNum = vbNullString Then Exit Sub
         On Error Resume Next
        lMin = Left(strNum, InStr(1, strNum, ","))
```

```
            If Not IsNumeric(lMin) Or lMin = 0 Then
                MsgBox "Error in your entering of numbers, or Min was a zero", ↵
        vbCritical, "Ozgrid.com"
                Exit Sub
            End If

            lMax = Replace(strNum, lMin & ",", "")
            If Not IsNumeric(lMax) Or lMax = 0 Then
                MsgBox "Error in your entering of numbers, or Max was a zero", ↵
        vbCritical, "Ozgrid.com"
                Exit Sub
            End If

            If lMax < lMin Then
                MsgBox "Min is greater than Max", vbCritical, "Ozgrid.com"
                Exit Sub
            End If


            If lMin + 1 = lMax Then
                MsgBox "No scope between Min and Max", vbCritical, "Ozgrid.com"
                Exit Sub
            End If


            If Selection.Cells.Count = 1 Then
                Set rCcells = Cells.SpecialCells(xlCellTypeConstants, xlNumbers)
                Set rFcells = Cells.SpecialCells(xlCellTypeFormulas, xlNumbers)
                Set rStart = Cells(1, 1)
            Else
                Set rCcells = Selection.SpecialCells(xlCellTypeConstants, ↵
        xlNumbers)
                Set rFcells = Selection.SpecialCells(xlCellTypeFormulas, ↵
        xlNumbers)
                Set rStart = Selection.Cells(1, 1)
            End If

            'Reduce down range to look in
            If rCcells Is Nothing And rFcells Is Nothing Then
                MsgBox "Your Worksheet contains no numbers", vbCritical, "ozgrid. ↵
        com"
                Exit Sub
             ElseIf rCcells Is Nothing Then
                Set rLookin = rFcells.Cells 'formulas
             ElseIf rFcells Is Nothing Then
                Set rLookin = rCcells.Cells 'constants
             Else
                Set rLookin = Application.Union(rFcells, rCcells) 'Both
            End If

            lCellCount = rLookin.Cells.Count
            Do Until lFound > lMin And lFound < lMax And lFound > 0
                lFound = 0
```

```
                    Set rStart = rLookin.Cells.Find(What:="*", After:=rStart, ↵
        LookIn:=xlValues, _
                        LookAt:=xlWhole, SearchOrder:=xlByRows, _
                        SearchDirection:=xlNext, MatchCase:=True)
                lFound = rStart.Value
                lcount = lcount + 1
                If lCellCount = lcount Then
                    bNoFind = True
                    Exit Do
                End If
            Loop

            rStart.Select

            If bNoFind = True Then
                MsgBox "No numbers between " _
                & lMin & " and " & lMax, vbInformation, "Ozgrid.com"
            End If
            On Error GoTo 0
    End Sub
```

Close the VBE, return to Excel proper, and save your workbook.

Running the Hack

To run the code, press Alt/Option-F8, select the macro, and press Run. The GETBETWEEN dialog will pop up (as shown in Figure 7-20) and ask you to "Please enter the lowest value, then a comma, followed by the highest value." Enter **1,10** and click OK. The number 2 will be highlighted because the number 2 is the *first cell* that has a value between (not equal to) the specified minimum (1) and maximum (10).

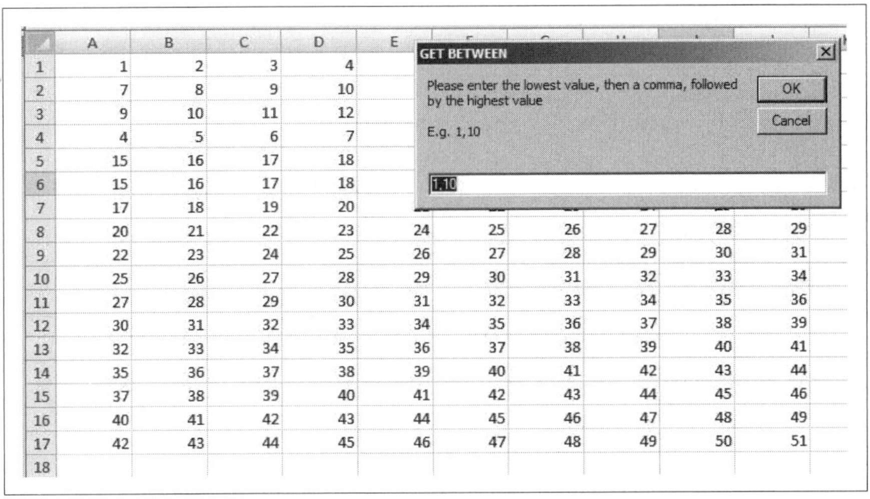

Figure 7-20. GETBETWEEN dialog showing the lowest value and highest value

This code will not locate a zero value.

Convert Formula References from Relative to Absolute

Change absolute formula references to relative references, vice versa, or a mix of absolute and relative columns and rows.

Wouldn't it be nice if you could easily convert your Excel formula references from absolute to relative and/or relative to absolute? Using the two methods in this hack, you can. You can even convert to a mix of relative row/absolute column references or absolute row/relative column references.

The fastest way works on less complicated formulas, but you'll need the second with mega and/or array formulas.

Less Complicated Formulas

Using the following code is the fastest method, but it can cause problems when used with more complicated formulas.

As with any code, always save your workbook before running the code.

The code. Right-click on your sheet tab and select View Code (pre-2007, Tools → Macro → Visual Basic Editor) or press Alt/Option-F11. To insert the following code into a standard module, select Insert → Module:

```
Sub MakeAbsoluteorRelativeFast( )
'Written by OzGrid Business Applications
'www.ozgrid.com

Dim RdoRange As Range
Dim i As Integer
Dim Reply As String

    'Ask whether Relative or Absolute
    Reply = InputBox("Change formulas to?" & Chr(13) & Chr(13) _
    & "Relative row/Absolute column = 1" & Chr(13) _
    & "Absolute row/Relative column = 2" & Chr(13) _
    & "Absolute all = 3" & Chr(13) _
    & "Relative all = 4", "OzGrid Business Applications")

    'They cancelled
```

```
    If Reply = "" Then Exit Sub

    On Error Resume Next
    'Set Range variable to formula cells only
    Set RdoRange = Selection.SpecialCells(Type:=xlFormulas)

    'determine the change type
    Select Case Reply
        Case 1 'Relative row/Absolute column
            For i = 1 To RdoRange.Areas.Count
                RdoRange.Areas(i).Formula = _
                Application.ConvertFormula _
                (Formula:=RdoRange.Areas(i).Formula, _
                FromReferenceStyle:=xlA1, _
                ToReferenceStyle:=xlA1, ToAbsolute:=xlRelRowAbsColumn)
            Next i

        Case 2 'Absolute row/Relative column
            For i = 1 To RdoRange.Areas.Count
                RdoRange.Areas(i).Formula = _
                Application.ConvertFormula _
                (Formula:=RdoRange.Areas(i).Formula, _
                FromReferenceStyle:=xlA1, _
                ToReferenceStyle:=xlA1, ToAbsolute:=xlAbsRowRelColumn)
            Next i

        Case 3 'Absolute all
            For i = 1 To RdoRange.Areas.Count
                RdoRange.Areas(i).Formula = _
                Application.ConvertFormula _
                (Formula:=RdoRange.Areas(i).Formula, _
                FromReferenceStyle:=xlA1, _
                ToReferenceStyle:=xlA1, ToAbsolute:=xlAbsolute)
            Next i

        Case 4 'Relative all
            For i = 1 To RdoRange.Areas.Count
                RdoRange.Areas(i).Formula = _
                Application.ConvertFormula _
                (Formula:=RdoRange.Areas(i).Formula, _
                FromReferenceStyle:=xlA1, _
                ToReferenceStyle:=xlA1, ToAbsolute:=xlRelative)
            Next i

        Case Else 'Typo
            MsgBox "Change type not recognised!", vbCritical, _
            "OzGrid Business Applications"
        End Select

        'Clear memory
        Set RdoRange = Nothing
End Sub
```

Now, click the top-right X (or press Alt/⌘-Q) to get back to Excel proper, and then save your workbook.

Running the hack. To run the code, select the range of cells you want to change, press Alt/Option-F8, select the macro name, and click Run. A dialog will pop up, giving you four options, as shown in Figure 7-21.

	A	B	C	D	E	F	G	H
			D10	fx =($C10-D$6)+($C$7*$C$2)				
1								
2		Discount		10%				
3								
4								
5		Membership Types	Today's Price	Gold Member	Silver Member	Bronze Member		
6				$100	$75	$50		
7		1 Year	$300.00	230	255	280		
8		2 Years	$600.00	530	555	580		
9		3 Years	$900.00	830	855	880		
10		5 Years	$1,500.00	1,430				
11		7 Years	$2,100.00	2,030				
12		10 Years	$3,000.00	2,930				
13		15 Years	$4,500.00	4,430				
14		20 Years	$6,000.00	5,930				
15		Life	$10,000.00	9,930				
16								
17								
18								
19								

OzGrid Business Applications

Change formulas to?

Relative row/Absolute column = 1
Absolute row/Relative column = 2
Absolute all = 3
Relative all = 4

OK
Cancel

Figure 7-21. Dialog showing choices of absolute/mixed/relative references

Depending on the result you are looking for, you will make a selection of 1, 2, 3, or 4, then click OK and your formula will be converted to comply with your selection.

There is no "Undo" option after you have run this macro.

Mega or Array Formulas

This method is slightly slower, but it's less likely to cause problems with more complicated code.

The code. Enter the following code by right-clicking on your sheet tab and selecting View Code (pre-2007, Tools → Macro → Visual Basic Editor) or pressing Alt/Option-F11, then selecting Insert → Module and pasting this code:

```
Sub MakeAbsoluteorRelativeSlow( )
    'Written for www.ozgrid.com
    'By Andy Pope
    'www.andypope.info/
```

```
Dim RdoRange As Range, rCell As Range
Dim i As Integer
Dim Reply As String

 'Ask whether Relative or Absolute
Reply = InputBox("Change formulas to?" & Chr(13) & Chr(13) _
& "Relative row/Absolute column = 1" & Chr(13) _
& "Absolute row/Relative column = 2" & Chr(13) _
& "Absolute all = 3" & Chr(13) _
& "Relative all = 4", "OzGrid Business Applications")

 'They cancelled
If Reply = "" Then Exit Sub

On Error Resume Next
 'Set Range variable to formula cells only
Set RdoRange = Selection.SpecialCells(Type:=xlFormulas)

 'determine the change type
Select Case Reply
Case 1 'Relative row/Absolute column

    For Each rCell In RdoRange
        If rCell.HasArray Then
            If Len(rCell.FormulaArray) < 255 Then
                rCell.FormulaArray = _
                Application.ConvertFormula _
                (Formula:=rCell.FormulaArray, _
                FromReferenceStyle:=xlA1, _
                ToReferenceStyle:=xlA1, ToAbsolute:=xlRelRowAbsColumn)
            End If
        Else
            If Len(rCell.Formula) < 255 Then
                rCell.Formula = _
                Application.ConvertFormula _
                (Formula:=rCell.Formula, _
                FromReferenceStyle:=xlA1, _
                ToReferenceStyle:=xlA1, ToAbsolute:=xlRelRowAbsColumn)
            End If
        End If
    Next rCell

Case 2 'Absolute row/Relative column
    For Each rCell In RdoRange
        If rCell.HasArray Then
            If Len(rCell.FormulaArray) < 255 Then
                rCell.FormulaArray = _
                Application.ConvertFormula _
                (Formula:=rCell.FormulaArray, _
                FromReferenceStyle:=xlA1, _
                ToReferenceStyle:=xlA1, ToAbsolute:=xlAbsRowRelColumn)
            End If
        Else
```

```
                If Len(rCell.Formula) < 255 Then
                    rCell.Formula = _
                    Application.ConvertFormula _
                    (Formula:=rCell.Formula, _
                    FromReferenceStyle:=xlA1, _
                    ToReferenceStyle:=xlA1, ToAbsolute:=xlAbsRowRelColumn)
                End If
            End If
        Next rCell

    Case 3 'Absolute all
        For Each rCell In RdoRange
            If rCell.HasArray Then
                If Len(rCell.FormulaArray) < 255 Then
                    rCell.FormulaArray = _
                    Application.ConvertFormula _
                    (Formula:=rCell.FormulaArray, _
                    FromReferenceStyle:=xlA1, _
                    ToReferenceStyle:=xlA1, ToAbsolute:=xlAbsolute)
                End If
            Else
                If Len(rCell.Formula) < 255 Then
                    rCell.Formula = _
                    Application.ConvertFormula _
                    (Formula:=rCell.Formula, _
                    FromReferenceStyle:=xlA1, _
                    ToReferenceStyle:=xlA1, ToAbsolute:=xlAbsolute)
                End If
            End If
        Next rCell

    Case 4 'Relative all
        For Each rCell In RdoRange
            If rCell.HasArray Then
                If Len(rCell.FormulaArray) < 255 Then
                    rCell.FormulaArray = _
                    Application.ConvertFormula _
                    (Formula:=rCell.FormulaArray, _
                    FromReferenceStyle:=xlA1, _
                    ToReferenceStyle:=xlA1, ToAbsolute:=xlRelative)
                End If
            Else
                If Len(rCell.Formula) < 255 Then
                    rCell.Formula = _
                    Application.ConvertFormula _
                    (Formula:=rCell.Formula, _
                    FromReferenceStyle:=xlA1, _
                    ToReferenceStyle:=xlA1, ToAbsolute:=xlRelative)
                End If
            End If
        Next rCell

    Case Else 'Typo
```

```
            MsgBox "Change type not recognised!", vbCritical, _
            "OzGrid Business Applications"
        End Select

         'Clear memory
        Set RdoRange = Nothing
    End Sub
```

Running the hack. Click the top-right X (or press Alt/⌘-Q) to get back to Excel proper, and then save your workbook.

Again, to run the code, select the range of cells you want to change, press Alt/Option-F8, select the macro name, and click Run. The dialog shown previously in Figure 7-21 will pop up, again enabling you to make your selection as required.

> If you want to change only one formula, you could toggle through the four reference types a formula can use by selecting the cell that housing the formula, clicking in the Formula bar, then clicking inside the reference part of your formula (e.g., A1, $A$1) and pressing F4. Each press of F4 will toggle the reference type.

HACK 127   Name a Workbook with the Text in a Cell

When you save your workbook, use the text of a selected cell as your filename.

ALL

It's quite common for Excel users to want to save an Excel file with a filename that corresponds to the text in a worksheet cell. This can be done with the help of a small amount of code inserted into a module.

Click in cell C1 on the worksheet and enter some text to save. We will use the codename Sheet1.

The Code

Open the Visual Basic Editor by selecting Developer → Code → Visual Basic, or right-clicking on the sheet name and selecting View Code (pre-2007, Tools → Macros → Visual Basic Editor), or pressing Alt/Option-F11.

Select Insert → Module and paste the following code:

```
Sub SaveAsCell()
Dim strName As String

On Error GoTo InvalidName
    strName = Sheet1.Range("C1")
    ActiveWorkbook.SaveAs strName
```

```
Exit Sub
InvalidName: MsgBox "The text: " & strName & _
        " is not a valid file name.", vbCritical, "Ozgrid.com"
End Sub
```

Now, click the top-right X (or press Alt/⌘-Q) to get back to Excel proper, and then save your workbook.

Running the Hack

Click anywhere on your worksheet and select Alt/Option-F8. Then, select the SaveAsCell macro from the dialog, click Run, and your workbook will automatically be saved as Sheet1. If you had a name other than Sheet1 in cell C1, the code will still work and your workbook will be saved as that name. The only time the code will fail is if you have an invalid filename in cell C1, as shown in Figure 7-22.

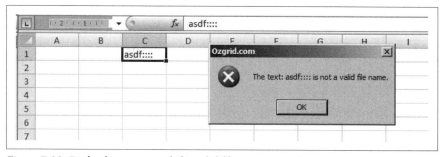

Figure 7-22. Dialog box generated if invalid filename entered in C1

Hide and Restore Toolbars in Excel

HACK 128

<2007

Attach a custom toolbar to your spreadsheet that doesn't get in the way of the end user's settings for other spreadsheets when yours is closed.

One of the most exciting parts of Excel is the customizability of its output to end users. For example, you might build your own custom toolbar to distribute it with your spreadsheets. However, the golden rule of when/if to change any part of Excel is to make sure everything for the user goes back to how it was when the user closes your specific spreadsheet—in other words, *restore the user's settings*!

There are many ways to do this, some of which are extremely complicated (often unnecessarily). This hack provides a cleaner, less complicated way.

Attaching Your Toolbar to the Workbook

Let's assume you have created a custom toolbar called MyToolbar and, for some purpose, want to hide all of Excel's built-in toolbars from the user, displaying only MyToolbar.

 Before starting, it is *vital* that you attach your custom toolbar to the workbook that will be using it. This will also stop users from being able to make changes stick and will ensure an error-free process.

Here's how to attach a custom toolbar that takes care of these requirements:

1. Open the workbook that should display the custom toolbar.
2. Right-click on any gray, unused part of any toolbar and select Customize.
3. On the Toolbars page, check MyToolbar (or the applicable name), to make it visible.
4. Select Attach, drag your tool toolbar from the Attach Toolbar dialog, and press Copy.
5. Press OK, then Cancel, and you're done!

You should now be aware that *any* changes made to your custom toolbar will not stick (between closing and reopening the workbook it's attached to, unless you first (before any changes) go back to the Attach Toolbar dialog, select your toolbar, this time from the right side (Toolbars in workbook), and press Delete. Then, make any changes needed and follow Steps 1 through 5 again.

Coding the Toolbar Show and Restore

The two following macros will display your toolbar (MyToolbar), remove all native toolbars and, most importantly, restore them for the user when your spreadsheet is closed.

To insert a standard module, right-click on the sheet name, select View Code → Insert → Module to insert a Standard Module, and paste the following code:

```
Sub RemoveToolbars()
    On Error Resume Next
        With Application
            .DisplayFullScreen = True
```

```
            .CommandBars("Full Screen").Visible = False
            .CommandBars("MyToolbar").Enabled = True
            .CommandBars("MyToolbar").Visible = True
            .CommandBars("Worksheet Menu Bar").Enabled = False
        End With
    On Error GoTo 0
End Sub
```

Then, insert another module with the following code:

```
Sub RestoreToolbars()
    On Error Resume Next
        With Application
            .DisplayFullScreen = False
            .CommandBars("MyToolbar").Enabled = False
            .CommandBars("Worksheet Menu Bar").Enabled = True
        End With
    On Error GoTo 0
End Sub
```

You aren't quite finished yet! You still need to make sure that both macros run at the correct time, so you'll have to place a Run statement in the Workbook_Activate and Workbook_Deactivate procedures of the Workbook object (ThisWorkbook). Right-click on the Excel icon (on the top left, next to File on the worksheet menu bar), select View Code, and insert the following code:

```
Private Sub Workbook_Activate()
    Run "RemoveToolbars"
End Sub

Private Sub Workbook_BeforeClose(Cancel As Boolean)
    On Error Resume Next
        Application.CommandBars("MyToolbar").Delete
End Sub

Private Sub Workbook_Deactivate()
    Run "RestoreToolbars"
End Sub
```

Note the deletion of the custom toolbar when the workbook closes. This is what prevents any changes from sticking unless you have first deleted it (as shown previously), made the changes, and then attached it again.

> Do not run the Application.CommandBars("MyToolbar"). Delete when the custom toolbar is *not* attached.

Sort Worksheets

129

ALL

One of the most commonly used functions in Excel, sorting is usually performed on a list, table, or range of cells, but you can take things a step further and sort your worksheets as well.

By using some code in an Excel workbook, or an Excel Add-In, you can sort all sheets in the active workbook, making it easier to locate sheets when you have many in your workbook.

The Code

Open the workbook for which you want to sort the sheets. Press Alt/Option-F11 to open the Visual Basic Editor, and insert a module by selecting Insert → Module and entering the following code:

```
Sub SortSheets()
Dim lCount As Long, lCounted As Long
Dim lShtLast As Long
Dim lReply As Long


lReply = MsgBox("To sort Worksheets ascending, select 'Yes'. " _
& "To sort Worksheets descending select 'No'", vbYesNoCancel, _
"Ozgrid Sheet Sort")
If lReply = vbCancel Then Exit Sub

lShtLast = Sheets.Count

If lReply = vbYes Then 'Sort ascending
    For lCount = 1 To lShtLast
        For lCount2 = lCount To lShtLast
            If UCase(Sheets(lCount2).Name) < UCase(Sheets(lCount).Name) Then
                Sheets(lCount2).Move Before:=Sheets(lCount)
            End If
        Next lCount2
    Next lCount
Else 'Sort descending
 For lCount = 1 To lShtLast
        For lCount2 = lCount To lShtLast
            If UCase(Sheets(lCount2).Name) > UCase(Sheets(lCount).Name) Then
                Sheets(lCount2).Move Before:=Sheets(lCount)
            End If
        Next lCount2
    Next lCount
End If

End Sub
```

Close the window to get back to your worksheet and save your workbook.

Running the Hack

To run the code, click in any worksheet, press Alt/Option-F8, select the macro, and press Run. You will be asked if you want to sort your sheets in ascending (A – Z) or descending order (Z – A), as shown in Figure 7-23.

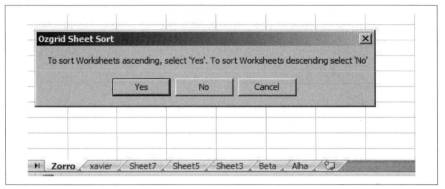

Figure 7-23. Dialog box presented when running macro to sort worksheets in ascending or descending order

Password-Protect a Worksheet from Viewing

HACK 130

Keep prying eyes from viewing a worksheet, unless they have the password.

ALL

With the aid of some Excel VBA code placed the Private module of the workbook object, you can protect a worksheet from viewing by anyone who doesn't know the password you select. The code stops after three failed attempts. A runtime error will occur, you will not be able to view the worksheet, and it does not mask the password entry. You'll need to close and reopen the workbook to try again.

> This method is far from secure and should *not* be used if the worksheet contains highly sensitive information. It only enhances the general worksheet protection and uses the UserInterfaceOnly option of the Protect method. You should also protect/lock Excel VBA code.

The code in this hack makes use of the worksheet's CodeName. The Workbook_Open procedure ensures that the workbook does not open with the unviewable worksheet being active.

The Code

Right-click on the sheet tab, select View Code, double-click on ThisWorksheet, and insert the following code:

```
Dim sLast As Object

Private Sub Workbook_Open()
    'Ensure Sheet1 is not the active sheet upon opening.
    If Sheet1.Name = ActiveSheet.Name Then Sheet2.Select
End Sub

Private Sub Workbook_SheetActivate(ByVal Sh As Object)
Dim strPass As String
Dim lCount As Long

    If Sh.CodeName <> "Sheet1" Then
        'Set sLast variable to the last active sheet _
        This is then used to return the user to the _
        last sheet they were on if password is not known _
        or they Cancel.
        Set sLast = Sh

    Else
        'Hide Columns
        Sheet1.Columns.Hidden = True
            'Allow 3 attempts at password
            For lCount = 1 To 3
                strPass = InputBox(Prompt:="Password Please", Title: ⏎
="PASSWORD REQUIRED")
                    If strPass = vbNullString Then 'Cancelled
                        sLast.Select
                        Exit Sub
                    ElseIf strPass <> "Secret" Then 'InCorrect password
                        MsgBox "Password incorrect", vbCritical, "Ozgrid.com"
                    Else 'Correct Password
                        Exit For
                    End If
            Next lCount

            If lCount = 4 Then 'They use up their 3 attempts
                sLast.Select
                Exit Sub
            Else 'Allow viewing
                Sheet1.Columns.Hidden = False
            End If
    End If
End Sub
```

The password used in this code is Secret.

Running the Hack

Save and close your workbook and reopen it. To run the code, enable your macros and then try selecting Sheet1. A blank screen and a dialog will appear, asking you for the required password. Remember, you only get three shots at it!

HACK 131 Change Text to Upper- or Proper Case

When using a built-in Excel function is impractical, you can use a custom macro to change any existing text to uppercase or proper case.

Excel already has two functions that change text to *uppercase* (all caps), or *proper case* (capitalizing the first letter of every word). Let's say we have the words hong kong disneyland in cell A1. The existing functions that can be used to change text are:

=UPPER(A1)

> Converts all text in cell A1 to uppercase (all caps), giving the result of HONG KONG DISNEYLAND

=PROPER(A1)

> Converts all text in cell A1 to proper case which would give the result Hong Kong Disneyland

These functions work well when referring to cells that house the text, but there are many instances when using the worksheet function approach is not practical, such as with massive amounts of data. We can fix this with the use of some simple code that displays a message box asking if we would like to convert to uppercase or proper case.

The Code

Right-click on your sheet tab, select View Code (or press Alt/Option-F11), insert a module by selecting Insert → Module, and enter the following code:

```
Sub ConvertCase()
Dim rAcells As Range, rLoopCells As Range
Dim lReply As Long

    'Set variable to needed cells
    If Selection.Cells.Count = 1 Then
        Set rAcells = ActiveSheet.UsedRange
```

```
    Else
        Set rAcells = Selection
    End If


    On Error Resume Next 'In case of NO text constants.
    'Set variable to all text constants
    Set rAcells = rAcells.SpecialCells(xlCellTypeConstants, xlTextValues)

    If rAcells Is Nothing Then
        MsgBox "Could not find any text."
        On Error GoTo 0
        Exit Sub
    End If

    lReply = MsgBox("Select 'Yes' for UPPER CASE or 'No' for Proper Case.", _
    vbYesNoCancel, "OzGrid.com")
    If lReply = vbCancel Then Exit Sub

    If lReply = vbYes Then ' Convert to Upper Case
            For Each rLoopCells In rAcells
                rLoopCells = StrConv(rLoopCells, vbUpperCase)
            Next rLoopCells
    Else ' Convert to Proper Case
            For Each rLoopCells In rAcells
                rLoopCells = StrConv(rLoopCells, vbProperCase)
            Next rLoopCells
    End If

End Sub
```

Click the X at the top-right side of the Visual Basic editor to close and return to Excel, and then save your workbook.

The code uses the STrConv function to convert the text. The StrConv function can take many forms, so if you want to convert to lowercase, for instance, you can substitute either vbUpperCase or vbProperCase in the code with vbLowerCase or any of the alternatives in the following list:

vbUpperCase
    Converts the string to uppercase characters

vbLowerCase
    Converts the string to lowercase characters

vbProperCase
    Converts the first letter of every word in the string to uppercase

vbWide
    Converts narrow (single-byte) characters in the string to wide (double-byte) characters

vbNarrow
> Converts wide (double-byte) characters in thestring to narrow (single-byte) characters

vbKatakana
> Converts Hiragana characters in the string to Katakana characters

vbHiragana
> Converts Katakana characters in the string to Hiragana characters

vbUnicode
> Converts the string to Unicode using the default code page of the system (not available on the Macintosh)

vbFromUnicode
> Converts the string from Unicode to the default code page of the system (not available on the Macintosh)

See the Excel VBA help for specifics.

Running the Hack

To run the macro, press Alt/Option-F8, select the macro name, and press Run.

The macro will run and display a message box that asks if you wish to change existing text to either uppercase or proper case, and depending on user selection the code will convert the text.

> If you run the macro with only a single cell selected, it will work on the entire worksheet. If you run the macro with more than one cell selected, it will work on only your selection.

HACK 132 Force Text to Upper- or Proper Case

Restrict all future entries in a spreadsheet or range of cells to uppercase or proper case only.

ALL

Rather than convert the existing contents of a spreadsheet to either uppercase or proper case [Hack #131], you can restrict all future entries to either uppercase or proper case for a range of cells or an entire spreadsheet.

With some VBA code in the Private module of the Worksheet object, you can force any text entered to be uppercase (all caps), or proper case (capitalizing the first letter of each word). This hack presents four Excel VBA procedures that will do the trick. The first two restrict the forcing of uppercase to a specified range on the worksheet, and then the entire worksheet. The last two procedures do the same but force text to be entered as proper case.

The Code

To insert one of the procedures, right click on the sheet tab, select View Code, and enter the procedure you require.

 It is very important that you insert one and one only procedure to prevent erroneous results.

Uppercase. If you want to force all future text in your worksheet to uppercase, but restrict the range, you can use the following procedure, which will force uppercase text in cells A1:B20 only:

```
Private Sub Worksheet_Change(ByVal Target As Range)

''''''''''''''''''''''''''''''''''''''''''''
'Forces text to UPPER case for the range A1:B20
''''''''''''''''''''''''''''''''''''''''''''

If Target.Cells.Count > 1 Or Target.HasFormula Then Exit Sub

    On Error Resume Next
    If Not Intersect(Target, Range("A1:B20")) Is Nothing Then
        Application.EnableEvents = False
        Target = UCase(Target)
        Application.EnableEvents = True
    End If
    On Error GoTo 0

End Sub
```

If, however, you want to force uppercase entry throughout your worksheet, use this procedure instead:

```
Private Sub Worksheet_Change(ByVal Target As Range)

''''''''''''''''''''''''''''''''''''''''''''
'Forces all text to UPPER case
''''''''''''''''''''''''''''''''''''''''''''

If Target.Cells.Count > 1 Or Target.HasFormula Then Exit Sub

    On Error Resume Next
        Application.EnableEvents = False
        Target = UCase(Target)
        Application.EnableEvents = True
    On Error GoTo 0

End Sub
```

Proper case. If you want to force all future text in your worksheet to proper case (capitalized first letter), but restrict the range, you can use the following procedure, which will force proper case text in cells A1:B20 only:

```
Private Sub Worksheet_Change(ByVal Target As Range)

''''''''''''''''''''''''''''''''''''''''''''''
'Forces text to Proper case for the range A1:B20
''''''''''''''''''''''''''''''''''''''''''''''

If Target.Cells.Count > 1 Or Target.HasFormula Then Exit Sub

    On Error Resume Next
    If Not Intersect(Target, Range("A1:B20")) Is Nothing Then
        Application.EnableEvents = False
        Target = StrConv(Target, vbProperCase)
        Application.EnableEvents = True
    End If
    On Error GoTo 0

End Sub
```

If you want all entries throughout your worksheet to be proper case, use the following procedure:

```
Private Sub Worksheet_Change(ByVal Target As Range)

''''''''''''''''''''''''''''''''''''''''''''''
'Forces all text to Proper case
''''''''''''''''''''''''''''''''''''''''''''''

If Target.Cells.Count > 1 Or Target.HasFormula Then Exit Sub

    On Error Resume Next
        Application.EnableEvents = False
        Target = StrConv(Target, vbProperCase)
        Application.EnableEvents = True
    On Error GoTo 0

End Sub
```

Once you have inserted the required procedure, click the top-right X (or press Alt/⌘-Q) to get back to Excel proper, and then save your workbook.

Running the Hack

To run the required procedure (we are using the first as an example), just enter text in any cell in the range A1:B20, and any entry you make will be forced to uppercase, as shown in Figure 7-24.

	A	B
1	RAINA	ADAM
2	RAINA	AIDEN
3	DAVE	BOB
4	DAVE	SALLY
5	FRED	JOHN
6	BILL	DAVE
7	JOE	JANE
8	ANGIE	ANNE
9	KELLY	MARGARET
10	KYLIE	GILES
11		

Figure 7-24. Entries in the range A1:B20 forced to uppercase

Hacking the Hack

To take things a step further, you can use the following Excel VBA code in an ActiveX TextBox control to force text within a textbox into uppercase or proper case. To do this, you must first insert the TextBox, so select Developer → Controls → Insert, select the TextBox tool under ActiveX Controls, and draw a textbox on your spreadsheet.

With the textbox selected, double-click it and place this procedure to force text to uppercase:

```
Private Sub TextBox1_Change( )
    On Error Resume Next
    TextBox1 = UCase(TextBox1)
    On Error GoTo 0
End Sub
```

or this procedure to force text to proper case:

```
Private Sub TextBox1_Change( )
    On Error Resume Next
    TextBox1 = StrConv(TextBox1, vbProperCase)
    On Error GoTo 0
End Sub
```

Exit the VBE and save your workbook.

Now, any text that you try to enter into the textbox will be forced to either upper or proper case.

This code can also be used in a textbox on a userform.

HACK 133

Prevent Case Sensitivity in VBA Code

Keep Excel from distinguishing between capital and lowercase letters in your text.

ALL

By default, Excel VBA code is case sensitive and uses what is known as *binary comparisons*. This means that it sees Cat and cat as two different words. There are many times, however, where you would like Excel VBA not to use binary comparisons like this (e.g., when counting entries) and you would like it to see Cat and cat as the same. You can do this easily in at least two different ways.

Ucase Function

The Ucase function can compare text in a range of cells, allowing us to write a macro that compares text case-insensitively. Here is one that displays a message box if it encounters any cell in A1:A10 of the active sheet containing any case variation of the word CAT.

The code. To insert the code, press Alt/Option-F11, select Insert → Module, and paste the following:

```
Sub CompareText( )
Dim rCell As Range

    For Each rCell In Range("A1:A10")
        If UCase(rCell) = "CAT" Then
            MsgBox rCell.Address & " has " & rCell & " in it"
        End If
    Next rCell
End Sub
```

Exit the VBE and return to Excel and save your workbook.

Running the hack. To run the macro, select Developer → Macros (pre-2007, Tools → Macro → Macros...), select CompareText from the list, and click Run. So if you had the word CAT (uppercase) in cells A1:A9 and the word cat (lowercase) in A10, the macro would display a message box for *each* instance of the word "cat," regardless of what case it is entered in.

Option Compare Text

The other method eliminates case sensitivity for *all* procedures (or macros) in a specified module. This means that if you have 20 macros in a module, each doing something different, running this code removes case-sensitivity from all macros. This means that if we have the word CAT entered in 20 macros doing different things, it will always be seen without regard to case sensitivity.

We do this by placing the words Option Compare Text at the *very top* of the module we want to make case insensitive. This will ensure that any procedures placed within the same module as the procedure in the following section will no longer be case sensitive.

The code. To insert the code, press Alt/Option-F11, select Insert → Module and paste the following:

```
Option Compare Text

Sub OptionCompareText( )
Dim rCell As Range

    For Each rCell In Range("A1:A10")
        If rCell = "CAT" Then
            MsgBox rCell.Address & " has " & rCell & " in it"
        End If
    Next rCell
End Sub
```

Exit the VBE and return to Excel and save your workbook.

Running the hack. To run the macro select Developer → Macros (pre-2007, Tools → Macro → Macros...), select OptionCompareText from the list, and click Run.

To make all procedures within the Module case sensitive again we would replace Option Compare Text with Option Compare Binary.

H A C K #134 Display AutoFilter Criteria

Use a custom function to display the criteria used for any column in a table with an AutoFilter applied.

Excel's AutoFilter is one of its most useful features, but one small drawback is that it's hard to tell the criteria being applied to the data at a glance. A custom function can display the criteria being used for each column of the table that has had an AutoFilter applied.

Let's say you have some data set up in a table and you have applied AutoFilters. First, you need to ensure that you have at least two rows above the table. Then, right-click on your sheet tab, select View Code (or press Alt/Option-F11), select Insert → Module, and paste the following code:

```
Function AutoFilter_Criteria(Header As Range) As String
Dim strCri1 As String, strCri2 As String
```

```
    Application.Volatile

    With Header.Parent.AutoFilter
        With .Filters(Header.Column - .Range.Column + 1)

            If Not .On Then Exit Function

                strCri1 = .Criteria1
            If .Operator = xlAnd Then
                strCri2 = " AND " & .Criteria2
            ElseIf .Operator = xlOr Then
                strCri2 = " OR " & .Criteria2
            End If

        End With
    End With

    AutoFilter_Criteria = UCase(Header) & ": " & strCri1 & strCri2
End Function
```

Close the window to get back to your worksheet and save your workbook.

Now to add the custom function to each cell two rows above the column heading. Click in cell B1, enter the following formula, and press Enter:

```
=AutoFilter_Criteria(B3)
```

Then, copy across to D3. Your data should something like Figure 7-25.

B	C	D
YEAR: =2007	DEPT: =Lab	AMOUNT: >500
Year 🔽	Dept 🔽	Amount 🔽
2007 Lab		520
2007 Lab		620
2007 Lab		530
2007 Lab		654

Figure 7-25. Data showing criteria selection in B3:D3

As you change the selection criteria via the AutoFilter switches in columns B, C, and D, the formula results in B3:D3 that show the criteria you selected will change accordingly, thus allowing you to always see at a glance the criteria used in your filter.

Remember that if you do not have AutoFilters applied, you will have nothing in these cells.

Cross-Application Hacks
Hacks 135–138

With the ever-increasing usage of computers in our society, it is fast becoming necessary for most people to use a combination of applications in their work. Microsoft Office 2007's enhanced capabilities for cooperation between its applications makes combining Excel with Word, Access, and Outlook easier than before. The hacks in this chapter cover some of the most common problems.

Import Data from Access 2007 into Excel 2007

VBA can be used to import data into Excel from an Access database, but Access 2007 has undergone some major, important changes that effect how we create connections to Access 2007 databases and also how we work with the Access 2007 Objects Model.

To communicate with Access 2007 databases via VBA, the preferable method is to use Data Access Objects (DAO), which is the object model written specifically for Access. It's an object library with a collection of database objects.

> This hack works with Excel 2007, Access 2007, Windows XP, and Windows Vista.

For the purpose of this hack, we will use the database file *Northwind 2007.accdb* (a database created and stored in Access 2007 that can be used for test purposes).

> If you installed Office 2007 via a downloadable link, you may need to download the Northwind 2007 example file from the Microsoft web site: *http://office.microsoft.com/en-us/templates/TC012289971033.aspx.*

The code we will use does the following:

1. Connect to the database (in this case *Northwind 2007.accdb*).
2. Send a Structured Query Language (SQL) question order to populate a recordset with the required records. A *recordset* can be thought of as a container used to hold a set of records from a database table, which is then copied and imported into Excel.
3. Close the connection to the database.
4. Display a message stating that the data successfully transferred.

The first step is to set a reference to the new library (Microsoft Office 12 Access Database Engine Object Library). In the Visual Basic Editor, go to Tools → References..., locate and check the Microsoft Office 12 Access Database Engine Object Library in the list, and then click OK and exit the VBE.

The following code example shows a few possible approaches to retrieve data in a flexible way:

Retrieve a whole table's data
> Tables in databases can contain a great number of records, so you should retrieve all records only when necessary and if the table is relatively small. For this purpose, the example we are using is a *table* recordset type and only a table name can be the source.

Retrieve a selected group of data based on SQL queries
> This is the most common approach, in which we create an SQL query that includes a specific WHERE clause to retrieve the wanted records. In the example, we use the *snapshot* recordset type. A snapshot-type recordset is *static*, which means it is not editable and therefore it can only be read.

> SQL is a powerful language, which we can use to create very complex questions, but it's beyond the scope of this hack to delve into it deeper.
>
> For more on SQL, see *SQL Hacks* by Andrew Cumming and Gordon Russell (O'Reilly).

Execute a stored report in the database

Instead of creating the SQL question in VBA, we can create and save the question in the Access 2007 database and then execute it from Excel 2007. Here we use the *forward* recordset type, which is efficient and allows us to move forward in the recordset (if this is what we require).

The Code

To insert the code, right-click on the worksheet name, go to View Code, select Insert → Module in the VBE and enter the following:

```
Option Explicit
'A reference via Tools | References... to Microsoft Office 12 Access
Database Engine Object Library
'must be set in order to get the below code to work properly.

Sub Import_Data_Access_2007()

'The pathway to and the name of the database.
Const stDB As String = "c:\Northwind 2007.accdb"

'The table to be retrieved all data from.
Const stWholeTable As String = "Shippers"

'The SQL query with one condition.
Const stSQL As String = "SELECT Company,City FROM Shippers " & _
                        "WHERE [Country/Region]='USA'"

'The name of the stored report that will be executed.
Const stStoredReport As String = "Order Summary"

'A general error handling routine.
On Error GoTo Error_Handling

'Variables for the DAO objects.
'The database object.
Dim db As DAO.Database
'The table defintion variable for a saved table object.
Dim tdf As DAO.TableDef
'The recordset object.
Dim rs As DAO.Recordset

'Variables for the Excel objects.
Dim wbTarget As Workbook
Dim wsOrders As Worksheet
Dim wsShippers As Worksheet
Dim wsProducts As Worksheet
Dim rnOrders As Range
Dim rnShippers As Range
```

```
Dim rnProducts As Range
Dim lnCounter As Long

'Instantiate the Excel objects.
Set wbTarget = ActiveWorkbook

With wbTarget
    Set wsOrders = .Worksheets(1)
    Set wsShippers = .Worksheets(2)
    Set wsProducts = .Worksheets(3)
End With

Set rnOrders = wsOrders.Range("A2")
Set rnShippers = wsShippers.Range("A2")
Set rnProducts = wsProducts.Range("A2")

'Instantiate the DAO objects and at the same time create
'a connection to the database and populate the 1st recordset.
Set db = OpenDatabase(stDB)
Set tdf = db.TableDefs(stWholeTable)
Set rs = tdf.OpenRecordset(dbOpenTable)

'To avoid that the screen flicker during dataprocessing.
Application.ScreenUpdating = False

'Populate the first row in the target worksheet with fieldnames.
For lnCounter = 0 To rs.Fields.Count - 1
    'The array of fieldnames is 0-based which we need to consider when
    'populating the worksheet.
    wsShippers.Cells(1, lnCounter + 1).Value = rs.Fields(lnCounter).Name
Next lnCounter

'Copy the retrieved records.
rnShippers.CopyFromRecordset rs

'Clear the recordset variable.
Set rs = Nothing
'Instantiate and populate the 2nd recordset.
Set rs = db.OpenRecordset(stSQL, dbOpenSnapshot)

'Populate the first row in the target worksheet with fieldnames.
For lnCounter = 0 To rs.Fields.Count - 1
    'The array of fieldnames is 0-based which we need to consider when
    'populating the worksheet.
    wsProducts.Cells(1, lnCounter + 1).Value = rs.Fields(lnCounter).Name
Next lnCounter

'Copy the retrieved records.
rnProducts.CopyFromRecordset rs

'Clear the recordset variable.
Set rs = Nothing
'Instantiate and populate the 3rd recordset.
```

```
Set rs = db.OpenRecordset(stStoredReport, dbOpenForwardOnly)

'Populate the first row in the target worksheet with fieldnames.
For lnCounter = 0 To rs.Fields.Count - 1
    'The array of fieldnames is 0-based which we need to consider when
    'populating the worksheet.
    wsOrders.Cells(1, lnCounter + 1).Value = rs.Fields(lnCounter).Name
Next lnCounter

'Copy the retrieved records.
rnOrders.CopyFromRecordset rs

'Close the objects.
rs.Close
db.Close

MsgBox "All data has been successfully transfered.", vbOKOnly

'Make sure that it only exist one exit point in the procedure.
ExitSub:
'Release the objects from memory.
Set rs = Nothing
Set tdf = Nothing
Set db = Nothing
Exit Sub

Error_Handling:
MsgBox "Error number: " & Err.Number & vbNewLine & _
       "Description: " & Err.Description, vbOKOnly
Resume ExitSub

End Sub
```

Now, close down the VBE, return to Excel, and save your workbook.

Running the Hack

To run the code, select Developer → Macros, highlight Import_Data_Access_2007 in the list, and click Run. You will see the required recordset populate your Excel spreadsheet, as shown in Figure 8-1.

Armed with this code, you can comfortably connect to an Access database from within Excel 2007 and import any information you require.

> The code as is assumes the *Northwind 2007.accdb* test file is saved to your C: drive. If you have saved it somewhere else, you will need to put the full pathname in the code.

—Dennis Wallentin

	A	B	C	D	E	F	G	H	I	J	K	L	M
1	Order ID	Employee	Customer	Order Date	Shipped Date	Sub Total	Shipping F	Taxes	Order Total	Ship Nam	Ship Addr	Paid Date	Status
2	81	2	3	25/04/2006		0	0	0	0	Thomas A	123 3rd Street		New
3	80	2	4	25/04/2006		380	0	0	380	Christina	123 4th Street		New
4	79	2	6	23/06/2006	23/06/2006	2490	0	0	2490	Francisco	123 6th St	23/06/2006	Closed
5	78	1	29	5/06/2006	5/06/2006	1560	200	0	1760	Soo Jung L	789 29th S	5/06/2006	Closed
6	77	9	26	5/06/2006	5/06/2006	2250	60	0	2310	Run Liu	789 26th S	5/06/2006	Closed
7	76	9	25	5/06/2006	5/06/2006	660	5	0	665	John Rodr	789 25th S	5/06/2006	Closed
8	75	4	8	5/06/2006	5/06/2006	510	50	0	560	Elizabeth	123 8th St	5/06/2006	Closed
9	74	6	6	8/06/2006	8/06/2006	510	300	0	810	Francisco	123 6th St	8/06/2006	Closed
10	73	7	9	5/06/2006	5/06/2006	96.5	100	0	196.5	Sven Mor	123 9th St	5/06/2006	Closed
11	72	1	28	7/06/2006	7/06/2006	230	40	0	270	Amritansh	789 28th S	7/06/2006	Closed
12	71	1	1	24/05/2006		736	0	0	736	Anna Bed	123 1st Street		New
13	70	1	11	24/05/2006		800	0	0	800	Peter Krsc	123 11th Street		New
14	69	1	10	24/05/2006		52.5	0	0	52.5	Roland W	123 10th Street		New
15	68	1	7	24/05/2006			0	0		Ming-Yan	123 7th Street		New
16	67	4	10	24/05/2006	24/05/2006	200	9	0	209	Roland W	123 10th S	24/05/2006	Closed
17	66	3	8	24/05/2006	24/05/2006		5	0		Elizabeth	123 8th St	24/05/2006	New
18	65	9	28	11/05/2006	11/05/2006		10	0		Amritansh	789 28th S	11/05/2006	New
19	64	8	6	9/05/2006	9/05/2006		12	0		Francisco	123 6th St	9/05/2006	New
20	63	4	3	25/04/2006	25/04/2006	620	7	0	627	Thomas A	123 3rd St	25/04/2006	Closed
21	62	3	29	12/04/2006	12/04/2006		7	0		Soo Jung L	789 29th S	12/04/2006	New
22	61	9	4	7/04/2006	7/04/2006		4	0		Christina	123 4th St	7/04/2006	New
23	60	6	8	30/04/2006	30/04/2006	1392	50	0	1442	Elizabeth	123 8th St	30/04/2006	Closed
24	59	4	12	22/04/2006	22/04/2006		5	0		John Edw	123 12th S	22/04/2006	New
25	58	3	4	22/04/2006	22/04/2006	3520	5	0	3525	Christina	123 4th St	22/04/2006	Closed

Sheet1 / Sheet2 / Sheet3

Figure 8-1. Data called from Access 2007 via VBA for Excel Code

Retrieve Data from Closed Workbooks

HACK #136

2007

Use VBA and a database approach to populate a workbook with data retrieved from closed workbooks. The same technique can be applied to Word and Access.

It's common for Excel users to consolidate data from several other workbooks into one main workbook. By using an approach combining VBA and a database, we can retrieve data from workbooks without opening them. There are several techniques you could use to do this, including links and query tables, but these techniques tend to be difficult to maintain and time consuming to update when working with a larger number of workbooks.

By contrast, the approach in this hack offers the following advantages:

- The underlying workbooks do not need to be open in order to retrieve data from them.
- The code is easier to maintain, because it is in the main workbook.
- It consumes resources only when the code is being executed.
- It forces Excel to create an identical structure for all involved workbooks.

A database approach comes with some general requirements to consider when designing the main workbook and the underlying workbooks. All worksheets (including the main worksheet) need to have the same design and setup:

- The data needs to be in an identical table structure, with identical names for each column in use.

- Each column needs to have only one data type—for instance, integer or string.

- All cells in each row must have values; i.e., the value #Null! cannot exist.

- An identical name for the worksheets can be used to increase the simplicity when creating the code.

Excel 2007 and Windows Vista

With Office 2007, Microsoft introduces a new data provider, Microsoft.ACE. OLEDB.12.0, which makes it possible to connect to Microsoft Access 2007 databases (file extension *.accdb*) and to Microsoft Excel 2007 workbooks (file extension *.xlsx*). When used with Microsoft Excel 2007, the workbooks are treated as database sources. In this hack, the data provider is used to connect to the underlying closed workbooks and is part of the connection string shown in this example:

```
"Provider=Microsoft.ACE.OLEDB.12.0;" & _
"Data Source=c:\Test\Data.xlsx;" & _
"Extended Properties=""Excel 12.0;HDR=YES"""
```

The first extended property in the connection string does not explicitly refer to Excel 2007, which has the version number 12; rather, it's an indication that the provider works with version 2007 and later versions of Excel.

The second extended property, HDR, indicates whether the tables in the underlying worksheets have column names (field names) or not. In general, it's highly recommended to use column names in the first row in the table, so the value of this property should be set to YES.

Windows Vista comes with a new version of the Microsoft ActiveX Data Objects library 6.0, which can be used with Excel 2007. This external library is used to create a recordset that holds the retrieved data from each underlying workbook and from which the data is copied into the main workbook.

When the connection has been established with an underlying workbook, we need to help Excel to both locate and select the required data. This is done via SQL statements. These statements can be rather complex, depending on the specific requirements. For our purpose, we set focus on the options we have to locate the data.

To select all data in one worksheet, we can use the following SQL expression:

```
"SELECT * FROM [WorksheetName$]"
```

The $ sign indicates that the worksheet exists.

To select all data in one range, we could use either of two alternatives. Here's how to use select data explicitly, using a range address:

```
"SELECT * FROM [WorksheetName$A2:A10]"
```

And here's how to use a named range (where the range name is unique for the workbook):

```
"SELECT * FROM [NamedRange]"
```

If we want to retrieve a value from only one cell, then we still need to refer to a range, like so:

```
"SELECT * FROM [WorksheetName$A2:A2)"
```

If we use a range name, it must cover a range, like A2:A2:

```
"SELECT * FROM [NamedRange]"
```

In our example, all workbooks are identical and all of them are placed in the same folder: *C:\Products*. A worksheet with the name Summary exists in all workbooks, and the range name ProductData refers to the range A2:D6, as shown in Figure 8-2.

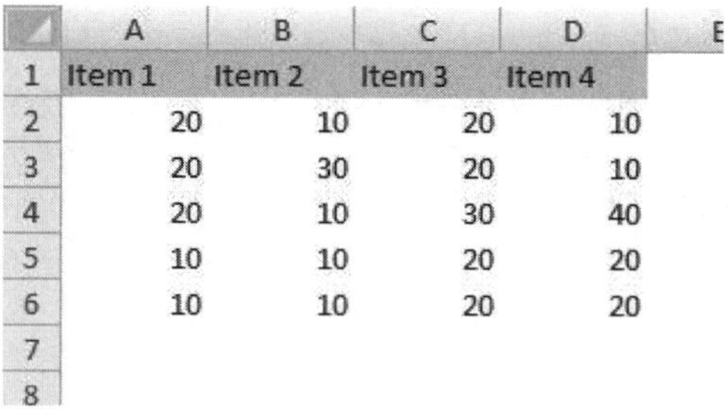

	A	B	C	D	E
1	Item 1	Item 2	Item 3	Item 4	
2	20	10	20	10	
3	20	30	20	10	
4	20	10	30	40	
5	10	10	20	20	
6	10	10	20	20	
7					
8					

Figure 8-2. One of the identical workbooks, showing data

The code. In the workbook into which you want to import all of your data (let's call it the final workbook), right-click, select View Code to take you to the VBE, select Insert → Module, and paste the following code:

```
Option Explicit

'A reference to Microsoft ActiveX Data Objects  Library 6.0 must be
'set via Tools → References...

Sub Retrieve_Data_Closed_Workbooks()
'Constant variable that holds the directory.
Const Con_stPath As String = "C:\Products\"
'The SQL statement string variable which only include the name for the range
```

```
'that contain the data in each worksheet and workbook.
Const Con_stSQL As String = "SELECT * FROM [ProductData]"


'The ADO Recordset variable.
Dim rst As ADODB.Recordset
'The connection string variable.
Dim stCon As String

'String variable that holds the located Excel files.
Dim stFile As String
'Variable to temporarily store the present calculation mode.
Dim xlCalc As Excel.XlCalculation
'Variable for this workbook.
Dim wbBook As Workbook
'Variable for the target worksheet.
Dim wsTarget As Worksheet
'Variable to get the last used row in the target worksheet
Dim lnLastRow As Long

'General error handling.
On Error GoTo Error_Handling

'Temporarily change some settings to increase the performance.
With Application
    'Store the calculation mode.
    xlCalc = .Calculation
    'Temporarily set the calculation mode to Manual.
    .Calculation = xlCalculationManual
    'In case any Events procedures exist.
    .EnableEvents = False
    'To avoid that the screen is flickering during the process.
    .ScreenUpdating = False
End With

'Instantiate the workbook variable.
Set wbBook = ThisWorkbook
'Instantiate the worksheet variable.
Set wsTarget = wbBook.Worksheets(1)

'Instantiate the Recordset object.
Set rst = New ADODB.Recordset

'Get the first Excel file.
stFile = Dir(Con_stPath & "*.xlsx", 7)

'Iterate through the collection of Excel files,
'open a connection to each file and retrieve the wanted data,
'copy the retrieved data to the target worksheet
'and close the connection.
Do While stFile <> ""
    'Create the connection string.
    stCon = "Provider=Microsoft.ACE.OLEDB.12.0;" & _
```

```
                    "Data Source=" & Con_stPath & stFile & ";" & _
                    "Extended Properties=""Excel 12.0;HDR=YES"""

            'Open the connection and execute the SQL statement.
            rst.Open Con_stSQL, stCon, adOpenForwardOnly, adLockReadOnly, adCmdText

            With wsTarget
                'The assumption here is that it will not be more then 500 rows.
                lnLastRow = .Range("A500").End(xlUp).Row
                'Copy the retrieved data into the first empty row in target worksheet.
                .Range("A" & lnLastRow + 1).CopyFromRecordset rst
            End With

            'Empty the connection variable.
            stCon = Empty
            'Close the recordset.
            rst.Close
            'Get the next Excel file.
            stFile = Dir( )
        Loop

        MsgBox "All the data has successfully been retrieved!", vbOKOnly

        'Make sure that it only exist one exit point in the procedure.
        ExitSub:
        'Release variable from the memory.
        Set rst = Nothing
        'Reset the settings.
        With Application
            .Calculation = xlCalc
            .EnableEvents = True
            .ScreenUpdating = True
        End With

        Exit Sub

        Error_Handling:
        MsgBox "Error number: " & Err.Number & vbNewLine & _
               "Description: " & Err.Description, vbOKOnly
        Resume ExitSub

    End Sub
```

Close down the VBE and return to Excel and save your workbook.

Running the hack. To run the code, select Developer → Macros. Highlight Retrieve_Data_Closed_Workbooks in the list, and click Run.

When you do this, the data in range A2:D6 (which we have given the name of ProductData) in each closed workbook will be pasted into your final workbook in the range A2:D16, as shown in Figure 8-3.

	A	B	C	D	E
1	Item 1	Item 2	Item 3	Item 4	
2	20	20	20	10	
3	10	30	10	10	
4	20	20	30	20	
5	10	10	40	20	
6	10	10	20	20	
7	10	10	20	20	
8	10	30	10	30	
9	20	40	20	20	
10	20	20	10	10	
11	20	10	10	10	
12	20	10	20	10	
13	20	30	20	10	
14	20	10	30	40	
15	10	10	20	20	
16	10	10	20	20	
17					

Figure 8-3. Final workbook showing result of importing the same data range in three different workbooks

Windows XP `2003`

You can use the previous method with Windows Vista and Excel 2007, but if you're running Windows XP and Excel 2003, you'll need to use a slightly different technical approach. Specifically, you'll need to use the external library, Microsoft ActiveX Data Objects 2.8 or a previous version. In addition, the connection string differs by including Excel 8 in the first extended property, as shown here:

```
Provider=Microsoft.Jet.OLEDB.4.0;" & _
"Data Source=" c:\Test\Data.xls;" & _
"Extended Properties=""Excel 8.0;HDR=YES"""
```

The first extended property's value does not explicitly refer to Excel 97, which has the version number 8; rather it's an indication that the data provider works with version 97 to version 2003 of Excel.

The code. To insert the code, right-click on your sheet tab and select View Code to take you to the VBE. Then, select Insert → Module, and paste in the following:

```
Option Explicit

'A reference to Microsoft ActiveX Data Objects  Library 2.8 and earlier
'must be set via Tools → References...
```

```
Sub Retrieve_Data_Closed_Workbooks( )
'Constant variable that holds the directory.
Const Con_stPath As String = "C:\Products\"
'The SQL statement string variable which only include the name for the range
'that contain the data in each worksheet and workbook.
Const Con_stSQL As String = "SELECT * FROM [ProductData]"


'The ADO Recordset variable.
Dim rst As ADODB.Recordset
'The connection string variable.
Dim stCon As String

'String variable that holds the located Excel files.
Dim stFile As String
'Variable to temporarily store the present calculation mode.
Dim xlCalc As Excel.XlCalculation
'Variable for this workbook.
Dim wbBook As Workbook
'Variable for the target worksheet.
Dim wsTarget As Worksheet
'Variable to get the last used row in the target worksheet
Dim lnLastRow As Long

'General error handling.
On Error GoTo Error_Handling

'Temporarily change some settings to increase the performance.
With Application
    'Store the calculation mode.
    xlCalc = .Calculation
    'Temporarily set the calculation mode to Manual.
    .Calculation = xlCalculationManual
    'In case any Events procedures exist.
    .EnableEvents = False
    'To avoid that the screen is flickering during the process.
    .ScreenUpdating = False
End With

'Instantiate the workbook variable.
Set wbBook = ThisWorkbook
'Instantiate the worksheet variable.
Set wsTarget = wbBook.Worksheets(1)

'Instantiate the Recordset object.
Set rst = New ADODB.Recordset

'Get the first Excel file.
stFile = Dir(Con_stPath & "*.xls", 7)

'Iterate through the collection of Excel files,
'open a connection to each file and retrieve the wanted data,
```

```
'copy the retrieved data to the target worksheet
'and close the connection.
Do While stFile <> ""
    'Create the connection string.
                stCon = "Provider=Microsoft.Jet.OLEDB.4.0;" & _
                        "Data Source=" & Con_stPath & stFile & ";" & _
                        "Extended Properties=""Excel 8.0;HDR=YES"""

    'Open the connection and execute the SQL statement.
    rst.Open Con_stSQL, stCon, adOpenForwardOnly, adLockReadOnly, adCmdText

    With wsTarget
        'The assumption here is that it will not be more then 500 rows.
        lnLastRow = .Range("A500").End(xlUp).Row
        'Copy the retrieved data into the first empty row in target worksheet.
        .Range("A" & lnLastRow + 1).CopyFromRecordset rst
    End With

    'Empty the connection variable.
    stCon = Empty
    'Close the recordset.
    rst.Close
    'Get the next Excel file.
    stFile = Dir( )
Loop

MsgBox "All the data has successfully been retrieved!", vbOKOnly

'Make sure that it only exist one exit point in the procedure.
ExitSub:
'Release variable from the memory.
Set rst = Nothing
'Reset the settings.
With Application
    .Calculation = xlCalc
    .EnableEvents = True
    .ScreenUpdating = True
End With

Exit Sub

Error_Handling:
MsgBox "Error number: " & Err.Number & vbNewLine & _
       "Description: " & Err.Description, vbOKOnly
Resume ExitSub

End Sub
```

Close down the VBE, return to Excel, save your workbook, and give it a try.

Running the hack. To run the code, select Developer → Macros, highlight Retrieve_Data_Closed_Workbooks in the list, and click Run.

When you do this, the data in range A2:D6 (which we have given the name of ProductData) in each closed workbook will be pasted into your final workbook in the range A2:D16, as shown previously in Figure 8-3.

> Remember that the code relies on all workbooks being stored in the same directory—in this case, *C:\Products*.

—Dennis Wallentin

Automate Word from Excel
HACK 137

Import and update a table and chart from Excel into Word, and create a report for the user to comment on.

2007
2003

Say you have a Word-based report (*Weekly Report.docx* in the folder *C:\ Reports*) that you distribute on a weekly basis. It contains a table and a chart from an Excel workbook, as shown in Figure 8-4, and you want to import and update the Word report regularly. This hack shows how to use VBA for Excel to transfer the table and the chart, automating the report in Word.

In order to get a smooth technical solution, the first thing we need to do is to create two bookmarks in our Word report. The first bookmark will be used to insert the table, and the second will be used for the chart object. You can do this easily in Word by selecting Insert → Links → Bookmark. We have used the names XLChart and XLTable. Ensure you have saved and closed the Word report (with bookmarks in it) in the folder *C:\Reports*.

In our code, we'll copy the table in the normal way, but for the chart we need to create a temporary image file, paste it into the Word report, and finally delete it. When the data has been transferred from Excel to Word, the Word report will be opened and the transferred data will be displayed for checking and saving purposes.

> This hack works with Excel 2007, Excel 2003, Word 2007, Word 2003, Windows Vista, and Windows XP.

The Code

In the workbook that contains the table and the chart, right-click on the sheet tab and select View Code. Then, select Insert → Module and paste the following code:

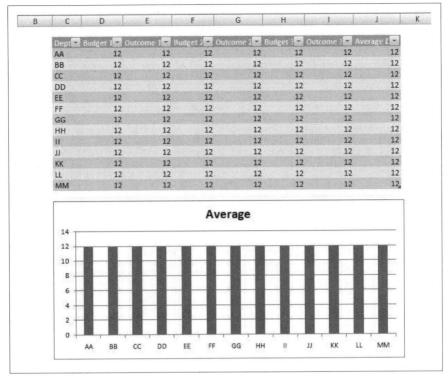

Figure 8-4. Table and chart in Excel workbook to be imported into Word document

```
Option Explicit

'A reference to the Microsoft Word 12.0 Object Library must be
'set via the Tools | References... in the VB Editor.

'For Office 2003 a reference needs to be set to Microsoft Word 11.0.

Sub Update_Word_Report( )
'The pathway to the Word report file and its name.
Const stReport As String = "c:\Reports\Weekly Report.docx"

'A general error handling.
On Error GoTo Error_Handling

'Variables for Word.
Dim wdApp As Word.Application
Dim wdDoc As Word.Document
Dim wdRange As Word.Range

'Variables for Excel.
Dim wbSource As Workbook
Dim wsSheet As Worksheet
```

```
Dim rnTable As Range
Dim chObject As ChartObject

'Instantiate the Excel variables.
Set wbSource = ActiveWorkbook
Set wsSheet = wbSource.Worksheets(1)

With wsSheet
    'A range name for the table is in use.
    Set rnTable = .Range("ReportTable")
    'A customized chart name is in use.
    Set chObject = .ChartObjects("ReportChart")
End With

'Instantiate the Word variables.
Set wdApp = New Word.Application
Set wdDoc = wdApp.Documents.Open(stReport)

'The first bookmark where the table will be inserted at.
Set wdRange = wdDoc.Bookmarks("xlTable").Range

'It's necessary to delete any existing table before
'inserting the new report table. If it does not exist an error will be ↵
generated
With wdDoc.InlineShapes(1)
    .Select
    .Delete
End With

'In order to avoid screen flickering.
Application.ScreenUpdating = False

'Copy the table.
rnTable.Copy

'Paste the table at the bookmark in the Word document.
With wdRange
    .Select
    .PasteSpecial Link:=False, _
                  DataType:=wdPasteMetafilePicture, _
                  Placement:=wdInLine, _
                  DisplayAsIcon:=False
End With

'Save the Word document.
wdDoc.Save

'The second bookmark where the chart will be inserted at.
Set wdRange = wdDoc.Bookmarks("xlChart").Range

'Export the chart object to a GIF file in the same folder as the workbook. ↵
chObject.Chart.Export Filename:=ThisWorkbook.Path & "\Chart.gif", ↵
FilterName:="GIF"
```

```
'Delete the existing chart object.
With wdDoc.InlineShapes(2)
    .Select
    .Delete
End With

With wdRange
    .Select
    'Insert the chartobject into the bookmark.
    .InlineShapes.AddPicture _
        Filename:=ThisWorkbook.Path & "\Chart.gif", _
        LinkToFile:=False, _
        SaveWithDocument:=True
End With

'Save the Word document.
wdDoc.Save

With Application
    'Release Excel from the "cut copy" mode.
    .CutCopyMode = False
    .ScreenUpdating = True
End With

'Make the document available for the user.
wdApp.Visible = True

'Delete the temporary GIF file.
Kill ThisWorkbook.Path & "\Chart.gif"

'Make sure that it only exist one exit point in the procedure.
ExitSub:
'Release objects from memory.
Set wdRange = Nothing
Set wdDoc = Nothing
Set wdApp = Nothing
Exit Sub

Error_Handling:
    'If a table or a chart object does not exist and when trying to
    'remove it it will generate an error with the number 5941.
    If Err.Number = 5941 Or Err.Number = 91 Then
        Resume Next
    Else
        MsgBox "Error number: " & Err.Number & vbNewLine & _
            "Description: " & Err.Description, vbOKOnly
        Resume ExitSub
    End If
End Sub
```

Close down the VBE, return to Excel, and save your workbook.

Running the Hack

To run the code, select Developer → Macros, highlight Update_Word_Report in the list, and click Run. The table and chart from the Excel workbook will be imported into the closed Word report and the Word report will be opened and displayed, as shown in Figure 8-5.

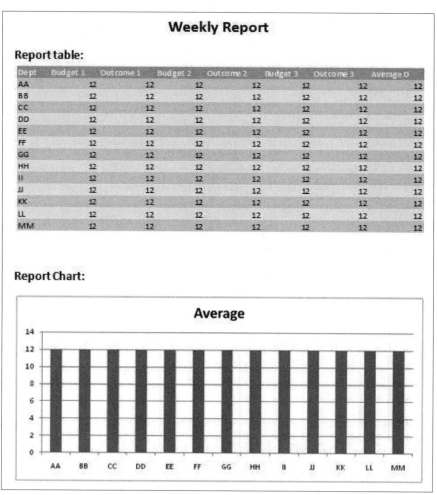

Figure 8-5. *Word report showing imported table and chart from Excel workbook*

The clever thing about this hack is that you don't even need Word open in order to import, update, and save information from Excel.

—Dennis Wallentin

Automate Outlook from Excel

Distribute weekly reports via Outlook, adding each worksheet in the workbook to an outgoing email.

2007
2003

One of the more common tasks for Excel users is report distribution. This hack shows how to leverage Outlook for automatic emailing of Excel worksheets, even creating a standard message in the body of the email.

> This hack works with Excel 2007, Excel 2003, Windows Vista, and Windows XP.

In our workbook, we want to email a valid recipient list (a list of email addresses), which is predefined in column A in each worksheet, as shown in Figure 8-6.

Figure 8-6. Excel spreadsheet with a list of email recipients in column A

The first thing we need to do is to set a reference to the new library (Microsoft Outlook 12.0 Object Library). In the Visual Basic Editor, go to Tools → References..., locate and check the Microsoft Outlook 12.0 Object Library in the list, and then click OK and exit the VBE.

> If you are running Outlook 2003, you need to check Microsoft Outlook 11.0 Object Library instead.

The Code

Right-click on the sheet name, select View Code → Insert → Module, and paste the following code:

```
Option Explicit

'A reference to Microsoft Outlook 12.0 Object Library must be set
'via the command Tools | References...

'If running Microsoft Outlook 2003 then replace the reference of 12.0 to
'11.0

'Make sure that the recipients exist in Outlook's Address book.

Sub Send_Mail_Outlook()
'A folder to temporarily store the created Excel workbooks in.
Const stPath As String = "c:\Attachments"

'The subject for all e-mails.
Const stSubject As String = "Weekly report"

'The message in the bodies of the outgoing e-mails.
Const stMsg As String = "The weekly report as per agreement." & vbCrLf & _
                        "Kind regards," & vbCrLf & _
                        "Michael"

'Variables for Outlook.
Dim olApp As Outlook.Application
Dim olNameSpace As Outlook.Namespace
Dim olInbox As Outlook.MAPIFolder
Dim olNewMail As Outlook.MailItem
Dim lnCounter As Long

'Variables for Excel.
Dim wbBook As Workbook
Dim wsSheet As Worksheet
Dim lnLastRow As Long

'Variable that holds the list of recipients for each worksheet.
Dim vaRecipients As Variant
'Variable that flag if the list of recipients only include one recipient.
Dim bFlag As Boolean
'Variable which holds each worksheet's name.
Dim stFileName As String
'Variable for each created workbook's path and name.
Dim stAttachment As String

'Set the flag to false.
bFlag = False

'General error handler.
On Error GoTo Error_Handling
```

```
'Freeze the screen so it will not flicker during execution.
Application.ScreenUpdating = False

'If Outlook is already open then the variable is instantiated to the
session.
Set olApp = GetObject(, "Outlook.Application")

'If Outlook is not running we here intantiate a new session for it.
If olApp Is Nothing Then
    Set olApp = New Outlook.Application
    'Get Outlook's work area.
    Set olNameSpace = olApp.GetNamespace("MAPI")
    'Access and display the Inbox folder.
    Set olInbox = olNameSpace.GetDefaultFolder(olFolderInbox)
    'Make Outlook visible.
    olInbox.Display
End If

'Instantiate the workbook's variable.
Set wbBook = ThisWorkbook

'Loop through the collection of worksheets in the workbook.
For Each wsSheet In wbBook.Worksheets

    With wsSheet
        'Retrieve the worksheet's name.
        stFileName = .Name
        'Locate the last used row in column A.
        lnLastRow = .Cells(.Rows.Count, "A").End(xlUp).Row
        'Set the flag to true if the list only includes one recipient.
        If lnLastRow = 1 Then bFlag = True
        'Grab the list of recipients.
        vaRecipients = .Range("A1:A" & lnLastRow).Value
        'Copy the worksheet to a new workbook.
        .Copy
    End With

    'Here we convert all formulas (and links) to fixed values.
    'The active sheet is the worksheet in the new created workbook.
    With ActiveSheet.UsedRange
        .Copy
        .PasteSpecial Paste:=xlValues
    End With

    'Clear the clipboard.
    Application.CutCopyMode = False

    'Create the full path and name of the workbook.
    stAttachment = stPath & "\" & stFileName & ".xlxs"

    'Save and close the temporarily workbook.
    With ActiveWorkbook
      .SaveAs Filename:=stAttachment
```

```
        .Close
    End With

    'Create the new e-mail.
    Set olNewMail = olApp.CreateItem(olMailItem)

    'Manipulate the main properties of the outgoing e-mail.
    With olNewMail
        'Set a flag for the e-mail degree of importance.
        .Importance = olImportanceHigh
        .Subject = stSubject
        'Add the list of recipients.
        If bFlag = True Then
            'Add the only recipient.
            .Recipients.Add vaRecipients
        Else
            For lnCounter = LBound(vaRecipients) To UBound(vaRecipients)
                .Recipients.Add vaRecipients(lnCounter, 1)
            Next lnCounter
        End If
        'Make sure that the recipients exist in the Address book.
        .Recipients.ResolveAll
        'Add the message.
        .Body = stMsg
        'Add the attachment.
        With .Attachments
            .Add stAttachment
            .Item(1).DisplayName = stFileName
        End With
        'Save the e-mail.
        .Save
        'Send the e-mail, i e place it in the outbox.
        .Send
    End With

    'Delete the temporarily workbook.
    Kill stAttachment

Next wsSheet

'Make sure that it only exist one exit point in the procedure.
ExitSub:
'Release objects from memory.
Set olNewMail = Nothing
Set olInbox = Nothing
Set olNameSpace = Nothing
Set olApp = Nothing
Exit Sub

Error_Handling:
    'If not Outlook is running then we need to resolve the error message in
    'order to continue.
    If Err.Number = 429 Then
```

```
                Resume Next
        Else
            MsgBox "Error number: " & Err.Number & vbNewLine & _
                   "Description: " & Err.Description, vbOKOnly
            Resume ExitSub
        End If
    End Sub
```

Close down the VBE, return to Excel, and save your workbook.

Running the Hack

To run the code, select Developer → Macros, Highlight Send_Mail_Outlook in the list, and click Run. Each sheet in your workbook will be emailed to the list of recipients in column A with a standard message, as shown in the Figure 8-7.

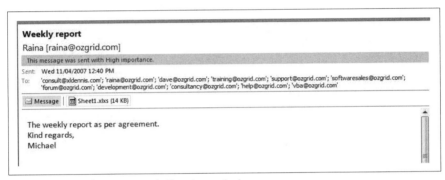

Weekly report

Raina [raina@ozgrid.com]

This message was sent with High importance.

Sent: Wed 11/04/2007 12:40 PM
To: 'consult@xldennis.com'; 'raina@ozgrid.com'; 'dave@ozgrid.com'; 'training@ozgrid.com'; 'support@ozgrid.com'; 'softwaresales@ozgrid.com'; 'forum@ozgrid.com'; 'development@ozgrid.com'; 'consultancy@ozgrid.com'; 'help@ozgrid.com'; 'vba@ozgrid.com'

✉ Message | 🗐 Sheet1.xlsx (14 KB)

The weekly report as per agreement.
Kind regards,
Michael

Figure 8-7. Email message with Sheet1 attached

When you run the code, due to Outlook's security model, you may get two security messages, as shown in Figures 8-8 and 8-9, which ask you to make a decision. Since we have initiated the process, we can allow access to Outlook, enabling it to send the emails and the worksheet attachments.

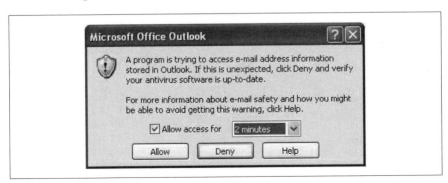

Microsoft Office Outlook [?][X]

A program is trying to access e-mail address information stored in Outlook. If this is unexpected, click Deny and verify your antivirus software is up-to-date.

For more information about e-mail safety and how you might be able to avoid getting this warning, click Help.

☑ Allow access for [2 minutes ▼]

[Allow] [Deny] [Help]

Figure 8-8. A possible Outlook error message

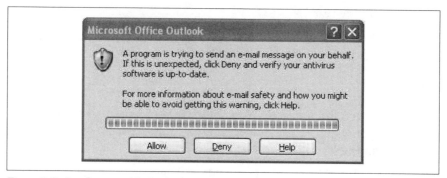

Figure 8-9. Another possible Outlook error message

There are tools (both free and commercial) that can eliminate these messages. One free tool is Express ClickYes, which you can download from *http://www.contextmagic.com/express-clickyes/*. If you prefer to manage it with VBA, you can use the commercial Outlook Redemption tool at *http://www.dimastr.com/redemption/*.

—Dennis Wallentin

Index

{ } braces, 57, 243
[ ] square brackets, 81
' apostrophe
    allows for worksheet names with
        spaces, 237
    with INDIRECT function, 49
* asterisk, 84, 277
$ dollar sign
    Average function made absolute
        with, 77
    for absolute formulas, 38, 194
    force ranges to be absolute, 108
    reference columns absolutely
        with, 59
= equal sign, for copying cells to any
        location, 194
() parentheses, 266
" quotation marks
    around formulas, 56
    removing around formulas, 56
; semicolon, for separating sections of a
        cell, 79
[*] to search for real external links, 39
_ underscore, 110

Numbers

1900 date system, Excel's default
        system, 94
3-D effects
    3-D pie, 140
    3-D Pie icon, 141
    applying automatically and
        dynamically, 62

data tables, 61
tables or cells, 60
80/20 Rule for planning spreadsheets, 1

A

A1 cell (Start name), 3
absolute column, 100
absolute references
    absolute column, 100
    cells, moving using relative references
        without making the references
        absolute, 38
    converting from relative to, 310–315
    converting references from relative to
        absolute, 312
    dollar sign ($), average function
        made absolute with, 77
    dollar sign ($) for absolute
        formulas, 38
    dollar sign ($), forces ranges to be
        absolute, 108
    dollar sign ($), reference columns
        absolutely with, 59
    F4 key, toggles through different
        absolute formulas, 194
    formulas for, 38
.accdb, 337
Access database
    Data Access Objects (DAO), 331
    execute a stored report in the
        database, 333
    forward recordset, 333

We'd like to hear your suggestions for improving our indexes. Send email to *index@oreilly.com*.

Access Database (*continued*)
   import data into Excel
      2007, 331–335
   Northwind 2007.accdb, 331
   recordset, 332
   retrieve a selected group of data
      based on SQL queries, 332
   retrieve tables in databases, 332
   snapshot recordset, 332
   static recordset, 332
   Structured Query Language
      (SQL), 332
Activate command, 263
ActiveSheet, 267
ActiveWorkbook, 284
ActiveX Controls, 267, 327
ActiveX TextBox, 327
Add, 71
add-ins
   adding labels to charts, 166
   Add-Ins, 97
   Add-Ins available: box
      (Add-Ins), 284
   Browse button (Add-Ins), 284
   Calendar Control, 274
   Chart Report, 167
   Chart size, 167
   Chart Tools, 163
   CommandButton, 277
   distributing macros, 283
   dynamic named ranges for new data
      in tables, 4
   EOMONTH, 253
   error handling, 284
   Excel Calendar Control, 274
   Excel Options → Add-Ins, 284
   Export, 167
   File → Save As... → Microsoft Excel
      Add-in (*.xla), 284
   IsAddin property, 284
   Label, 269
   legend, 169
   menu item, adding
      (pre-2007), 285–289
   Office button → Save As... →
      Microsoft Excel Add-in
      (*.xlam), 283
   Picture, 167
   protecting, 285
   Super Code, 286
   Text Size, 167

   TextBox, 277
   ThisWorkbook, 284
   toolbars and, 284
   Tools → Add-Ins
      installing add-ins, 286
      viewing add-ins, 284
      Workbook_AddinUnInstall, 285
Additional Controls (Controls
      toolbox), 275
ADDRESS functions, 65
Advanced Filter
   data manipulation, 75
   pre-Excel 2007 versions, 66
Alignment tab, 3, 69
All Open Workbooks, 18
Allow: box (Data Validation), 32
Alt/Control-~, shows actual formulas
      on the worksheet, 164
Alt/⌘-Q, 10, 55
alternating row colors, 58
alternating row colors dynamically, 59
alternative paths, 57
Alt/Option-F11, 55, 70
Alt/Option-F8, to bring up macro
      list, 18
Amount field, 135
Analysis ToolPak, 96, 118
AND function, 60, 64
apostrophe ('), 237
Application.OnTime method, 264, 265
Application.ScreenUpdating
      property, 263, 271
arguments
   COUNTA argument, 146
   criteria argument, identification of
      cells with conditions, 204
   database argument, identification of
      cell ranges, 203
   field argument, indicates columns in
      functions, 204
   Height argument, 113
   Schedule argument, 265
   SUBTOTAL argument, 213
   summing cells by fill color, 274
   UserInterfaceOnly, 98, 282
Arrange All, 5
arrays
   array formula, to SUM every second
      cell in the range, 208
   array formulas, 56

array formulas, slows recalculations, 57

array formulas, using { } braces, 57

braces { }, 243

converting references from relative to absolute, 312

Ctrl-Enter, 196

Ctrl-Shift-Enter, 57, 208, 244

curly brackets ({ }), inserted manually causes formulas to fail, 208

Enter, avoid when entering array formulas, 57

formulas, 243

formulas in spreadsheets, 4

formulas, overusing, 246

multiple arrays and large reference ranges in spreadsheets, 4

arrows

directional, 175

placing on the end of an axis, 177–180

Assign Macro dialog box, 267

asterisk (*), 84, 277

At maximum category, 183

auto-fill features in Excel, 64

AutoFilter tool, 289–291

creating a custom function for, 329

limitations of, 75

auto-generate indexes, 24

AutoOutline, 98

axis

Axis Label Range, 146

axis labels, changing position of, 181

Axis Options, 161

B

Basic Shapes, 71

Before Print, 14

Before Save, 12

blank cells

filling in using macros, 198

filling with cell values, 100

for repeated data, 2

blank columns and rows in tables of data, 2

blank default workbook, restoring, 23

blank entries in tables, 100

Blanks option, 198

Block Arrow, 71

boldface

boldface for column headings, 73

using to identify subtotals, 85

Border, 60

Border Color, 167

bounding area, extend or reduce by dragging, 155

braces ({ }), 57, 243

Browse button (Add-Ins), 284

built-in lists, 84

built-in number formats, customizing, 79

buttons, 268

assigning buttons to macros, 268

attaching a code to a button, 305

macros for managing several buttons with a single button, 267

C

Calculation, 80

calculations, avoiding error values, 203

Calendar Control, 274

Callouts, 71

Camera icon, 130

Caption property, 275, 277, 302

Cascade option, layering workbooks on top of each other, 5

case sensitivity in VBA Code, preventing, 328

Categories in reverse order, 183

Category option, 55

CELL function, 279, 280

Cell-Link box, 214

cells

= equal sign, for copying cells to any location, 194

;;;, for hiding cell contents, 149

3-D effects in cells, 60

A1 cell (Start name), 3

based on fill color, 273

blank cells, avoid within data, 127

blank cells, filling in a list, 197

blank cells, filling in using macros, 198

blank cells for repeated data, 2

blank cells, removing quickly, 134

Blanks option, 198

calculations, avoiding error values, 203

cell comments, adding pictures, 72

cells (*continued*)

cell comments, customizing content, 71

cell comments, extracting text, 73

CELL function, 236, 279

Cell Style, 61

cell style, saving in pre-Excel 2007 versions, 61

cell styles, 60

Cell Value Is, 63

Cell Value Is for pre-Excel 2007 versions, 52

Cell-Link box, 214

center across selection for merged cells, 3

checkboxes, creating ticked or unticked upon selection, 271

conditional formatting, 280

containing formulas, locking and protecting, 30

converting text numbers to real numbers, 68

counting cells with specified fill color, 273

counting with multiple criteria, 243

counting words in a cell or range of cells, 234

criteria argument, identification of cells with conditions, 204

Ctrl-~, shows correct formulas for cells, 161

Ctrl-Enter, 196

data sources, removing unused cells, 44

database argument, identification of cell ranges, 203

date and time, automate insertion of information into a cell, 297

dirty (contain data), 146

DSUM, adds numbers in a column of a list, 240

empty cells, prevent plotting of, 173

Format Cells, 3

formatted as text, avoiding, 3

formatting as text only when necessary, 3

formatting selected cells, 50

formulas, identifying cells with conditional formatting quickly, 54

In-Cell drop-down checkbox, 49, 67

Last cell, 43

Lock Cell, 31

merging, 3

=NA( ), for plotting blank cells, 174

#N/A, for plotting blank cells, 174

New Cell Style, 61

numbers and text, mixing in the same cells, 70

recalculations, global, 54

reference cell addresses, 49

relative references, moving cells without making references absolute, 38

SaveAsCell, 316

searches, 307

second space character in a cell, locating automatically, 224

semicolon (;) for separating sections of a cell, 79

Show formulas in cells instead of their calculated result, 161

SpecialCells, 306

subtotals, 85

sum cells, based on multiple criteria, 239

sum cells, with specific fill colors, 273

sum every nth cell or row, 208

sum or count cells with conditional formatted data, 56

sum or counting while avoiding error values, 4

SUMIF function, 239

SUMPRODUCT function, 242

text elements, linking to a cell, 171

ticking, 272

ticking upon selection, 271, 272

Use a formula to determine which cells to format option, 50, 54, 86, 88

using Lookup function within a cell, 259

volatile functions, 54

workbooks, naming with the text in a cell, 315

worksheet name, using in a cell, 236

Cell Value Is, 63

Cell Value Is for pre-Excel 2007 versions, 52

center across selection for merged
cells, 3
Change AutoShape, 71
Change Shape button, 71
Change Shape tool, 71
characters
extracting a range of characters from
a string, 225
second space character in a cell,
locating automatically, 224
Chart → Data Labels → Legend
Key, 169
Chart Tools → Format → Current
Selection → Format Selection
→ Secondary Axis, 158
Chart Tools → Layout → Analysis →
Error Bars → More Error
Bars, 162
Chart Tools → Layout → Labels → Axis
Titles → Primary Vertical Axis
Title, 160
Chart Type, 141
charts
;;;, for hiding cell contents, 149
-1, omits heading in the named
range, 146
3-D pie, 140
3-D Pie icon, 141
Alt/Control-~, shows actual
formulas on the
worksheet, 164
arrows, placing on the end of an
axis, 177–180
At maximum category, 183
Axis Label Range, 146
axis labels, changing position of, 181
Axis Options, 161
bar chart, displaying two sets of
data, 184
bar chart labels, 182
Border Color, 167
bounding area, extend or reduce by
dragging, 155
bubble charts, 154
Categories in reverse order, 183
Change Chart Type, 141
Chart Report, 167
Chart Size, 167
Chart Tools, 146
downloadable Chart Tools, 163

Chart Type, 141
column charts with variable widths
and heights, 160–163
column lines, 162
narrow columns, correcting when
using dates, 180
columns, creating, 161
columns, hiding, 173
customizing controls, 148
COUNTA argument, 146
Current Selection options, 143
data point formatting, removing, 177
Design tab, 140
directional arrows, 175
doughnut charts, 164–166
dragging and dropping data, 152
drop-down list, linking to dynamic
named range, 149
dynamic named ranges, 144
empty cells, prevent plotting of, 173
End Type, 176
Error bars, 162
Error Bars option, 162
Export, 167
FALSE formula cells, prevent plotting
of, 173
Fill, 167
fill-less plot area, 161
adding flexibility to, 148
Format Axis dialog, 161
Format Plot Area, 161
Format tab, 143
Formula bar, 154
Gap Width, 158
Gauge chart, 186
gridlines, removing, 161
horizontal axis labels, removing, 185
Horizontal (Category) Axis
Labels, 146
include new data
automatically, 144–147
making interactive, 148
invalid dates and, 274
labels, changing the position of, 182
labels, reversing order of, 182
legend
adding, 169
removing, 161
Legend Entries (Series), 142
links, finding and deleting, 39

charts (*continued*)
  Male series, 185
  Maximum settings, 161
  Minimum settings, 161
  More Error Bars, 162
  =NA( ), for plotting blank cells, 174
  #N/A, for plotting blank cells, 174
  Negative Error Value settings, 162
  No Fill, 167
  OFFSET function, 149
  Outside End, 192
  Paste Special Function, 156
  Picture, 167
  exploded pie chart, 140
  pie chart, creating two sets of slices in one, 142–144
  pie chart, creation of, 140
  pie charts, 140
  plot new data automatically, 144–147
  Positive Error Value setting, 162
  readings, plotting the last x number of, 147
  rows, hiding, 173
  scenarios, testing, 155
  scrollbar, 170
  scrollbar, inserting, 149
  scrollbar, linking to dynamic named range, 148–151
  Select Data Source Dialog, 146
  SERIES function, 154
  Series X values, 163
  Sheet name, for entering named range in formulas, 147
  Show formulas in cells instead of their calculated result, 164
  speedometer chart, 164–171
  stacked chart, displaying totals of, 190
  Temperature Data Series, 157
  text elements, linking to a cell, 171
  Text size, 167
  thermometer chart, 157–158
  Tick mark labels, 182
  tornado chart (population pyramid), 184–186
  Type options, 141
  unexplode pies, 141
  updating quickly, 152
  Value (y) axis crosses at maximum category, 183
  Walkenbach, John, downloadable Chart Tools for adding labels to charts, 166
  X-axis category labels, highlight with color, 188–190
  XY scatter chart, 160
Charts → Other Charts, 164
checkboxes
  Check Box, 62
  checkbox icon for pre-Excel 2007 versions, 62
  CheckBoxLink, 52
  CheckBoxLink, changing font color of, 53
  creating ticked or unticked upon selection, 271
  numbers, highlighting with toggle on and off via a checkbox, 52–54
  setting up for conditional formatting, 50
  uses for, 271
Choose Commands From, 71
Choose Commands From: box, 130
CHOOSE function, 257, 260
Clear All, 42
Clipboard options, 61
Close button, 55
code
  attaching a code to a button, 305
  attaching a code to a shortcut key, 305
  case sensitivity in VBA Code, 328
  CODE function, 68
  Code options, 18
  color-code for visual identification, 35
  creating an advanced Find feature, 300–306
  exceeding the conditional formatting three-criteria limit, 280
  IndexCode, 26
  list of date and time codes, 82
  list of miscellaneous codes, 83
  loops causing slow code, 271
  performance of, 270
  range changes and, 280
  speeding up, 263
  speeding up results in macros, 263

Super Code, 286
user's workbook, never use code to
    unprotect workbooks, 284
View Code, 9
Visual Basic code, running
    automatically, 11
Code → Macros, 199
CodeName
    ActiveWorkbook and, 284
    Edit → Replace, for changing to
        CodeNames, 266
    referencing worksheets via, 266
    to references specific sheets, 266
    VBE (Visual Basic Editor), 266
codes
    list of formatting codes, 81
    list of text codes, 82
collapse tool, 85
ColorFunction custom function, 273
colors
    Border Color, 167
    color-code for visual
        identification, 35
    ColorFunction custom function, 273
    Colors and Lines, 72
    conditional formatting, 34
    for data identification, 35
    fill, 273
    icolor, 282
    summing cells by fill color, 274
    Vary colors by point, 46
columns
    absolute column, 100
    avoid referencing entire, 3
    blank columns in tables of data, 2
    blanks, filling in columns, 198
    boldface for column headings, 73
    column charts with variable widths
        and heights, 160–163
    COLUMN function, 201
    column limits, 26
    column lines, creating, 162
    columns, creating, 161
    deleting, avoiding the #REF!
        errors, 43
    DSUM, adds numbers in a column of
        a list, 240
    file bloat, 42
    formatting, eliminating
        extraneous, 43

Hide Columns, 27
hiding, 26, 173
incrementing cell references by rows
    across columns, 199–201
Names column, use dynamic range
    names, 229
#NUM! error, returned with two or
    more identical names in name
    column, 229
#REF! error, 43
Refers To: column, 39
narrow columns, correcting when
    using dates, 180
ComboBox, changing lists with, 64
CommandButton, 277
Commands Not in the Ribbon, 130
comments
    cell comments, customizing content
        of, 71
    cell comments, extracting text, 73
    Comment border for pre-Excel 2007
        versions, 72
    Comment for pre-Excel 2007
        versions, 71
    Comments, 71
    New Comment, 71
CompareText, 328
comparison operators, use
    interchangeably, 231–233
conditional formatting
    color coding for visual
        identification, 35
    colors, 34
    Conditional Formatting dialog
        box, 34
    Conditions for pre-Excel 2007
        versions, 36
    controling with checkboxes, 50
    criteria limits, 280
    for comparing ranges, 196
    for finding duplicate data, 34
    identifying cells with, 54
    sum or count data cells, 56
    three-criteria limit, code for
        exceeding the limit, 280
    turning on and off with a
        checkbox, 62
    turning on and off with a switch, 63
Conditions for pre-Excel 2007
    versions, 36

Controls → Insert, 149
Controls toolbox (UserForm)
    buttons and, 267
    for running macros, 269
    Label control (Controls
        toolbox), 269
    to create a splash screen, 269
converting
    dates and times to real numbers, 97
    dollar values, displaying as
        words, 83
    Excel dates to formatted dates, 202
    functions to values, 89
    negative (right-aligned) numbers to
        Excel numbers, 215
    numbers to dollars and cents, 83
    references from relative to
        absolute, 310–315
    text numbers to real numbers, 68
copy
    Copy (Ctrl-C), 198
    copy formula results, 89
    Copy Here as Values Only, 89
    Copy to Another Location
        option, 78
COUNT cells, 273
COUNT function
    named ranges, 113
Count of Product, 133
COUNTA argument, 146
COUNTA function
    counts all nonblank cells, 113
    defining the range of, 112
    dynamic highlighting, 60
COUNTIF function, 272
criteria
    conditional formatting limits, 280
    filtering two or more in a table, 230
    identification of cells with
        conditions, 204
Ctrl key
    create incremented lists by 1, 107
    for grouping worksheets manually, 8
Ctrl-~, shows correct formulas for
        cells, 161
Ctrl-C (copy), 187
Ctrl/⌘-K, insertion of hyperlinks, 24
Ctrl-Enter, 196
Ctrl-G, 32, 198
Ctrl-R (View Project Explorer), 266

Ctrl-Shift-Enter, 57, 208, 242, 244
Ctrl-V (paste), 187
curly brackets ({ }), 208
Current Selection options, 143
Custom, 80
Custom → Specify Value, 162
custom functions
    and conditional formatting, 56
    ColorFunction, 273
    for sliding tax scale
        calculations, 249–251
    SheetName, 279
    workbook name/path, 279
Custom Lists for Months, 102
Custom Lists for pre-Excel 2007
        versions, 85
Custom Lists for Weekday, 102
custom toolbar, deleted when workbook
        closes, 318
Customize, 71
Customize → Commands → Macros →
        Custom Button, 306
customized toolbars, 37
customizing cell contents, 71

D

DAO (Data Access Objects), 331
data
    blank cells for repeated data, 2
    blank rows in tables of data, 2
    conditional formatted cells, 56
    data fields, sorting more than three
        fields, 73
    data manipulation with Advanced
        Filter tool, 75
    data matches, finding in Excel, 78
    data sources, removing unused
        cells, 44
    data tables, 3-D effects, 61
    data tables, defining as dynamic, 113
    Data Tools, 32, 48
    data validation, 32, 48
        turning on and off with a
            checkbox, 62
        turning on and off with a
            switch, 63
    database argument, identification of
        cell ranges, 203

database functions for setting up
    lists, 126
database functions, replacing other
    functions with, 227–229
excluding duplicate data in lists,
    excluding, 207
deleteting data permanently, 41
dragging and dropping data, 152
duplicated data for pre-Excel 2007
    versions, 34
duplicated in multiple worksheets, 8
dynamic named ranges for new data
    in tables, 4
Excel Help for large data tables with
    multiple criteria, 4
extract statistical information from
    raw data, 124
extraction from corrupt
    workbooks, 45
finding duplicates, 34
flagged as incorrect, 62
identifying data that appears two or
    more time, 35
import from an Access
    database, 331–335
incorporating in continuous
    rows, 112
keeping related data in one
    continuous table, 2
lookup functions for setting up
    lists, 126
pivot data for immediate results, 125
raw data, 124
removing duplicates, 62
spreading over different tables
    unnecessarily, 2
spreading over many different
    workbooks unnecessarily, 2
spreading over numerous worksheets
    unnecessarily, 2
tables with multiple criteria, 4
validation list and decreasing list of
    options, 101
workbooks, saving before deleting
    data permanently, 41
Data → Data Options → Data
    Validation, 238
Data → Data Tools, 212
Data → Data Tools → Data
    Validation, 209, 230

Data → Data Validation, 32
Data → Edit Links, 41
Data → PivotTable, 133
Data → PivotTable Report, 133
Data Access Objects (DAO), 331
Data Labels → Below, 189
Data Series → Data Labels → Value, 191
date and time
    1900 date system, Excel's default
        system, 94
    adding and subtracting months from
        specific dates, 251
    additional information links for, 97
    Analysis ToolPak, 96
    automate insertion of information
        into a cell, 297
    Calendar Control and, 274
    CHOOSE formula, 257
    converting to real numbers, 97
    Date & Time, 96
    current date, and NOW
        function, 205
    date, and NOW function, 205
    date and time calculations, 95
    date and time features, 94
    date bugs, 97
    date codes, list of, 82
    date extensions, adding, 214
    DATE function, 252
    DATEDIF function, 96
    Day variable, 252
    dd/mm/yy, date format, 202
    decimal fractions, treated as time, 94
    default date system, changing, 218
    Display Negative Time Values, 96
    EDATE function, 251
    EOMONTH, finding the last day of
        any given month, 253
    European date format, 202
    Excel dates, convert to formatted
        dates, 202
    finding the last day of any given
        month, 253–255
    manipulating with magic
        numbers, 95–96
    MAX function, 96
    MIN function, 96
    Month variable, 252
    negative time values, displaying, 217

date and time (*continued*)
    negative times, displaying using a
        custom format, 219
    number of specified days in any
        month, determining, 222
    setting numeric values, 94
    starting dates, 218
    SUM function for adding time
        beyond 24 hours, 94
    TEXT formula, 257
    time codes, list of, 83
    time, treated as decimal fractions, 94
    total time, show as days, hours, and
        minutes, 221
    "Use 1904 date system"
        checkbox, 218
    .Value = Now, 298
    showing a weekday as a
        number, 256
    showing a weekday as weekday
        name, 257
    showing the weekday as weekday
        text, 257
    finding the weekday associated with
        any date, 256
    WEEKDAY formula, 257
    WEEKDAY function, 256, 257
    Year variable, 252
DATEDIF function, 255
DCOUNT function, 230
dd/mm/yy, date format, 202
decimal fractions, treated as time, 94
default date system, changing, 218
default workbook, customizing, 23
default workbook, restoring to a blank
    default, 23
defined name link, finding and
    deleting, 39
Defined Names, 66
Defined Names → Create from
    Selection, 110
Defined Names → Define Name, 108
Defined Names → Name Manager, 109
Defined Names option, 39
Delete for pre-Excel 2007 versions, 87
Delete Links Wizard, 39
Delete Rule, 87
deleteting data permanently, 41
Design → Data → Add, 163
Design → Data → Select Data, 142, 146

Design → Type → Change Chart
    Type, 168, 189
Design tab, 140
Developer, 12
Developer → Code → Record
    Macro, 275
Developer → Controls → Insert, 169,
    267
Developer → Controls → Insert → Form
    Control, 213
Developer → Macros, 18, 29
Developer → Macros, highlight Import_
    Data_Access_2007, 335
Developer → Macros, highlight
    Retrieve_Data_Closed_
    Workbooks, 340
Developer → Macros, highlight
    Retrieve_Data_Closed_
    Workbooks, 344
Developer → Macros, highlight Send_
    Mail_Outlook, 353
Developer → Macros, highlight Update_
    Word_Report, 348
Developer → Macros or
    Alt/Option-F8, 15
Developer → Visual Basic, 16, 30
Developer tab, 50
Dfunction (database function), 246
directional arrows, 175
Disable all macros with notification, 11
Display Negative Time Values, 96
Display options for this Workbook, 164
DoIt macro, 271
dollar sign ($)
    Average function made absolute
        with, 77
    for absolute formulas, 38
    force ranges to be absolute, 108
    reference columns absolutely
        with, 59
dollar values, displaying as words, 83
double-clicking
    ticking cells upon selection, 272
    .xla file, 285
doughnut charts, 164–166
dragging and dropping data, 152
Drawing, 71
Drawing toolbar, 71, 271
drop-down list, linking to dynamic
    named range, 149

DSUM function, 57, 203, 209
dTime, 265
duplicate data, removing, 62
duplicated data for pre-Excel 2007
     versions, 34
DWORD Value, 84
dynamic formula identification, 55
dynamic named range
     adding new data to tables, 4
     expand and contract, 112
     Name box, 112
     PivotTable, 138
     to decrease refresh time, 137
     types of dynamic named range
          examples, 117

E

Edit → Copy → Picture, 129
Edit → Go To..., 198
Edit → Paste, 129
Edit → Replace, 266
Edit Custom List, 85
Edit mode, 72
Edit mode and pre-Excel 2007
     versions, 71
Editing → Find & Select → Replace, 194
Enable, 38, 99
Enable All Macros, allows for dangerous
     code infiltration, 15, 99
Enabled property, 301
End Type, 176
Enter, avoid when entering array
     formulas, 57
entries with text and numbers, 70
EOMONTH, 253
equals key (=), 198
Error Alert tab, 92, 100
Error bars, 162
Error Bars option, 162
error handling, add-ins and, 284
error values, 203
European date format, 202
EVALUATE function, 258
Events, 11
Excel
     2007, new changes in Excel, xv
     automate comparisons for ranges
          in, 195

automate Outlook from
     Excel, 349–354
automate Word from
     Excel, 344–348
converting negative (right-aligned)
     numbers to Excel
     numbers, 215
dates, convert to formatted
     dates, 202
default date system, changing, 218
Excel Help for large data tables with
     multiple criteria, 4
ExcelFix program, 47
finding exact data matches, 78
OpenOffice.org, 47
PivotTable feature, 4
PivotTables online tutorial, 124
placing on the end of an axis in Excel
     2007, 177–180
placing on the end of an axis in older
     versions of, 177–180
sheet events, 9
True or False, using to compare
     ranges, 195
View Microsoft Excel tool, 10
Excel Calendar Control, 274
Excel icon (View Code), 264, 283
Excel Options → Add-Ins, 284
Excel Options → Customize, 130
exploded pie chart, 140
Export, 167
Express ClickYes, 354
extended property, 337
extensions, adding date extensions, 214
extract numeric portions of cell
     entries, 70
extracting a range of characters from a
     string, 225

F

F4 key, 194, 269
F5, 32
F7 (View → Code), 276
F9 key when recalculating
     spreadsheets, 4
FALSE formula cells, 173
FALSE value, 50
field argument, indicates columns in
     functions, 204

File → Import File, 44
File → Save As... → Microsoft Excel
    Add-in (*.xla), 284
File Name box, 5
files, unable to open, 46
Fill, 167
fill colors, 273
Fill Effects, 72
Fill Handle, 102
Fill Handle, adding Custom Lists, 102
Fill Without Formatting, 228
Filter the List in Place, 66
filtering, two or more criteria in a
    table, 230
Find feature
    button, attaching a code to a
        button, 305
    Caption property, 302
    creating an advanced Find
        feature, 300–306
    Enabled property, 301
    finding a name between two
        numbers, 306–310
    finding data matches in Excel, 78
    GETBETWEEN, 309
    shortcut key, attaching code to
        a, 305
    SpecialCells, 306
    UserForm, 301
Find featureQuick Access Toolbar, 305
FIND function, 69, 224
Find What, 68
Find What: box, 38, 194
First Name field, 132
Flow Chart, 71
Font Style, 87
Font tab, 87
Form Controls, 50, 52, 62, 64
Format → Cells, 219
Format → Cells → Protection, 31
Format → Conditional Formatting, 34,
    280
    overcoming limitations, 280
Format → Conditional Formatting... →
    Select Formula Is, 196
Format → Protect sheet, 32
Format → Source Data → Series, 142
Format Axis → Axis Options, 185
Format Axis → Patterns, 182
Format Axis dialog, 161

Format Cells, 3
Format Data Labels → Alignment, 192
Format Data Labels → Label Options →
    Label Position → Above, 192
Format Data Point → Line Style, 176
Format Data Series → Line Color → No
    Line → Close, 192
Format Data Series → Series Options →
    Secondary Axis, 185
Format Painter tool, 61
Format Plot Area, 161
Format tab, 71, 143
Format values where this formula is
    true, 58, 63, 88
formats
    built-in number formats,
        customizing, 79
    color coding, 34
    color coding for visual
        identification, 35
    Conditional Formatting dialog
        box, 34
    eliminating superfluous formats, 43
    finding duplicate data, 34
    Format dialog, 3
    Format tab (Format button on Mac
        OS X), 34
    Format values where this formula is
        true, 55, 58, 86
    formatting cells as text only when
        necessary, 3
    formatting codes, list of, 81
    formatting, eliminating
        extraneous, 43
    tips for spreadsheets, 2
    Use a formula to determine which
        cells to format option, 50, 86
Forms for pre-Excel 2007 versions, 62,
    75
Forms toolbar, buttons and, 268
Forms toolbar for pre-Excel 2007
    versions, 50, 52
Formula → Defined Names → Use in
    Formula → Paste Names, 121
Formula bar, 80, 154
formula cells, accidentally
    overtyping, 32
Formula Is in pre-Excel 2007
    versions, 50

formulas

$ dollar sign, for absolute
  formulas, 194
absolute formula, 38
Alt/Control-~, shows actual
  formulas on the
  worksheet, 164
and cells formatted as text,
  avoiding, 3
array formulas, to SUM every second
  cell in the range, 208
cells containing formulas, locking
  and protecting, 30
CHOOSE formula, 257
columns, filling blanks in, 198
converting references from relative to
  absolute, 310–315
converting to values, 89
copying quickly, 57
dollar sign ($) for absolute
  formulas, 38
dynamic identification, 55
EDATE formula, 251
Excel ranges, automate
  comparisons, 195
F4 key, toggles through different
  absolute formulas, 194
Find What: box, 194
finding the last day of any given
  month, 253–255
Format values where this formula is
  true, 58
formula cells, accidentally
  overtyping, 32
Formula Is in pre-Excel 2007
  versions, 50
and headings, 77
highlight automatically in custom
  formats, 55
identifying cells with conditional
  formatting quickly, 54
incrementing cell references by rows
  across columns, 199–201
macro for converting to values, 89
Match Entire cell contents
  option, 194
mega-formulas,
  constructing, 224–226
mega-formulas, converting references
  from relative to absolute, 312

mega-formulas, referencing another
  workbook, 226
N function, 194
Refers To:, 109
relative formulas, 38
relative formulas with references,
  moving, 194
Replace With: box, 194
reproduce in another range on the
  same worksheet, 194
text, adding descriptive text, 193
TEXT formula, 257
tips for spreadsheets, 3
Use a formula to determine which cells
  to format option, 50, 54, 86
using { } braces, 57
using lists, 237
value derived from a formula,
  determining, 54
VLOOKUP function, using across
  multiple tables, 219–221
WEEKDAY formula, 257
Formulas → Defined Names → Create
  from Selection, 231, 238
Formulas → Defined Names → Define
  Name, 146, 149, 151, 229,
  261
Formulas → Defined Names → Name
  Manager, 107
Formulas → Defined Names → Name
  Manager → New, 119
forward recordset, 333
Function Library, 55
Function Wizard pre-Excel 2007
  versions, 96
functions
  ADDRESS functions, 65
  AND function, 60, 64
  blank cells, deleting from lists, 197
  CELL function, 236, 279
  CHOOSE function, 260
  CODE function, 68
  ColorFunction, 273
  COLUMN function, 201
  COUNT function, 113
  COUNTA function, 112, 113
  custom function, 56
  custom functions, create by using
    names, 108

functions (*continued*)

custom functions, for sliding tax scale calculations, 249–251

database functions, replacing other functions with, 227–229

DATE function, 252

DATEDIF function, 96, 255

DCOUNT function, 205

DCOUNT function, filtering with two criteria, 230

DCOUNTA function, 205

Dfunction (database function), 246

DMAX function, 205

DMIN function, 205

DPRODUCT function, 205

DSUM function, 57, 209

DSUM function, error values, 203

DSUM function, use with a variety of error values, 204

EDATE function, 251

EVALUATE function, 258

field argument, indicates columns in functions, 204

FIND function, 69, 224

finding the last day of any given month, 254

Function Library, 55

Function Wizard pre-Excel 2007 versions, 96

functions, converting to values, 89

GETPIVOTDATA function, 135

IF function, for sliding tax scale calculations, 246

IF functions, 219

INDIRECT function, 49, 221

Insert Function, 55

INT function, 222

LEFT function, 69

LEFT function, to return first character or characters in a text string, 234

LEN function, to return the number of characters in a text string, 235

Lookup and Reference functions, 112

macro for converting to values, 89

MATCH function, 114–116, 260

MAX function, 96

MID function, 225

MIN function, 96

MINUTE function, 222

MOD function, 60, 208, 209

MyFullName, 279

MyName function, 279

N function, 194

nested functions, 226

nonvolatile functions, nested withing volatile functions, 205

NOW, 205

Now( ), 17

OFFSET function, 112, 113

Paste Special Function, 156

RAND function, 74

RAND function, major flaw in, 75

ROW( ) function, 60, 208

SheetName function, 279

SMALL functions, to extract figures from PivotTables, 136

STrConv function, 323

SUBSTITUTE function, 216

SUBSTITUTE function, for counting words in a cell or range of cells, 235

SUBTOTAL function, 212

SUBTOTAL function, making it dynamic, 212

SUM function, 57

SUM function, adding time beyond 24 hours, 94

SUM function, error values, 203

SUM function for adding time beyond 24 hours, 94

SUM function, for sliding tax scale calculations, 246

SUM function, simplify summing with use of, 108

SUMIF function, 56, 239

SUMPRODUCT function, 242, 245

TEXT function, 69, 218

TODAY, 205

Today( ), 17

TRIM function, ensures no space characters in a cell, 216

TRIM function, nesting to remove superfluous spaces in counting, 236

user-defined functions (UDF), 54, 249

using Lookup function within a
cell, 259
VLOOKUP function, 210–212
volatile functions, 17, 54, 60
recalculations, reducing when
using volatile functions, 205
WEEKDAY function, 256

G

Gap Width, 158
Gauge chart, 186
General, 71, 81
General for pre-Excel 2007 versions, 71
GETBETWEEN, 309
GETPIVOTDATA function, 135
global recalculations, 54
Go To Special dialog, 32
Grand Total, 87, 135
gridlines, removing, 161
Group, 98, 99
Group feature, using manually, 8
grouping worksheets, 98
grouping worksheets automatically, 9

H

hacks (quick and dirty solutions to
problems) downloads, xvi
headings
-1, omits heading in the named
range, 146
boldface for column headings, 73
required for PivotTables, 127
row headings, dynamic
references, 200
using formulas with, 77
Height argument, 113
hidden name links, finding and
deleting, 39
Hide, 19, 138
Hide & Unhide, 27
Hide Rows, 27
hiding, 27
columns in charts, 173
finding and deleting hidden name
links, 39
Hide, 19
Hide & Unhide, 27
Hide Columns, 27
hiding cell contents, 149

rows, 27
rows in charts, 173
toolbars, hiding and restoring, 316
Unhide, 19
Unhide under Window options, 17
workbooks, 283
worksheets, keeping hidden from
unseen users, 19
hiding workbooks, 283
HKEY_CURRENT_USER, 84
Home → Cells → Format Cells, 219
Home → Cells → Insert, 116
Home → Clear → Clear All, 42
Home → Conditional Formatting →
New Rule, 35
Home → Defined Names → Name
Manager → New, 118
Home → Editing → Find & Select → Go
To Special, 198
Home → Editing → Find & Select →
Replace, 195
Home → Find & Select → Go to
Special, 32, 40
Home → Format → Lock Cell, 31
Home → Styles → Conditional
Formatting → New Rule, 196
Home tab → Find & Select →
Replace, 38
Horizontal alignment, 97
horizontal axis labels, removing, 185
Horizontal (Category) Axis Labels, 146
Horizontal for viewing workbooks in a
single stack, 5
HTML features lost for pre-Excel 2007
versions, 46
HTML, lost features when saving in
HTML, 46
hyperlinks
avoid using URLs as a base, 25
Ctrl/⌘-K for insertion of, 24
Hyperlink, 24
hyperlink base for pre-Excel 2007
versions, 25
hyperlinked index, creating, 24

I

icolor, 282
IF functions, 219
Import button, 85

Import File, 44
In-Cell drop-down checkbox, 49, 67
index of sheets, 23
indexes
    auto-generate, 24
    hyperlinked index, creating, 24
    index numbers, 266
    index sheet, creating manually, 24
    IndexCode, 26
    linking from a context menu, 25
    linking indexes from a context
        menu, 25
    worksheets and, 266
INDIRECT function, 49, 221
Initialize, 269
Initialize event, 269
Insert, 75
Insert → Chart → Line, 186
Insert → Charts → Columns, 146, 190
Insert → Charts → Scatter, 160
Insert → Illustration → Shapes, 271
Insert → Illustrations → Insert → Shapes
        → Block Arrows, 186
Insert → Links → Bookmark, 344
Insert → Module, 26, 134, 217
Insert → Module, creates a new
        module, 268
Insert → Module (VBE)
    accessing standard modules, 265
    adding Calendar Control, 276
    assigning buttons to macros, 268
    password protecting
        worksheets, 278
    summing cells by fill color, 273
Insert → Name → Create, 231, 238
Insert → Name → Define, 39, 107, 146,
        261
Insert → Pivot Table, 132
Insert → UserForm, 269, 275
Insert → UserForm, opens the VBE, 269
Insert Function, 55
Insert tab, 128
Inset → Picture → AutoShapes → Block
        Arrows, 186
INT function, 222
intersect operator, 110
IsAddin property, 284

K

keys, attaching a code to a shortcut
        key, 305
keystrokes, macro recorder and, 263

L

labels
    add-ins, 269
    changing the position of, 182
    Label control (Controls
        toolbox), 269
    Label Controls Property
        window, 269
    reversing order of, 182
Labels → Data Labels → More Data
        Label Options, 189
LARGE function, 136
LargeScroll command, 263
Last cell, 43
Layout → Labels → Legend, 169
Layout button, 133
LEFT function, 69, 234
left-align text in spreadsheets, 3
left-aligned text, avoid changing, 81
legend, 169
    removing, 161
Legend Entries (Series), 142
LEN function, 235
LetterNames, 120
Line box, 60
Lines, Colors and, 72
lists
    adding data automatacally to a
        validation list, 91
    blank cells, filling in a list, 197
    changing with options buttons and
        ComboBox, 64
    containing numeric data only, 113
    creating a list of workbook
        hyperlinks, 298–300
    creating custom lists, 84
    creating unique items in, 66
    Ctrl key, create incremented lists by
        1, 107
    custom lists for Months, Weekdays
        and numeric sequences, 102
    Custom Lists for pre-Excel 2007
        versions, 85

data, excluding duplicate data in lists, excluding, 207
database functions for setting up lists, 126
entries, counting multiple entries only once, 206
Filter the List in Place, 66
guidelines for creating tables or lists, 126
lookup functions for setting up lists, 126
multiple lists, 64
PivotTables, to produce unique names in lists, 207
turning sorted lists upside down, 85
user-friendly validation (pick) list, 67
validation list and decreasing list of options, 101
validation lists, changing based on another selected list, 66
with formulas, 237
Lock Cell, 31
long-term planning of spreadsheets, 1
Lookup and Reference functions, 112
Lookup functions, 259
lookup functions, creating, 110
loops
cannot be created with the macro recorder, 271
causing slow code, 271
getting a number between a nominated range, 306
macro recorders and, 271
password protecting worksheets, 278

M

Macintosh, accessing private modules, 283
macros
ActiveSheet, 267
ActiveX Controls and, 267
Alt/Option-F8, to bring up macro list, 18
Application.OnTime method, 264
Application.ScreenUpdating property, 263
assigning buttons to, 268
checkboxes, creating ticked or unticked upon selection, 271
code, speeding up results in, 263

CodeNames to references specific sheets, 266
converting negative (right-aligned) numbers to Excel numbers, 216
counting cells with specified fill color, 273
Disable all macros with notification, 11
displaying messages, 271
distributing, 283
DoIt macro, displays please wait message, 271
dTime, 265
eliminating screen flicker, 263
Enable All Macros, 15
enabling deleted macros, 15
Excel Calendar Control, 274
distributing a macro's functionality, 283
using an index number, 266
index numbers and, 266
Macro Settings Button, 11
Macros under Code options, 18
managing several buttons with a single button, 267
OnTime method, 264
Personal.xls file and, 274
please wait message, displaying, 270
protected worksheets and, 282
recorded macros, 18
Run statement, 318
running, 264, 271
running at predetermined times, 264
Schedule argument, 265
screen flicker, 263
ScreenUpdating property, 263
Select command, 264
selecting a range outside scrollable areas, 29
volatile functions, avoid storing in personal macros, 17
Warning Prompts, stopping, 18
workbook splash screen, 268
Workbook_BeforeClose event, 265
workbooks, personalizing, 23
workbooks, retrieving name and path of, 279
worksheets, password-protect and unprotect with one application, 276–279

Male series, 185
Manage Rules, 87
manual calculation mode for
    spreadsheets, 4
Marlett font, 272
Match Entire cell contents option, 194
MATCH function, 114–116, 260
MAX function, 96, 113
Maximize button, 8
mega-formulas, constructing, 224–226
memory conservation with
    PivotTables, 126
menu item, adding (pre-2007), 285–289
messages, displaying, 270
Microsoft
    Microsoft Access 2007
        databases, 337
    Microsoft ActiveX Data Objects
        2.8, 341
    Microsoft ActiveX Data Objects
        library 6.0, 337
    Microsoft Excel 2007
        workbooks, 337
    Microsoft folder, 84
    Microsoft Office 12 Access Database
        Engine Object Library, 332
    Microsoft Office Download
        Center, 39
    Microsoft query link, finding and
        deleting, 39
    Microsoft Word, automate from
        Excel, 344–348
    Microsoft.ACE.OLEDB.12.0, 337
MID function, 225, 279
MIN function, 96
MINUTE function, 222
miscellaneous codes, list of, 83
missing fields in tables, 100
MOD function, 60, 208, 209
modules
    accessing, 265
    Module, 55
    protecting add-ins, 285
More Error Bars, 162
MsgBox, 14
MsoFileType constants, 298
msoFileTypeAllFiles, 298
msoFileTypeBinders, 298
msoFileTypeCalendarItem, 298
msoFileTypeContactItem, 298

msoFileTypeCustom, 299
msoFileTypeDatabases, 299
msoFileTypeDataConnectionFiles, 299
msoFileTypeDesignerFiles, 299
msoFileTypeDocumentImagingFiles, 299
msoFileTypeExcelWorkbooks, 299
msoFileTypeJournalItem, 299
msoFileTypeMailItem, 299
msoFileTypeNoteItem, 299
msoFileTypeOfficeFiles, 299
msoFileTypeOutlookItems, 299
msoFileTypePhotoDrawFiles, 299
msoFileTypePowerPointPresentations, 299
msoFileTypeProjectFiles, 299
msoFileTypePublisherFiles, 299
msoFileTypeTaskItem, 299
msoFileTypeTemplates, 299
msoFileTypeVisioFiles, 299
msoFileTypeWebPages, 299
msoFileTypeWordDocuments, 299
multiple lists, changing with options
    buttons and ComboBox, 64
MyFullName function, 279
MyName function, 279

N

N function, 194
=NA( ), for plotting blank cells, 174
#NA, for plotting blank cells, 174
Name box (Formula bar), 268
Name Manager, 39, 66
Name tab, 8
named constants, 260
named range
    address data by names, 105
    advantages of using, 49
    apostrophe (') around names, 107
    COUNT function, 113
    counting all nonblank cells with
        Counta, 113
    creating, 48
    Ctrl key, create incremented lists by
        1, 107
    custom functions, create by using
        names, 108
    data, incorporating in continuous
        rows, 112
    data tables, defining as dynamic, 113
    Defined Names, 107

disadvantages of using, 49
dollar sign ($), force ranges to be
    absolute, 108
drop-down list, linking to, 149
dynamic named range, 112
types of dynamic named range
    examples, 117
dynamic named ranges, 112
Height argument, 113
identifying named ranges, 121
intersect operator, 110
LetterNames, 120
long lists of names, using dynamic
    names for, 118–120
lookup functions, creating, 110
MATCH function, 114–116
MAX function, 113
Name a Range, 107, 108, 116
name a range of cells, 105
Name box, 105
Name Manager, 107
names refer to specified range on a
    specified worksheets, 106
naming a cell, 105
OFFSET function, 112, 113
range address, making it
    variable, 238
ranges, expanding or
    contracting, 112
Refers To:, 109
Refers To: box, 107
relative references, 107
scrollbar, linking to dynamic named
    range, 148–151
underscore (_), 110
use of exclamation mark (!), 107
use of zoom, 122
using formulas as your Refers
    To:, 109
using meaningful names for specific
    ranges, 121
using names in place of cell
    identifiers or ranges, 105
using the same name for ranges on
    different worksheets, 106
workbook level names, 106
worksheet name and including
    spaces, 107
names
    macro recorders and, 266
    Name, 65

Names in Workbook for pre-Excel
    2007 versions, 65
retrieving for workbooks, 279
workbooks and, 279
Names column, use dynamic range
    names, 229
Negative Error Value, 162
Negative Numbers, 79
nested functions, 226
New, 66
New Cell Style, 61
New Comment, 71
New Rule, 35, 88
New Worksheet, 132
Next button, 133
No Fill, 167
No Text Please message, 80
Northwind 2007.accdb, 331
Now( ), 17
NOW functions, 205
#NUM! error, returned with two or
    more identical names in name
    column, 229
Number Sold field, 135
numbers, 68
    and text, mixing in the same cells, 70
    Average, High, or Low headings,
        displaying with numbers, 83
    built-in number formats,
        customizing, 79
    converting dates and times to, 97
    converting negative (right-aligned)
        numbers to Excel
        numbers, 215
    converting to dollars and cents, 83
    counting cells with specified fill
        color, 273
    Ctrl key, create incremented lists by
        1, 107
    DSUM, adds numbers in a column of
        a list, 240
    entries, counting multiple entries
        only once, 206
    extracting numeric portions of cell
        entries, 70
    finding a name between two
        numbers, 306–310
    highlighting, 52
    highlighting with toggle on and off
        via a checkbox, 52–54
    index numbers, 266

numbers (*continued*)
  lists containing numeric data
    only, 113
  lookup numbers on a scale, 261
  macro to convert negative
    (right-aligned) numbers to
    Excel numbers, 216
  magic numbers for manipulating
    dates and times, 95
  Number, 80
  number formats, customizing, 79
  number formats for text and
    numbers, 79
  numeric value, setting for date and
    time, 94
  right-aligned numbers, avoid
    changing, 81
  SUM function, simplify summing
    with use of, 108
  sums, simplify, 108
  showing a weekday as a
    number, 256
numeric sequences, custom lists
  for, 102
numeric value, setting for date and
  time, 94

O

object links, finding and deleting, 39
Objects folder, 19
Office button → Excel → Formulas, 4
Office button → Excel Options →
  Add-Ins, 253
Office button → Excel options →
  Add-ins, 118
Office button → Excel Options →
  Advanced, 161
Office button → New, 21
Office button → Open, 5
Office Button → Prepare → Properties →
  Document Properties →
  Advanced Properties, 25, 43
Office button → Prepare → Properties →
  Document Properties
  drop-down → Advanced
  Properties, 44
Office button → Save → Tools Button →
  General Options, 11
Office button → Save As, 13

Office button → Save As... → Microsoft
  Excel Add-in (*.xlam), 283
Office folder, 84
OFFSET function, 112, 113, 149
OnAction property, 288
OnTime method, 264
OnTime method (Application), 264,
  265
OpenOffice.org, free version of, 47
Option, 64
option buttons (radio buttons), 64
Option Compare Text, 329
Options, to assign shortcut keys, 199
Outline, 85
Outlook, automate from
  Excel, 349–354
Outlook Redemption tool, 354
Outlook's security model, 353
Outside End, 192

P

parentheses (), 266
password protection, 276, 282, 320
password Secret, always avoid using, 98
PasswordChar property, 277
passwords, 33, 320
Paste, 89
Paste Function dialog box
  (Shift-F3), 279
Paste Name dialog, 40
Paste Special, 69, 89
Paste Special Function, 156
Paste Special... → Transpose, 201
Paste Special... → Values, 129
Paste Values, 89
pathnames, retrieving, 279
paths, alternative, 57
Patterns → Line → None → OK, 192
Patterns page tab for pre-Excel 2007
  versions, 35
Patterns tab, 34, 61
personal macro workbook, 17, 23, 276
  creating Personal.xls file, 274, 276
Personal.xls file, 274, 276, 283
phantom links, finding and deleting, 41
phantom workbook links, removing, 39
Picture, 72, 167
pictures, adding to cell comments, 72
pie charts, 140

PivotCharts, 126
PivotTable feature, 4
please wait message, displaying, 270
plot areas, fill-less, 161
Pope, Andy, 192
Popular, 71, 85
Positive Error Value, 162
Positive Numbers, 79
Precision as Displayed option, 80
printing workbooks, preventing, 14
private modules
    macro ease of use and, 285
    Private module, 324
    protected workbooks, 283
    Workbook_Open event, 264
Procedure box (VBE), 269
procedures, running, 282
progress meters, 270
Project Editor (VBE), 283
Project Explorer (VBE), 16
    splash screens, 270
prompting to save nonexistent
        changes, 17
prompts, preventing unnecessary
        prompts, 15
proper case text, 322–327
Properties Window, 19, 275
Protect method, 282, 283
Protect Workbook, 15
Protect Worksheet, 32
protected worksheets, 98, 282
Protection, 31
Protection method, 98

Q

Quick Access Toolbar, 305
Quick Access toolbar, 71
quotation marks (")
    around formulas, 56
    removing around formulas, 56

R

RAND function, 74
RAND function, major flaw in, 75
range address, 238
ranges, VBA code and, 280
raw data, 124
Read-only recommended, 11
real numbers, 68

recalculation speeds of spreadsheets, 4
recalculations, global, 54
recalulations, slowing with array
        formulas, 57
recorded macros, 18
    performance of, 270
recordset, 332
Refers To: box, 40, 107
Refresh option, 126
Regedit, 84
relative references
    converting to absolute
            references, 310–315
    formulas and, 194
relative row, 100
Replace, 68
Replace for removing unwanted
        characters, 68
Replace With: box, 38, 194
ResetScrollArea, 30
restore workspace, 5
Review, 71
Review → Changes → Protect Sheet, 276
Review → Changes → Protect
        Workbook, 15
ribbon, results-oriented interface, xv
ribbons, 284
right-aligned numbers, avoid
        changing, 81
right-aligned numbers in
        spreadsheets, 3
right-clicking Excel icon, 264
ROW function, 208
rows
    AutoFilter, 289–291
    blank rows in tables of data, 2
    colors of, alternating, 58
    and columns, hiding, 27
    deleting, avoiding the #REF!
            errors, 43
    deleting in worksheets without
            AutoFilter, 291–293
    deleting rows in worksheets with
            specified criteria or
            conditions, 289–293
    dynamic colors, 59
    headings, dynmaic references, 200
    Hide & Unhide, 27
    Hide Rows, 27
    hiding, 26, 173

rows (*continued*)

incorporating data in continuous rows, 112

incrementing cell references by rows across columns, 199–201

leave at least three blank rows above tables, 3

left-align text in spreadsheets, 3

relative row, 100

right-aligned numbers in spreadsheets, 3

ROW( ) function, 60

scrolling range limit, 26

sum every nth cell or row, 208

Run statement, 318

running

macros, 264, 271

procedures, 282

runtime errors, 282

S

Save As, preventing in workbooks, 11

Save Workspace, 5

SaveAsCell, 316

saving workbooks, before deleting data permanently, 41

scales, look up numbers on, 261

scenarios, testing, 155

Schedule argument (OnTime method), 265

screen flicker, 263, 263

Application.ScreenUpdating property, 263

ScreenUpdating, setting to false to prevent, 263

ScreenUpdating, setting to true, 264

ScreenUpdating

Application.ScreenUpdating property, 263

macro for ScreenUpdating property, 263

ScreenUpdating property (Application), 263, 271

setting to false to prevent screen flicker, 263

setting to true, 264

Script window, 134

scroll area, limiting to used range on worksheets, 30

ScrollArea, 27

scrollbars

inserting, 149

linking to dynamic named range, 148–151

for speedometer charts, 170

searches, and cells, 307

security

Disable all macros without notification, 11

Enable All Macros, 15

Select command, 263, 264

Select Data Source Dialog, 146

Select Home → Clipboard → Paste → As Picture → Copy Picture, 129

Select Number → Category → Custom, 185

semicolon (;) for separating sections of a cell, 79

SERIES function, 154

Series X values, 163

Shadow Settings, 71

sheet events, 9

Sheet Name tab, 9

accessing View Code, 281

Sheet object, 9

SheetName custom function, 279

SheetName function, 279

Shift key, prevents normal files from running, 284

Shift-F3, 279

shortcuts

assigning, 278

shortcut key, attaching code to a, 305

shortcut keys, using Options to assign, 199

Show Developer tab in the Ribbon, 12

Show formulas in cells instead of their calculated result, 161, 164

ShowPass, 278

Single, 88

single apostrophe ('), with INDIRECT function, 49

size handles, 213

SMALL functions, 136

SmallScroll command, 263

Smart Art Tools, 71

snapshot recordset, 332

Software folder, 84

sorting
  more than three data fields, automating with a macro, 73
  Sort, 73
  sort, random sorting, 74
  sorted lists, turning lists upside down, 85
  sorting more than three data fields, 73
  tables, 127
  worksheets, 319
Source: box, 231
SpecialCells, 306
speedometer chart, 164–171
Spreadsheet viewer, 46
spreadsheets
  [*] to search for real external links, 39
  3-D effects, 61
  80/20 Rule for planning spreadsheets, 1
  Alignment tab, 3
  All Open Workbooks, 18
  Alt/⌘-Q for closing module window, 10
  Alt/Option-F8, to bring up macro list, 18
  array formulas, 4
  arrays, multiple arrays and large reference ranges, 4
  Before Print, 14
  Before Save, 12
  blank cells for repeated data, 2
  blank columns and rows in tables of data, 2
  blank default workbook, restoring, 23
  Cascade option, layering workbooks on top of each other, 5
  cells containing formulas, locking and protecting, 30
  cells, moving with relavite references without making absolute references, 38
  center across selection for merged cells, 3
  chart links, finding and deleting, 39
  Clear All, 42
  code for creating customized toolbars, 37
  code for creating hyperlinked index, 24
  code for linking indexes from a context menu, 25
Code options, 18
columns, avoid referencing entire, 3
Conditional Formatting dialog box, 34
conditional formatting for finding duplicate data, 34
conditional formatting, turning on and off with a switch, 63
conditions, color coding for visual identification, 35
Ctrl key for grouping worksheets manually, 8
Ctrl/⌘-K, insertion of hyperlinks, 24
data duplicated in multiple worksheet, 8
data, finding duplicates, 34
data, identifying data that appears two or more time, 35
data sources, removing unused cells, 44
data, spreading over different tables unnecessarily, 2
data, spreading over many different workbooks unnecessarily, 2
data, spreading over numerous worksheets unnecessarily, 2
Data Tools option, 32
Data Validation, 32
data validation, 32
data validation, turning on and off with a switch, 63
default workbook, customizing, 23
defined name link, finding and deleting, 39
Defined Names option, 39
Delete Links Wizard, 39
deleteting data permanently, 41
Developer, 12
Disable all macros with notification, 11
dollar sign ($) for absolute formulas, 38
dynamic named ranges when adding new data to tables, 4
Enable, 38
Enable All Macros, 15

spreadsheets (*continued*)
    Events, 11
    Excel Help for large data tables with
        multiple criteria, 4
    ExcelFix program, 47
    Excel's PivotTable feature, 4
    F9 key when recalculating, 4
    File Name box, 5
    files, unable to open, 46
    Format Cells, 3
    Format dialog, 3
    Format tab (Format button on Mac
        OS X), 34
    formatting cells as text only when
        necessary, 3
    formatting, eliminating superfluous
        formats, 43
    formatting tips, 2
    formula cells, accidentally
        overtyping, 32
    formula tips, 3
    formulas, absolute, 38
    formulas and cells formatted as text,
        avoiding, 3
    formulas, relative, 38
    Go To Special dialog, 32
    Group feature, using manually, 8
    hidden name links, finding and
        deleting, 39
    Hide, 19
    Hide & Unhide, 27
    Horizontal for viewing workbooks in
        a single stack, 5
    HTML, lost features when saving in
        HTML, 46
    Hyperlink, 24
    hyperlinks
    hyperlinks, avoid using URLs as a
        base, 25
    Import File, 44
    index, auto-generate, 24
    index of sheets, 23
    index sheet, creating manually, 24
    IndexCode, 26
    indexes, linking from a context
        menu, 25
    keep related data in one continuous
        table, 2
    Last cell, 43

    leave at least three blank rows above
        tables, 3
    left-align text, 3
    Lock Cell, 31
    long term planning for, 1
    macro, enabling deleted macros, 15
    Macro Settings Button, 11
    Macros, 18
    macros, selecting a range outside
        scrollable areas, 29
    manual calculation mode, 4
    Maximize button, 8
    merged table cells, merging, 3
    Microsoft query link, finding and
        deleting, 39
    MsgBox, 14
    Name Manager, 39
    Name tab, 8
    New Rule, 35
    Now( ), 17
    object links, finding and deleting, 39
    Objects folder, 19
    OpenOffice.org, free version of, 47
    passwords, 33
    Paste Name dialog, 40
    Patterns tab, 34
    personal macro workbook, 17, 23
    phantom links, finding and
        deleting, 41
    phantom workbook links,
        removing, 39
    Project Explorer, 16
    prompting to save nonexistent
        changes, 17
    prompts, preventing unnecessary
        prompts, 15
    Properties Window, 19
    Protect Workbook, 15
    Protect Worksheet, 32
    protected worksheets, grouping
        on, 98
    protected worksheets, outlining
        on, 98
    Protection, 31
    Read-only recommended, 11
    recalculation speeds, 4
    recorded macros, 18
    reproduce another sheet in the same
        workbook, 194
    ResetScrollArea, 30

restore workspace, 5
right-aligned numbers, 3
rows and columns, hiding, 27
Save As, preventing in
    workbooks, 11
Save Workspace, 5
saving workbooks, before deleting
    data permanently, 41
scroll area, limiting to used range on
    worksheets, 30
ScrollArea, 27
sheet events, 9
Sheet Name tab, 9
Sheet object, 9
sheets, repairing corrupted
    sheets, 44
Show Developer tab in the
    Ribbon, 12
Spreadsheet viewer, 46
structural tips for setting up and
    laying out spreadsheets, 2
template tab, 21
templates, 21
templates, grouping, 21
ThisWorkbook, 12
tiled view, 5
Today( ), 17
toolbars, customizing, 36
Trust Center, 11
Trust Center Settings, 11
Ungroup Sheets, 8
Unhide, 19
Unhide under Window options, 17
updated values, 4
users, bypassing limited access, 11
users, limiting privileges, 11
users, preventing from inserting
    worksheets, 14
VBA code for grouping worksheets
    automatically, 9
versus PivotTables, 125
Vertical option places workbooks
    side by side, 5
View Code, 9
View Microsoft Excel tool, 10
Visible property, 19
Visual Basic code, running
    automatically, 11
Visual Basic Editor (VBE), 13
volatile functions, 17

warning prompts, stopping, 18
Workbook bloat, 42
workbook customization, 5
workbooks, extracting data from
    corrupt workbooks, 45
workbooks, opening more than one
    at a time, 5
workbooks, prevent printing of, 14
workbooks, reducing the size of, 42
workbooks, repairing corrupted
    workbooks, 44
workbooks, saved as read-only, 11
workbooks showing muliple ones
    simultaneously, 5
worksheet protection,
    auto-toggling, 33
worksheet_Activate, 27
worksheets, grouping
    automatically, 9
worksheets, grouping manually, 8
worksheets, keeping hidden
    worksheets unseen from
    users, 19
worksheets, limiting scrolling
    range, 26
worksheets, specify a valid range, 27
worksheets, ungrouping, 8
workspace, 5
XLSTART folder, 23
xlVeryHidden, 19
.xlw extension for saving
    workspace, 5
SQL (Structured Query Language), 332
square brackets ([ ]), 81
stacked chart, displaying totals of, 190
standard toolbar for pre-Excel 2007
    versions, 61
Stars and Banners, 71
static recordset, 332
static value, determining, 54
Store macro in: box (Record
    Macro), 274, 276
stored values, permanently changing
    with Precision as Displayed
    option, 80
STrConv function, 323
structural tips for setting up and laying
    out spreadsheets, 2
Structured Query Language (SQL), 332

Styles merging from other
workbooks, 61
SUBSTITUTE function, 216, 235
subtotals
boldface, using for identification, 85
identifying in worksheets, 85
SubTotal Button, 85, 88
SUBTOTAL function, 212
SUBTOTAL function, making it
dynamic, 212
Subtotals, 85
Subtotals, identifying Grand Total
from, 87
Subtotals pre-Excel 2007
versions, 85
SUM cells, 273
SUM function, 57
SUM function, adding time beyond 24
hours, 94
SUMIF function, 56
Summarize value field by, 133
summing
based on fill color, 273
calculating a person's exact age, 255
calculating sliding tax scales, 246
calculations, avoiding error
values, 203
counting cells with multiple
criteria, 243
custom functions, for sliding tax
scale calculations, 249–251
DATEDIF function, 255
DSUM function, adding numbers in a
column of a list, 240
DSUM function, 209
DSUM function, error values, 203
finding the nth occurrence of a
value, 210
IF functions, for sliding tax scale
calculations, 246
SUBTOTAL function, 212
SUM and IF, slowing down
recalculations, 242
sum cells, based on multiple
criteria, 239
sum every nth cell or row, 208
SUM function, error values, 203
SUM function, simplify summing
with use of, 108

SUM functions, for sliding tax scale
calculations, 246
Sum of Amount field, 135
sum or counting cells while avoiding
error values, 4
sum totals, and error values, 203
SUMIF function, 239
SUMPRODUCT function, 209, 242,
245
SUMPRODUCT, overusing, 246
SUMPRODUCT, slows down
recalculations, 242
VLOOKUP function/formula, for
sliding tax scale
calculations, 247
showing a weekday as a
number, 256
showing a weekday as a weekday
name, 257
SUMPRODUCT function, 209
Super Code, 286
Super Code menu items, 286

T

Table Style, 62
tables
3-D effects, 61
blank cells, avoid within data, 127
Camera icon, 130
columns, 127
comparison operators, use
interchangeably, 231–233
Count of Product, 133
database functions for setting up
lists, 126
dynamic named range based
PivotTable, 138
dynamic named range, to decrease
refresh time, 137
Existing Worksheet, 128
extract statistical information from
raw data, 124
First Name field, 132
generate and extract data while
conserving memory, 126
GETPIVOTDATA function, 135
Grand Total, moving to top of the
table, 135
Grand Totals, 135–136

guidelines for creating tables or
lists, 126
headings, 127
Hide, 138
high row numbers, avoid using, 138
Insert tab, 128
invalid dates and PivotTables, 274
LARGE functions, to extract figures
from PivotTables, 136
Layout button, 133
leave at least three blank rows above
in spreadsheets, 3
list, creating, 126
lookup functions for setting up
lists, 126
macro, creating PivotTables
with, 133
Names column, use dynamic range
names, 229
New Worksheet, 132
Next button, 133
#NUM! error, returned with two or
more identical names in name
column, 229
pivot data for immediate results, 125
pivot data from another
workbook, 137
PivotChart Wizard for pre-Excel
2007 versions, 128
PivotCharts, 126
PivotCharts, unavailable for
Macintosh in Excel, 126
PivotTable, automate creation
of, 131–133
PivotTable creating, 128
PivotTable for pre-Excel 2007
versions, 128
PivotTables, classic table formats
required, 124
PivotTables, formatting and color
coding, 129
PivotTables online tutorial, 124
PivotTables, restricting shared
data, 129
PivotTables, to produce unique
names in lists, 207
PivotTables versus spreadsheets, 125
preventing blank entries and missing
fields in, 100

producing summary information
from a table, 125
range selected automatically, 128
raw data, 124
recordset, 332
Refresh option, 126
retrieve tables from databases, 332
rows, 127
SMALL functions, to extract figures
from PivotTables, 136
sorting, 127
static picture of PivotTables, 129
Summarize value field by, 133
tables, creating, 126
Values area, 132
View code, 134
VLOOKUP function, using across
multiple tables, 219–221
"What kind of report do you want to
create?" for Windows
PCs, 133
TakeFocusOnClick property, 277
Target.Interior.ColorIndex, 282
tax scales, calculating, 246
Temperature Data Series, 157
template tab, 21
templates, 21
templates, grouping, 21
text
changing to upper- or proper
case, 322–324
extract a specified word from a text
string, 234
extracting from a cell, 73
first word from a text string,
returning, 234
forcing to upper- or proper
case, 324–327
last word in a string of,
returning, 233
LEFT function, to return first
character or characters in a
text string, 234
left-aligned numbers, avoid
changing, 81
LEN function, to return the number
of characters in a text
string, 235
list of text codes, 82

text (*continued*)
  number entries and, extracting
      numeric portions of cells, 70
  numbers and, mixing in the same
      cells, 70
  STrConv function, 323
  text equations, evaluation of, 258
  TEXT function, 218, 257
  text numbers, converting to real
      numbers, 68
  Text Size, 167
  text string, extracting specified words
      from, 233
  text string, extracting the numeric
      portion, 70
  showing the weekday as weekday
      text, 257
TEXT function, 69
Text Size, 167
Text Values, 79
TextBox, 277, 327
thermometer chart, 157–158
ThisWorkbook, 12
  add-ins, 284
  macro ease of use and, 285
  pre-2007 Excel, 99
  private module, 264, 283
  Workbook_Open event, 264, 283
Tick mark labels, 182
ticking cells, 272
Tile button, 5
tiled view of spreadsheet, 5
TODAY function, 17, 205
toolbars
  attaching to a workbook, 317
  coding Restore, 317
  coding Show, 317
  creating a custom toolbar, 317
  custom toolbars, 37
  customizing, 36
  displaying, 317
  hiding and restoring, 316
  native toolbars, removing, 317
  pre-Excel 2007 versions and, 36
Tools → Add-Ins, 253
  installing add-ins, 286
  viewing add-ins, 284
Tools → Macro → Macros → FillBlanks →
    Run, 199

Tools → Macro → Macros
    (Alt/Option-F8), 263
  adding Calendar Control, 276
  password protecting
      worksheets, 278
  running macros, 271
Tools → Macro → Record New
    Macro, 274, 275, 276
Tools → Macro → Visual Basic
    Editor, 13, 19, 37, 134, 217,
    223
Tools → Macro → Visual Basic Editor
    (Alt/Option-F11), 266
  assigning buttons to macros, 268
  retrieving workbook name/path, 279
  splash screens, 269
  summing cells by fill color, 273
Tools → Options → Calculation, 218
Tools → Protection → Protect
    Sheet, 276
Tools → Protection → Protect
    Workbook, 15
Tools → References..., 332
Tools → VBAProject Properties →
    Protection, 285
tornado chart (population
    pyramid), 184–186
Track Changes, 293
tracking changes, track, report, and
    overcome limits to, 293
TRIM function, 216, 236
True or False, using to compare
    ranges, 195
TRUE value, 50
true value for calculations, 80
Trust Center, 11
Trust Center Settings, 11
Type → Change Chart Type, 191
Type options, 141

U

Ucase function, 328
UDF (user defined functions), 249
UDF (user-defined functions), 54
Underline, 88
underscore (_), 110

Undo
adding up to 100 mistakes to the
Undo feature, 84
Undo History, 84
Undo Stack, 84
unexplode pies, 141
Ungroup Sheets, 8
ungrouping worksheets, 8
Unhide, 19
Unhide under Window options, 17
Unique Records Only, 66, 78
unprotecting worksheets, 282
unwanted characters, removing, 68
updated values in spreadsheets, 4
uppercase text, 322, 324–327
URLs, avoid using as a hyperlink
base, 25
"Use 1904 date system" checkbox, 218
Use a formula to determine which cells
to format option, 50, 54, 55,
58, 88
UserDefined, 55
UserForm (VBE), 301
splash screens, 269
UserInterfaceOnly argument, 98, 282,
283
UserInterfaceOnly option, 320
users
bypassing limited access, 11
limiting privileges, 11
prevent printing of workbooks, 14
preventing from inserting
worksheets, 14
restoring settings, 316
user-defined functions (UDF), 54,
249
user-friendly validation (pick) list, 67
worksheets, keeping hidden
worksheets unseen from
users, 19

V

valid recipient list, 349
validation
validating data, 48
Validation, 48
validation list, decreasing list of
options, 101

validation lists, adding data
automatically to, 91–93
validation lists, changing based on
another selected list, 66
.Value = Now, 298
value derived from a formula,
determining, 54
#VALUE!, returned if cells contain
text, 209
Value (y) axis crosses at maximum
category, 183
Values area, 132
values, finding the nth occurrence of a
value, 210
VBA (Visual Basic for Applications)
auto-generate indexes, 24
code for grouping worksheets
automatically, 9
code performance, 270
data, sending to multiple places, 8
Excel, incompatibility with, 47
OpenOffice.org, incompatibility
with, 47
ticking cells upon selection, 272
VBA code, unrecoverable due to
incompatibility, 47
VBA Projects, HTML and HTM
formats, 46
worksheet index numbers and, 266
VBE (Visual Basic Editor)
CodeNames and, 266
hidden workbooks, 283
splash screens, 269
vbFromUnicode, 324
vbHiragana, 324
vbKatakana, 324
vbNarrow, 324
vbProperCase, 323
vbUnicode, 324
vbUpperCase, 323
vbWide, 323
Vertical option places workbooks side
by side, 5
View → Code, 12
View → Code (F7), 276, 278
View → Macros, 29
View → Project Explorer, 19
View → Project Explorer (Ctrl-R), 266

View → Properties (F4)
  adding Calendar Control, 275
  password protecting
    worksheets, 277
  splash screens, 269
View → Properties Window, 19, 269
View → Toolbars → Customize...., 130
View → Toolbars → Forms, 149, 213,
    267
View → Toolbox, 269
View → Unhide, 17, 40
View Code
  code for creating customized
    toolbars, 37
  code to specifying a specific
    worksheet in a custom
    toolbar, 37
  conditional formatting, 281
  grouping worksheets
    automatically, 9
  index, auto-generating, 24
  pre-Excel 2007 versions, 99
  protected worksheets, 283
  ranges, activating only the used
    ranges, 30
  running macros, 264
  Save As, preventing in a
    workbook, 12
  ticking cells upon selection, 272
  valid ranges, establishing boundaries
    to, 27
  worksheet protection, auto-toggle
    for, 33
View Microsoft Excel tool, 10
Visible property, 19
Visual Basic code, running
    automatically, 11
Visual Basic Editor (VBE)
  code for customizing toolbars, 36
  code to prevent users from printing a
    workbook, 14
  menus, quick access to, 13
  pre-Excel 2007 versions, 55
  prompts, preventing unnecessary, 16
  worksheet protection, 19
VLOOKUP function, 210–212
VLOOKUP function, using across
    multiple tables, 219–221

volatile functions
  COLUMN function, 201
  nonvolatile functions, nested withing
    volatile functions, 205
  Now(), 17
  personal macro workbook, avoiding
    storing in, 17
  RAND function, 74
  RAND function, major flaw in, 75
  recalculating, 17
  recalulations, reducing when using
    volatile functions, 205
  ROW( ) function, 60
  spreadsheets, 17
  Today(), 17
  Use a formula to determine which
    cells to format, 54

W

Walkenbach, John
  downloadable Chart Tools for adding
    labels to charts, 166
  web site for downloadable Chart
    Tools, 163
warnings
  array formulas, overusing, 246
  error values, 203
  SUMPRODUCT, overusing, 246
  warning prompts, stopping, 18
WEEKDAY function, 256, 257
"What kind of report do you want to
    create?" for Windows
    PCs, 133
Window → Unhide
  Personal.xls file, 274, 276
  viewing hidden workbooks, 283
Window → View → Arrange, 5
Windows → Save Workspace, 5
Windows → View → Unhide, 276
Windows of active workbook, 5
Windows XP, retrieve data from closed
    workbooks, 341–344
word-based reports, 344
Workbook Open, 98
Workbook_AddinInstall event, 285,
    287
Workbook_AddinUnInstall, 285
Workbook_AddinUninstall( ), 287

Workbook_AddinUnInstall event, 285, 287
Workbook_BeforeClose event, 265
Workbook_Open event, 264, 283
workbooks
    ActiveWorkbook, 284
    All Open Workbooks, 18
    attaching a toolbar to, 317
    blank default workbook, restoring, 23
    Calendar Control, 274
    Cascade option, layering workbooks on top of each other, 5
    code, never use to unprotect user's workbook, 284
    CodeName and, 266
    creating a list of hyperlinks, 298–300
    customization of, 5
    customizing default workbooks, 23
    data extraction from corrupt workbooks, 45
    Display options for this Workbook, 164
    Excel Calendar Control, 274
    hiding, 283
    Horizontal for viewing workbooks in a single stack, 5
    macro workbooks, personalizing, 23
    retrieving name and path of, 279
    naming with the text in a cell, 315
    opening more than one at a time, 5
    personal macro workbook, 17
    prevent printing of, 14
    Protect Workbook, 15
    reducing the size of, 42
    repairing corrupted workbooks, 44
    reproduce another sheet in another workbook, 194
    retrieve data from closed workbooks, 336–344
    retrieving names/paths, 279
    Save As, preventing in workbooks, 11
    saved as read-only, 11
    saving workbooks, before deleting data permanently, 41
    showing muliple workbooks simultaneously, 5
    splash screen, 268
    ThisWorkbook, 12

track changes on all worksheets in a given workbook, 295
tracking changes in a specific workbook, 293–295
Vertical option places workbooks side by side, 5
Windows of active workbook, 5
Workbook bloat, 42
Workbook_AddinUninstall( ), 287
Workbook_Open event, 283
workbooks names for pre-Excel 2007 versions, 40
worksheets
    Alt/Control-~, shows actual formulas on the worksheet, 164
    AutoFilter, 289–291
    avoid selecting entire worksheet, 55
    code for worksheet protection, 33
    Ctrl key for grouping worksheets manually, 8
    data duplicated in multiple worksheets, 8
    data, spreading over numerous worksheets unnecessarily, 2
    deleting rows with specified criteria or conditions, 289–293
    Existing Worksheet and tables, 128
    grouping manually, 8
    grouping worksheets automatically, 9
    index numbers and, 266
    keeping hidden worksheets unseen from users, 19
    limiting scrolling range, 26
    macro recorders and, 266
    named ranges, identification of, 121
    password protection for, 276
    password-protect and unprotect with one application, 276–279
    Private module, 324
    protect from viewing without a password, 320
    Protect Worksheet, 32
    referencing via CodeName, 266
    retrieving names, 279
    rows, deleting in worksheets without AutoFilter, 291–293
    running procedures on protected worksheets, 282

worksheets (*continued*)
scroll area, limiting to used range on worksheets, 30
sorting, 319
specify a valid range, 27
track changes on all worksheets in a given workbook, 295
tracking changes in a specific workbook, 293–295
ungrouping, 8
unprotecting, 282
UserInterfaceOnly, 282
users, preventing from inserting worksheets, 14
VBA code for grouping worksheets automatically, 9
Worksheet and tables, 128
worksheet name, using in a cell, 236
worksheet names, creating a list of, 236
worksheet names, extracting, 237
worksheet_Activate, 27
worksheets protection with auto-toggling, 33

xlSheetVisible, 295
xlVeryHidden, 295
worksheets, referencing via CodeName, 266
workspace, 5
workspace, restoring, 5

X

X-axis category labels, highlight with color, 188–190
.xla extension, 283, 285
xlSheetVisible, 295
XLSTART folder, 23
.xlsx, 337
xlVeryHidden, 19, 295
.xlw extension for saving workspace, 5
XY scatter chart, 160

Z

Zero Values, 79

Colophon

The tool on the cover of *Excel Hacks* is a trowel. The trowel shown is the type that is generally used in everyday gardening tasks such as removing stones from dirt, planting, and removing weeds.

The cover image is from the Stockbyte Work Tools CD. The cover font is Adobe ITC Garamond. The text font is Linotype Birka; the heading font is Adobe Helvetica Neue Condensed; and the code font is LucasFont's TheSans Mono Condensed.

Better than e-books

Buy *Excel Hacks,* 2nd Edition, and access the
digital edition FREE on Safari for 45 days.

Go to www.oreilly.com/go/safarienabled
and type in coupon code FILKIXA

Search
thousands of
top tech books

Download
whole chapters

Cut and Paste
code examples

Find
answers fast

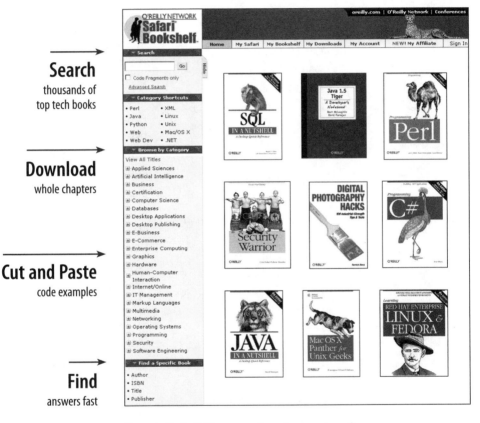

Search Safari! The premier electronic reference
library for programmers and IT professionals.

Related Titles from O'Reilly

Hacks

Access Hacks

Ajax Hacks

Amazon Hacks

Astronomy Hacks

Baseball Hacks

BlackBerry Hacks

BSD Hacks

Car PC Hacks

Digital Photography Hacks

Digital Video Hacks

eBay Hacks, *2nd Edition*

Excel Hacks, *2nd Edition*

Firefox Hacks

Flash Hacks

Flickr Hacks

Gaming Hacks

Google Hacks, *3rd Edition*

Google Map Hacks

Greasemonkey Hacks

Halo 2 Hacks

Hardware Hacking Projects
  for Geeks

Home Theater Hacks

iPod & iTunes Hacks

IRC Hacks

Knoppix Hacks

Linux Desktop Hacks

Linux Multimedia Hacks

Linux Server Hacks

Linux Server Hacks, Volume 2

Mac OS X Panther Hacks

Mapping Hacks

Mind Hacks

Mind Performance Hacks

Network Security Hacks,
  2nd Edition

Nokia Smartphone Hacks

Online Investing Hacks

Palm & Treo Hacks

PayPal Hacks

PDF Hacks

Perl Hacks

PC Hacks

PHP Hacks

Podcasting Hacks

PSP Hacks

Retro Gaming Hacks

Skype Hacks

Smart Home Hacks

Spidering Hacks

SQL Hacks

Statistics Hacks

Swing Hacks

TiVo Hacks

Ubuntu Hacks

Visual Studio Hacks

VoIP Hacks

Web Site Measurement Hacks

Windows Server Hacks

Windows XP Hacks,
  2nd Edition

Wireless Hacks, *2nd Edition*

Word Hacks

XML Hacks

Yahoo! Hacks

O'REILLY®

Our books are available at most retail and online bookstores.
To order direct: 1-800-998-9938 • *order@oreilly.com* • *www.oreilly.com*
Online editions of most O'Reilly titles are available by subscription at *safari.oreilly.com*

The O'Reilly Advantage

Stay Current and Save Money